LEGENDS
of the
ASH

Do not seek to follow in the footsteps of the masters; seek what they sought.

Zen wisdom

BRENDAN FULLAM is a native of Ardagh, Co. Limerick, and a retired bank manager, who served in that capacity in Killorglin, Co. Kerry, the Crescent in Wexford, and New Ross. In his younger years his banking career took him to Killorglin, Kilrush, Clifden, Ballyshannon, Wexford and Tralee, and in each of these towns he played with the local hurling team. The game of hurling is his greatest interest, and his vision in meeting and interviewing the legends of the game over the past eighteen years has resulted in three unique and invaluable records of the game and its players — *Giants of the Ash, Hurling Giants* and now the final book in the series, *Legends of the Ash* — treasures for all sports followers.

To my children:
Helena, Deirdre, Brendan, Máire, and Gráinne,
with affection.

Tribute to the Fallen
In football, hurling, handball, whichever game you've tried,
You try your best to win it and bring honour to your side,
But why be disappointed if you fail to make the grade?
To win or lose is not what counts, it's how the game was played.

And when the final whistle blows, and your heart begins to glow,
Show respect for your opponent, whose heart is full of woe.
Go shake his hand in friendship, say there'll be another day,
And trust that he'll do likewise when things go the other way.

LEGENDS

of the

ASH

Brendan Fullam

WOLFHOUND PRESS
& in the US and Canada
The Irish American Book Company

First published in paperback 1998
First published 1997
Wolfhound Press Ltd
68 Mountjoy Square
Dublin 1
Tel: (353-1) 8740354
Fax: (353-1) 8720207

Published in the US and Canada by
The Irish American Book Company (IABC)
6309 Monarch Park Place
Suite 101
Niwot, Colorado 80503
USA
Tel: (303) 652 2710
Fax: (303) 652 2689

British Library Cataloguing in Publication Data
A catalogue record for this book is available from the British Library

ISBN 0-86327-619-9 hb
ISBN 0-86327-667-9 pb

10 9 8 7 6 5 4 3 2 1

The author and publishers are grateful to hurlers and their families who supplied photographs and to all who assisted in research for this book. The photographs on pages 17, 44, 45, 50, 64, 69, 93, 107, 135, 148, 161, 164, 172, 179, 206, 209 and 286 are reproduced with the kind permission of Jim Connolly. Those on pages 75, 86, 112, 167 and 252 with the permission of Inpho. The colour photographs are reproduced with the permission of Inpho and Sportsfile. While every effort has been made to contact holders of copyright material, in a few instances we have been unable to contact the relevant persons. We request that they write to the publishers.

Cover design: Slick Fish Design, Dublin
Cover photographs: Inpho and Sportsfile
Typesetting: Wolfhound Press
Printed in the Republic of Ireland by Colour Books, Dublin

CONTENTS

Foreword by Con Houlihan

Innocent people such as myself like to speculate about pre-history, about the world of which we have no records. When we speak about the 'dawn of history', we mean more or less the time when records began to be kept.

I have a theory concerning the ball-and-stick games that were part of our ancestors' culture — it may be no more than fantasy but I will give it to you.

Early man was a gatherer and a hunter; his hunting was done with his bare hands for a long time. Thus he caught fish and birds and little animals. The next step came when he learned to use missiles, such as rounded stones. Then came a great leap forward in evolution when he began to use tools and weapons. I wasn't around then but I can see my ancestors using a stick to drive rounded stones at flocks and herds.

Man learned to draw before he learned to write; there is an a abundance of depictions to show that ball-and-stick games were widespread in early civilisation.

Hurling was well established in pre-Christian Ireland. In the Brehon Laws you will find sophisticated provisions to compensate the families of any man killed by a hurley or a hurling ball. King Cahir The Great of Tailteann left 50 brass hurleys and 50 brass hurling balls in his will.

There were two forms of hurling in Ireland: winter hurling was played with a narrow stick and a hard ball; summer hurling was played with a broad-bladed stick and a soft ball. You weren't allowed to handle the ball in the former; it was very much a feature of the latter.

Michael Cusack pondered long and deeply when the time came to decide which version he would make official; he chose the summer version probably because it was more widespread at the time and was more attractive.

Winter hurling survived in the odd nook and occasional cranny; it was played in south-west Kerry until about forty years ago, mainly on the roads and with improvised camáns. It is probably fair to say that summer hurling was played in the better land and by the better-off people — the winter game was favoured more by the working class.

It was played too in our part of Kerry, a few miles north of Castle Island. There was little traffic in the War years; we engaged in fierce battles on the Dublin Road — for a ball we used the bottom half of a small polish box.

Many years later I was delighted to discover that we have been playing winter hurling, much as the two men in one of Molière's plays were thrilled when they found out that they had been speaking prose all their lives.

When Cusack wrote that the GAA swept the country like a prairie fire, he was thinking mainly of Gaelic football; it proliferated phenomenally. Hurling is our national game in that it is old and unique to us — Gaelic football is the more widespread.

The bogey of tradition has hindered the growth of hurling; there is a mystique about the game that inhibits the so-called lesser counties. We are almost given to believe that every boy in Kilkenny and Cork and Tipperary is born with a wee hurley in one hand and a tiny sliotar in the other; no other county can attain their expertise — so we are told.

In this generation we have seen the ancient game make some progress. A big factor was the emergence of the Faithful County in 1981. The emergence of Waterford in 1948 hadn't the same impact because it had always been deemed a hurling county.

Incidentally, some of the traditionalists looked on Offaly's great achievement as some kind of freak happening; I heard them called 'scoopers'. This word probably comes from scuaibín, the name given to cross-country hurling, the counterpart of caid in football.

Television has given a great boost to the ancient game — and so, of course, has the coming of headgear. It is such a good idea that you wonder why it wasn't adopted long ago.

I know of no game that arouses more passion than hurling and I know of no game that evokes more dedication in its exponents; around it there is a kind of healthy madness, fiabhras na fuinseoige. Imprinted on my mind there are three images that tell a lot about the game.

I see Lory Meagher putting a ladder up against a cock of hay and going back about fifty yards and pucking a sliotar under the bottom rung — and pucking another under the next rung, and so on — and sometimes starting again until he has got it all right.

When Christy Ring drove an oil lorry around the roads of Cork, he kept a hurley and a bucket of sliotars in his cab; the bucket was flattened on one side; he put it down in a field during his lunch hour — that was his target.

Then there was the occasion when Galway, long out of the centre court, were on the way to winning the Final of the League. The three Connolly brothers, natives of Connemara, were on board. Mícheál Ó'Muircheartaigh broke into Gaelic and delivered the last twelve minutes of his commentary in the old tongue.

We all love to speculate about who was the greatest hurler of all time — it is good and endless fun. I prefer to name the man who for me most symbolises all that is great in the game. He is Tony Doran, the Happy Warrior.

Brendan Fullam has gone into the forest that he has so long loved and that he knows so well and brought back great stories. Mo bheannacht.

Con Houlihan
Sportswriter, journalist & author

Foreword by Liam Griffin

'The credit belongs to the man who is actually in the arena, whose face is marred by dust and sweat and blood; who strives valiantly; who errs and comes short again and again, who knows the great enthusiasms, the great devotions, and spends himself in a worthy cause; who at the best, knows the triumph of high achievement; and who, at the worst, if he fails at least fails while daring greatly, so that his place shall never be with those cold and timid souls who know neither victory nor defeat.'

Roosevelt's words — it must always be about the players.

I feel honoured but somehow unworthy between the covers of a Brendan Fullam book. 'Gods of the Game' — 'Hurling is magic in game form' — so many words could be used. The unique way that Brendan has set out his books is fascinating in its simplicity. The players tell their stories and all so differently. John T. Power who won his first All-Ireland with Kilkenny in 1907 was interviewed in his 99th year (*Giants of the Ash*); the oldest living player interviewed is Jim Power of Galway who will be 102 next November (*Giants of the Ash*) — all the way to the great George O'Connor and Martin Storey of Wexford 1996 and some of the great camogie players also. Some extremely interesting statistics are also presented in *Giants of the Ash*. Two leather-bound journals of seven hundred pages each have captured for posterity the autographed personal written contribution of each player interviewed.

How did Brendan Fullam even think of doing this? How much effort has it taken to get to all of these great players? How can hurling people thank this man for his priceless work? Who will keep it up? Perhaps the GAA should take it on board; Brendan Fullam is owed that much. To hurling people these are the records of the 'Masters', more important to me than the 'Book of Kells'.

Read Doctor Croke's letter of 1884 in *Giants of the Ash*: how relevant it is today!

Open a page — games played before you were born come to life. I see Terry Leahy's point to win the '47 All-Ireland against Cork as clearly as if I was there. I see Bobby Rackard's performance at full-back at the end of the '54 All-Ireland and I can smell the rain as Jimmy Kelly of Carrickshock sends over the winning point to win the famous Thunder and Lightning All-Ireland of '39. Billy Rackard was the greatest centre-back I ever saw — I never knew John Keane — I feel I do now. The names and events my father spoke of in the old Morris Minor ZR 338 on the way to and from matches all those years ago — people I never really knew — Tyler Mackey and his famous sons, 'Fowler' McInerney, Tommy Doyle, Joe Salmon, Jim Langton, Matt Nugent (why Clare lost in '55 — Dermot Kelly). The bicycle Munster final of '44.

'Over the bar' says Lory Meagher. 'Into the square' says Charlie Ware.
'Now Cork is beat; the hay is saved the thousands wildly sing — they speak too soon,
my sweet garsún, For here comes Christy Ring'.

The place and club names — Bennetsbridge, Thurles, Mooncoin, Mount Sion, Rathnure, Glen Rovers, Ahane, Antrim, Cork and all counties between. The hair stands on the back of your neck, goose pimples on your arms — beautiful wonderful work — 'Nectar'.

I started with Roosevelt. I'll give the last word to his wife Elenor.

'The future belongs to those who believe in the beauty of their dreams'.

Thank you for your dream, Brendan, and thank you for giving us the dreams of so many of the greats of the Riverdance of Sport.

Liam Griffin, Former Wexford hurling manager

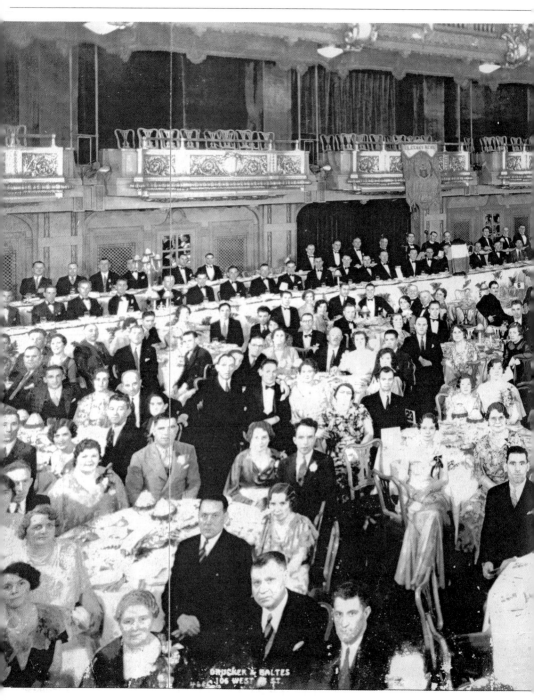

Testimonial dinner dance tendered to the Kilkenny All-Ireland champions by the Kilkenny Men's S. and B. Association, at the Hotel Astor, 13 June 1934.

TESTIMONIAL DINNER-DANCE
TENDERED TO THE
KILKENNY HURLING TEAM
ALL-IRELAND CHAMPIONS
BY THE
KILKENNY MEN'S S. AND B. ASSOCIATION
HOTEL ASTOR   JUNE 13, 1934

Anthony Daly on 14 September 1997 became the ninth captain to lift the MacCarthy Cup for the second time. The twenty-seven-year-old six-footer from Clarecastle played at minor and under-21 level for his native Clare and made his senior début in the National League of 1989/90.

In his school days he won the Dr Harty Cup and All-Ireland medals with St Flannan's in 1987.

Further successes to date include county titles, Railway Cup honours, All Stars, Munster titles and All-Ireland titles.

He now enters the hurling records as the first captain to take home the new MacCarthy Cup on two occasions.

He has proved himself an influential figure on the Clare team, an inspirational captain and a player always most gracious in victory.

Preface

With its two sister books, *Giants of the Ash,* published in 1991, and *Hurling Giants,* published in 1994, this book completes a trilogy of works on the great game of hurling.

The three books deal with over two hundred of the game's greatest personalities since the foundation of the GAA in 1884. These people, together with so many others — for there were so many great hurlers — contributed to making hurling the magnificent spectacle that it is: the greatest field game in the world; a game that stands on its own, superb and peerless.

Legends of the Ash is full of household hurling names from every decade and from many counties, names that conjure up splendour and magic and courage and supreme skill: names such as Paddy Clohessy, Matty Power, Paddy Molloy, Jim Hurley, Mickey Byrne and Tom Cheasty from earlier days, Pat Fox, George O'Connor, Pete Finnerty, Ray Cummins and Aidan Fogarty of more recent times.

Nor have I forgotten the brilliant hurling men of the lesser counties, like Paddy Quirke of Carlow, Pat Dunny of Kildare, Christy O'Brien of Laois, and Terence 'Sambo' McNaughton of Antrim.

For the first time I have included some of the players now playing: D.J. Carey, Billy Dooley, Ger Cunningham, Martin Storey, Gary Kirby, Joe Cooney, Brian Lohan and Ciarán Carey — all brilliant exponents of the modern-day game.

Remembered too are some of our camogie players, Mary O'Leary, Mairéad McAtamney, Órla Ní Shíocháin, Liz Neary, and Margaret O'Leary-Lacey. And speaking of camogie players, it is with much sadness that I record the death of that genial star of the camogie world, Kathleen Mills, who featured in *Hurling Giants.*

This trilogy is probably the most comprehensive compilation of the personalities of the hurling world ever undertaken. I know from comments I have received that the two earlier books have given immense pleasure to hurling lovers. Stories of the joy and entertainment they have brought to old-timers have been most rewarding and in some cases very moving. And little wonder, for we are talking of a game that is so much part of what we are: it courses through our very veins; it permeates the very parish soil.

Recorded now for all time, in two original leather-bound journals, are the written personal contributions of these wonderful ambassadors of the great game of hurling whom I had the pleasure of meeting.

Michael Cusack, founder of the GAA, had this to say: 'When I reflect on the sublime simplicity of the game, the strength, the swiftness, of the players, their apparently angelic impetuosity, the apparent recklessness of life and limb, their magic skill, their marvellous escapes and the overwhelming pleasure they give their friends, I have no hesitation in saying that the game of hurling is in the front rank of the Fine Arts.'

'Carbery' — player and renowned journalist — once wrote of hurling: 'It teaches reckless courage, initiative, speed of thought and action; it encourages collective effort, mutual respect, gallant sportsmanship, discipline, fair play, self-control, agility and uniform development.'

> *'Camáin á luascadh ar fud na páirce,*
> *Is an sliotar ag imeacht ar luas in airde.'*

Mícheál O'Hehir & President Mary Robinson.
Holding Hurling Giants *and* Giants of the Ash
respectively.

Mícheál was so much part of hurling that it seems only appropriate that he should be part of this trilogy.

I can still hear that voice: 'Bail ó Dhia oraibh go léir, a chairde, agus fáilte romhaibh,' welcoming, enthusiastic and dramatic, ringing and echoing in my ears. It will always be there, for it was stored computer-like in my very young and impressionable years, years when so much about the world seemed simple, the pace pedestrian, and the magic voice of Mícheál O'Hehir entertained and excited scores of people in every parish with a dramatic account of the thrills and the tensions as they unfolded on the hurling pitch.

He spared no effort to give his listeners as vivid a picture as possible of the action on the pitch and the location of that action. This he did by indicating at the outset that the pitch was divided into six sections — sections 1, 3 and 5 and sections 2, 4, and 6 — and the location of these in relation to his own position.

Those broadcasts enlivened our Sunday afternoons, and I always remember that at half time, having summarised the first half, he would say, 'And now I will let you listen to the music of the band.'

He loved the word 'shemozzle'; he used it to describe action on the ground in front of goal. Once he said 'shemozzle' you could picture the scene: hurleys, bodies, legs, shoulders, hips, swinging and surging and clashing ...

'Well, your guess is as good as mine' was an expression he often used. 'And it's a 21-yard free to Cork slap-bang in front of the Limerick goal. Christy Ring is coming up to take it. Will he go for the goal, or will he be satisfied with the point? Well, your guess is as good as mine ... Backs line the goal. He bends, he lifts, he strikes, low and hard — and it's saved! Oh, a great save, a great save ...'.

Another phrase one often heard was 'The game isn't over yet.' This would come, well into the second half, after a score that heralded a comeback, and would be followed by Mícheál asking, 'And can they now pull the game out of the fire?'

Mícheál was born on 2 June 1920 in Dublin of Clare parents, and as he grew up Limerick's Mick Mackey was his hero. His father, Jim, was associated with the Clare All-Ireland success of 1914.

Following a successful test, Mícheál made his first broadcast on 14 August 1938, the All-Ireland football semi-final between Monaghan and Galway at Mullingar. From that day onwards he became the 'Voice of Sport' in Ireland, a household name, a revered figure — a man who all his life remained a tee-totaller and non-smoker.

His broadcast of the All-Ireland football final from the Polo Grounds in New York in 1947 between Cavan and Kerry will always be remembered as a feat that bordered on the miraculous at the time, in technological achievement but more so for his repeated appeals to the American authorities not to cut him off at 5 p.m. when he suddenly realised that at 4:55 p.m. there were still ten minutes left to play and air time had been booked and paid for up to 5 p.m. only. The style and nature of his appeal was such that it was responded to.

When Telefís Éireann was set up in 1961 Mícheál became Head of Sports Programmes, and he remained in that position for eleven years.

His radio broadcasts made him part of hurling folklore, and his name will for ever remain synonymous with the great game. To the generation that grew up in the forties and fifties the name Mícheál O'Hehir will always carry with it a ring of nostalgia. As a tribute to him, the new hurling pitch in Cratloe, County Clare, opened in 1991, is named after him.

At the photo call for my book *Hurling Giants* at Áras an Uachtaráin in 1994 President Mary Robinson arranged for Mícheál to be present. It was a lovely gesture. Kathleen Mills and Una O'Connor of Dublin camogie fame approached him with a view to introducing themselves, but as they approached he, to their amazement, said, 'Ah, Kathleen Mills and Una O'Connor.'

In 1985 he suffered a stroke, an affliction that denied him the distinction of broadcasting his hundredth All-Ireland final. He died on 24 November 1996, aged seventy-six. As I listened to the many tributes paid to him and said a silent prayer for his gentle soul I remembered those words that used to conclude all his hurling broadcasts in the faraway days of my youth: 'Agus seo é Mícheál O'Hehir ag rá, slán agaibh go léir.'

Croke Park 1939, as Mícheál O'Hehir would have described it to his listeners.

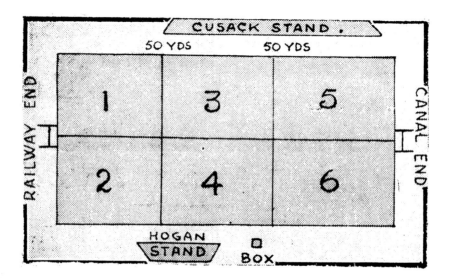

16

Mícheál was born and reared a short distance from Dingle town. It would have been a Gaeltacht locality. He grew up in a bilingual atmosphere and learned from an early age to communicate effectively in both Irish and English.

The scene was set for a career in National teaching when he went to Coláiste Íosagáin in Ballyvourney, County Cork.

From there he went to St Patrick's Training College in Drumcondra. It was while in the college that he made his first broadcast. It was St Patrick's Day 1949 and, following a trial ten days earlier — done for a bit of craic rather than serious intent — he was called upon to broadcast in Irish the Railway Cup football final between Munster and Leinster.

That day we heard for the first time his distinctive style as he painted pictures of the footballing prowess of 'Weeshie' Murphy, Paddy 'Bawn' Brosnan, Jackie Lyne, Batt Garvey, Paddy O'Brien, Jack Bell, Peter McDermott, Seán Boyle,

'Boiler' White agus na h-imreóirí eile freisin, i gcluiche a bhí ar có scór ag deireadh na h-uaire. On that day in 1949 as the players names echoed in Irish throughout the land we learned that Batt Garvey was Partholán Ó'Garbhfí and that Peter McDermott — 'the man with the cap' — was Peadar Mac Diarmada. And when the final whistle blew it was clear that a new voice was emerging in sports broadcasting.

Mícheál saw his first All-Ireland football final in 1948 — viewed from Hill 16 — between Cavan and Mayo, on a day when a gale was blowing from the Canal to the Railway goal and the attendance was a little over 300 short of 75,000. Cavan, with the breeze, led by eleven points at half time. But with time almost up and the scoreboard reading Cavan 4:5, Mayo 4:4, Mayo got a close-in free taken by Pádraig Carney — 'the flying Doctor'. It was charged down by Mick Higgins — some say illegally — and the game was won and lost. Little did Mícheál realise, as he made his way out of Croke Park, that within six months he would be broadcasting the next major football match to be played in those grounds.

Subsequent to St Patrick's Day 1949, Mícheál gave commentaries on Oireachtas hurling games — some great games involving Clare, Galway and Wexford. We all became familiar with phrases like — an poc amach ón gcúl — ceann árd fada ag tuitim isteach sa chearnóg — an sliotar in a laimh aige agus é imithe leis féin — glanta amach ar an dtalamh thar an dtaobh líne — ceann beacht, cruinn, buailte thar an dtrasnán — poc sleasa agus an sliotar imithe ar fóiríol — ceann deas buailte go h-aclaí.

It wasn't until 1956 that he made his first broadcast in English. It was the Munster football final replay between Cork and Kerry — won by Cork on the score 1:8 to 1:7. Thus was established the foundation of a brilliant career in broadcasting. He holds his listeners spellbound as he relates the unfolding drama on the playing field — drifting effortlessly from time to time between English and Irish without ever losing his listeners — for even those with only very basic Irish can readily understand the well-delivered, clear diction.

Mícheál, a non-smoker and non-drinker all his life, has been blessed with a fabulous memory and tremendous stamina. Those close to him affirm that the public man and the private man are the same — always a gentleman who has time for everyone, a man who radiates a warmth in his dealings with people, an easy-going manner that reflects a great inner calm and confidence. He has always had an enormous rapport with players and is highly respected by them. His marvellous detail has often astounded his listeners and his colourful style of expression has been enriched by his Gaelic roots.

His interests have been many and diverse. Greyhound racing has a great appeal for him and he has broadcast from that field of sport too. He has over the years trained and coached Kerry footballers resident in Dublin and prepared them for championship fare. He has a musically talented family, deeply involved in Irish music. Mícheál himself is at present Cathaoirleach of Bord na Gaeilge.

It is hard to believe that in less than two years it will be fifty years since he made his first broadcast at the age of 19.

The story is told of a tourist who tuned into Radio Éireann one Sunday afternoon and was so captivated by what he heard that he pulled in to the roadside and listened enthralled, to the end of the game — the flow of words, the choice of words (I wonder was it one of those days that a player took four truslóga fada down the field), the soft Kerry accent, the detail, the expression, the clarity.

Mícheál intrigued and fascinated the tourist. For several decades he has entertained and enlivened many a Sunday afternoon for his regular listeners.

Beatha agus sláinte chugat a Mhíchíl Uasail agus go mba fada buan thú.

Born 1935

Tipperary. In 1952 and 1953 I played with Cork minors but again we were beaten in Munster finals in both years by Tipperary.

From 1954 on to 1964 I played senior with Cork, except in 1955, when I was out of bounds, which unfortunately were very lean years — some very unlucky. However, I played seven years inter-provincial, winning six Railway Cup medals. In between I won two county championship medals with Blackrock — the first one, in 1956, was the first county the club had won for twenty-five years.

Since my first involvement with the GAA I have seen many changes, some for the better but some I would begin to worry about. The game itself has got faster and the players fitter, but I think the skills have suffered a bit. Also, I am very worried about the new set-up at inter-county level. I think championships should be knock-out, and I'm afraid the league set-up will have a fierce effect on club championship.

I hope these few lines will be of interest to you, and I am proud and happy to have played a part in a great association.

Jimmy Brohan

"

From my earliest days I have always had a huge interest in hurling, earliest recollections being ballboy at Church Road in Blackrock, following the sliotars behind the goals when they were training for their championship matches, then later on at school in Sullivan's Quay and at juvenile level with Blackrock.

At Sullivan's Quay and Christian Brothers a Brother Bridges from Wexford had a great influence on my game in school shield competitions.

Some of my earliest heroes at club would have been the Riordan brothers, Gerry and Mossie, and John Quirke, who was one of the greatest of all time.

From school shield I gravitated to Harty Cup and in 1951 caused a sensation in reaching the final, but we were beaten by Thurles CBS — a team captained by Paddy Croke and which also included Tony Wall, later a star with

After the Munster semi-final of 1958 — won by Tipp on the score 2:6 to 2:4 — John D. Hickey, writing in the *Irish Independent,* had this to say:

'Jimmy Brohan convinced me that he is the best cornerback I have ever seen.'

In Cork the local paper made him 'Cork Star of the Week', adding:

'Jimmy Brohan's display against Tipp. in the Munster semi-final, last Sunday, established him as probably the best cornerback in present day hurling. Often-times, he electrified the vast crowd by clearing

the ball upfield while two or three opponents strove to prevent him.'

Writing in the *Sunday Review* on 4 January 1959, Paddy Downey picked his hurling team of 1958. In selecting Jimmy Brohan he said:

'Right-full-back must go to Cork's Jimmy Brohan. This angular frail-looking man improves with each season. He is now at the peak of his power.'

Jimmy Brohan's hurling talents came from his own natural abilities — shaped and moulded in his early youth through watching his heroes practising on the local pitch at Blackrock. He paid particular attention to Johnny Quirke, one of hurling's all-time greats, equally brilliant in defence and attack — a man for whom Jimmy still holds a special feeling of affection and admiration. 'Johnny used tell a story about one of his first matches with Blackrock. It was a county final. Paddy "Balty" Aherne, star Cork forward of the twenties and early thirties, sent across a lovely pass from the wing. Johnny pulled and missed — opportunity lost. Balty came across and gave Johnny a little smack on the face, saying, "Don't do that again, boy".'

Jimmy's memory of games goes back to 1944. He remembers in particular the Munster final of 1945 between Limerick and Tipperary. It was an age when forwards could charge the goalkeeper; he can still clearly see John Mackey thundering in on little Jimmy Maher in the Tipperary goal and belting the crossbar with his hurley. 'He had Jimmy terrified. Jimmy wore a cap. John would grab it and throw it into the back of the net.'

Another story in a similar vein is told. John Mackey was full-forward and marking Ger Cornally, the Tipperary full-back. He had the heart crossways in Jimmy Maher from charging in on him. One fast ball came along the ground. Jimmy put down the hurley to stop it but lifted his head as Mackey came thundering in. The sliotar hopped over Jimmy's hurley to the net. John's rush stopped. He looked at Jimmy, lifted up

Jimmy's hurley, examined the bos, and said in surprise: 'Jaysus, Jimmy, there's no hole in that.' Those were the days!

Jimmy Brohan arrived on the county scene just when Cork were ending a great three-in-a-row sequence of victories. Even though he gave a very sound display against Galway in the All-Ireland semi-final of 1954, he found himself back on the subs' bench for the final, when Cork had a somewhat fortunate three-point victory over a still emerging Wexford fifteen.

Then Cork hit one of their rare lean spells. Twelve years passed before their next All-Ireland win, in 1966. With the label of underdogs firmly attached to them, they played first-time, no-nonsense hurling and surprised a hotly fancied Kilkenny team. But by then Jimmy had departed the scene, and the glory that every hurler dreams of — winning an All-Ireland medal on the pitch — had evaporated. It is his only regret. 'I was on the panel in 1965 as Cork prepared for the Munster final against Tipp. I opted instead to go on a holiday to Wales. That finished me with the selectors.'

And yet during those lean years Cork came quite close to major honours on a few occasions. In 1956 they had a dramatic Munster final win over Limerick, Ring scoring three goals in the space of about five minutes in the closing stages, when Limerick seemed set to retain their Munster crown. Against Wexford in the All-Ireland final there was more drama in the final moments, involving Ring and a timely save by Art Foley, following which Wexford clinched a great victory.

In 1957 and 1959 Cork failed in the Munster final to a wonderful Waterford fifteen. Very close it was: 5 points and 3 points, respectively. In 1960 they lost the league final to Tipperary at Cork by 4 points, 2:15 to 3:8. There followed later that year a torrid Munster final battle with Tipperary at Thurles; it ended 4:13 to 4:11 in Tipperary's favour. 'Ring always blamed the Cork County Board for that Munster final loss. In return for Tipp playing the league final in Cork, the Cork County Board agreed to Thurles as the venue for the Munster final. It was worth a few points to Tipperary, of course. Ring always maintained it was a big mistake. He claimed it would have been won if played at Limerick, a neutral venue.'

Cork again reached the league final in 1962 but lost to Kilkenny on the score 1:16 to 1:8. By this time frustration was building up in Ring at the failure to collect a major title. Following the defeat by Kilkenny he is reputed to have said that he carried more passengers in the previous eight years than CIE.

Christy always had a fierce, burning desire to win, no matter what was at stake — same passion in a tournament game as in an All-Ireland final. And he could motivate too. Let Jimmy illustrate. 'It was a team talk at training, before the third-in-a-row success of the 1976 to '78 era, the opponents Kilkenny. All the selectors, including myself, said what we would expect from the team. Ring was last to speak. Everyone was listening intently. "We were playing Kilkenny," said Ring. "It was a terrible day. The rain was falling from the sky. I was left-half-forward. The ball fell behind the half-backs. I ran in, collected the ball, and ran ten yards. The next thing the rain was falling from the back of the net." End of talk. Message? Go do in like manner.'

Jimmy got on very well with Christy, both on and off the pitch. 'In the 1954 county final, which the Glen won, I was playing corner-back on Ring. But only for part of the hour. Ring would switch about from time to time as he saw fit. He had a very big pair of hands and extraordinary strength. He was a shy man in many ways, but on the pitch he was able to let the hurley do the talking. In 1956, when we beat them in the county final, I believe he was genuinely delighted for us. It was Blackrock's first county title in twenty-five years. The club hadn't won since 1931 and the great days of Eudi Coughlan. We had

Jimmy Brohan in action for Munster with Mícheál Maher (M) and Christy O'Brien (L).

two Wexfordmen at centrefield in 1956: John Redmond and Séamus Hearne.'

Few if any players who spent a decade in Cork senior hurling teams won as little as Jimmy did in the red-and-white jersey. But he fared well in other areas. He demonstrated his undoubted defensive talents in the blue-and-white jersey of Munster when honoured by the provincial selectors for seven successive years, from 1957 to 1963, inclusive — and always at right-full-back. He missed out on the final in 1958 having broken a bone in his hand in the semifinal against Connacht. He recalls that in 1962, with time ticking away, Munster were leading Leinster by 1:9 to 0:10. 'Then Leinster got a seventy. It came dropping into the square. I joined the bunch that attempted to cover and clear it. It broke, however, to Denis Heaslip of Kilkenny — always an opportunist — who found the net and with it victory for Leinster, who added another point. If I had stayed in my position I might have prevented the goal.' Though defeated, Jimmy sees it as probably his best game for his province. It was the only time he played on a losing Railway

Cup side. The *Cork Examiner* in its report on the game said:

> *'Jimmy Brohan, more adventuresome than ever in the first half, cleared wonderfully.'*

He was an automatic choice on Rest of Ireland teams in the years from 1957 to 1962, missing out only in 1958.

This excerpt from Mick Dunne's report in the *Irish Press* after the 1960 Railway Cup final makes interesting reading. He gave the game a one-star rating out of a possible five:

> *'This was the biggest hurling flop for many a St. Patrick's Day ... There was the irritating spectacle of missed strokes, fluffed catches, wild swings and shots with neither direction nor length ... How thankful we were then for Jimmy Brohan, a five star performer in a game that needed some more of his impeccable hurling. From the throw-in Brohan was unbeatable, no matter where he turned up in the Munster defence ... on the ground and in the air he was faultless.'*

Jimmy feels that his greatest game for Cork — lost on the score 3:6 to 0:7 — was in the 1961 Munster final against Tipperary in Limerick. 'I played a lot of ball that day. I suppose when you are on song things go well and you go from strength to strength.'

Tony Wall, in the *Gaelic Weekly* of 5 August 1961, wrote:

> *'From the Cork point of view Jimmy Brohan was easily the man of the match. His hurling is really delightful to watch and his clearances, even when under pressure, were wonderful. I saw him get away with picking the ball off the ground, but even this he accomplished with aplomb.'*

But there was much more to the 1961 final. Tension filled the air. A record attendance crammed the grounds, officially 60,177, but thousands more gained entry after the crowd broke down the gates. Everyone knew it would be a game where little quarter would be given: memories of the 1960 clash between the two sides were fresh and vivid in all minds. In less than twenty minutes Tipp had scored three goals and at half time led by 3:3 to 0:1 — on the run of play slightly flattering. The tension exploded in the eighteenth minute of the second half when John Doyle and Christy Ring — then in his forty-first year — became entangled in each other. A free-for-all followed. The Tipperary corner-forward Tom Moloughney had to leave the pitch with a nasty wound from a stroke of a hurley that required twelve stitches to his face. It was never established who struck him.

Jimmy was also a footballer of note. This led to his suspension in 1955 by the city divisional board following his failure to turn out for his club, Seandún; the suspension caused him to miss the first-round senior hurling game at Thurles, when Clare caused a mild surprise by dethroning the reigning All-Ireland champions, Cork. He captained Cork junior footballers to a Munster title in 1957, only to fail to Mayo in the home final. He played one game at senior level with Cork footballers.

He was a Cork hurling selector from 1976 to '79 and again in 1986. A Munster title was won in all of those years. Only 1979 failed to produce an All-Ireland

---

This is Jimmy Brohan's team, excluding Corkmen,
'but I felt I couldn't leave out Christy Ring.'

	Ollie Walsh (*Kilkenny*)	
Jimmy Brohan (*Cork*)	Bobbie Rackard (*Wexford*)	John Doyle (*Tipperary*)
Jimmy Finn (*Tipperary*)	Billy Rackard (*Wexford*)	Tony Wall (*Tipperary*)
	Phil Grimes (*Waterford*)	Joe Salmon (*Galway*)	
Jimmy Doyle (*Tipperary*)	Christy O'Brien (*Laois*)	Seán Clohossey (*Kilkenny*)
Jimmy Smyth (*Clare*)	Christy Ring (*Cork*)	Seán McLoughlin (*Tipperary*)

title, Cork going down to Galway in the semi-final.

Two of his brothers played League of Ireland football: Bobby as goalkeeper for Evergreen United, John at full-back for Cork Hibernians. The Westham manager showed interest in Bobby, but at the time he was very young and decided against going overseas. Might he have played soccer himself? 'I might if I had come after Bobby and John.'

Well, perhaps it was just as well he didn't. Otherwise hurling lovers would have missed the hurling skills of this tall, lightly built, brilliant right-full-back — with the white legs — whose timing in the pull was superb, who always played the ball — a gentleman of modest demeanour on and off the field, a credit to the game.

Born 1912

I am indebted to Billy Burke (son) and Liam Burke (nephew) for much of the information in this article about the late Billy Burke, who died in January 1995.

Billy was born in 1912 on the night the *Titanic* went down. A native of Dunmore — a football stronghold in his youth — he didn't become involved in hurling until he went to Kilkenny CBS. From there he progressed through colleges hurling to the Kilkenny minor team of 1930 — beaten by Tipp in the final, 4:1 to 2:1.

In 1934 he played on the county junior team beaten by Kildare at Athy. Fate then took a hand in his introduction to senior ranks. Kilkenny stepped in at short notice — after Limerick had indicated that they couldn't fulfil the engagement — to play Clare in the Cusack Shield final at Ennis for the official opening of Cusack Park. Kilkenny hadn't time to notify all the regulars, so Billy was among the newcomers called upon. The medal he won that day always remained a cherished possession, ranking with the pride he felt as a nineteen-year-old in 1931 when Lory Meagher asked him to hurl with Tullaroan, and his great sense of achievement in 1939 when he won his first and only All-Ireland medal.

He always looked back on 1935 with a sense of regret. He played at left-half-back in all the games up to the All-Ireland final. Because of a dispute between the county board and the James Stephens Club, Paddy Larkin and Peter Blanchfield didn't play in those games, but matters were resolved for the final. Billy was then among the subs. In atrocious weather, Kilkenny beat Limerick in a thriller by one point, 2:5 to 2:4. Billy, who was about to get married, returned home after the final and wasn't present at the celebrations in the Ossory Hotel. He never got a medal.

In 1936 Limerick and Kilkenny again met in the final. Billy came on as a sub in that game, but Limerick reversed the result of the previous year with a great second-half performance. By 1937 Billy had a regular place on the team; but by then it was an aging one, and they went down heavily to Tipp in the All-Ireland final at Killarney.

But a heavy defeat has never fazed Kilkenny hurling men. There is always new talent coming to hand; and so in 1939 they were back again to contest the final with Cork on the first Sunday in September. It was the day of the outbreak of the Second World War; it is said that some of those travelling to the game heard the news and turned back at Carlow. It was a day of thunder and lightning and rain. It was the day of a memorable final won by Kilkenny on the call of time with a point from Jimmy Kelly of Carrickshock, 2:7 to 3:3.

Billy had a great game at centre-back. He was equally brilliant at centre-back that year in the Leinster final against Dublin, a game that he always described as the best game of hurling he played in. For the eighth time since 1931

Kilkenny reached the final in 1940 and were opposed by Limerick — contesting their fifth final since 1933. It turned out to be a very exciting final. At half time Kilkenny led by 1:4 to 1:2, and Billy Burke at centre-back was having a great game on the mighty Mick Mackey — and was acknowledged by Mick as one of the great opponents he encountered. A Limerick switch in the second half took Mackey to centrefield. Other Limerick switches paid dividends too, and when the final whistle blew it was Limerick 3:7, Kilkenny 1:7. It was understandable after the game that some Kilkenny folk would say that Billy Burke should have been sent to police Mackey; but centrefield is different from centre-back, and Billy had never played there.

After 1940 Kilkenny hit a lean patch. Because of an outbreak of foot and mouth disease, Kilkenny weren't allowed to take part in the championship of 1941. The following year they lost the Leinster final to Dublin, 4:8 to 1:4, and Billy finished up that day manning the goal. That result was reversed in 1943 in a game in which Billy received a broken jaw. As a result he was unavailable for the All-Ireland semi-final against Antrim in Belfast, a day when Antrim shocked Gaeldom with a sensational win, 3:3 to 1:6.

1945 was Billy's last year in the black and amber. He didn't play in the Leinster championship but was brought on as a sub against Galway in the All-Ireland semi-final, a game won by Kilkenny by one point. And so the final against Tipp. Billy, playing in his fifth final, was at centre-back. Down four goals at half time, Kilkenny made a great second-half rally and came within four points with ten minutes left, before losing in the end by 5:6 to 3:6. A knee injury caused Billy to leave the field of play.

He has been described as a stout-hearted hurler, strong, utterly dependable, very determined, committed to fitness. His medals he bequeathed to the Lory Meagher Heritage Centre.

He played with three senior clubs in

Billy Burke (right) with Jack Lynch.

Kilkenny — Tullaroan, Éire Óg, and Dicksboro' — but never won a county senior medal. It was an era when there was no parish rule. His sons Billy and Gerard played at minor level for Kilkenny in 1962 and 1969, respectively.

Throughout his life Billy was a keen follower of Gaelic football and regarded Tommy Murphy of Laois and Paddy Kennedy of Kerry as the two finest footballers he had seen.

Having established himself on the Kilkenny team in 1937, he became an automatic choice on the Leinster Railway Cup team from 1938 onwards. From 1938 to 1943 Leinster contested every Railway Cup final with Munster. It was, however, an era when Munster dominated. Only in 1941 did Leinster win. They defeated Munster by one point, 2:5 to 2:4; but fortune frowned on Billy on that occasion, and injury kept him from lining out. John and Mick Mackey were absent from the Munster selection. They had played in the semi-final on 16

February against Connacht; three days later their brother Paddy died. In accordance with the custom of the time, neither played with club or county until the following year.

Billy was unlucky again in 1943. The Railway Cup final of that year is remembered as one of the best and most exciting the competition has known. With about ten minutes to go Leinster were six points ahead and looking good. But a Munster rally brought two goals, and Christy Ring got the winning point, leaving the score 4:3 to 3:5 and the Leinster players and Billy Burke very disappointed.

I asked Billy and Liam to select a team they felt Billy might have chosen to captain, based on chats and discussions they had with him down the years. This they sportingly did, and here is their selection.

Ollie Walsh *(Kilkenny)*

Bobbie Rackard *(Wexford)*   Nick O'Donnell *(Wexford)*   Billy Burke *(Kilkenny)*

Séamus Cleere *(Kilkenny)*   John Keane *(Waterford)*   Paddy Phelan *(Kilkenny)*

Frank Cummins *(Kilkenny)*   Lory Meagher *(Kilkenny)*

Jack Lynch *(Cork)*   Pat Delaney *(Kilkenny)*   Mick Mackey *(Limerick)*

Christy Ring *(Cork)*   Nicky Rackard *(Wexford)*   Eddie Keher *(Kilkenny)*

And then they added that any of the following might also have found favour:
Jackie Power *(Limerick)*, Jimmy Finn, Tommy Doyle and Jimmy Doyle
(Tipperary), Christy Moylan *(Waterford)*, and Jimmy Langton *(Kilkenny)*.

Born 1923

For fifteen years at county senior level Mickey Byrne was a key figure in 'Fortress Tipperary'. I am referring of course to the Tipperary hurling full-back line, where Mickey played at right-full. Those were the days when a full-back line guarded and covered their goalkeeper almost with their lives and in the process took no prisoners. Dust would fly in the square; body would crunch on body; ash would flail on ash; spectators would marvel at the hardihood of the human frame and revel in the intensity of the exchanges.

In the early days the line read: Mickey Byrne, Tony Brennan, John Doyle. Later and with equal effectiveness it read: Mickey Byrne, Mícheál Maher, Kieran Carey. 'Tony Brennan, who was about 6 foot 3 tall, would never play a high lobbing ball. At the crucial moment he would deflect the opponent's hurley away from the ball and let Reddan gather it behind him. We had a great understanding with Reddan — a wonderful goalkeeper, whom John Killeen, the former Galway midfielder, was indirectly instrumental in bringing to Tipp. We also had an understanding among ourselves in the backs that if an opposing half-forward slipped his man we would revolve either clockwise or anti-clockwise as a unit so as to head him off and tighten the defence.'

66

I was born in 1923, went to school at Thurles CBS. When I was growing up in Thurles I had to get interested in hurling, as it was in Thurles that the GAA was founded and hurling was always a topic at corners and in the pubs around Thurles.

I won my first hurling medal in the CBS in 1939 in what was called the Dean Ryan Cup. In 1940 I won my first county championship (minor) with Sarsfields. In 1941 I was picked on the county team and was beaten by Cork in the Munster final in Limerick.

In 1944 I won my first senior county championship, winning fourteen in all up to 1965 (twenty-one years). I went on to win numerous championships etc.

I can tell you they were the happiest years of my life and I would not swop them for anything else. I must say my hardest opponents on the field were my greatest friends, and when I meet them from time to time we go back and play those games over and over again, and it brings back great enjoyment.

99

Mickey Byrne

Mickey, whose height was 5 feet 7 and who never weighed more than ten-and-a-half stone in his playing days, was like a pocket battleship at right-full-back. He encountered many opponents during his long career and held his own with them all, including the Maestro himself, Christy Ring — 'the most complete hurler I ever played on.' An opponent's size or reputation never fazed him. In many ways he was indestructible, and during his career he never left the field because of injury. 'Oh, I often got some stitches after a match. I remember one day in a league final going in close to hook my man in the opening five minutes. I got a belt on the thumb and knew it was injured. I pulled a hankie from a pocket in the back of the togs and wrapped it round the thumb. After the match a doctor came in with Paddy Leahy, examined it, and said it was broken. We came home through Cashel that night and at about eleven o'clock Surgeon Hogan set it for me.'

Uppermost in Mickey's mind remains the first-round Munster championship marathon encounter with Cork at Limerick in 1949. It went on for two-and-a-half hours — a draw; a replay — draw; thirty minutes' extra time. 'For the replay it was a sweltering hot day, the sun boiling out of the heavens. It was said that empty lemonade bottles were being filled with water and sold to spectators for a tanner [six old pence]. At full time we retired to the dressing-room. In there were two great athletes, Dick and Mick Blake of Coolquill, who had brought along a few tankards of cool spring water. We pulled off our jerseys and they sponged us down. Then they rubbed us with a concoction of their own that included methylated spirits and wintergreen. We were new men: we went out like kangaroos. Jim Barry slipped up badly: he let the Cork players stay out on the pitch under the sweltering sun.'

Though they didn't know it at the time, Tipp had cleared the first hurdle that would lead them to three successive All-Ireland titles, the second such achievement by the county.

Mickey recalled some moments from his youth that will always live in his memory. 'I was at Clonmel in 1937 — my father took me there — when Limerick, the reigning All-Ireland champions, faced Waterford in the first round. That day I witnessed the greatest individual duel I have ever seen between two players: John Keane at centre-back for Waterford versus Mick Mackey at centre-forward for Limerick. It surpassed and still surpasses all others. I

was in Thurles in 1940 for the Munster final — the draw and replay between Limerick and Cork. They were the two greatest games I have seen. I saw Paddy Scanlon puck out the ball, and Timmy Ryan doubled on it to send it over the bar. I have never seen a centrefield man like Timmy Ryan. You don't see the kind of overhead hurling he did nowadays.'

Mickey's own hurling career took off in Thurles CBS, where in 1939 the school won the Dean Ryan Cup. In 1941 he played minor for Tipp. By 1945 he had progressed to the senior panel and was a sub on the All-Ireland winning team. Later that autumn he played his first competitive game in the blue and gold when Tipp beat Galway in the Oireachtas final, 4:6 to 4:3. There followed four Munster and All-Ireland successes, 1949, '50, '51, and '58, and seven National league wins. With fourteen county senior hurling titles, he holds a Tipperary record that may never be equalled.

Between 1949 and 1954 a fierce rivalry developed between Tipperary and Cork. After the first-round marathon of 1949 they met every year for the next five years in the Munster final. The occasions were great, even if some of the games fell short of greatness. These were games that at times demanded raw courage. Adverse comment in the form of letters to the newspapers followed the 1949 meeting; and yet out of those clashes of intense rivalry there grew friendships that blossomed brightly and that continued to endure and have an even greater meaning and affection as the years roll on into old age. Mickey has friends from his playing days in every hurling county. 'I remember in one of the 1949 games someone placed a Cork red-and-white cap on the net behind Tony Reddan — probably to annoy him. When I saw it I went round and sliced it down with my hurley.'

Mickey retired after the 1960 National league win over Cork — a victorious exit. 'I told Paddy Leahy I was calling it

Right:
*Mickey
Byrne (on the
left) with
former
Tipperary
star Mutt
Ryan.*

a day — our mentor and commander-in-chief, one of the brainiest men ever involved in the game: many a winning switch he made.' But Mickey returned a short time later for just one last hour of glory — a winning one — when he captained Tipperary in a tournament game against Cork in Birmingham.

Mickey's sitting-room is adorned with trophies and pictures. There is a large picture of Michael Collins — 'my favourite character in Irish history.' There is a photograph of himself, Tommy Doyle and Jim Devitt taken at the funeral of Jim Langton. He pointed to one taken at Christy Ring's graveside of Mick Mackey, Tommy Doyle, and himself — all sombre and reflective. On parade before the National League final against Waterford in 1959 was a fine shot of Jimmy Finn, John Doyle, Mícheál Maher, Mickey Byrne, and Kieran Carey. On the social scene was a photograph of Jack Lynch and Mick Mackey at Thurles Golf Club. 'I took that photograph,' says Mickey.

Hurling has always been good to Mickey Byrne. In his playing days he got three trips to America and twelve trips to London, where they played games at Wembley, New Elton, and Mitcham Stadium. In the 1950 trip to America they played New York at the Polo Grounds — 'the last game to be played there: after that it was Gaelic Park.'

In 1992 he was invited by the Tipperary Association to Manchester, where he was honoured as a player of the past and presented with a bronze statuette similar to that given to the All-Stars. In 1995 he received a Hall of Fame award, presented to him by Bob Stakelum on behalf of the Mid-Tipperary Board of the GAA. In June the same year he received an invitation — the only Tipperary man to receive one — to attend at City Hall in Cork on the occasion of Con Murphy being made a Freeman of Cork. There Mickey linked up with Willie John Daly. Dave Guiney reported that he met them but, with both in full verbal flight, he didn't get a word in. Memory Lane was at work and dust was flying in the square again — this time nostalgic dust.

Mickey is a great raconteur and has a spontaneous wit and sense of humour. He told me he had his two hips replaced — did a few swaggers to show how successful they were, and added, 'I joined the hippy club.' He tells a story about Christy Ring. 'It was in a league game against Cork and both teams were level. Cork won a sideline cut about forty-five yards out. Cathal McLoughlin, the referee, told Ring it would be the last puck of the game. Ring took two steps back; looked at the posts; and from the moment he hit it, it was on the way for a point. Afterwards Ring walked into the hotel with Jim Barry. I turned to him and said, "By God, Christy, we'll have to shoot you." "Oh, sure ye might as well, Mickey," said Ring. "Ye've tried everything else."'

Witticisms associated with Mickey would fill an entire volume — comments like 'The first half was even, and the second half was even worse.' 'The only hamstrings in my day were the ones hanging outside a butcher's shop.' And of course the unfortunate referee who wouldn't see a 'foul' in a henhouse. If the poet Alexander Pope had met Mickey he would almost certainly have dedicated the following rhyming couplet to him:

> 'True wit is nature to advantage dress'd,
> What oft was thought, but ne'er so well express'd.'

Born 1920

For much of the information in this article I am indebted to three Antrim Gaels who were most helpful. First is Seán Campbell, the late Noel's brother, who in our telephone conversation told me that Jack Lynch paid a visit to Noel in the mid-forties and during his stay 'they had a few wee deohanna together as they reminisced and talked about the great game they both played so well — well, a good few wee deochanna.' Next is Joe Cooper, a wonderful 82-year-old veteran in 1996. 'I visit the "Rossa" club every Tuesday night for a yarn and a glass with the hurlers of yesteryear, and we play many a match over again.' He is still a regular visitor to Croke Park. In the forties he cycled annually to Thurles for a number of years to the Munster final — a round trip of four hundred miles from Belfast. On 4 July 1995 he was awarded the honorary degree of doctor of science in education by Queen's University. Awarding the doctorate, the dean of the Faculty of Theology, Professor Bernard Cullen, described him as 'a voice of reason and calming influence on the community' through some of the

more terrible years of violence. The third person is Brendan Harvey, a lecturer in mathematics at St Malachy's College, Belfast. Like Joe Cooper he visits the 'Rossa' club on Tuesday evenings. His father, Liam, was a founder-member of the O'Connell Club in 1916. He was twice County Antrim chairman in the twenties and thirties; he first represented Antrim at Ulster level in 1924 and finally retired from GAA office in 1970. The Ulster hurling championship cup is named after him. Brendan's mother was secretary of the first organised Antrim Camogie Board. 'I suppose it should surprise no-one that I was reared in a teaghlach fíor-Ghaelach.'

Now to Noel Campbell. Down the decades Antrim has been the chief standard-bearer of hurling in Ulster. Derry (1902 and 1909), Cavan (1908) and Donegal (1923) between them made a total of four appearances in the All-Ireland semi-final, but they never developed into a force. By contrast, the game always flourished in Antrim and particularly in Belfast and the Glens. The enthusiasm was there in abundance; so was the raw material; what was missing was regular competition against the leading hurling counties, coupled with coaching by an expert from one of those counties.

Creditable performances by Antrim juniors against Cork in the home final of 1938 and by their minors against Limerick in the All-Ireland final of 1940 suggested that Antrim hurling was in the ascendant. This was confirmed in 1943 when Antrim was admitted to the senior championship. A quarter-final meeting with Galway ended on the score Antrim 7:0, Galway 6:2. Noel Campbell at midfield — ably supported by his schoolmate and club colleague Jackie Bateson — had a brilliant game and scored a goal direct from a

The Antrim team of 1943 which defeated Kilkenny at Corrigan Park, Belfast. Back row: *Tom Walsh, Mannix McAlister, Donal Boylan, Dan McKillop, John Currie, Kevin Murphy, John Butler,* **Noel Campbell,** *Willie Graham.* Middle row: *John McNeill, Joe Mullan, Sam Mulholland, Kevin Armstrong, Paddy McGarry, Jimmy Walsh, Paddy McKeown, John Hurl, Jackie Bateson, Danny McAlister.* Front row: *Fred Delaney, Gerry McAteer, Billy Best.*

The Railway Cup final 1945, Ulster against Munster. Noel Campbell leads the parade.

sideline cut to win. The Antrim full-forward Dan 'Baxter' McAllister, who scored four goals, in 1995 attended the Ireland v. Scotland game in Fort William.

In the All-Ireland semi-final in Belfast, Antrim beat Kilkenny, 3:3 to 1:6. It was one of hurling's greatest sensations, all the more so because it was Antrim's first appearance in a semi-final since 1924. Again, Noel was outstanding at midfield, and his display would in modern times have won him the Man of the Match award.

Expectations and hopes were high in Antrim after the historic defeats of Galway and Kilkenny. In preparation for the final showdown with Cork a former Dublin hurler was engaged for two weeks to train the Antrim team. They were brought together by the Antrim County Board in Belfast and put up in a hotel. Unfortunately the recipe proved to be unsuccessful. A combination of Croke Park nerves caused by a first All-Ireland appearance, a suspicion that they were overtrained and muscle-bound, and exceptional opponents in a highly talented Cork outfit, now appearing in their third All-Ireland final in a row, all contributed to an overwhelming defeat, 5:16 to 0:4. Campbell was one of a few on the Antrim side whose class was in evidence; many considered him the equal of the hurling giants of that era.

Antrim hurling men were to the fore again in 1945. Ulster, backboned by ten Antrim men, created another sensation by defeating Leinster in the Railway Cup at Belfast, a Leinster team with Nicky Rackard and Jimmy Langton in their ranks. Noel was the Ulster captain and gave his usual polished display at midfield. That day Ulster wore an old-style Antrim jersey: horizontal hoops of green and gold.

In the other semi-final, at Galway, Connacht drew with Munster but lost the replay at Limerick, 4:8 to 3:7. So there was a unique hurling pairing on St Patrick's Day: Ulster v. Munster. For half an hour Ulster fared very well, showed a good turn of speed, first-time pulling, some grand ground balls. Noel's class stood out, and he was one of Ulster's shining lights. Unfortunately two rather soft goals were conceded early in the second half, and the final score read Munster 6:8, Ulster 2:0. Noel had played against the cream of Munster hurling and was not found wanting. The line-out is worth recording:

Noel Campbell probably reached his hurling peak in 1945. He was playing brilliant hurling. In the All-Ireland semi-final against Tipperary he ruled supreme at midfield, and Tipp replaced their midfielder, Tom Wall; but in the end Tipperary's superior forces won the day, 5:9 to 1:6. It was, however, a very creditable performance by Antrim.

Noel learned his hurling at St Mary's CBS and played for the school. Later he played his club hurling with Mitchels and won a junior and intermediate league in 1939. In 1942 Mitchels were promoted to senior status, and in 1947 Noel led them to their only Antrim senior hurling success. He was still playing good hurling but beginning to slow down. His working life, as a telephone engineer, did not lend itself to steady training. In his final years he played at full-back. He went to work in England in the early fifties but returned to Dublin every All-Ireland day to relive the scene.

Noel was a very stylish player. Adept at first-time hurling, he could hold his own at midfield with the best in Ireland. He had speed and flair — the skill and touch of a genius that distinguishes the ace player from the ordinary.

He retired in 1980 and came back to Cushendall on the Antrim coast. In the words of Brendan Harvey, 'he was still the same confident extrovert that he was on the hurling field.'

D'éag sé i 1985 in aois a cúig bliana is seasca. But he will live in hurling folklore and always be remembered in his native Belfast and 'the high hills of Antrim, the glens and the streams' as one of Ulster's all-time hurling greats.

The Munster Team 1945

Jim Ware *(Waterford)*

| Andy Fleming *(Waterford)* | Willie Murphy *(Cork)* | Peter Cregan *(Limerick)* |
| Paddy O'Donovan *(Cork)* | Jackie Power *(Limerick)* | Jim Young *(Cork)* |

Paddy McCarthy *(Limerick)*   Con Cottrell *(Cork)*

| Tommy Purcell *(Tipperary)* | Christy Ring *(Cork)* | Dick Stokes *(Limerick)* |
| Mick Mackey *(Limerick)* | Johnny Quirke *(Cork)* | P.J. Quane *(Clare)* |

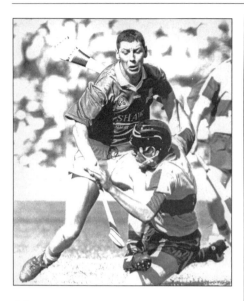

Born 1970

"

I have many memories of hurling, both good and bad, but my most vivid memory was when I was first taught how to rise a ball by a certain man called Anthony Carmody, who also happens to be my cousin. I was eight years of age at the time and Anthony was a skilful thirteen-year-old who was making a name for himself at under-age. I lived in 43 Marian Park and Anthony lived two doors down in 45 Marian Park, and it couldn't have been more ideal, as the hurling-field was situated at the back of our houses. For good measure Gary Kirby's house was opposite me and Phil Bennis's house just up the road. I would be up in the field every day with my brother Nigel after school, practising and playing hurling into the late hours of the evening.

My very first taste of competitive hurling came in the form of the local parish league, where games were contested with fervour and plenty of excitement at weekends. While I always enjoyed these games I was still looking forward to the thrill of representing my club, Patrickswell, at under-age level. But before I was to savour any thrill representing my club I was to have the unique distinction of captaining the lo-

cal national school to its first hurling title at under-twelve. It was this team which set the ball rolling, so to speak, as it formed the nucleus of our first victorious under-fourteen hurling team in our Centenary year of 1984, which I also had the distinction of captaining. This was indeed not only an exceptional year for the club in other grades (under-eighteen hurling, senior hurling) but it was also extra special for me, as I played in the minor team and was to get my first taste of inter-county hurling.

It was in this year, to the best of my knowledge, that the Tony Forrestal Memorial Trophy was inaugurated. This tournament, which could be considered an All-Ireland under-fourteen competition, was run very successfully over a weekend, and we were delighted to emerge eventual winners over a gallant Cork team in a closely contested final. I was also to experience a great personal achievement by being selected as Player of the Tournament.

I was to experience varying degrees of success at under-age level for my club before being elevated to minor inter-county status. But the following is one of my most cherished memories, which will live with me for ever. The year was 1987. I was just turned seventeen and I was to make the jump into manhood. The senior team were, as more often than not, making a strong challenge for the championship, and as I watched them training that evening, little was I to know what was about to unfold. The regular senior goalkeeper, Joe Murphy, suffered a serious hand injury at work and was unable to hurl. I was catapulted from watching the team training into standing in goal in my school uniform for the regular training. How could I have dreamed that I would be selected in goal for the senior team, let alone go on and win the county championship? Which is exactly

The winning point against Clare in '96.'The greatest winner ever scored.'

whathappened. Happily, Joe recovered and resumed his usual number 1 spot.

On the inter-county front I represented my county for two years at minor level and had the unenviable record of losing four consecutive under-21 Munster hurling finals. It was amidst these intervening years that I got that dream call-up to represent my county at senior level against Dublin in 1988 in the National League quarter-final. While it was a privilege to hurl in the league, my real blooding was to come at Páirc Uí Chaoimh when I was selected to play at corner-forward against a Tipperary team at the pinnacle of its power, which boasted such luminaries as Nicholas English, Pat Fox, and Bobby Ryan, to mention but a few. That same Tipperary team was to continually frustrate us as they defeated us for four consecutive years ('88 to '91) in the Munster championship. While I would never be a defeatist or a person to drop the head, even I began to have nagging doubts as to when we would ever make that breakthrough. That eventual breakthrough came sooner than expected when we triumphed over Tipperary in the National League final in 1992 after overturning an eight-point deficit at half time. Words cannot describe the emotion I experienced that day.

While I hurled and trained with countless people over the years and still continue to do so, I feel there are two people in particular I must pay tribute to: John Enright, who guided me faultlessly through the under-age ranks and still continues to do so to many others, and last, but by no means least, Phil Bennis, a man who has influenced my career immensely, for his unerring guidance and advice and who was always there for me, and still is.

My uncle Éamon, my father, Pa, and my brother Pa all played at county senior level for Limerick. It is an honour for me to follow in their footsteps.

35

On our visit to Ciarán we met his wife, Miriam, who played minor camogie for Limerick and who was preparing young Barry for bed. We also met Sara, their four-year-old daughter, who a week earlier had won her first two medals for dancing — and very proud she was of them. She danced a few steps for us, with particular emphasis on doing the 'heel'. She then reeled off the names of the Limerick players and when asked who was the best didn't hesitate: 'Daddy is the best on the Limerick team: he won two cups.'

Miriam too is an avid hurling fan. Why wouldn't she be — wife of Ciarán, daughter of Phil Bennis? But she suffers the tortures of tension at many of the games. It was Sunday, 16 June 1996. Clare, All-Ireland champions, versus Limerick at Páirc na nGael, Limerick, in the Munster semi-final before a capacity attendance of 43,534. With five minutes to go Limerick trailed by three points and looked like losing. Three points from play brought them level. The game was in injury time when the Clare goalie, David Fitzgerald, pucked out the ball. Miriam saw Ciarán soar into the air for the ball. She couldn't look; she buried her head in her lap. She heard the rising cheers of the Limerick fans; still she kept her head buried. Then Damien Quigley's wife, who was beside her, shouted, 'He's scored!' She looked up. Someone had thrown Sara up in the air. The place was a mass of green and white. Soon the agony was over.

Let's recount that last score. As the puck-out from David Fitzgerald descended, Ciarán rose lynx-eyed into the air. Cleanly he caught the sliotar. He set off on a solo run like a greyhound from the traps. He was on a mission. A point or a free, he thought to himself. He veered slightly left. Fergal Hegarty, in hot pursuit, fell. Clare backs retreated to cover their men. Ciarán had now run all of sixty yards and handled the ball twice. Now, about thirty yards from goal, he turns to his right — his weak side — clips the sliotar off the hurley,

and strikes the winner with control and composure. The Guinness advertisement summed up the feelings of all Clare supporters: 'This man can break hearts from seventy yards.'

Kevin Cashman, writing in the *Sunday Independent*, described it as 'the greatest winner ever scored,' and continued:

'a truly unique occasion; made so by excitement and tension and passion and sportsmanship (not whiter than white, but still terrific) and a pre-match atmosphere, in the grounds and its environs, such as many of us had thought had gone with the days of the fifties.'

The Clare captain, Anthony Daly, described the solo run as the four most agonising seconds of his life. And Ciarán's recollection of the day? 'I had to change my boots at half time. The ground was rock-hard. I was wearing boots with steel cogs. My feet were cut to ribbons from the studs and took a couple of weeks to heal. I changed to rubber cogs. When I caught the ball I saw a big space and said, here goes. I headed towards the left post, then darted to the right. It was the hottest day I ever hurled — unbelievable heat. I don't know where I got the energy to run.'

More agony for Miriam at the Munster final against Tipperary at Páirc na nGael on 7 July. Down ten points at half time, playing poorly, looking uncertain, Limerick had a huge task on their hands. Miriam went to the back of the stand. She cried and prayed to her grandmother. She was listening to the men who were coming and going. They'll come back; they'll come back all right, they were saying. It gave her a bit of hope. When she returned to her seat, Limerick had cut the deficit to seven points. A long nail-biting road lay ahead. But Limerick were now playing valiantly and scored ten points without reply. In the dying seconds Frankie Carroll scored the equaliser. Miriam's prayers were answered — and on the eve of the replay she said a few more.

Tom Humphries in the *Irish Times* the day after the drawn game had this to say:

'Extraordinary. A game which jangled the nerves and brought the memory of great days vaulting out from the recesses of the mind. Unbelievable. An afternoon of jack-knifing fortunes and twisting, lurching narrative. Incredible. A game with jagged edges and a deservedly even finish ... The greatest Munster hurling final of recent times ... There will be the sceptics who will sniff that the hurling lacked purity, that the striking lacked sweetness, that the game lacked texture. Bah. May their air lack oxygen.'

As Ciarán glanced through my leather-bound journal of six hundred pages in which so many great hurlers had made a written contribution, he came upon the name of the late Bobbie Rackard. Glancing at his two All-Ireland wins of 1955 and '56, he said: 'It would do me if I could get one.' The might-have-beens of '94 and '96 were in his mind. 'I thought I was consistent through the two games and got three points from centre-back against Wexford. I think '94 would have to be my biggest disappointment. That day we hurled well as a team — not so in '96. '94 looked good for us.' Miriam interjected to say: 'I never want to experience another loss.'

Ciarán, a keen Liverpool soccer fan, was from his infancy surrounded by a hurling atmosphere — in his home, in his parish, in school at Limerick CBS and Croom Vocational School. Then to under-age with Limerick. 'I played in four under-21 Munster finals and lost all to Cork and Tipperary.' In the 1996 senior hurling championship there were six Careys on the Patrickswell panel, five playing: Patrick, Seán, Ciarán, Kevin, Paul, and Nigel. When Limerick beat Tipp in a thrilling National League final in 1992 Patrick was full-back and Ciarán was centre-back. 'It was the first season I was placed at centre-back and I have special memories of our quarter-final win over Kilkenny, the semi-final win over Cork, and the final win over Tipp.' It was the beginning for Limerick of a series of victories over the old rivals Cork and Tipp.

Indeed, he feels those wins over Tipp might have come sooner if Limerick hadn't had Mike Barron, their full-back, sent off in the Munster championship game against Tipp in 1990 at Limerick. 'I was only a garsún that day — playing at right-corner-forward. We were hurling well and having the better of it. We would have rattled them if he was left on.' What did he feel was his best display? He paused; it was a difficult one. 'Miriam, give me a hand.' And she did. 'I felt he had a brilliant game against Cork in '94.' Well, he certainly had, for he hunted all over the field: fielding, passing, linking; and in the closing moments he sent in the ball that Pat Heffernan flicked to the net for a great overhead goal. 'Yes, I played well that day.' Miriam was wearing the watch he won as RTÉ Man of the Match.

The opponents he most admired are Martin Storey of Wexford, Brian Corcoran of Cork, and Tony O'Sullivan of Cork. His top three to date other than opponents are Brian Whelehan of Offaly, Brian Corcoran of Cork, and D.J. Carey of Kilkenny. 'I rate them very highly.'

Hurling trophies and photographs are much in evidence in their home: three All-Star awards; a crystal sliotar on a pedestal, awarded following his selection on the *Sunday Independent* team of 1992; a pair of copper boots on a lovely base, presented to him as Hurler of the Month in May 1992 by National Irish Bank; a beautiful crystal plaque incorporating a silhouette of himself presented by *Gaelic World* in a consistency ratings award in 1992; inscribed Waterford Glass vases for Runner-Up Hurler of the year in '92 and '96.

In 1996 he captained Limerick and led them through as testing and demanding a Munster campaign as any team ever encountered. First it was Cork in their own back yard, Páirc Uí Chaoimh, where they hadn't suffered a championship defeat since 1922. The final score made everyone blink, for Limerick had beaten their bogey team, 3:18 to 1:8. Next it was Clare, reigning All-Ireland champions, at Páirc na nGael — a game with which the name of Ciarán Carey will be for ever linked; and in years to come when the story is retold who knows how much longer that solo run of sixty yards will have grown, and perhaps the heat will have passed 100 degrees Fahrenheit. Who knows! It was Tipperary, the league finalists, in the Munster final at Páirc na nGael. Ciarán proved his calibre as captain that day when he spoke to his team colleagues at half time and lifted their spirits. It was a memorable moment for him when he lifted the cup after the replay defeat of Tipp, and Limerick were crowned Munster champions.

It had been a superb Munster championship, demonstrating to the full the peerless spectacle that is hurling. The ancient game — in craft and skill and heroics, thrills and excitement and drama — was never seen to better advantage. And at all times Ciarán was an inspirational captain.

He is a utility man, one of the great hurlers of the present-day game, who has displayed his repertoire of skills in the backs, at centrefield, and among the forwards. Before a game he likes a few quiet moments to himself: to focus his thoughts, to concentrate, but in particular 'to have a little chat with Himself.' At times on the pitch he seems like a hurling magician as he bobs and floats and wafts and glides through the field. A man of pace, artistry, and courage, he can execute deeds of skill while moving at great pace. One of his favourite ploys is to sally forth from defence, make a sortie into the opposing lines, and complete the incursion by picking off punishing and inspiring scores.

A delight to watch is Ciarán.

Born 1970

"

My first memories of travelling to hurling matches were with my uncle, Martin Carey. He was the first big influence on my hurling career. Martin was a hurler of note with our local club, Young Irelands, Gowran. It was with him that we learned our hurling at a young age. I have three brothers and three sisters, and all would be very interested in the game. This year three of us won the local senior club championship for the first time with Gowran. Most of that local team came through, under the supervision of two great schoolteachers and hurling people, John Knox and Dick O'Neill. They were largely influential in our local club winning the championship, because of their hard work and dedication down the years in producing hurlers from a very small pick.

Leaving my local school for secondary level, I went to St Kieran's College. St Kieran's was and is a great school for hurling and it provides an awful lot of Kilkenny hurlers. There are a lot of great men in there, such as Nicky Cashin, Séamus Knox, Tommy Lanigan, Denis Philpott, Father Paddy Bollard, Father Fergal Farrell, and many more. All of these people worked at some time or another with the legendary Father Tommy Maher.

Hurling has always been very good to me. I suppose, because I have always been so involved in hurling, football, and handball, it has kept me out of any trouble. It has been a great time because I have got so much out of the game and hopefully, barring injury, I will be able to play the game for as long as possible. I would encourage every parent in the country to get the children playing our sport. It gives a great sense of pride to be able to go out and achieve something for their local parish, whether that be at local or national level.

The great thing for me is that our games will never die, because the interest at grass-roots level will always be there. I would encourage the young people to get involved, and even if they are not good at the games they might be very good administrators.

I would like to see more counties getting better at hurling. Gaelic football is very strong at national level, but unfortunately there's only a handful of teams in contention for glory every year.

Play hurling, football, handball, camogie etc. for enjoyment. Every game gets very serious and the problem is nowadays that sport in general is being based on fitness a lot, which means some of the enjoyment is going away from it. I hope that this will not happen, but not everyone will reach that level; so whether you do or don't, get as much enjoyment from it, because a career is very short. Some people go through their careers and get a good few years out of it, but unfortunately for some, a lot of players get injured and have to give up the game. So that's why I suggest you enjoy the time you have on the field.

People who influenced me most in my career or who I looked up to were my parents, my uncle Martin Carey, and

Peggy Muldowney (née Carey), who won four All-Ireland camogie championships with Kilkenny, John Knox, and Dick O'Neill (schoolteachers). Players I admired most were Ger Henderson (Kilkenny), Nicky English (Tipperary), and Joe Cooney (Galway). I was very lucky to play with or against all these players. I also got to play with a lot of great Kilkenny players, such as Liam Fennelly, Richie Power, Joe Hennessy, Christy Heffernan, John Henderson, and many more.

,,

G rowing up in Gowran, D.J. Carey — nicknamed the 'Dodger' — was introduced at an early age to the game of hurling, and before he went to St Kieran's College he had tasted success at under-age level. Hurling brilliance was of course in the genes. His grand-uncle Paddy Phelan, who featured in Hurling Giants, gave many dazzling displays at left-half-back for great Kilkenny teams in the thirties and played into the early forties. His aunt Peggy Muldowney (née Carey) played camogie for many years with Kilkenny and won four All-Ireland titles. She was on the 1974 team that brought Kilkenny its first senior camogie title, a team that sowed the seeds for many future successes that made Kilkenny a camogie power.

Two days before I met D.J. his sister Caitríona was stealing the limelight. She scored the winning goal for Hermes hockey team to give the club its first Irish senior cup in their first appearance in the final of the competition. Mary Hannigan, reporting on the game, wrote: 'Up until Saturday afternoon she was known as D.J. Carey's sister who "plays a bit of hockey." After she scored the goal that won Hermes the Irish senior cup, D.J. better get used to life as Caitríona Carey's big brother, the one who plays a bit of hurling.'

At St Kieran's, D.J. further developed

his hurling skills and won two senior All-Ireland college titles in 1988 and '89 with victories over Midleton CBS and St Flannan's, respectively. In 1988 he won an All-Ireland minor title with Kilkenny, and in 1990 — the year after he made his début in goal for Kilkenny seniors in a game against Offaly — he won an All-Ireland under-21 title. So at a young age the medals were beginning to accumulate.

At the same time he was having a successful run in the handball court. This was a game he played from a very early age; as with hurling, he blossomed into a master. His list of twenty major successes is highly impressive and includes All-Ireland titles at under-12, under-14, under-16, college, club, minor, junior, senior, and two under-23 world titles. The handball activity was of course tremendous for building up stamina. It also created a keen eye, sharp reflexes, and strong wrists.

But back to hurling. A technically brilliant player, he is a classical performer and an outstanding artist of the modern game. Modest and genial, he is blessed with a placid temperament — a factor, no doubt, that contributes immensely to his powers of concentration. He has flair, perception, pace, and creativity. In his solo runs you are treated to grace of movement, tremendous acceleration once he rounds his man, the side-step, the dummy, magical control, and a deadly clinical finish. It all adds up to a superbly fit hurling master — a teetotaller and non-smoker — who is the ultimate in sportsmanship and a most worthy holder of five All-Stars in a row, from '91 to '95. He rarely fails to find the net, can engineer goals from any quarter on the field, and can on occasions cause havoc, as he did against Offaly in the league final of '95. He did it again with a display of genius and wizardry in a league game against Galway at Ballinasloe in March 1997, scoring 2:9 out of a total of 3:11 and, to quote from Clíona Foley's report on the game, giving 'a new meaning to the phrase "playing a captain's part" ... that had even

Galway's most loyal supporters in the 6000 crowd singing his praises.' And Seán Kilfeather in the *Irish Times* wrote: 'What can be said of Kilkenny's captain D.J. Carey? What more can he do to join those great players like Ring, Mackey, Power and his fellow Kilkennyman Keher?' Well, he advanced his cause still further with a virtuoso performance against the same opposition in the All-Ireland quarter-final at Thurles on 28 July 1997. He scored 2:8 of Kilkenny's 4:15 in their two points win and in the process teased, tortured and tormented the hurling men of Galway, who will have some nightmares about a game in which they held a nine points lead at half-time.

He showed his class and coolness in the All-Ireland final of 1992 against Cork when just before half time Kilkenny were awarded a penalty. It was a vital moment, and Kilkenny badly needed a score. The sliotar was wet. A point was there for the taking. D.J. addressed the ball and with the confidence of a veteran despatched it to the net. I wondered if he considered his options when awarded a penalty. 'No. Your mind is made up beforehand for you in every game. It is agreed if we get a penalty you go for a goal — unless of course it's in the dying moments and the position might be such as to make it better to take the certain point.' Offaly and Wexford have also, to their cost, seen the net bulge from D.J.'s hurley.

Sunday 20 October 1996 will always live in his memory. It was the day he captained Young Irelands of his native Gowran to their first county senior hurling title, in a replay with James Stephens — a success that had its roots in an under-12 team of the early eighties. That day, out of a total of 3:9 he scored 2:4. His goals were a study in psychology. Twice his marker, Philip Larkin, remonstrated with the referee and twice the referee moved the ball forward. So a 40-yard free became a 21-yard free. D.J. placed the ball. Then he stepped back a few yards. He stood and gazed at the James Stephens players

who lined the goal. Then he advanced. His intentions were clear. He was moving at pace as he tossed the sliotar goalwards. With a swing and perfect co-ordination — well inside the 21-yard line — he struck the ball with force. The green flag waved. Within three minutes Young Irelands were awarded a penalty. This time only three players could line the goal. D.J. went through the same drill and ritual — mesmeric stuff. The attendance of fifteen thousand watched in anticipation. The net shook again.

Sharing that county success with D.J. were his brothers Martin, who kept a fine goal, and Jack, who, as the game was heading towards the final whistle and another draw seemed likely, took a pass on the run to score the winning goal. Earlier in the championship another brother, Kieran, was on the panel.

Every competition, irrespective of level, has its own Everest. Those who participate want to reach the highest point. To conquer the top leaves its own trail of special memories. D.J. has many of them and finds it hard to pick one above the other. 'I still remember the under-12 handball success; the All-Ireland win of '92 — my first; I remember the defeat of '91. You know you're better off losing in the first round than in the final. When you get to the final you're there to win. The club win of '96 was great. I would say to people that there is nothing greater than a win with your club, because it's the parish you grew up in. You step onto a higher level when you play with your county, and of course the biggest honour is to win the All-Ireland title.'

D.J. believes that the better team never loses. 'Whoever scores the most is the winner. That's how the winner is decided. Having more possession or being more stylish isn't what counts. You need a bit of luck, but you must score if you are to win.' His magnificent displays during '93 brought him a treble of personal awards: Texaco Hurler of the Year; Player of the Year; Players' Player of the Year.

So much of what D.J. does on the hurling-pitch is aptly summed up by an admirer, Michael Massey, in the following poem:

Better than the Best

A clean slap of hurls
A collision of colour
And out the sliotar spurts
Skittering stark-white
Along crew-cut green
In expectancy's split-second
He's a mental step ahead
A black-and-amber blur
With the merest hint of a shoulder dip
The flick of a stick
The sliotar slips
Snug into his fist
And he dances away on laughing feet
And we are where dreams begin

Where the lines have been erased
Where all things are possible
We glimpse the promise of
  perfection
Then in the hush of our held
  breaths
We marvel at the graceful ease of
  the hurl's arc
The sweet thud of leather on
  wood
And the net exults
In the self-expression
Of the artist's perfected craft
And we swell with pride.

Born 1931

Mick Dunne wrote in the *Irish Press* on the 1960 decider:

'Only slightly behind Brohan in Munster's merit list was Mick Cashman. He completely outshone Ollie Walsh and his cat-like agility foiled Leinster repeatedly in the second half.'

Imagine outshining Ollie! Mick was in his class.

A two-point defeat by Leinster in 1962 denied him seven in a row. The damage was done by Denis Heaslip of Kilkenny, who came on as a sub and in the closing moments was in the right spot to finish a seventy to the net in a relatively low-scoring game, 1:11 to 1:9. Mick's only real challengers preceded him: Paddy Scanlon of Limerick, who won five between 1934 and 1940, and Tony Reddan of Tipperary, who won five between 1950 and 1955.

His years with Cork were lean ones — among the leanest in the history of the county. A Munster title came his way in

Mick Cashman succeeded two great goalkeepers: Dave Creedon in the county jersey in 1956, and Tony Reddan in the provincial jersey in 1957. To both he was a most worthy successor. He gave many superb goalkeeping displays.

And yet it is a well-known fact that he had no great love or preference for goalkeeping, even though his senior club career began in his early teens. His talents were spotted by the great Johnny Quirke. Centre-back was where Mick liked best. He played there for his club and played a key role in the county final of 1956 when Glen Rovers were defeated 2:10 to 2:2 — Blackrock's first county title in twenty-five years. In 1961, when a no longer youthful Blackrock faced Avondhu in the county final, he was the outstanding man on the field, giving a magnificent performance, to which the opposition had no reply. He won his second county title. Mick played in the half-back line in the Cork junior team that defeated London in the final of 1950.

As a goalkeeper with Munster he set a record that is unlikely to be equalled, never mind surpassed. He won six Railway Cup medals. He was the automatic choice on the Munster team for seven successive years, from 1957 to 1963.

Mick with two sons Tom and Jim holding the McCarthy Cup.

1956, but Wexford defeated them in the All-Ireland final. Cork didn't win again in Munster until 1966, and by then Mick had departed the scene. And yet a twist of fate may well have deprived him of three All-Ireland titles. In 1952 he had to cry off the Cork team because of illness. Dave Creedon, who had made up his mind to retire, was coaxed back into action. So successful was he that he held his place and played a significant part in Cork's great three-in-a-row of 1952, '53, and '54. In 1953 and '54 Mick was a sub on the All-Ireland winning teams.

He married Jimmy Brohan's sister, Anne. Given the pedigree, it is no surprise that their sons Tom and Jim turned out to be wonderful hurlers — skilled, stylish, and sporting. 'They take after me,' remarked Jimmy to me with an impish laugh. Tom arrived on the county scene in 1977. He made an immediate impression and went on to play in six All-Ireland finals with Cork, winning four and captaining them in 1986 when they surprisingly defeated a very talented Galway team. Other honours included National Leagues, Railway Cups, county titles, eight Munster titles, and a recognition by the All-Star selectors on three occasions. Special too were the All-Ireland minor medal of 1974, the All-Ireland under-21 medal of 1976, and the All-Ireland club victory of 1979 — close, exciting and hard-earned over the famed Shamrocks of Kilkenny. Those who saw Tom play witnessed in action a great stick man, a wonderful ball player, equally adept left and right, master of the ground and air stroke, an excellent long-distance point-taker, a true sportsman who adorned our ancient game.

As I write, Jim is still playing the game. He partnered John Fenton at centrefield in 1986. In his second All-Ireland final, in 1990, he was centre-back, just as his brother Tom was in 1986. It was Cork's first final since 1986, and by coincidence the opponents were again Galway. As in '86, Cork, the underdogs, won. Jim is a classy hurler, possessing many of the attributes of his brother Tom. He does the basics with an art that conceals art — making hurling look simple. Who will forget his equalising point for Cork from surely eighty yards in the league final of 1993 following a hasty Wexford clearance? It was taken coolly and calmly, with aplomb and assurance, with the confidence of a master who knew his craft. In addition to the honours already mentioned, this most sporting of players also has Munster, county and Railway Cup medals and two All-Star awards. Here is how one hurling journalist summed him up:

'Splendid stickman, comparable to the best of any generation. He excelled in almost every position including goalie. Hardy, exemplar of John Keane's immortal dictum: — Take it, give it, and forget it.'

Ní raibh Mick ach 59 bliain d'aois nuair a d'imigh sé ar Shlí na Fírinne sa bhliain 1990.

Born 1934

Power, who was one of our best players at midfield, worked with us, so I always had somebody to train with when the evenings were too short to go down to the field in Kildermody.

The first game I played senior hurling for Waterford was a bit unusual. I had gone to the sports field to see Waterford playing Kilkenny in the league. Some players did not turn up. I remember the late Tom Penkert looking around for somebody to tog out. At that time, playing for a junior club, I was glad to be asked. That was October 1954. I was on the panel for the championship against Limerick in 1955. I came on as a sub; we were beaten narrowly.

I was on the team that played against Cork in Fermoy in 1956. It was a bit of a breakthrough for me, as I scored five points from play. Cork beat us by a few points. I was picked for the Rest of Ireland team later that year. After that then we won the Munster final in 1957; were beaten a bit unluckily against Kilkenny; won in Munster in 1959; beat Kilkenny after a replay; won in Munster in 1963; won the League final against Tipp; were beaten by Kilkenny in the All-Ireland final.

As a young fellow, working on a fairly big mixed farm in the late forties and early fifties, there was still a lot of manual work to be done; physical strength was an asset, whether you were at a threshing, in a hayfield or a cornfield. Strong, hardy men were what was wanted. As a man of 5 foot 8 plus and around 13 stone I was able to hold my own with most of them. You need to be strong, fit and tough to survive playing with a middling junior club.

Looking back now on all the years of hard training with club and county and many disappointments, I often wonder whether it was worth it or not. At times you think maybe it was: you meet people

"

I was born in Ballyduff, Lower, County Waterford, in 1934. My father, Geoffrey, was a native of the parish. My mother, Kathleen (Walsh), was from Mooncoin in south Kilkenny. At about the age of four I went to live with my mother's aunt and uncle, who were from south Kilkenny. They had bought a farm about a mile from my father's place. As with most Kilkenny people, there was always talk about hurling — mostly the old Mooncoin team, the Doyles, and 'Drug' Walsh.

I probably played my first hurling in a small field near my grandmother's house in Grange, near Mooncoin. There was little organised hurling at juvenile level. When I was growing up in Ballyduff I started to play minor hurling when I was fifteen years. I played for the Waterford minors the year after at wing half-forward. I played full-back for the minor footballers. I don't think I was very skilful but I was fairly strong and a fast runner. I never had match success playing minor.

My brother Edmond also played a bit. He was on goal when Ballyduff won the junior championship in 1961. Mick

and make friends, have something to have a bit of a chat about. I wasn't really that happy with my life on the land, so hurling, football and a bit of running — this was my life. That's about it.

In the days of my youth the men I looked up to were John Keane, Mick Hickey, Christy Moylan, Mick Hayes, Andy Fleming, Charlie Ware, Éamon Moynihan — a close friend and neighbour, a man I looked up to who won a junior All-Ireland with Westmeath — and Fad Browne, a native of Ballyduff, a player with Ballyduff in his early days and very prominent with the great Erin's Own team in the twenties and thirties — his grandson Tony is now a very good inter-county hurler; and the Foran family, who live near us in Knockaderry and played with Ballyduff in the forties and early fifties.

"

Tom Cheasty

Tom was four years old when Waterford made the breakthrough in Munster in 1938. His only recollection of the final against Dublin centres around his uncle going to a neighbour's house to listen to the broadcast on the wireless. But he does remember the triumph of ten years later when the Decies captured their second Munster crown and then went on to win their first All-Ireland senior title with a victory over Dublin. And he remembers in particular some of the great names associated with that historic win — 'although by then quite a few had gone past their best' — John Keane, Jim Ware (captain), Andy Fleming, Christy Moylan, Vin Baston, and Mick Hickey.

The circumstances surrounding Tom's début in the Waterford jersey can only be described as akin to something you would read in a novel or see in a film. 'It was the autumn of 1954. I was standing on the embankment of Walsh Park, awaiting a league game between Waterford and Kilkenny. Waterford were short — stuck for players.

I was approached to play, given a loan of a hurley and boots, and togged out.'

Thus started the senior county career of a player destined to make his mark at centre-forward. Strong, fit, and fast, uncompromising in exchanges, he held his own with the leading centre-half-backs of the day. Unorthodox in style, he would gain possession, surge forward, and scoop the ball ahead or over the bar.

An indestructible hurler was Tom. He was always exceptionally fit: used to win 100-yard competitions; won cross-country races; worked on the farm at home. 'I can remember opening up the headland with a scythe in preparation for the harvesting, and the sound of the scythe being sharpened echoed like music around the field. My father was a perfectionist, and the work I did didn't always satisfy him. He was a hard taskmaster. I'd be sent out picking turnips and would take the hurley and boots with me. I'd do a quick job on the turnips — wouldn't be as good as my father would like. I would then do a few rounds of the field, go on a few solo runs and then puck around for a while with the workman. That would be when the evenings were short and I wouldn't have time to go to the field.' No wonder he had speed and stamina and was as hard as nails!

'I always took the view that as well as scoring and distributing the ball, I should at least neutralise my opponent. No good in a forward playing a good game if his opponent is allowed to get in telling clearances to his forwards. When you line out for a game, any one of three things can happen to you on the day: you can meet someone you just can't manage; you can find yourself in the wrong place the whole time; everything — well, almost everything — runs right for you.'

Tom played well when going under to Cork in the championship of 1956, and even though he didn't know it then, Waterford were on the threshold of a great era, which was to bring an All-Ireland title in 1959, Munster titles in

Tom Cheasty receiving the cup at the Waterford County Championship.

1957, '59, and '63, Oireachtas victory in 1962, National League honours in 1963 and Railway Cup honours to Munster and in which Waterford players figured prominently, particularly in 1960, when they supplied seven of the team that defeated Leinster by 6:6 to 2:7. And yet Tom isn't happy. 'I now look back with a sense of overriding disappointment. Only one All-Ireland; we lost 1957 by one point; we lost 1963 by one goal after scoring 6:8 — each time to Kilkenny. I feel we could have won both; tradition, I suppose, won it for Kilkenny. Yes, I'm disappointed.'

I reminded Tom that I had travelled from Ballyshannon, where I was stationed, for the final of 1957. It was the era of 'first come first served' where entry to Croke Park was concerned. I took up position under the Cusack Stand — standing room only in those days — and close to the canal goal. It was a breathtaking final — epic in many ways. When the final whistle blew I was as stunned and numbed as any Waterford supporter, for my heart

was with the underdog. It seemed unreal — unreal that Waterford had lost. They led by six points entering the last quarter and were hurling as if they would increase it. Despite Kilkenny pressure, they still led by four points with nine minutes remaining. Full time, and Kilkenny a point in front: All-Ireland champions for the fourteenth time; victory by one point in their last four All-Ireland triumphs. My abiding memories of that final are the splendour of Waterford's hurling; the brilliance of Ollie Walsh in the Kilkenny goal; the feeling that a draw would have left everyone happy; the desire of all to see a repeat of a hurling thriller.

Tom looks on 1959 as being Waterford's best hurling year of that era. And no wonder. 'We trounced the All-Ireland champions, Tipp — revenge for a sixteen-point defeat the previous year. We beat Cork in a pulsating Munster final at Thurles, 3:9 to 2:9. A draw with Kilkenny in the final and victory in the replay by a margin of eight points sealed our greatness in 1959. Very few can claim to have beaten the "Big Three" on the way to All-Ireland success.' That comment set me thinking, and as far as I can trace it is the only time it happened. Because of the structure of the championship, it could of course only be achieved by a Munster team other than Tipperary or Cork.

After the drawn game with Kilkenny, Tom and Ollie Walsh were joint Sports Stars of the Week, and in the replay Tom recalls scoring a personal tally of 2:2 from play. He sees the year ending in September 1963 as probably their most successful twelve months. 'It began with the winning of the Oireachtas in the Autumn of 1962 with a good win over Tipp. We beat them again in the home final of the league. I probably played my best ever game for Waterford that day. It was one of the few days I got the better of Tony Wall. It brought me a Sports Star of the Week award.

'I wasn't on the team for the drawn game and the victorious replay against New York. There is a story behind that. I went to a soccer dance in the Olympia and got suspended. I got no league medal. If they offered it to me now I don't think I'd take it.

'We beat Tipp in the Munster final. That was our fourth major victory over Tipp — and remember they were a very good team. We beat them in the championship of 1959; the Oireachtas of 1962; the league of 1963; the Munster final of 1963. We felt confident for the All-Ireland final of 1963. Going onto Croke Park that day I felt fitter than in 1959. But I didn't have a good game on Ted Carroll. We nullified each other. Kilkenny dominated at midfield. I regret I didn't switch to midfield — I played mainly there for my club. Sometimes now, when I look back, I regret I didn't spend my career hurling in defence at county level. I think the half-back line would have suited me best, given my physique, temperament, and style of play.'

Tom then reminisced and mused about great hurlers and great teams. 'I had a great grá for the Wexford team of the fifties and early sixties — big men and exceptionally sporting. I played on one of the Hennessys in New York — both good hurlers: they came from the Kerry Ballyduff. Ollie Walsh was a magnificent goalkeeper: there was great style about him. Jack Lynch was one of the nicest men I ever met — a gentleman; never forgot his hurling roots; always willing to attend a function. I always found Paddy Barry of Cork hard to mark: he was elusive. Philly Grimes would be my outstanding man of that era: he had a great turn of speed — more effective in the loose than in the tight.

'The best teams I have seen were Tipperary in the sixties, Kilkenny in the early to mid-seventies, and the Cork team of Seánie O'Leary, Jimmy Barry Murphy and Ray Cummins in the late seventies. The Clare team of the seventies were most unlucky, so I was glad to see them win the All-Ireland this year [1995]. Their backs won it for them. John Horgan of Cork was a marvellous corner-back — great to read a game and clear from the full-back line. Jimmy Doyle could do anything he liked with the ball; I think I'd put him after Mackey and Ring.'

For a man who came from a predominantly football area, I wondered what it was that attracted him in his young days to hurling. 'I think it was to a great extent my mother. She came from Mooncoin. I used to go on holidays there in the summer time and play local matches. Even though Mooncoin hadn't then a great team, hurling was very important. They talked about nothing else. No matter where you went, the subject was hurling, and of course you heard about 'Drug' Walsh and the Doyle brothers — Mick Doyle was a personal friend of my mother's family. They lived on hurling.'

It certainly rubbed off on Tom in a big way. He played senior hurling for his club into his early forties. In 1982 he was asked to train the Ballyduff junior team; he agreed, and jokingly added, 'and I'll play with them next year.' Well, play he did, and a couple of months before his fiftieth birthday he won the county junior title with his native Ballyduff — operating, would you believe, at centre-forward, and nursing a broken bone in his hand from an earlier game.

We'll leave the last word on this great-hearted player to Pat Fanning, president of the GAA, 1970 to 1973. He wrote the following tribute in the programme on the occasion of the first-round Munster championship match against Clare on 24 May 1992. 'No man in Waterford's hurling story symbolises the spirit and the style of Decies hurling at its best than does Tom Cheasty of Ballyduff/Portlaw. Few will forget the many towering displays of the man during the great years of a great team between 1957 and 1963. His distinctive style marked him apart as, in turn, he jinked and weaved his way through the tightest defence, or burst through for a decisive score, seemingly impervious to personal danger. He was as brave as he was strong, and he was happiest when the battle was at its fiercest. A man of tremendous physical strength, he was, nevertheless, a ball player, who spearheaded a Waterford attack noted for its teamwork.

'With Waterford he won All-Ireland, National League and Oireachtas honours, was an outstanding Railway Cup player when the Railway Cup competition packed Croke Park on St Patrick's Day, and was an automatic choice for the Rest of Ireland teams. Tom Cheasty was, too, the most durable of players, whose hurling career spanned three decades. He achieved prominence in the fifties, starred through the sixties, while he was the inspiration of Ballyduff/Portlaw county championship triumphs in the seventies.

'Through all these years the word most used to describe Cheasty was "indestructible". It was a fitting description of a man whose name and fame will be for ever remembered in the county he served with such commitment and dedication. Always a great fan of Waterford hurling, he will be in Thurles today, hoping for a Decies victory.'

Tom's team is as follows:

Ollie Walsh *(Kilkenny)*

Bobbie Rackard *(Wexford)*   Pat Hartigan *(Limerick)*   John Doyle *(Tipperary)*

Jim English *(Wexford)*   Tony Wall *(Tipperary)*   Jimmy Finn *(Tipperary)*

Phil Grimes *(Waterford)*   Frank Cummins *(Kilkenny)*

Eddie Keher *(Kilkenny)*   Tom Cheasty *(Waterford)*   Jimmy Doyle *(Tipperary)*

Christy Ring *(Cork)* Ray Cummins *(Cork)*   Michael Keating *(Tipperary)*

And having picked it, he was still looking for places for Éamon Grimes *(Limerick)*, Jimmy Barry-Murphy, John Horgan and Gerald Murphy *(Cork)*, Frankie Walsh *(Waterford)*, and Billy Rackard *(Wexford)*.

Born 1940

ings afterwards. During that time I made many friends — friendships that have endured over the years.

It is with a great sense of loss that I recall the passing in recent times of the late Ted Carroll, Ollie Walsh, and Cha Whelan, whom I will always remember with great admiration and affection. **"**

Séamus Cleere

Séamus belonged to a wonderful club, with which he won six county titles. It's a club that has much to be proud of. Between 1952 and 1974 it appeared in sixteen county senior finals and won eleven. 'Those were great days, and there were tournaments played involving the leading clubs in Ireland — some really outstanding games. I was on the sideline with Dan Kennedy (then retired) for a tournament final at Nowlan Park in '57 between Bennettsbridge and Thurles Sarsfields, who were thirteen points ahead at half time. Frank Ryan of our team was having a hard time on Mickey "Rattler" Byrne. Dan, who in his playing days was in the same mould as Mickey, shouted in to Frankie: "If you don't give the Rattler a rattle, I'll go in and do it myself." It was a brilliant game that we won in the end by one point.

'Two years later I was to have the great honour of playing in a tournament final in Nowlan Park. The purpose was to put a roof on the Black Abbey church. Paddy Johnson of Kilkenny was referee. Our opponents were Glen Rovers, and at centre-back I was opposing Christy Ring. Speed was my great asset. As the game progressed I was getting some physical attention, so Jim Dobbyn on the wing said to me, "Come out here

"

Growing up in Bennettsbridge in the late forties and fifties, it was every young boy's ambition to wear the green and gold of his native club. Bennettsbridge were fortunate to have the services of men of the calibre of Ned Lyng and the legendary Father Patrick Nugent. Ned Lyng was principal of the local national school, and his arrival in Bennettsbridge marked the beginning of a historic era for the club. Under the inspirational leadership of Father Nugent, the 'Bridge' went from strength to strength, achieving many honours during the glory years of the fifties, sixties, and early seventies.

In the early sixties I started playing for Kilkenny, and for almost ten years I was privileged to wear the black and amber. 1963 would probably be the highlight of my hurling career, when I had the honour of captaining Kilkenny to a glorious win over Waterford in the All-Ireland final. In the same year I won the Caltex Award. It gives me a great sense of pride to have taken part in our national game at county level for ten years. I enjoyed every minute of it — on the field and also the great social gather-to the wing, I'll go in there." We won a great game by one point, and I collected a beautiful gold medal that had been minted in 1905.'

In 1973 Bennettsbridge produced three All-Stars in the persons of Jim Treacy, Noel Skehan, and Pat Lalor. Between 1947 and 1972 five Bennettsbridge men captained Kilkenny to All-Ireland success: Dan Kennedy (1947), Michael Kelly (1957), Séamus Cleere (1963), Jim Treacy (1967), and Noel Skehan (1972). Seventeen Bennettsbridge men, including substitutes, have between them won forty-one All-Ireland medals, ranging from Johnny Dunne, otherwise lovely Johnny Dunne, in 1933 to Liam Simpson, a nephew of Séamus, in 1993.

Séamus recalled the central role played by the late Father Patrick Nugent in the success of the club after he came to the parish as a curate in 1946. 'He was a master tactician. He had a great understanding of the game and knew what it took to succeed. Above all he realised that you had to have a blend of different qualities in a team unit: stoppers, crafty lads, stylish players, robot lads, and some no-nonsense fellows.'

When it came to travelling to Ballybofey to play Antrim in a league game in 1959, Paddy Grace sent a taxi for Johnny McGovern and Liam Cleere with instructions to collect whoever he could around Bennettsbridge. Thus did Séamus make his début in the black and amber. 'I was handed boots in the dressing-room, and we played the game in sleet and snow.'

Séamus doesn't recall having any interest in hurling before becoming involved with the Bennettsbridge under-16 team. He was a sub on the Kilkenny minor team that lost to Galway at the semi-final stage in 1958. 'I was mad to get in, to play beside Keher; instead I found myself in the goal. Anything I learned as a young lad about the game came from Johnny McGovern. He had great heart as a player and always encouraged young lads. He was tremendous at reading a game and spotting a weakness in the opposition. I remember one day playing a game against Mount Sion. Our half-back line of Johnny, myself and Jim Dobbyn were taking a roasting from Mick Flannelly, Phil Grimes, and Frankie Walsh. They were racing past us. At half time, Johnny, having studied what was happening, decided to line up our half-back line at a diagonal rather than straight across the field. In that way we were able to cope with the attacking tactics of the Mount Sion half-forward line, and we won the game.'

Séamus was involved in five All-Ireland final days. In 1963 Kilkenny faced Waterford in the final for the third time in seven years. Victory went to Kilkenny in 1957 and to Waterford in 1959 after a replay. All three games were tremendously exciting and most entertaining. So the question was, who would succeed in '63. The final score was quite remarkable: Kilkenny 4:17, Waterford 6:8. Séamus proved to be a superb captain at right-half-back and in the course of the game found time to sally downfield to score two great points.

The quality of his hurling throughout the championship was such that he received a Texaco Hurler of the Year Award. 'It was a great honour, but it couldn't have been achieved without the support of all of the other players, and it's an honour I share with every one of them.' Before the game the Kilkenny half-back line were concerned about Tom Cheasty of Waterford and how best to subdue this fast, strong, bustling centre-forward. 'Ted Carroll said to me to fall in behind him — he said the same to Martin Coogan — and I'll keep him out; you be there to collect. That way we closed him down. Ted could read a game real quick: he had a brilliant head, great ability to stick with a fellow. Very early in the second half we went eleven points up, but Waterford pegged us back, and with a minute to go we were only two points in front. Then Eddie Keher got his last point — his fourteenth of the day — from out under the stand, and I said to myself, we'll win it now. We needed the point; Waterford were coming at us.'

The 1964 result of Tipperary 5:13, Kilkenny 2:8, probably does an injustice to Kilkenny from the point of view of outfield exchanges. The Kilkenny selectors took the strange option of moving Séamus from right-half-back to right-half-forward for the game. Why? 'I hurled centre half-back for my club and used nip upfield and get a few scores. Maybe they thought it would add scoring power to the attack. I started the game on Tipp's captain, Michael Murphy, and finished up on Mick Lonergan, who came on as a sub. I remember in the first half I collected a ball; went on a solo run; seemed to be clear, when I ran into a shoulder from Michael Maher, the Tipp full-back. It was like running into a fireplace. I was looking at stars for the remaining fifteen minutes or so of that half. Martin Coogan had to go off injured — that was a big loss. In general we were poor that day.' Regarding that out-of-course switch to the half-forward line, it is interesting to note that the Leinster Railway Cup selectors never made such a move: for six successive years, from 1963 to 1968, Séamus 'owned' the right-half-back position on the Leinster team — a tribute to his consistency and brilliance in that position.

All-Ireland final day 1966 was a very disappointing one for Kilkenny. They were favourites. They wanted to atone for 1964; they didn't want two losses in a row. But that's how it turned out. 'We had a good team, and Cork had been struggling for quite a while to make an impact. We prepared well, but things didn't work out. Colm Sheehan got three goals for Cork. We missed sitters.'

Kilkenny were back again for final day in Croke Park in 1967 and faced their arch-rivals, Tipperary. 'We had to do something about beating Tipp. It was a needle affair. For us it was a good day but it wasn't a great match. It was tough, rugged, and close marking. Looking back, I didn't get a lot of the ball. I started off on Donie Nealon; then McKenna; after that Jimmy Doyle; and I think Devaney was on me for a while. That can upset you.' The final score was Kilkenny 3:8, Tipperary 2:7. The jubilant Kilkenny captain, Jim Treacy, collected the McCarthy Cup to record their first All-Ireland win over Tipperary since 1922.

In 1968 Séamus damaged a ligament in his knee. 'After the 1969 Leinster final and All-Ireland semi-final against London, the knee was in a bad way. I wasn't able to turn on it. I failed a fitness test and took my place with a strapped-up knee among the subs. The selectors were about to make a third substitution in the second half, and I was told to go on. I went three or four yards onto the pitch, and it suddenly struck me that if the knee went we would be down to fourteen men. I came back, and Paddy Moran, who was recovering from flu, went on. It was the best thing ever: he played a fine game.' Séamus as a sub collected his third All-Ireland medal. Later that year he retired from inter-county fray.

Séamus was a classical hurler: 'poetry in motion' is an expression that aptly describes him. His displays epitomised all that is graceful and gracious in the ancient game. This great hurler and sportsman came to be acknowledged as one of the outstanding exponents and gentlemen of the game.

Born 1910

Patrick Clohessy

by the narrowest of margins, 3:2 to 2:4. It is said that the final whistle denied Young Ireland what would have been the equalising point.

No doubt it was in the hurling field at Fedamore that Paddy Clohessy first gripped a camán and pucked a sliotar; but it was in the team of Sexton Street CBS, Limerick, that he made his first big impact on the hurling world — the 'schoolboy wonder'. At centre-back he played a key role in the CBS Harty Cup (Munster Colleges) victories of 1925 and 1926. A star was born.

In the jersey of his native parish he gave many a superb display in county championship matches against the leading senior clubs of those days. Rivalry could be intense, and in a particular match between Fedamore and Ahane the referee, Jim Roche of Croom, sent Paddy and John Mackey to the sideline. The acrimony caused by the sending off led to Paddy not lining out for Limerick against Cork in the Munster final of 1939. A hectic encounter — one of the great southern deciders — was lost by Limerick on the score 4:3 to 3:4. In a match that left the scribes searching for superlatives to describe the game and the performance of the Limerick goalkeeper, Paddy Scanlon, it was generally felt that the absence of Paddy Clohessy was the difference between victory and defeat. 'Green Flag' wrote in his report:

'Hats off to Cork on their brilliant victory. I still hold that Paddy Clohessy would have made the world of difference. The Fedamore man's lengthy clearances and anticipation were sadly lacking in a period when the game was in the balance. Jackie Power played well in Clohessy's old berth, but one missed Paddy's lightning drives and accurate frees, and I think his absence

The parish of Fedamore is a few short miles south of Limerick. It has a long hurling tradition, with players from the parish — most notably Egan Clancy, Mick Harrington, Ned Treacy, Con Scanlon, and Stephen Gleeson — helping Limerick to Munster title victories as far back as 1910 and 1911. Emigration took its toll on clubs in those days too, and among those who went to America was Egan Clancy. There he played with the Young Emmet Hurling Club of Philadelphia and was known in Gaelic circles as the wizard wielder of the crooked ash. He also wrote a GAA column in a leading American weekly. His brother, Seoirse Clancy, became Mayor of Limerick and while in office was murdered by British forces.

The Fedamore club is one of the oldest in the GAA, established in 1885. It was re-formed in 1894, and the colours were changed from purple and gold to green and white.

The parish won two Limerick senior hurling titles, and the second of those, in 1927, coincided with the arrival of Paddy Clohessy, who participated in the success and who the previous year had won a county junior title with his native Fedamore. In the 1927 championship Fedamore had three hectic games with Young Ireland — 3:1 to 3:1, 3:2 to 3:2, and in the third meeting victory

had as much to do with Limerick's defeat as had Cork's speed.'

It probably cost Limerick a Munster and All-Ireland title, for later that year, with Paddy back in the fold, Limerick beat the then All-Ireland champions, Kilkenny, in the Oireachtas final, 4:4 to 2:5; and the following year in the autumn of his inter-county career he gave evidence of his superb centre-half-back qualities in a championship campaign that saw Limerick engaged in a series of teak-tough encounters. A draw and a two-point replay victory over Waterford was only clinched in the closing moments, and there was a draw with Cork in the Munster final and a two-point victory in the replay, 3:3 to 2:4, a game in which the half-time score incredibly read Cork 0:3, Limerick 0:0.

And here is an excerpt from an article by 'Carbery' in the *Cork Weekly Examiner* of Saturday 4 August 1940:

'I thought Cork opened like a super team. Their hitting was sweet and true as at a practice match; their pace was electric. Ball after ball rained in on Limerick's granite backs. For ten minutes Cork were downfield looking for scores. Scanlon, Kennedy, Cregan, McCarthy, and Clohessy met every ball four square and slashed them back with sweeping ash ... Hurling was of real Munster championship timbre. Tackling was severe, but honest enough, though a few bucking jumps with the ball an absentee could have been cut out ... [Limerick] had switched about again. Paddy Clohessy was marking John Quirke, Cork's most dangerous marksman ... Limerick seized the chances with both hands — a hard side to beat, and worthy winners.'

There followed a hard game against Galway. Then came the final against Kilkenny and victory on the score 3:7 to 1:7 in a game where Paddy Clohessy gave a regal display at centre-back, one of many that assured him a place among the immortals. 'Carbery' reported:

'Nothing there is to compare with a hurling final and tell us how sound is the heart of the nation ... For a brief session

Limerick looked tied to the ground by comparison. Kilkenny were sweeping along wing and centre like brown bees bursting out of a hive at a sudden blast of Summer sun. Limerick's backs were rocklike, but Terry Leahy, of Urlingford and Faughs, found a way past with the long, swerving strides of an evasive antelope through brushwood. He had the ball in fine control at his feet as he tore through to the 14 line and whipped the leather well out of Pat Scanlon's reach. Four minutes' dazzling hurling and a roar like the Nore in Winter flood greeted the green flag.

'Kilkenny were snapping up balls just as nimbly as swallows would grab flies in June. An easy swing, and the ball was sailing goalwards. Limerick's backs were tested. They were like the walls of St John's Castle in a siege. They couldn't stop Terry Leahy's deadly free for a point — Kilkenny four points up in six minutes of typical Noreside hurling.

'Pat Clohessy now hunched his tall shoulders, pulled that grey cap down on his eyebrows and 'spat on his stick.' 'This won't do,' said the Fedamore man. As if to put the 'comether' on opponent Terry, Pat borrowed his hurley for a second while the ball was out of play to flatten an imaginary nail in the band of his own.

'The charm worked. Thenceforward we saw not a lot of Terry, but a hell of a lot of Fedamore elbow, corners and flail-like arms, that tore through and drove raking balls goalwards. Clohessy's second 70 was a joy to see, and oh so easy on the eye, for hurling lovers. Straight and true the ball sailed home for a point, dropping 15 yards behind the crossbar at the fifteenth minute — first Limerick score.

'There followed ten minutes of gloriously level hurling; cut and parry, charge and slap and hook; long-ground driving, severe tackling — real championship stuff ... More brilliant hurling we may have seen; but never a game where supreme manhood, virility and skill were tested in scale and crucible. Skill and power; power and skill; all locked in close embrace. And the stronger team won.'

Paddy was a key and commanding figure on the great Limerick team of the thirties, a litany of names that spelt every skill in the game: Paddy Scanlon, Micky Cross, Garrett Howard, Timmy Ryan, John and Mick Mackey, Paddy McMahon and Tom McCarthy are just some of them. He won three All-Ireland medals — 1934, '36, and '40, four National league titles, an Oireachtas and five Munster titles. He was one of a select band of Limerick men to have played in five All-Ireland finals: four in a row, 1933–36, and 1940. Only Garrett Howard surpassed it, having played in the finals of 1921, '33, '34, '35 and '36 with his native Limerick and 1924 and '27 with Dublin — seven in all.

Paddy made his début for Munster in the Railway Cup of 1932, and from then until 1940 he never lost his place on the Munster team. And from nine final appearances he was on the winning side on six occasions.

He set standards. His consistently high performances — a sure mark of greatness — placed him among the élite of centre-backs. His style was direct and first-time. He never flinched. There was steel and fire in his play — 'the Fedamore firebrand'. His approach was fearless and uncompromising. His temperament and range of talents enabled him to combine the rugged with the classical to telling effect. He was capable of scaling great heights, and there were even occasions when he stole the limelight and the headlines from the maestro himself, Mick Mackey. In long-range free-taking he was very reliable and accurate. He was Fedamore's pride — one of the all-time greats.

A Dublin hurling enthusiast wrote to me in recent times as follows: 'I am intrigued by the magnificence of the players that adorned the great Limerick team of 1934–44, particularly Paddy Clohessy and Paddy Scanlon, who seemed to have been overshadowed by the greatness of Mackey. Clohessy is continuously being referred to as unmatched in his position and had no parallel as a centre-back. Even great players from other counties who played against him say he was a player of exceptional skill, power and passion.'

Paddy had three brothers: Dave, Jack, and Andy. Andy emigrated to America. Jack didn't hit the headlines at county level. Dave won All-Irelands in 1934 and '36; in 1934 he had the distinction of scoring four goals in the All-Ireland replay against Dublin, out of a total of 5:2. Interestingly, Limerick had the benefit of the coaching services of the renowned Cork trainer Jim Barry in their preparation for the 1934 replay.

In later life Paddy turned to politics and represented Limerick East on the Fianna Fáil benches in Dáil Éireann. He was also a referee of note, spent a few terms as chairman of the East Limerick Board, and in 1950 was elected vice-chairman of Limerick County Board.

Nuair a fuair sé an glaoch deireanach ó Dhia, sa bhliain 1971, ní raibh sé ach bliain agus seasca — óg go leor. Is beag iománaí a bhí inchurtha leis i rith a ré. Go dtí an lá inniu féin deir na seanóirí nach raibh a shárú ann riamh mar chosantóir.

Fedamore

When all alone I often think
And dream on days of yore,
And my thoughts go quickly o'er the seas
To dear old Fedamore;
For it's many the pleasant stroll I took,
With ashen stick in hand,
To spend the day in manly play
With the lads in Con's command.

And when the practice match was o'er
To Jamesy's we'd repair,
To discuss the coming conflict,
And Shaun would take the chair.
And Mick would read the minutes
Of the meeting that passed o'er,
Oh! God be with those happy times,
And bless you, Fedamore.

Joe is one of a family of fourteen children — six boys and eight girls. When Sarsfield's — a rural club located a few miles from Loughrea town — won the All-Ireland senior club hurling final in 1993, all six boys participated in the great victory. Jimmy, who won an All-Ireland medal with Galway in 1980, with a brilliant display at cornerback, was among the subs. The fullback line was an all-Cooney one, Packie (Capt), Brendan and Michael. Joe was at midfield and Peter was corner-forward. That victory over Kilmallock by 1:17 to 2:7 ranks as Joe's greatest hurling moment and rivals the All-Ireland triumphs with Galway in 1987 and '88. The following year the club repeated the success with a two-point win over Toomevara and in so doing created a number of records that may never again be repeated. The exact same fifteen lined out in the exact same positions. They were led by the same captain. It was the only time to date that the same club won the title in successive years. 'After being beaten by Ballyhale Shamrocks (they had seven Fennellys in the team) in the semi-final of the 1990 championship, I thought we'd never win a club title'. The successes generated immense parish pride in a club that 'depends on six or seven families for its playing members'.

1996 was the Silver Jubilee year of the club championship and Joe felt very honoured to have been chosen on the AIB Silver Jubilee team.

Joe's journey into hurling greatness began when he played in goal for Galway under-16s in 1980. That year, he watched his brother Jimmy win his All-Ireland senior medal and it became his ambition to emulate that success some day. In 1983 he was left half forward in the Galway minor team that beat Dublin by 0:10 to 0:7 in the All-Ireland final — the only occasion in the competition

"

I started playing hurling in national school in Bullaun. We trained after school hours because our teacher had no interest in hurling. I did not win much at under-age level but once we reached minor we won a few county championships. From minor on, our team improved and we won a good few medals. David McGann was one of my biggest influences in the game. He was a teacher from the other side of the parish. Everything he taught us, we remembered and we never forgot it. I first went to an All-Ireland final in 1980. My brother Jimmy was playing for Galway in that match. I was sitting in the stand and thinking would I ever get a chance to play in Croke Park. Galway won that match and I played three years after that for Galway, in a minor final which we won also. Winning a club final in 1993 was one of my proudest memories, which I will never forget. Mick Jacob, Seán Silke, Iggy Clarke, Jimmy Barry-Murphy, Tony Doran and Sylvie Linnane were some of my idols in those years. I love the game and met many many fine people through the game of hurling. 99

that both teams failed to score a goal. That day, as Galway captured its first minor title, Joe showed evidence of his sharp shooting skills and polished hurling potential. Three years later he won an under-21 title with a victory over Wexford.

He entered county senior ranks for the league campaign of '84/'85. Soon, this richly talented player, holding his hurley right-hand under, caught the eyes of the All-Star selectors. He won his first of three in a row and five in all to date, in 1985. Hurling followers were witnessing one of the all-time greats of the game — a player of vision with a penchant for despatching 'killer' precision passes.

In many respects Joe had his greatest year in 1987. It began with a league title win over Clare. This was followed by an All-Ireland title in a tense struggle with Kilkenny. Leinster were defeated in the Railway Cup final in October. He received his third successive All-Star award. And, finally, to crown everything, he had the wonderful personal honour of being chosen Texaco Hurler of the Year. 'Yes, it was a fantastic year. It isn't too often things happen that way for you — it was probably my best year'.

His career is dotted with great performances. In the league of '87 against Clare he got two great first-half goals — both brilliantly taken. He added something like five points to claim a major share of Galway's 3:12 to 3:10 scoreline. In the All-Ireland final win of that year — 1:12 to 0:9 — in a game of no quarter against Kilkenny, he scored five points and was involved in the build-up that led to Noel Lane scoring an excellent goal less than ten minutes from the end, to clinch a Galway title.

Joe played some splendid hurling in the second half of the 1988 final against Tipperary. That, combined with the work of the indestructible Brendan Lynskey, paved the road to victory — a victory that only became assured when Noel Lane, as he had done the previous year, found the net in the closing moments. It ended 1:15

to 0:14. It is interesting to note that in both of those finals Galway conceded no goals and each time it was substitute Noel Lane who, in sealing the issue, demonstrated his goal-scoring capabilities.

The year 1989 will always conjure up in Galway memories of a lost opportunity — memories of a three in a row that might have been. Galway faced Tipperary in the All-Ireland semi-final — minus outstanding left-half-back Tony Keady — suspended in controversial circumstances for having played in the US. Reduced to thirteen men in the second half, Joe moved to midfield where he played a stormer — inspired hurling, that almost turned the tide. It wasn't his fault that Galway lost a game that was within their capacity to win.

The most painful year of Joe's hurling career was 1990. They faced Cork in the final and were firm favourites. Joe was Captain. He gave a scintillating first-half performance, scoring 1:6 — all but one point from play. Galway dominated much of the game and at times looked rampant. 'We scored 2:21 — it would have won most finals'. But they had costly lapses — the first before the game was one minute old. They conceded five goals — most of them due to lapses of concentration and lack of attention to key basics. But when your luck is out even the gods can frown on you. Less than ten minutes from half time, Joe sent one of his 'killer' passes to Éanna Ryan, whose shot bulged the net — but the referee blew for a foul on Joe — no goal. Then in the second half Martin Naughton bore down on the Cork goal and his rasping shot, with goal written all over it, glanced off the forehead of the advancing Ger Cunningham, and the umpire, instead of giving a seventy, signalled a wide. Joe's recollection is that from the puck out Cork scored a point. He knows that a game that was lost by three points could have been won and won well. 'Yes it is my most painful memory'.

In the 1996 league final against Tipperary at Limerick, we caught glimpses of his hurling genius from time to time

and in the closing stages of the game a flash of brilliance that brought a great goal — a winning one. 'Joe Rabbitte gave me a pass — you only get a split second — you have to have a go at it. I couldn't see whether it had gone in or not — then I heard the crowd shouting.'

He sees the rules as 'fairly OK' and wouldn't make any changes but he would wish for 'greater consistency in refereeing' and would 'severly penalise the hand chop.'

He sees hurling as 'going through a great era — great games — with Offaly, Wexford, Galway, Clare and Limerick all contributing and challenging seriously for major honours — has to be good for the game.'

Now at 32 this genial and exemplary sportsman can look back on a career to be proud of — a career in which he has won every honour in the modern-day game and stood shoulder to shoulder with 'great defenders like Ger Henderson, Joe Hennessy and Tom Cashman'. Looking ahead — well, he knows that Father Time is catching up — 'the training gets harder — the amount of training is nearly full-time now'. Still, with the amount of hurling talent available in Galway, Joe could well add yet another All-Ireland to his list of honours.

Born c. 1901

In the Claughaun jersey — horizontal bars of green and white — he won a county medal in 1926. It was a championship in which he gave outstanding displays and none more so than that against the old rivals, Young Ireland. The campaign was a gruelling one, as the following scores suggest; and even in the final at Croom the clinching scores came only in the last quarter:

v. Fedamore, 3:4 to 2:5

v. Kilfinnane, 4:3 to 3:2

v. Young Ireland, 2:6 to 1:6

v. Newcastle West, 5:3 to 1:4

On five occasions between 1925 and 1935 he won Thomond Feis honours (an annual early-summer tournament, now defunct, held in Limerick, the contestants Limerick, Cork, Clare, and Tipperary. It produced many epic games and blooded players for the championship).

Micky was selected on the first Munster Railway Cup team of 1927 that lost to Leinster in the final, a game, to quote the late Séamus Ó Ceallaigh, 'that left a fragrant memory with those lucky enough to witness what many regard as the outstanding hurling match of all the great ones Croke Park has witnessed.' In all, he was chosen for his province on eight occasions, the last in 1936, missing out only in 1928 and again in 1935, when he was a substitute, and winning on four occasions: 1929, '30, '31, and '34.

At county level a golden era dawned in 1933. In the years 1933–36 the Limerick half-back line read: Micky Cross, Paddy Clohessy, Garrett Howard.

It was the finest in the land — one of the great half-back lines of hurling. In those years Micky added four Munster titles to his 1923 victory, and also two All-Ireland titles: 1934, the jubilee year of the GAA, and 1936. To these were added four successive National League medals from 1934 to 1937.

Micky Cross, one of the all-time greats, was born into a hurling environment. He was a product of the Claughaun club that won Limerick County senior titles in 1914, '15, '16, and '18. He was one of a family of six, the others being Jimmy, Pa, Kathy, Maria, and Biddy.

When Limerick lined out against Dublin on 4 March 1923 to contest the final of 1921 and win on the score 8:5 to 3:2, Micky Cross wasn't on the team; but he was there on 14 September 1924 when Limerick contested the 1923 final against Galway. Defeat was his lot that day, but he could look back with satisfaction on a Munster medal won at the expense of Tipperary — one of his first inter-county games. From then until 1937, when he played his last game with Limerick in the Munster final against Tipperary, he was a regular on the Limerick team, and as he matured as a hurler he developed into one of the finest right-half-backs of that era, indeed of any era.

He arrived on the county scene at the end of a strong era in Limerick hurling. They had contested the eight Munster finals between 1917 and 1924, winning three, losing two after replays, losing three others that might have gone either way. There followed some lean years.

In 1932 he was selected for the Tailteann Games team — the last of the modern Tailteann — to play an American selection; Ireland won by 9:7 to 3:6. He was a member of the Limerick team that travelled on the *Manhattan* when Limerick set out on 8 May 1936 on their first American tour. It was a great hurling combination — one of the greatest in the history of the game. Three of them were later to receive All-Time All-Star Awards: Mick Mackey (1980), Garrett Howard (1982), and Jackie Power (1991). Micky was the veteran of the team, and his popularity is reflected in the fact that he was one of the most sought-after by Limerick exiles in America.

It is said that before the trip his mother had a word with him. He would have been in his mid-thirties; the household was matriarchal, and none of the family ever married. Anyway, his mother called him aside and told him there was a dangerous woman in America named Mae West and to stay away from her. After all, she was known to invite her menfolk to 'Come up and see me some time.'

Despite the threat of Mae West, the tour was a great success. Games were played at Yankee Stadium, New York, before an attendance of 40,000, and in Cambridge, Massachusetts — all victorious. A month later, on 9 June, the team arrived back in Ireland to a public reception. The Cavan footballers were also on the tour — the first time that both codes had toured together.

Micky was a talented and gifted hurler. He would lift and strike in the one movement and drive the sliotar with perfect direction. As often as not, he would strike on the ground — firm, well-timed strokes that displayed first-touch mastery and turned defence into attack. It was all done with the minimum of effort and perfect timing. He played in an era when first-timing the sliotar was the norm. The precision and skill associated with that came from regular practice, and in his day this was a daily routine, loved and relished. To him — as to many of his contemporaries — the game was second nature: he was never taught how to play it. Those who dallied with the ball invited physical aggression, and the rules and the refereeing were liberal in this regard.

The 1937 Munster final against Tipperary — one of the greatest games of the thirties — heralded the end of Micky Cross's county career. Youth won the day for Tipperary, and Micky Cross had as his immediate opponent a hurler half his age — Tommy Doyle, full of speed and energy. And to add to his woes he played that day under considerable personal stress. The previous night fire had destroyed his stables and some valuable horses. Tipperary won a thriller, 6:3 to 4:3.

Micky took with him into retirement hurling memories and achievements to be proud of. Often it was truly said of him, 'A great striker and a great man is Cross.' The late Séamus Ó Ceallaigh once wrote: 'Every honour the game could bestow was secured by this unassuming Gael, who was a hurler to his fingertips. Strong and fearless, very quick to turn and hit, he was a brilliant tactician. Pluck, stamina and grit were the big factors in his make-up and he

Limerick team aboard the Manhattan, *1936 trip to America.. Mickey Cross is third from left, back row.*

delighted in a hard, vigorous match, for the crash of the ash was the sweetest of music to him. Blessed with plenty of dash and resource, he shone in ground-work and from his position at right-half-back often drove balls to the opponents' goalmouth, and that on the sod, off either hand.'

'Carbery' had this to say:

'I met the smiling hurling veteran, Micky Cross, as stout and clever a wing-back as ever swung ash. Always the "big game" man, he was twenty years in the limelight and was never out of trim, Summer and Winter. He just loved hurling and lived for it — like successful men in every walk of life. A hospitable hostel was nearby but Micky Cross is almost a pussyfoot and we just thrashed out old and new matches "on the flags" in the mid Summer eve, oblivious to happenings around us.'

I will end on a personal note. My mother always enjoyed a night at the dogs in Limerick — a shilling each way was her bet. After one such occasion she met Micky Cross and told him of my interest in the game. He got a hurley made for me. It was the most perfect specimen I had, or have, ever seen. It had all the key attributes: excellent grip, great balance, beautifully shaped, the grain curving perfectly at the bos. Foolishly, I took it away to school with me. It was bound to be a source of temptation — and it was. The seventh commandment was breached. I still lament the loss of that hurley — the kind gesture of a hurling giant to a young enthusiast. Little did either of us realise that I would one day write about him. Solas na bhFlaitheas ort, a Mhíchíl uasail.

Michael Cross

Here are four verses of a lovely poem called
'The Old Hurler's Song to His Ash'.

I'm eighty years come Michaelmas,
*   and shaking is this hand of mine;*
Your shape recalls the happy days
*   when I was young and gay;*
Last eve at dusk when stripping thatch,
*   I found you on the rafter-line —*
My old camán, that served me well,
*   from Cork to Ballyhay.*

'Twas coming from the Fair of Ross, I
*   saw that bend of growing ash,*
And swore I'd cut the makings true,
*   before the night was done;*
Tho' tyrants held the woodland then,
*   close guarded by Black Tady Nash*
I shouldered home the 'soople' tree
*   before the morning sun.*

It was upon this homely hearth I
*   fashioned you most lovingly,*
And planed your sides with patient
*   hand, till every vein did shine;*
Your sole was wide; your nose was slim;
*   your graceful waist was maidenly,*
And sweetly balanced was the spring of
*   beauty every line.*

You made your name in championships,
*   when Gaelic men ranged side by side,*
St Finbarr's Reds, Dungourna men
*   with Blackrock in the van;*
Tip'rary fame, Kilkenny's pride, the
*   fearless men from Shannon's tide —*
But by my word, my honest ash, you
*   never maimed a man!*

Born 1950

Martin Cuddy (right) with his brother Jackie — both Oxford Players 1972 — and their father Jack.

“
As the second-youngest of seven brothers, I had a lot to live up to. As soon as I came home from school I went out on the green hurling. Father Seán Collier and George Leahy were a big influence on me. Father Seán used come to train us. He would get in among us, pulling right and left and showing us how it should be done.

I went to England when I was seventeen and played with Oxford with my brother Jack. We used to bring a seven-a-side team to play in a tournament at Camross. We had some great games.

In 1988 in the month of June I played a match in Mountrath on a Friday evening. We got the one o'clock plane from Shannon to San Francisco, arriving at midnight. On Sunday we played the Californian final. At half time, full time and half way into extra time it was level pegging; in the end we won by one point. Celebrations went on until ten o'clock Monday morning, when we got the plane back to Shannon via New York. We arrived in Shannon on Tuesday morning. I didn't know whether I was coming or going for a week.

I played with the Fenians in San Francisco against the Gaels, who had in their ranks Paddy Quirke of Carlow, whom I was playing on, and Pádraig Horan, who was their coach.
”

Martin Cuddy

Laois, for the second year running, contested the All-Ireland final of 1915 before an attendance of 14,000 and defeated a much-fancied Cork combination — Laois's only All-Ireland title. Cork led by 3:0 to 2:2 at half time, but in the second half Laois lifted their game and, with a fine display of dash, combination, and opportunism, ran out worthy winners on the score 6:2 to 4:1. 'Vigilant', writing of the game, reported as follows:

'I have witnessed a good many hurling finals and I can truthfully say that I never saw one that was played out from start to stop in a finer or more admirable sporting spirit. There was no denying the fact that Cork was confronted with the biggest and most amazing surprise that has ever been effected on the Gaelic athletic arena. There was no luck in it, and beyond all possible shadow of doubt the better team won, and

won conclusively and in the most decisive manner imaginable.'

Since that great victory Laois has contributed much to hurling and produced many fine hurlers. Martin Cuddy ranks among the great ones; but major honours, so richly merited, have eluded him. Martin hails from Camross, a parish that has been to the forefront of Laois hurling for almost forty years now. He participated in their successes from the seventies and in that time won ten county titles.

His proudest moment came in 1977 at Carlow, when he captained his native Camross to a Leinster senior hurling club title with a one-point victory over the reigning All-Ireland champions, James Stephens of Kilkenny. They were beaten in the final by Glen Rovers of Cork. Seven Cuddys, from two families — distantly related — lined out with Camross: Martin and his brothers, Tim, Ollie, and Michael; P.J. of Laois full-forward fame, and his brothers Ger and Seán.

Martin emigrated to England at the age of seventeen; there he played with Oxford in the company of his brother Jack and won four county titles. He

Martin Cuddy receiving the Leinster Club Cup in 1977.

played with Hertfordshire in two All-Ireland junior finals. They lost to Meath after a replay in 1970. In 1971 something unique happened in the final against Wicklow. The game ended in a draw, and the referee declared that the next score would decide the winners. The 'winning' point came to Hertfordshire, and the score stood at 4:9 to 3:11. The referee's decision led to a dispute, and a replay was ordered. Again it ended in a draw. The second replay was won by Wicklow by one point on the score 4:6 to 3:8.

When Martin returned from England he joined the Laois senior panel, and All-Ireland B titles were won in 1977 and 1979. There were signs that Laois were moving towards competing with the best. 'Between '81 and '85 we were unlucky not to have made the breakthrough. There was the goal for Offaly that shouldn't have been — that lost us the game — when Pádraig Horan's shot went in on the outside of the post to the net. And there was the point from all of ninety yards by Paddy Kirwan with the last puck of the game — a free that should have gone the other way. We were doing well in league games too and lost a semi-final to Kilkenny in Thurles in '83. In 1984 we reached the final of the Centenary open draw competition. In '85, after beating Dublin in the first round and Wexford in the Leinster semi-final, we gave away rather easy goals early on to Offaly in the final. It was lost at half time.'

Four times in the early eighties Martin was selected to play with Leinster in the Railway Cup, but defeat was Leinster's lot on each occasion. 'Sometimes I used to think to myself that I wasn't supposed to win.'

Martin made a number of trips across the Atlantic to play hurling matches with a variety of clubs. He won a Californian title with San Francisco in 1988. Hurling games in America have tended to be very physical, and Martin found this to be particularly so in games he played in Chicago.

In a career that saw him nominated for the All-Stars he named some of the great centre-backs he encountered: 'Seán Silke, Pat Delaney, Ger Henderson, Seán Stack, Mossie Carroll, and Tom Cashman — some fair men to handle.'

Here is how Canon Seán Collier of Borris-in-Ossory — coach, trainer, and mentor, winner of three Leinster Colleges titles with St Kieran's of Kilkenny, Leinster Colleges player in 1943, and Kildare hurler after he was ordained — remembers Martin:

'Apart from the fact that we both hail from the foot of the Slieve Bloom mountains, where hurling is on the menu for breakfast, dinner and tea, Martin Cuddy, like his six brothers, was one of the greatest standard-bearers of hurling in Camross and Laois that I know. I had the pleasure and honour during the eighties of helping Camross to restore their great tradition of success and I must say that Martin Cuddy played a major role in the success, whether at centre-back or centre-forward. He set the club on the road to success in '85 and they have not looked back since.

'Needless to say, his ability and skills did not go unnoticed at county level and very soon he was to become one of the greatest wearers of the Blue and White. He will always be remembered for his grafting at number 11. His distribution of the ball led to many scores and indeed should have led to greater success for so much dedication. He was of course one of the few men of Laois to be chosen for Leinster. Opponents in Kilkenny, Offaly and Wexford will recall many of their great duels with Martin and will be the first to admit that his feats deserve the ultimate reward. Despite his success and achievements at inter-county and inter-provincial level I think his greatest joy was to captain Camross to a Leinster club championship success in 1977. Perhaps with a little good fortune his team might have won the All-Ireland club championship.

'I am glad to see that the magnificent efforts of Martin and his little rural club are recorded in this book, which I am sure will be read and treasured by all connected with hurling and will be a source of encouragement to the youth of today. Mol an óige agus tiocfaidh sí.'

This is Martin's team from the men he played against:

	Damien Martin *(Offaly)*	
Sylvie Linnane *(Galway)*	Eugene Coughlan *(Offaly)*	Dick O'Hara *(Kilkenny)*
Joe Hennessy *(Kilkenny)*	Ger Henderson *(Kilkenny)*	Ger Coughlan *(Offaly)*
Frank Cummins *(Kilkenny)*		Joachim Kelly *(Offaly)*
Mark Corrigan *(Offaly)*	Martin Cuddy *(Laois)*	Pat Carroll *(Offaly)*
Billy Fitzpatrick *(Kilkenny)*	Liam Fennelly *(Kilkenny)*	Johnny Flaherty *(Offaly)*

Born 1948

❝

As long as I can recall we had hurleys in our hands, not surprising since our parents were steeped in a hurling background. Willie Cummins of Carrigtwohill had won two All-Ireland minor medals ('38 and '39) with Cork. Mary Walsh of Glounthane was apparently no mean camogie player and a niece of 'Bowler' Walsh who was a very successful Chairman of the Cork County Board.

Ballinlough was a 'Buffers Zone' between a city starting to expand and a countryside of Mahon and Blackrock. Planners of that era didn't appreciate the value of green areas, so our 'Croke Park' graduated from the modest back gardens of our home (and numerous broken panes of glass!) to the road on which we lived.

The games played there were often as intense as I have ever played in and ended only as a result of a disputed decision, darkness, breaking of a neighbour's window or the appearance of a garda at the bottom of the road. We had great neighbours who never seemed to mind the noise and the banter on the road, the damage to flowers and shrubs or the invasion of property in the course of evading the forces of the law!

Derry Cremin entered our young lives as the organiser of teams in the parish leagues run by the Blackrock national hurling club — our first involvement in organised competition. Derry was to become the greatest influence, not alone in my hurling life, but in that of scores of young lads of our era. Indeed, the backbone of one of the most successful Blackrock hurling teams ever, consisted of Derry's prodigies. The number of county, provincial and All-Ireland medals won as a direct result of the influence of this man must count in dozens. What makes this all the more remarkable is that Derry was paralysed from his hips down and depended on a pair of crutches for mobility and generous club members for transport to training sessions and matches.

Unable to sit because of his condition, he used to perch himself on a wall near O'Driscoll's shop on the Ballinlough Road and around him our world revolved — discussion, debate and argument on hurling matters of the present and past were interspersed with the selection of teams, and organisation of transport, hurleys and gear for the upcoming games. The highlight of the summer weeks came on Sunday evening after Benediction when a full-blooded match would be played on the road, with Derry at centre stage acting as coach, mentor, referee, first-aid man etc. We were like bees around a honeypot! We were rarely interrupted by traffic (Sunday was a day of rest!) and the gardaí must have been on a five-day week! Invariably, however, there would be one halt to proceedings to allow John Joe Curry's horse and butt pass by as it careered from side to side like a Roman chariot returning John Joe from his day's drinking — how nobody was ever killed remains a mystery to me and a tribute to the old horse, for he was surely on auto pilot.

As twilight arrived, Derry, in the company of some of the older club members would make his way to an old two-room cottage down the road, known to us as Jack's House. We would follow. I never knew what illness afflicted Jack, but whatever ailed him, he was confined to bed and obviously enjoyed the invasion of his cottage at night and the banter that followed. It was here in front of a big open fire that we learned our history of hurling — the deeds of the great Lory Meagher, Eudi Coughlan, the Doyles, Stakelums, Mahers, and Leahys of Tipp, the Wares and Powers of Waterford, the Mackeys and Powers of Limerick, the Rackards of Wexford and the Langtons of Kilkenny, not to mention our own Ring, Lynch, Quirke and so on.

Derry would interrupt his repair and splicing of hurleys, to listen to Seán Óg's result of the day. 'Where's Oulart -The Ballagh?' some youngster would ask. This would trigger off a lecture on Vinegar Hill and Fr Murphy followed by a bar or two of 'Boulavogue' from one of the late arrivals from the pub! Not to be outdone, John Farnan, a staunch Kilkenny man (and a strong advocate of the pioneer pin), who lost his eye while playing with Blackrock, would give a full rendering of the 'Rose of Mooncoin'. Derry, balancing his rigid frame against the edge of the table, would have a roguish glint in his eye and beaming from ear to ear, happy in the knowledge that us young folk were getting our history, geography and cultural lessons all in one — and indeed, sensing that the 'craic' was starting! We hated going home as we too sensed that the fun had just begun — they were innocent times.

Kevin, the eldest in our family and two years older than me, arguably the most talented of the three of us, was making a name for himself at colleges level with Coláiste Chríost Rí. I recall him scoring five goals in a Dean Ryan (Munster Colleges Junior Hurling) Final, despite having a broken hand and a plaster cast. I was a sub on the team and gained my only colleges medal of note. Chríost Rí was a relatively new Secondary School run by the Presentation Brothers and quickly established itself as an excellent college in the academic, cultural and sporting fields. Many outstanding hurlers and footballers represented the school — John O'Halloran, Billy Morgan, Frank Cogan, Eric Philpott, Martin O'Doherty, Seamus Looney, Brian Murphy to name just a few. Indeed, half of the first Cork minor football team to win an All-Ireland at that grade were present or past pupils of the school. Brother Denis, late of Offaly fame, and Dick Tobin, were the main motivators of the games in the early days and, indeed, the latter was still involved this year when the school regained the Munster Colleges football crown after a lapse of many years — the team consisting of a number of sons of past pupils, including my own. The pinnacle of the schools sporting success came in 1968 when the All-Ireland football crown was won and the double was narrowly missed when the hurlers, captained by my younger brother Brendan, lost narrowly in the final after a replay.

So the seeds sown by Derry were well nurtured during secondary school years and our horizons expanded. Kevin won a county minor hurling title with Blackrock in '63 and captained Cork to All-Ireland success the following year. Brendan and I were part of a phenomenally successful under-age team which won every honour available in both hurling and football at under-15, juvenile and minor levels. I suffered a huge disappointment when six of my team mates were selected for the Cork under-15 hurling team. I alone, of the seven who attended the trials, was not chosen.

Looking back on this experience later, it was to be a great lesson on the ups and downs of life and sport in particular and I resolved to work hard on my game. The reward came at a minor level when I represented Cork in both hurling and football (1966), losing the hurling final after a replay to Wexford. Our disappointment at not winning on the day of the final was lightened by the success of the seniors over a much-fancied Kilkenny — the first senior All-Ireland for Cork in a dozen years and the first

Ray Cummins of Cork gains possession in the 1977 All-Ireland semi-final, Cork v. Galway. (Photo: Jim Connolly)

of any significance to me as I was too young to recall the three in a row of '52–'54.

I may have dreamt of it but little did I realise I would be part of the next success. The minors of '66 made up for their loss by winning the All-Ireland under-21 in '69 — a repeat of the previous year. At this stage I had made the transition from half-back to full-forward in hurling, a position I had played in football for quite a number of years. I enjoyed the freedom of forward play but did not relish the traditional role of full-forwards standing in the square, wrestling with the full-back and 'raising dust'! A couple of good games with UCC in the county championship got me onto the Cork senior panel for the Munster final of '69. I was brought on as a sub in the second half of the game but can't recall touching the ball. Nevertheless, Cork won and laid the Tipp bogey.

It's amazing how counties' fortunes change. In fourteen years of senior championship hurling I was never on a losing team to Tipp. A motor-cycle accident to Justin McCarthy in the lead-up to the All-Ireland final meant a reshuffling of the team with yours truly at full-forward. It was obviously a huge gamble in a crisis situation. After all, I had about four months' experience at full-forward at club level — ten or fifteen minutes at inter-county level — not even a league match played and facing the experienced Pa Dillon and behind him Ollie Walsh. We lost an All-Ireland we could have won — an indescribable disappointment. Again, a hard lesson learned, allied to a 'battle' of a league final success over New York during which the character of the team was tested to the limit (and Clem Foley, the Dublin referee, getting his jaw broken) resulted in All-Ireland success in 1970, defeating Wexford in the first eighty-minute final and the highest score in a final (6:21 to 5:10).

The same year I graduated from UCC as a civil engineer and UCC won the Cork county hurling championship for only the second time in its history. Around this time a number of Blackrock players who had been 'lost' to UCC in the sixties had graduated and returned to the club and the county championship was won in 1971 for the first time in ten years and only the second time in forty years — an unbelievable low period for a club that leads in the number of county titles won in Cork.

The most successful decade in the club's glorious history had dawned. The seventies produced five county championships, five Munster club championships and three All-Ireland club championship successes. We had a star-studded team which included players of the calibre of John O'Halloran, Fr Mick Waters, Frank Cummins, Simon Murphy, Paddy Moylan, Eamon O'Donoghue, Brendan Cummins, Tom Cashman and Dermot McCurtain, all of whom won senior inter-county All-Ireland medals on the field of play. Others had won All-Ireland medals as subs and most of our panel would have played at inter-county level at senior, under-21 or minor level. Such was the standard of club hurling in Cork during the seventies we needed more than star-studded players to reap success. The vital cog in our machine was our coach Joe McGrath. Joe was a revelation and an inspiration to us all, demanding the highest standards of fitness, skill, determination and commitment — all of which he portrayed in his role as coach, trainer, physiotherapist, tactician, psychologist and motivator. Any sacrifice Joe asked of us, he was prepared to give himself, two hundred fold.

There is no doubt in my mind that involvement in team sport is the best possible form of preparation for the ups and downs of life. Apart from the obvious benefits derived from physical fitness as a result of team sport, the character formation developed as a result of the self-discipline, commitment, loyalty, self sacrifice, dependence on others, respect for team mates, opponents and those in authority, the ability to handle pressure, suffer defeat in a manly fashion and with resolve to do better next time, treat success with dignity, is not found on the curriculum of any university, college or school. I will be eternally grateful to those who sowed the seeds, nurtured and cultivated my interest in hurling and football. They and their likes in other clubs and codes are due an enormous debt of gratitude by society.

Sadly, they often are the unsung heroes of our games and forgotten when the bouquets are given out or the tickets distributed. As I try to live up to their example, I am shocked by the number of parents of the present generation who don't seem to appreciate the benefits of team sports for their kids and who fail to help organise and run under-age clubs.

The excitement and hype surrounding provincial and All-Ireland finals as seen by the general public must give the impression of life being a bed of roses for the players. The reality of life is, oh, so different. There is little glamour in the endless hours of hardship in training during wet, cold and miserable conditions. Nor is there anything attractive about the self sacrifices made by the player or his family during a season which never seems to end. I was lucky that my wife, Bernadette, came from a hurling background and she appreciated, understood and most of all, supported me in meeting the demands, made on my career. Even so it was not easy, for her being at home alone, rearing our family, while I went from work to training, returning home at ten or eleven at night tired after a long day with little energy to be enthusiastic about her issues of the day. Weekends were little better as invariably there were games to be played involving travel and time away from home.

Our social life during those years was near to non-existent as I had a golden rule of being in bed before 10.30 p.m. from the Wednesday night before a game. As a result, many a party, birthday or wedding was missed or cut short

— the glamour of it all! However, on reflection, one tends to think of the good times more then the bad and I am sure if given a choice, I would do it all again.

No medal won or victory gained has given me more pleasure than the friendships made through the medium of hurling. Hurling folk are unique and nothing I have experienced binds people together quite like the love of hurling or the mutual respect of the honest hurler whatever his skill level. I consider myself privileged and honoured to have had the opportunity to play with and against so many many wonderful hurlers and great characters on and off the field. Too many in fact for me to mention, as it would need a book of its own and to leave out any would be an injustice.

99

W e met Ray Cummins in the beautiful coastal town of Kinsale. The setting is idyllic. Ray took us on a mini-tour. We saw where Don Juan Del Aquila and his Spanish fleet dropped anchor in 1601. And we saw, too, the position occupied by the Chieftains O'Neill and O'Donnell. Failure at Kinsale ended an era in Irish history. A new era began. Its ripples are still with us. We paid a visit to the hurling field — named after the stout-hearted Jack Barrett who played with Cork in the thirties. Kinsale is also the native place of Jim O'Regan, one of the game's outstanding centre-half-backs of the late twenties and early thirties.

Ray's father, Willie, won an All-Ireland minor title with Cork in 1938 in the exalted company of Alan Lotty, Christy Ring, Éamon Young, Ted Sullivan, and Jim Sadlier from Buttevant, who later played with Limerick and Munster. He won a second minor title the following year. Ray's mother played camogie at club level. He grew up in the atmosphere of a Blackrock club that was very successful in under-age competitions. In that background lay the basic ingredients of his future success.

Ray got his baptism of fire in senior championship hurling when he lined out at full-forward in the All-Ireland final of 1969 against Kilkenny and was faced by the experienced and uncompromising Pa Dillon. 'I was completely green. Such a scene was new to me.'

His début was not a winning one, but a remarkable dozen years of successes lay ahead. Ray was a dual player: he excelled at hurling and football and demonstrated during his playing career that he was one of the greatest dual players in the history of the GAA. And it is interesting to note that he had as contemporaries three fellow-countymen who were also outstanding dual performers: Jimmy Barry Murphy, Brian Murphy, and Denis Coughlan. His eleven Munster titles in a row, from 1969 to 1979, must surely constitute a record. Three of these were in football — 1971, '73, and '74 — despite the fact that 'they only played football seriously in Blackrock when out of the hurling championship.' The pressures of playing both games began to take their toll, and in 1975 he concentrated solely on hurling, having played football since the league of 1967. 'My first loyalty was to hurling. From day one I had a passion for hurling.'

Here is Ray's full list of achievements:

- Cork county hurling and football championships at under-15, under-16 and minor with Blackrock and St Michael's

- Played minor hurling and football with Cork, runners-up in All-Ireland hurling, 1966 (after a replay)

- Played under-21 hurling and football for Cork, winning All-Ireland hurling championships in 1968 and 1969

- Cork county senior hurling championships: UCC, 1970; Blackrock, 1971, '73, '75, '78, and '79

- Cork county senior football championships: UCC, 1969

- Munster club championships, hurling, 1971, '73, '75, '78, and '79

- All-Ireland club championships, hurling, 1972, '74, and '79

- Fitzgibbon Cup, UCC, 1967

- Sigerson Cup, UCC, 1969

- Munster senior hurling titles, 1969, '70, '72, '75, '76, '77, '78, '79, and '82

- Munster senior football titles, 1971, '73, and '74

- Railway Cup, hurling, 1970 and '76; football, 1972

- National Hurling League, 1970, '72, '74, '80, and '81

- All-Ireland senior hurling titles, 1970, '76, '77, and '78

- All-Ireland senior football title, 1973

- Oireachtas hurling titles, 1973, '74, and '75

- All-Star Awards: hurling, 1971, '72, and '77; football, 1971 and '73.

Ray reflected for a while when I asked him to recall three events from his career that conjure up something special. 'I remember going to Croke Park for the first time ever. We had won an under-16 ground hurling competition — no handling. The reward was a trip to Croke Park on All-Ireland final day in 1964. I was fascinated by Croke Park. My brother Kevin was playing with Cork minors, who won, and that was an added attraction.

'Meeting Jimmy Doyle was special. It was on one of the All-Star trips to the States in the early seventies. Jimmy Doyle was like a god to me. Neither of us were drinking, so we gravitated towards each other. Here was my boyhood hero — so natural, so unassuming. In the sixties I saw him destroy Cork in Munster finals. I remember coming out of Limerick as a spectator after Cork lost the '68 Munster final to Tipp by nine points and saying I will never again go. But there I was, back the following year, as a sub, with Cork.

'To captain Cork in '76 to the first of three in a row was a great honour. I was the first Blackrock man to do so since the days of Eudi Coughlan in 1931. Wexford were 2:2 up after seven minutes. It was a physically exhausting match; I felt drained after it. Ring was always great for sizing up the opposition and he used concentrate too on referees' 'weaknesses'. He told us we'd get away with four or five steps that day. I remember before half time rounding Willie Murphy. He had me hooked. I decided I would take a few more steps. I got away with it and scored a vital goal. My brother Brendan was centre-forward that day on Mick Jacob, who had a great game for Wexford. We still get onto Brendan and tell him he didn't hit a ball that day.'

Sportsmanship and whole-hearted endeavour are qualities Ray looks for, both in teams and individuals. 'I always wanted effort. I found it frustrating to see players with ability and talent giving a half-hearted display. The hurley of course is a weapon, and a coward can use it as such; it takes a man of character to use it for the skills of hurling.

'There is a bond between hurling men that is born out of respect. To me, hurling has meant involvement, excitement — there is no place like Thurles on a Munster final day — and friendship. I can go to Limerick and knock on Pat Hartigan's door and feel welcome. Pat was the best full-back I ever met. He was a great hurler and sportsman — physically strong and very committed. We played hard against each other, but we always played the ball. I would be comfortable meeting an honest hurler any time. At club level in Cork I had some great battles with Martin Doherty, a full-back for whom I had great respect too.'

Ray introduced a new strategy to full-forward play. He had a great sense of position; wonderful hands; anticipation and vision, especially peripheral vision. He demonstrated this to the full when he advanced outfield to grasp an incoming sliotar and laid off passes of telling importance to forward colleagues. His own abilities, coupled with his intelligent use of his forward teammates, placed opposing defences under extreme pressure, on occasions tearing them apart and opening up gaps that led to vital scores. When the occasion was right he took his own scores; and, as with all masters, he made it look simple.

The All-Star selectors were captivated by his approach to full-forward play and made the following observations in awarding him his three All-Stars.

Ray picked two teams

a) Best Cork team during his playing career (his to captain):

	Paddy Barry	
Brian Murphy	Martin O'Doherty	John Horgan
Tom Cashman	Johnny Crowley	Con Roche
Denis Coughlan		Tim Crowley
Gerald McCarthy	Willie Walsh	Jimmy Barry Murphy
Charlie McCarthy	Ray Cummins	Seánie O'Leary

b) best Munster team (excluding Cork) during his playing career:

	Jim Hogan *(Limerick)*	
Jackie O'Gorman *(Clare)*	Pat Hartigan *(Limerick)*	Jim Greene *(Clare)*
Ger Loughnane *(Clare)*	Mick Roche *(Tipperary)*	Sean Stack *(Clare)*
Bernie Hartigan *(Limerick)*	Eamon Grimes *(Limerick)*	
Johnny Callinan *(Clare)*	Noel O'Dwyer *(Tipperary)*	Jimmy Doyle *(Tipperary)*
Michael Keating *(Tipperary)*	Joe McKenna *(Limerick)*	Éamon Cregan *(Limerick)*

- 1971: 'For introducing a new degree of subtlety into full-forward play. His perfect co-ordination and the wide variety of his attacking play continually setting up scores.'
- 1972: 'For the supremely high standard he continues to set for full-forward play; for his utter unselfishness in bringing his team-mates into the game.'
- 1977: 'For the superb leadership and inspiration he provides for Cork as well as the intelligence of his skilful play.'

He quit after the All-Ireland final of 1982. 'I never had great speed or stamina. I remember in the '82 final Brian Cody [the Kilkenny full-back] got the ball towards the end. He took off downfield. I followed — not too far behind. Our centre-forward was missing, so I kept going. We passed the half-forward line; then passed midfield; on to the half-back line, still chasing. I felt burned out. After that I decided I had enough. Time to quit.'

As a full-forward, Ray's name will be remembered as one that fits comfortably into the company of Martin Kennedy of Tipperary, Paddy McMahon of Limerick and Nicky Rackard of Wexford from bygone days, together with Tony Doran of Wexford and Joe McKenna of Limerick from more recent times.

As a hurler and sportsman Ray ranks with the élite of the game.

Born 1961

Another great influence on my hurling at this stage was Brother Moloughney — a Tipperary-born Christian Brother, whose love for hurling outweighed even the academics at school.

A graduation to Coláiste Iognaid Rís continued my hurling education and it was here that the influence of the great Billy Morgan helped me to think seriously about playing in goal. Up to this I was playing in the forwards. The goalkeeping training and tips that I received from Billy continued long after I left school.

Winning the under-16 County with the 'Barrs in 1977 for the first time in the Club's history led to my call for the Cork minors in 1978. This began my connection with Canon Michael O'Brien who was to have a major influence in my hurling career over the next fifteen years.

My senior career with the 'Barrs and Cork followed on from winning minor All-Irelands in 1978 and '79 and under-21 in 1982. In 1979 I took over in goal from Jim Power, who had played for the 'Barrs since 1959.

My début for Cork seniors came in 1980 in Carrickshock against Kilkenny, in a challenge game, with my first league game to follow against Wexford in New Ross in October 1980. There have been many highlights in the intervening years. All-Ireland victories in 1984 (Centenary Year) 1986 and 1990 versus Galway, together with some disappointments — losing in 1982, '83 and '92 to Kilkenny. Captaining my club to county-final victory in 1988 will always be remembered.

Through the years I have had the pleasure to play with and against some great players within and outside Cork. The All-Star and Cork trips to places like San Francisco, New York and Toronto, gave the opportunity to get to know well, players from other counties.

"

My memories of my early hurling days are of the bell ringing to signify the end of the ten o'clock Sunday Mass at the Lough Church. At the base of the hill leading up to the Church, the Lough Leagues run by The 'Barrs Under Age were taking place. It was here that I first played in goal for 'Earlwood'. It was here at the Lough that many players who were later to play for the 'Barrs, first played. When the 'Barrs opened their premises in Togher in 1970, the Lough Leagues were no more.

The Lough area, with its vast green space, was the ideal place to practise and it was here that I played hurling with my Dad, Jim, whose interest and love for hurling was passed on to me and my brother Brian at an early age. Jim, together with Mum's family, the Finn's from Lough Road, were deeply involved with the 'Barrs. Indeed, the Finn connection goes back to the early 1900s when Tim 'Gas' Finn played for the 'Barrs.

I regret their passing, as it gave the opportunity to meet players other than on the playing pitch.

Over the years, it has been my privilege to play for a great club like the 'Barrs and to play for Cork. The games have taken me to many parts of Ireland and abroad and I have enjoyed every minute of it. It would not be possible to thank everybody who helped me in my career personally, but being involved in the GAA has given many opportunities that I may never have had.

I wish to thank Brendan for giving me this opportunity. Continued success to Brendan.

"

Ger Cunningham

D own through the decades Cork has produced some outstanding net minders. In the early years of this century Andy Fitzgerald was a household name. John Coughlan will always be associated with the successes of 1926 and 1931. In the forties it was Tom Mulcahy, who shared in the All-Ireland victories of 1943, '44 and '46. The early fifties produced fairytale stuff when all round sportsman and veteran Dave Creedon took over in goal in 1952, in his thirty-third year, and gave sparkling displays in Cork's three-in-a-row All-Ireland victorious campaigns of 1952, '53 and '54. He was followed by Mick Cashman — a brilliant custodian — Munster Railway Cup goalkeeper for seven successive years from 1957 onwards. After that came Paddy Barry and Martin Coleman. Paddy won titles in 1966 and '70 when he was captain. Martin is especially remembered for his part in the three-in-a-row titles of '76, '77 and '78.

Then came Ger Cunningham. He ranks with the greatest and is Cork's longest-serving goalkeeper. He made a winning début in a 1980/81 National League game against Wexford at New Ross. His height, agility and athleticism, combined with sharp reflexes and a hawk-like eye, have made him one of the most consistent and outstanding goalkeepers of his era — indeed of any era.

What background, ingredients and influences shaped this hurling giant? On his mother's side the genes and the blood would have played a significant role — 'her brother, Mossie Finn, starred with St Finbarr's and played with Cork in the early fifties — her father played with the 'Barrs in the twenties and was involved in a big way.'

Ger's father, Jim, has always been a tremendous enthusiast, a keen follower and has a great interest in the game. 'He would always attend at club and county training sessions. His experienced eye would be cast over the various players and he would make an assessment of their potential. He loves the game so much that he has often gone to three matches in the same day.' For Ger he has always had words of support and encouragement — never negative criticism.

At Coláiste Iognaid Rís Ger had visions of making his mark as a midfielder or half-forward. It was then that he 'became a goalie by accident. Pat McDonnell who was a teacher in the school and who played for Cork, reversed myself and the goalkeeper and that was more or less it.' Just like that — 'more or less it'. Well, lucky for Cork, for Ger has given magnificent service since he first wore the red of Cork as a minor in 1978. And in recent times, who will ever forget his superb goalkeeping against Limerick in the championship of 1996 when he saved the seemingly impossible?

His puck out from goal has always been of prodigious length. Little wonder that he won the Poc Fada competition for seven successive years. He dethroned Pat Hartigan — twice winner — and retired undefeated in 1991.

A goalkeeper has a rather unique view of a game as he observes proceedings from his goal line so I asked Ger to recall some of the players who had made a really lasting impression on him over the years. Understandably, he went mainly for forwards. 'A goalkeeper tends to keep his eye on corner-forwards and full-forwards. There was my boyhood hero Charlie McCarthy — brilliant corner-forward — I carried his bag for many years. Ray Cummins was a fabulous player — played against him in club games with Blackrock'. Did he send many goals past? 'No, no he didn't,' Ger affirmed with a smile of satisfaction. 'Eddie Keher was a big hero of mine. I wrote to him in my young days looking for tips on free-taking and he answered. I have always had great admiration for George O'Connor. We toured the States together and I liked his honesty and toughness. Éamon Cregan had a great hurling brain and was very sharp. Nicholas English was a forward of superb skills — probably at his best in the years before '87. Pat Fox was as good in a different way — an under-rated corner-forward. D.J. (Carey) is tremendous and of course there was big-hearted Tony Doran and the very dangerous Joe McKenna'.

Since 1978 when Ger won his first of two All-Ireland minor medals, hurling honours have flowed on a regular basis and every honour in the game has come his way. Some have special significance. 'I was captain of the 'Barrs when we won the county title in 1988. My brother Brian, who was eighteen, was playing the same day. The win gave so much pleasure to my father — it was very special for him. Winning my first All-Ireland in the Centenary year in Thurles in '84 was very special too. We beat Tipp. in the Munster final that year — my first final against them. The win meant so much but I hadn't a particularly good game. I was overtrained — I had no appetite for it — I remember staying back doing extra training — I was overprepared. I played well in the final against Offaly — I had learned a great lesson from the Munster final.' Glancing through his achievements I was particularly taken by the range of honours that came his way in 1986. It began with a Munster title win over Clare in July, followed by an All-Ireland medal in September when Galway were defeated. His performance that year brought him his third All-Star award and he was chosen as Texaco Hurler of the Year — 'it was a lovely accolade to be adjudged the best hurler in the country.' Add to the foregoing the Poc Fada success and '86 was surely a year for Ger to remember and be very proud of.

Losing to Galway in the All-Ireland semi-final of 1985 stands out as the biggest disappointment in Ger's career. 'I was captain. 'Twas a very wet day. The game shouldn't have been played in such weather. We lost by four points. To get so close after leading Cork to victory over Tipp in the Munster final, was a great disappointment. Jimmy Barry Murphy didn't play because he was injured, although he did come on in the last ten minutes. I had expected we would go on to win the All-Ireland final. When I look back now, on the fact that we won in '84 and '86, I feel it could well have been a three in a row.'

Before we parted I discovered that Ger was no mean footballer in his younger days. To prove it he has an All-Ireland under-21 medal won in 1981 that he is very proud of. 'I trained very hard for that medal. I didn't play any game. But I trained as a forward — trained very hard.' And what's more, it took a replay against Galway — and the hard training that went with it — before he pocketed that medal.

Half-time 1967 All-Ireland final (left to right)   *Born 1938*
Ted Carroll, Pa Dillon, Jim Treacy, and Ollie Walsh.

"

From the first time I caught a hurl and from the time I started to puck around, I loved hurling. From listening to Mícheál O'Hehir in the mid-forties and onwards, broadcasting about the stars of the day, notably Jim Langton, Jack Mulcahy, Terry Leahy, Christy Ring, Gerry O'Riordan, and Mattie Fouhy, we young fellas imagined ourselves as those great hurlers.

Hurls and hurling-balls were hard to come by in those days; but we were very lucky that just up the road from our house, outside Freshford, worked Martin Lalor and his son Jack, who was known all over Ireland and beyond.

Martin himself had won All-Ireland medals with Kilkenny in the early days of the association. At this time Martin was a well-known hurley-maker. Many was the hour we gave on our way home from school watching him and his workman shaping and finishing the hurls; many was the new hurl he gave me.

In the late forties Tom Waldron was transferred from Clontubrid school to Freshford and set about organising the local hurling scene. At that time we didn't have a set of jerseys, no spare hurls, or hurling-balls. So we all sold tickets, had a raffle, and made the princely sum of £12 6s 8d. Tom bought a set of jerseys, hurls, balls, and we were on the road to success. We organised our own hurling matches each day at lunch-time. After three o'clock we continued on. We played great games on the village green. I got every support from Tom Waldron, my parents, and also my uncles Jim and Bill Farrell. Jim and Bill gave me every support down through the years; they told me if I played well or badly, or if I misconducted myself (which I never did).

Our team won under-14, 16 and minor in a few years and progressed to the local junior team. At that time junior hurling was pretty tough going. It was badly organised: bad pitches, bad referees, no training; and almost every junior team in the county was illegal. You would often see fellas of forty-plus playing, the togs down to their knees, the wellie turned down; and usually the big full-back or full-forward wore the cap with the peak on the back — and during the game was given a lift with a Baby Power or two.

Our first major title was a junior hurling championship won on 20 March 1960 against a strongly fancied Thomastown side who had on their side one Ollie Walsh. That was a fantastic team achievement. It was the first major win for St Lactain's, Freshford, at adult level in the history of the club. The celebrations went on for weeks, and it laid the foundation for better things to come.

1960: I got my first call-up for Kilkenny. I was absolutely thrilled. I was going to play with Ollie, Séamus Cleere, Martin Coogan, Eddie Keher, and John McGovern. I was selected at full-back. The opposition was Waterford, whose line-up included Dook Whelan, Johnny O'Connor, Tom Cheasty, Frankie Walsh, Séamus Power, and Philly Grimes. The prize was a trip to Wembley, which we won. I wasn't great that day, as the speed of the Waterford forwards bearing down on goal and the speed of Ollie coming off the goal line, dodging the incoming forwards, left me dazzled. It was a big step up in class.

1961 was a great year for our club. Father Holohan was appointed CC to Freshford and he took a great interest in hurling. He amalgamated Threecastles and Freshford to form a powerful senior team, and in September 1961 we won our first senior hurling title. It was a dream come true to win a Kilkenny senior title. We beat a great divisional team in the final, consisting of players like Ollie Walsh, Link Walsh, his brother Tom, Denis Heaslip, and many other stars. We had a team of very good hurlers: strong, determined, and very fit. Alfie Hickey captained us to victory, and he went on to become the first Freshford man to captain a Kilkenny senior team, leading them to a league victory in 1962.

1963: I was glad to be a sub on a great Kilkenny team which beat Waterford in the final. The highlight of that great win was an invite to New York the following spring. It was a trip I really looked forward to and really enjoyed. We were three weeks out between New York and Chicago. We had some great games with New York, who had some brilliant players. My club also won its second senior title that year, beating Bennettsbridge in the semi-final, the best club team I ever saw, and beating a strong Tullogher team in the final.

I became a regular on the Kilkenny

team in 1964, but we were beaten badly by a great Tipp team in the All-Ireland. They had players of the calibre of John Doyle, Len Gaynor, Mick Roche, Theo English, Liam Devaney, Donie Nealon, and Jimmy Doyle.

1965: I retained my position at full-back on the team and was also selected full-back for Leinster. We defeated Munster in a great game. A few years previous to that my club were playing Moycarkey in a challenge. After the game we were having a drink in the local and I was talking to this man who I did not know at the time. He had a beautiful medal on a chain in his lapel. I asked him about the medal, to be told it was a Railway Cup medal. He was none other than the great Johnny Leahy. So it was a wish come true to win my own and to play with the stars of Kilkenny; also Tom Neville, Ned Colfer, Phil Wilson and Tony Doran of Wexford, Des Foley of Dublin, Paddy Molloy of Offaly, Christy O'Brien of Laois, and Red Willie Walsh of Carlow. In 1965 we were beaten by Wexford.

1966: I was selected at full-forward in a trial game for Leinster. I scored three goals and was picked at full-forward for Leinster against Munster on Patrick's Day. We were beaten by two points. I played on Austin Flynn of Waterford fame. I didn't care what position I played in: just to play hurling was all I wanted. That year we played Cork in the league final 'home' and we won well. We played New York twice in the league final proper — in Croke Park and in Kilkenny. I wasn't on in Croke Park but was recalled for the Kilkenny game at full-forward. I was delighted to be on, and we won well. Cork, who were classed as no-hopers, beat us in the 1966 All-Ireland.

1967: Dublin gave us a terrible fright in the first round, but Ollie was outstanding on that day. We went on to win the Leinster final against a great Wexford team. The final was against Tipp. I felt I would never win an All-Ireland. I was at full-back again. We were well on top in the first half against the wind, and Ollie was brilliant. We lost our two best forwards, Tom Walsh and Eddie Keher; and although we were on top we weren't showing it on the scoreboard. We won it. It was my first All-Ireland win. I could not describe the feeling, it was just great.

1969 was another great year. We won the Leinster final against Offaly. It was Cork in the final. This was the beginning of a great Kilkenny team, consisting of six great forwards: Keher, Delaney, Purcell, Dunne, Brennan, and Crotty. It was a thrill to beat Cork.

1972: Cork looked to have it in the bag with twenty-five minutes to go. Keher was switched to half-forward. Martin Coogan came on. Kilkenny were transformed, and we won another All-Ireland. After this I decided to retire from inter-county hurling and to finish my hurling years with my club, St Lactain's. I enjoyed about ten more years with the club. I enjoyed all the years and all the games immensely. I made great friends through the games and still meet them regularly. Due to hurling I had the pleasure of playing in Wembley Stadium, New York, Chicago, San Francisco; and those were places I would never have seen only for hurling. If I could roll back the years I would play all over again. There is no game like hurling.

Pa Dillon ”

Pa was a goalkeeper's dream. He played in the days when the rules allowed the inrushing forwards to bundle the goalkeeper into the back of the net. He saw to it that such activity was kept to a minimum: those who chose to indulge in it had to deal with Pa — if not on the way in, certainly on the way out.

Pa was tall and spare and physically strong. 'I never missed a night's training or a match, and hurling never caused me to miss a day's work.' He was a versatile performer, a rock-solid defender, who saw no danger and feared no opponent.

The late Ollie Walsh always felt extremely comfortable playing behind Pa. They had a great understanding. Ollie knew Pa would do his duty; Pa, well aware of Ollie's brilliance, knew when to let the ball go to him. It was a partnership that bred mutual confidence. Never was this more in evidence than in the 1967 All-Ireland final against Tipp. Pa was superb in his covering. It was the day the Noresiders overcame adversity (Ollie, with an injured hand, was brilliant and heroic; Eddie Keher and Tommy Walsh departed the scene injured in the second half) to win a famous victory. Down six points at half time, they won by four and conceded only one point to Tipp in the second half — and that in the dying moments. 'It was as good a Kilkenny team as I ever hurled with.'

Gentle promptings bring memories flowing from Pa. 'I remember the night before the second leg of the league final of 1966 against New York, which was played in Nowlan Park. I hadn't played in the first game in Croke Park, and I didn't expect to be playing in Nowlan Park either. Anyway, on the eve of the match I was at the social gathering and having a few drinks and chatting with the New York lads. When I told them I wouldn't be playing they seemed relieved, and I wished them well. The following day didn't Paddy Grace and Jimmy Langton meet me going to the match and asked me to play. The New York lads were amazed to see me. I scored two goals and missed what would have been the goal of the century. I doubled on an outcoming high ball that travelled like a bullet and hit the crossbar over the goalie's head. It must have rebounded about fifty yards out the field; 'twould have been the goal of the century.'

Pa felt honoured when he was picked to play for his province in the Railway Cup. He still thinks it is a great honour for any player and regrets that these games have lost the tremendous appeal they had in his day. He would like to see special efforts made to restore the attractiveness of the competition to spectators. One of the things Pa liked about the Railway Cup was that it gave players like Jobber McGrath of Westmeath, Paddy Molloy of Offaly and Willie Walsh of Carlow an opportunity to display their hurling skills to a wider audience. For Pa, one of the most thrilling and exciting games he played was the Railway Cup final of 1965, when they defeated Munster. 'I had a good game that day — several different lads on me — one of those days that everything went right. Coming off the field Ted Carroll said to me, "Did you ever think we'd win a Railway Cup medal together?"' And talking of Ted Carroll, Pa feels he was 'a very under-rated player — a player that was quietly effective; very good tactically and in his day played brilliant matches and many a blinder.'

Talking of opponents, he felt Jimmy Doyle was 'a lethal forward who wielded his hurley as if it was a magic wand.' He had many a confrontation with Tony Doran — 'a mighty man who when he got the ball in his hand was nearly impossible to stop. And he'd travel out the field to get the ball, and you'd have to follow him. He held the hurl right-hand under like myself, so he would go up for the ball with the right hand; the left elbow would be stretched out and nearly inside in your mouth — hard to manage.'

Pa has a room that displays a wide range of trophies, medals, and photographs. They range from the humble competition to the pinnacle of success. Prominent in their midst is a silver-plated trophy that holds a special place in Pa's hurling world. 'I won it when I was seventeen — a seven-a-side hurling competition; clubs from all over the county. Some of the teams had seven brothers on them — some very tough games; I shed tears and sweat and blood winning that.' And that from a man who togged out for eight All-Ireland finals — twice as a sub, in '63 and '73 — and won

Pa Dillon's daughter Gillian (centre) in action

four All-Ireland medals, three on the field and one as a sub.

Father Time, however, catches up with all mortals, even the yet very trim and fit-looking Pa. 'It was the very exciting 1972 final against Cork. I went for a ball that Charlie McCarthy let fly on — it was like a bullet. I'll get this one, I said to myself, but the reflexes let me down. They were just that split second off. It was the first time I experienced it.'

Yet Pa was still playing junior hurling at forty-six. It was against Muckalee. 'A high ball came in. I went up for it, still thinking I was twenty-one or twenty-two. I got a belt of a hurl in the forehead — blood everywhere.' Pa felt it warranted an investigation — just a personal one: no need to call witnesses or anything like that. 'I got up and asked the full-forward if he had hit me. He said no. Then I asked three or four more forwards. They all said no. I began to feel I must have hit myself. I was taken to hospital, into casualty. The nurse was filling a form and asked what age I was. I didn't want to say forty-six, so I said, "Put down 'Over 40'." As she walked away I heard her say to another nurse, "They never get sense, do they?" I felt then it was time to retire.'

Pa's hurling skills were inherited by his daughter Gillian, who has won three All-Ireland senior camogie medals with Kilkenny. In the second of those victories, in 1991, she scored two magnificent goals that were object lessons in converting fleeting opportunities. Twice the sliotar came her way. Each time she first-timed it on the bounce, and the green flag waved. It was innate skill — instinctive reaction. It was textbook stuff that many a county senior hurler would have envied and wished he could emulate: no stopping; no lifting; no handling. She deserved Kilkenny Sports Star of the Year in 1991 for camogie.

Billy Dooley with the All-Star trophy

Born 1969

66

I started off in Clareen national school in 1982, where we won our first school final. We hurled Lusmagh, the second-smallest parish in Offaly. Brendan Kelly, John Troy and Pat Temple were hurling with Lusmagh at that time. That was the start for me. Damien White was the hurling instructor at national school level; he helped me a lot at skills. After that I went to Birr Community School, where I hurled under-age with them.

My first All-Ireland medal was won with the college when we beat North Mon of Cork in the senior colleges final in Portlaoise in 1986. The same year we won the minor hurling final with Offaly by beating Cork, and the next year we beat Tipperary in the final. Pat Joe Whelehan had a big influence on my hurling career. He trained us to the two minor finals, when I never thought I could get to play in All-Ireland finals. In 1989 we played Tipperary in the All-Ireland under-21 final and I feel we could have won that match. But we were beaten by two points.

After that I started on the senior panel. My first success with the senior team was in 1991, when we won the first league final — Offaly's first and only one. Dublin beat us in the same year in the championship. It was 1994 before Offaly made the breakthrough again and we went on to win the All-Ireland. This was the highlight of my career up to date. In 1995 we were beaten in the All-Ireland final by Clare, which was the most disappointing day of my life. As for last year, Wexford beat us in the Leinster final, but I was delighted to see them win the All-Ireland final.

Éamon Cregan and Derry Donovan had a big influence on me over the last four years and helped me to become a better hurler. At club level I won my third championship medal this year. Up to 1988 we had won only a junior championship in Seir Kieran. But we were lucky to get a group of good players at one time. We have beaten Birr in the 1995 semi-final and Banagher in the final, which are the two strongest club teams in Offaly at the moment. That was the highlight of my career with Seir Kieran. But this year I won my third medal with four more of my brothers.

99

Billy Dooley

B illy Dooley comes from what is believed to be the smallest parish in Ireland but a parish that has given the game of hurling two of the finest full-backs in the history of the game, Eugene Coughlan and Kevin Kinahan. Eugene gave sterling performances for Offaly all through the eighties when his county emerged to take its place among the élite of the game and performed with distinction. Kevin followed in his footsteps. He has a different style but is equally brilliant. Who will ever forget his display against Kilkenny in the Leinster final of 1995, when he curbed the ever-present threat of D.J. Carey? And an equally magnificent performance against Clare in the All-Ireland final of that year, when Clare rained in a succession of high balls to the Offaly goalmouth that Kevin fielded superbly and cleared with aplomb.

Billy comes from a great hurling family, and the name Dooley will rank in hurling lore with the other great family names in the history of the game. His Uncle Joe played with Offaly in the fifties, while his grandfather, Jim Carroll, won an All-Ireland junior title with Offaly in 1929 with a win over Cork. His eldest brother, Joe, has played with Offaly seniors since 1984, winning All-Ireland titles in 1985 and 1994. Johnny, the youngest, has, like Billy, been with Offaly seniors since 1991, having won All-Ireland minor titles in 1987 and '89 and also three Leinster under-21 titles, in 1989, '91, and '92. The senior successes of Johnny and Billy run hand in hand: an All-Ireland title in '94, All-Star awards in '94 and '95, National League '91, Oireachtas '94, county titles '88, '95, and '96, and Leinster titles '94 and '95. All three played for Offaly in the forward line in the successive All-Ireland finals of '94 and '95 — possibly a family record. They were joined by Séamus and Kieran when the club won the county title in 1996. When Billy arrived at county senior level he had already notched up two All-Ireland minor successes and one under-21 Leinster title.

The players who have influenced him so far are his fellow-countyman Mark Corrigan, Tony O'Sullivan of Cork, and in particular Ger Henderson of Kilkenny, who was from his youth his favourite hurler: 'He influenced me by his attitude towards the game.'

In a career that still has quite a few years to run, Billy looks back on four games that were particularly memorable. 'All three of us played in the Leinster semi-final of 1994 against Kilkenny.

It was great to beat the All-Ireland champions.' That was the day Offaly led comfortably entering the closing moments, but Kilkenny got two late goals to leave the final score Offaly 2:16, Kilkenny 3:9. 'I was very satisfied with my play in the Leinster final against Wexford. Things went well for me that day.

'Of course the All-Ireland final of '94 against Limerick has to be memorable. We were lucky to be in the game at half time. We were down six points — could have been twelve; we were hurling bad. It all happened for us in the last five minutes.' Well, it certainly did. Limerick were leading by five points. The score read Limerick 2:13, Offaly 1:11. The McCarthy Cup seemed destined for the Shannonside — just a matter of concentrating and keeping it tight until the final whistle. The Offaly goal had come from a penalty in the opening five minutes, described by Con Houlihan as follows: 'Joe Quaid parried Johnny Dooley's penalty; Joe Dooley pounced like a hawk on a chicken too far from its mother.' Now with five minutes to go Billy Dooley is fouled by Joe O'Connor to the right of the railway goal 21-yard line. Not an unduly threatening position really. Johnny Dooley stands over the ball, seems set to take a point; then he lifts and strikes low — not a bullet, but it beats defenders and goalkeeper for a green flag.

Thirty seconds later the Limerick defence is caught flat-footed as a ball from midfield runs ahead of Pat O'Connor, who pulls first time to despatch it for another green flag. Offaly one point up, Limerick in disarray; Offaly supporters suddenly delirious, Limerick followers stunned. A vapid performance was suddenly transformed, and more was to follow. In the space of ninety seconds Billy sent over three glorious points, all with effortless ease from well out the field — target practice; manna from heaven. Not a drop of sweat was shed, either in the obtaining of possession or the execution of the scores. It was all unreal. 'I feel the play got out of hand

The three brothers Johnny, Joe, and Billy.

for Limerick: no-one marking; everyone doing their own thing all over the field; it suited Offaly.' Two other Offaly points gave the scoreboard at the final whistle a remarkable appearance: Offaly 3:16, Limerick 2:13.

In decades to come the Dooleys will be remembered in Offaly. Hurling fans will talk about their deeds and feats on the field. Those who saw them in action will eulogise and romanticise about the gaiscí of Billy and Johnny and Joe in the final of '94. All through the '94 hurling championship the Dooley clan was to the fore, and particularly so in the field of scoring. In the four games Offaly played, the Dooleys between them accounted for 6:41 of Offaly's total of 8:63 — each of them a handful for any defender.

Billy's next memorable game is the 1995 Leinster final against Kilkenny. Kilkenny were favourites. It will certainly live in my mind as one of the great games of hurling. Billy got five magnificent points that day, and Johnny got three. Billy's performance in that game earned him the Man of the Match award. When he scores, and he does so with clinical precision, he

makes it look easy — surely a sign of a master of his craft. We look forward to many more fine displays from this intelligent player, who thinks and reads a game very well.

What an absorbing contest we witnessed in 1995. Best game of the year it was — hurling in all its grandeur, where ash was swung with freedom and abandon in sporting, manly spirit. It was as if the gods knew what was in store and sent the elements to oblige us with a stirring prologue just as Kilkenny took the field: thunder, lightning, torrential rain, fans in the new Cusack Stand scattering and scurrying for cover. Right from the throw-in it was eyeball-to-eyeball stuff. No quarter anywhere on the pitch. Every score would be hard-earned: sweat and toil; sweat and toil. Offaly pressure was sustained and unrelenting. Every man had a task; the sum of all the tasks was a game plan — a team effort. Co-ordination; concentration; no panic; grim resolve — it all produced a synergy that slowly and gradually wore down the Kilkenny resistance. At half time it was five points to three points — low scoring but

Billy Dooley (Offaly) battles against Joe O'Connor (Limerick).

breathtaking and energy-sapping stuff. We marvelled at the splendour of the hurling — splendid and absorbing despite the atrocious weather.

The first score and the first goal could be crucial in the second half — and so it proved. Both came to Offaly in the second and seventh minutes. The goal, a probing outfield shot from Dáithí Regan, was a little fortuitous — but fortune favours the brave. Onward Offaly surged, their grip on the game growing more vice-like as the second half progressed. Between the tenth and eighteenth minute they were scoring at the rate of one point a minute and, as 'Carbery' would have said, 'moving like mowers in a meadow'. Kilkenny probed and prodded; they contested and counter-attacked. But the Offaly defence was phalanx-like, blocking, hooking, parrying, harassing, droppucking, covering, batting, chasing. No way through.

About the twenty-seventh minute Pat O'Connor scored a smashing Offaly goal. He won the pull as he doubled on an overhead dropping ball on the edge of the square. The scoreboard read 2:14 to 0:5, and it was still that way with five minutes to go. Spectators blinked in disbelief.

For about three-quarters of the game Kevin Kinahan had been magnificent on D.J. Carey, and then D.J. moved outfield. In the last five minutes two flashes of D.J. genius brought two consolation goals, and the final score read Offaly 2:16, Kilkenny 2:5.

Éamon Cregan must have felt very proud of his Offaly team. He had seen his hurling philosophy translated into visible action by a dedicated and disciplined group of hurlers who responded to his promptings and gave us a performance that matched all the epics we had heard and read about from bygone years. It was entertainment at its best from the aristocrats of modern hurling — aristocrats who specialise in playing vintage hurling when they face Kilkenny. We had witnessed a Homeric contest — compliments of Offaly and Kilkenny. The spellbound Yank was right when he exclaimed, having witnessed a game in the thirties: 'It's a game for the gods.'

For Johnny Dunne, like many of his generation, the emigrant ship beckoned, and he made his way to the United States in the late twenties. Up to then he had hurled with a team called Killarney, based near Bennettsbridge. He carried with him his hurling skills and continued to develop and fine-tune them during his stay there; in his heart he always hoped he would one day return to Ireland.

*'Rachaidh mé ar cuairt nó is luath mo
shaol*

*Don talamh bheag shuairc sin is dual do
Ghaeil.'*

And return to Ireland he did, with the American Tailteann team of 1932. Such was his class and brilliance that he immediately found favour with the Kilkenny selectors and won his first and only National League medal when Kilkenny, with a great second-half flurry, defeated Limerick in the final at Nowlan Park on 9 April 1933. Kilkenny were by then an established hurling power, full of class and in the big time. Limerick

Born 1905

were only emerging: their potential lay ahead. Both counties would dominate the thirties.

They met again in the All-Ireland final of 1933, which was destined to put Johnny's name among the immortals of the game. In Munster, Limerick had a testing campaign. In the first round they surprised everyone with an easy 6:8 to 1:1 victory over the All-Ireland finalists, Clare. The next encounter was with Cork, All-Ireland champions of 1931, in whose ranks were some of hurling's greatest names: Jim Regan, George Garret, and Paddy 'Fox' Collins — staunch defenders; Jim Hurley — great midfielder; and Dinny Barry Murphy — equally brilliant at half-back and half-forward. The Shannonsiders won a hard march, 2:9 to 1:6. And so to the Munster final against Waterford, with Limerick victorious on the score 3:7 to 1:2.

In Leinster, Kilkenny seemed in real trouble at half time in the final against Dublin when they trailed by four goals. But a typical rally in which they displayed all their craft and cunning saw them emerge winners on the score 7:5 to 5:5. After that they conquered Galway, 5:10 to 3:8.

The scene was now set for what promised to be a great final between Limerick and Kilkenny — the first such meeting since 1897. The prospect gripped the imagination of hurling followers, and a record crowd of just over forty-five thousand — the biggest up to then for either a hurling or a football final — crammed Croke Park, and it is estimated that about five thousand disappointed followers of the game were locked out when the gates had to be closed almost half an hour before the throw-in. It was an era when the singing of 'Faith of our Fathers' formed part of the prelude to our games. With the preliminaries concluded and amid intense excitement, the referee, Stephen Jordan of Galway, threw in the ball.

At half time it was four points each — hard, fast, exciting and pulsating; backs in the ascendancy; Kilkenny defending the railway goal and playing with wind advantage. Now there are less than five minutes to go. Only one point separates the teams. Scores are at a premium; each one is worth a king's ransom. It has been a second half of thrills, spills, great hurling, and some fine individual performances — Kilkenny defensively superb, Limerick offensively wasteful. Limerick, backed by the breeze and with a plentiful supply of the ball, are attacking, and all their lines have advanced upfield. From this position Kilkenny counter-attack. Matty Power despatches a pass. Johnny Dunne is away at speed. His rasping shot beats Paddy Scanlon in the Limerick goal — the only goal of the game. The green flag waves, and claims of over-carrying count for nothing. 'The field is fought and won.'

On one occasion when Johnny was asked about the goal, he described it as follows. 'When I got the ball I rounded McCarthy [Tom, the full-back] and just kept going and put the ball in the cage.' Cage! A Yankeeism, no doubt. A great Wexford hurling enthusiast who was at the game, and who is now no longer with us, recalled the scene for me. 'When the ball hit the net a bunch of Kilkenny lady supporters in the sideline jumped up in sheer delight and shouted, "Lovely, lovely, lovely Johnny Dunne." In that fleeting moment he was renamed and wrote himself into hurling legend.

The goal proved to be the turning-point in a game that ended 1:7 to 0:6. Johnny was top scorer of the day, with 1:1, and he added an All-Ireland medal to his growing collection — the first son of Bennettsbridge to win an All-Ireland senior medal. The victory was rewarded with a trip to America for the team the following year.

Johnny played in the finals of the Railway Cup in 1933, '34, '35, and '36, coming on as a sub in '33 and winning medals in '33 and '36. He won his second All-Ireland medal when Kilkenny beat Limerick 2:5 to 2:4 in a thriller played in a downpour in 1935, but he failed in his attempt for a third the following year when Limerick had revenge on the score 5:6 to 1:5. Some time after the 1936 campaign Johnny again emigrated, this time to England. The records show that he won a junior All-Ireland hurling title with London in 1938 when they defeated Cork by 4:4 to 4:1.

He returned home after the war and got a job as a postman. He played with Thomastown against his former club, Mooncoin, in the senior championship of 1946, aged forty-one. It isn't clear whether he played in the final of that year, when Thomastown won the county title.

This wily and talented forward, with a great turn of speed and flair for the big occasion, died young in September 1954.

For some of the detail in this article I am indebted to the Kilkenny GAA historian, Tom Ryall.

Born 1945

"

Growing up in Prosperous in the early fifties, I was fortunate that Tom Johnson, a Kilkennyman, came to live in the area. He, along with Paddy Power, a schoolteacher in Caragh, started hurling in the area. My earliest memories of hurling were of riding a bicycle up to Lalor's field to play and practise. The games seemed to start at seven o'clock and did not finish till dark. Weeknights were divided between hurling and football, and every night was a games night.

The under-age teams I played on enjoyed great success. The local parish priest of the time, Father Bennett, organised an under-age hurling tournament with neighbouring counties. The pride I felt from playing with my county made me determined that I would represent Kildare at adult level, both at football and hurling.

Growing older and playing against players from the strong hurling counties who were in the Army Apprentice Schools made me realise how much more skilful they were and the amount of practice it would take to be as good as they were.

I was fortunate to play and win an All-Ireland junior title with Kildare in 1962. Quite a few of the players were from the Army Cadet School, some of whom were to win senior medals in later years.

One of our greatest achievements was to win an All-Ireland intermediate championship, beating Cork in the final in Thurles.

In the early 1960s I was fortunate to be selected to play in the Cardinal Cushing Games in New York. I was lucky enough there to play both football and hurling with the late Christy Ring. Even then to see the skill and ability he displayed left a lasting impression with me, but above all was his willingness to help a young hurler from a non-hurling county to try and improve his hurling skill.

The sixties and seventies were great times in Kildare hurling. We were winning junior, intermediate and senior B All-Irelands and playing against most of the top teams in the leagues and championships. It was terrific to play against these teams, and we always acquitted ourselves well. Éire Óg, my hurling club, were also doing well in these years, and we were lucky enough to win ten hurling championships and quite a few leagues as well.

In the early seventies I was chosen to play for my province in the Railway Cup and was lucky to win medals in both football and hurling. To play on Leinster teams with the top players and against the top people from Munster and Connacht was a great source of pride for me, a Kildare man. The help and advice I got from the late Paddy Grace, the camaraderie of the Wexford, Offaly, Kilkenny, Laois and Dublin players and the friends I made then have endured to this day.

To be selected as a replacement All-Star in the mid-seventies to travel to America was the ultimate honour for me, and they hold some of the most treasured memories of my hurling career. I sometimes find it difficult to believe that hurling has been so good to me, and I hope the honours we won will be repeated in the future with Kildare hurling teams.

Pat Dunney "

M ention the name Kildare in GAA circles and immediately everyone will, understandably, think of football and footballers. And old-timers will remember with pride and affection great names from a glorious past: names like Matt Goff, Paul Doyle, Jack Higgins, and of course Larry Stanley — footballer supreme, athlete, high-jump champion, Olympic competitor at Paris in 1924, and captain of his native Kildare when defeating Galway in the 1919 All-Ireland football final.

Mention the name Pat Dunney in GAA circles and everybody calls to mind Kildare's greatest dual player of modern times — a worthy successor to his fellow-countyman Frank Burke (featured in *Giants of the Ash*), who achieved fame on Gaelic fields with his adopted Dublin, winning hurling titles in 1917 and 1920 and football in 1921, '22, and '23. Pat Dunney captained the Kildare under-21 football team of 1965 to All-Ireland victory over Cork. His inter-county football career stretched from 1962 to 1978, 'and in that period we were beaten in five Leinster finals by

Meath, Offaly, and Dublin.'

But Kildare had its hurlers too. No golden eras — just little pockets of success — and Pat shared in them all.

He was only seventeen in 1962 when he played in goal for the Kildare junior hurling team that beat London in the final to bring the Lily Whites their first hurling title. Also on that team was the army man Larry Kiely, who later excelled at centre-forward with his native Tipperary, winning All-Ireland senior honours with them in 1964 and 1965.

The Kildare success was repeated in 1966 with victory over Warwickshire at Birmingham. Pat, as captain and centre-half-back, had a brilliant game. Hurling was improving in Kildare, and further honours came Pat's way in 1969 with a division 2 National Hurling League and an All-Ireland intermediate success. 'One thing I remember about the intermediate win was that we beat Cork in Thurles, and about five of the Cork team subsequently won All-Ireland senior medals.'

His performances on the hurling field brought him to the notice of the Leinster Railway Cup selectors. He was picked for trial games; he impressed. It led to him being chosen at centre-back in 1971 and 1972 and at left-full-back in 1974, '75, and '76. He won Railway Cup medals in every year except 1976.

In those years Kilkenny and Wexford produced outstanding teams and several wonderful hurlers. It is therefore a measure of Pat's hurling ability that he was sufficiently accomplished and proficient to be numbered among them in Railway Cup selections. He had the temperament and talents to adjust to the pace and demands of the game at that level. He lined out in those years with some of the greats of the game, among them Pat Nolan, Damien Martin, Noel Skehan, Jim Treacy, Dan Quigley, Pa Dillon, Frank Cummins, Pat Delaney, Eddie Keher, Tony Doran, Fan Larkin, Martin Coogan, Barney Moylan, Kieran Purcell, Pádraig Horan, Pat Henderson, and Mick Jacob. He was surrounded by hurling stars from established strongholds; but he was at home in their midst and blended beautifully into their defensive structure.

For three years, from 1974 to 1976, the Leinster full-back line read: Paddy Larkin (Kilkenny), Pádraig Horan (Offaly), Pat Dunney (Kildare).

I queried his absence from the Leinster line-out in 1973: it broke what would have been six successive years at interprovincial level. 'We were playing a Leinster club game against Borris-in-Ossory. I went to block a fellow at the sideline; we both slipped. He hit me on the shoulder, I hit him on the head — both accidental. The referee put me off. I never forgave him for it. The man I hit played on; we are great friends. But I never forgave the referee.'

That apart, the Railway Cup competition conjures up all kinds of pleasant memories for Pat. It enabled him to play with and against the leading hurlers of his time. It brought him honours at the highest level. In his day it was still a very prestigious competition. But most of all it reminds him of his early youth, when his father used to take him to Croke Park and he saw in the flesh his heroes, who until then he had only heard about on the radio, through the magical voice of Mícheál O'Hehir; and in his young mind's eye they were giant-like figures, each a sporting colossus: Tony Reddan saving shots from all angles; Mick O'Connell soaring to the sky to fetch a football; Ned Wheeler sending a sideline cut over the bar; Nick O'Donnell rocklike at full-back. Understandably, he wants the Railway Cup competition to remain, and he likes the innovation of taking it to a provincial venue.

1974 was a most fruitful year in Pat's career. He won an All-Ireland senior hurling B medal and a division 2 National League football medal. On St Patrick's Day he won his first and only Railway Cup football medal when he came on as a sub in the defeat of Connacht, 2:10 to 1:7. On the following day he won his third Railway Cup hurling title when Leinster defeated Munster, 2:15 to 1:11. That dual Railway Cup success placed him among a select band.

Twice in the mid-seventies he was chosen as a dual All-Star replacement. It was a tremendous honour — a fitting reward for a great exponent of our Gaelic games.

'When to the sessions of sweet silent thought
I summon up remembrance of things past,'

Pat will reflect with relish on those days in the Leinster jersey and the never-to-be-forgotten All-Star trips to America. 'It was like home from home all the way. When we arrived in Chicago I met Jimmy Mitchell. We had gone to school together. We didn't sleep at all — stayed up all night talking. In San Francisco I stayed with J.J. Whelan. Himself and his wife were from Kilcullen. They gave me a car and off I went to visit Las Vegas and other sights. I stayed with Tom Stanley, a second cousin of mine in New York. We won school championships together in our young days. His father and Larry Stanley were brothers. The hospitality everywhere was incredible.'

And what about the games? 'Oh, they were great too — an honour to be in such company. I played on Ray Cummins in all the hurling games. I managed all right on him. He was a great player; very fair — a true sportsman.'

The junior and intermediate successes of the sixties were built on, and the senior team of the seventies was showing considerable promise. 'We were beating Offaly, Clare and Laois in league games. We lost by five or six points to Tipp and Galway, at National League and All-Ireland quarter-final stages, respectively. The seventies was our best time. We were showing real promise. I think 1976 was our best championship. We beat Dublin in Aughrim in the first round. We were reasonably good. The ref blew half time after thirty minutes; someone shouted in, "Five minutes more to go." Play resumed, and we scored two goals before half time. We won in the end by two points, and then we faced a great Wexford team that included Tony and Colm Doran, Martin Quigley, Ned Buggy, Mick Jacob, Willie Murphy, and Teddy O'Connor. For almost sixty of the seventy minutes we led them and had them beaten until they made a vital switch. They brought Tony Doran out to wing-forward. He drifted in to the middle and caught three or four balls and scored a goal and a few points. He had great hands and was very strong. If we were smart enough we would have responded to the switch — inexperience. We lost in the end by four points.'

Wexford went on to trounce Kilkenny by seventeen points in the Leinster final and failed narrowly and somewhat unluckily to Cork in the All-Ireland final. Unfortunately for Kildare it was an aging team, and there were no young players emerging to replace men of the calibre of Tommy and Tony Carew, Johnny Christian, Peter Connolly, Bobby Burke, Mick Dwane, Johnny and Ned Walsh. 'After '76 we started to go back.'

Pat played his club hurling with Éire Óg and his football with Raheen. In 1964 they won the county double, and in 1984 he made a comeback with a view to repeating the double in the Centenary year. He had 50 per cent success: the hurling was won.

He sees hurling as 'a better game to play than football'. As to which he was better at, 'I would like to think I was a better hurler, but probably I was a better footballer.'

GAA affairs are still central to Pat's life. He spent about eight years as chairman of Kildare County Board; at present he is the Kildare delegate to the Central Council. Much of his time is given to coaching the youth, and to young hurlers he advocates letting the ball do the work, coupled with minimal handling. This affable and quietly spoken Kildare man has been a wonderful ambassador for hurling and the GAA.

This is his team:

Noel Skehan *(Kilkenny)*

Fan Larkin *(Kilkenny)*   Pat Hartigan *(Limerick)*   Brian Murphy *(Cork)*

Mick Jacob *(Wexford)*   Pat Dunney *(Kildare)*   Iggy Clarke *(Galway)*

Frank Cummins *(Kilkenny)*   John Connolly *(Galway)*

Gerald McCarthy *(Cork)*   Paddy Delaney *(Kilkenny)*   Francis Loughnane *(Tipperary)*

Jimmy Barry Murphy *(Cork)*   Tony Doran *(Wexford)*   Eddie Keher *(Kilkenny)*

Born 1931

of the 1961 All-Ireland hurling final against Tipp.

"

Des. Ferguson

Des was a dual player — and a right good one he was too. My meeting with him took me back all of forty-four years to the All-Ireland hurling final of 1952. It was my first final. I had been listening to Mícheál O'Hehir's broadcasts since 1946 and used to long for the day when I would be in Croke Park for a final. I was stationed in Dún Laoghaire and travelled by bus to Croke Park. Those were the days when you queued at Croke Park: first come, first served. I took up position behind the canal goal. The attendance was seventy-one thousand — not a capacity crowd in those days. It was standing room only under the Cusack Stand; and in 1954, when Cork met Wexford, the attendance reached almost eighty-five thousand.

The teams emerged and presented a fine contrast in colours, Dublin in their sky-blue and white, Cork wearing red and white. Dublin hadn't won a hurling title since 1938, even though they subsequently contested four finals. Cork, on the other hand, had dominated the forties in Munster and took the McCarthy Cup to the Leeside on five occasions. They had in their ranks the great Christy Ring; marking him was Des Ferguson. The crowd looked forward to the clashes between them: Christy the wily warrior, the seasoned campaigner, Des the raw youth of indomitable spirit.

How did Des feel at the prospect of facing the maestro? 'Well, I was young — just twenty-one. I saw it as just another game, Christy as just another opponent. I was a senior hurler, given the

"
I recall the happy hours of yesteryear spent hurling on the streets of Donnycarney, practising the skills with many of the lads who afterwards made the St Vincent's and Dublin teams — players like Norman Allen, Pat Lillis, Tony Young. No boredom in those days! All activity, from dawn to dusk.

The GAA, I feel, owe a huge debt to the Christian Brothers for the dedication and unselfishness of their time spent coaching and training school teams. I am full of admiration for the mentors of the so-called weaker hurling counties who struggle with pleasure in promoting the game year after year, hoping always to make the big breakthrough.

The GAA has been part of my life for so long, stretching from my parents to my own family. Máire my wife, sons, daughters — all are involved and enjoy the spirit and traditions of the GAA.

I have no regrets, other than the losing

task of marking him, and that was it. My policy always was to get to the ball first; play the ball; let the opponent worry about me. Ring or anyone else — all the same. Sure if they had God on the team, you'd mark him.'

Des had a superb first half, and I can still see him in my mind's eye winning the tussles, gaining possession, clearing with confidence, and time and time again drawing cheers of admiration from the crowd. In the second half Dublin had to give second best to a fine Cork team under the captaincy of the ace forward Paddy Barry and inspired by the goalkeeping of Dave Creedon, who foiled many a Dublin effort.

Des emerged with reputation enhanced and added to it as the years passed. He was still there in 1961 when Dublin faced Tipperary in the final. By then he had moved back to right-full-back. He gave a great display of defensive hurling in a game that hung in the balance throughout and was lost in the end by only one point. Many felt that the sending off of Lar Foley that day may have cost Dublin the title; but there were other factors too. Here is an excerpt from a letter containing many reminiscences that I received in March 1992 from Brother T.N. O'Brien, a Christian Brother in Buenos Aires, after he had read *Giants of the Ash*. 'Two very doubtful frees against "Snitchy" Ferguson for picking the ball off the ground gave Tipp two golden points which made all the difference in the end. I was young at the time and my eyesight was nearly perfect but the referee's must have been exceptional. I thought the ball was that wee bit above the ground on both occasions. I would place "Snitchy" among the great dual players of the GAA.'

Des — otherwise known as 'Snitchy' — remembers those frees that should never have been and confirmed that the ball was not on the ground when he grasped it. But he accepted it all philosophically and in a spirit of positive sportsmanship. For him, playing the game was everything: the personal satisfaction; the comradeship; the friendships; the enjoyment and glory associated with wearing the club jersey, and the added status when you were handed a county or provincial jersey. Des doesn't think in terms of lows in his hurling career — not even the losing of the 1961 All-Ireland. 'It was a great achievement to reach the final. You go out to do your best. When you do that there is no such thing as a low. I always did my best; a good game was a bonus, a bad game — well, you did your best: you can't do any more.'

Des was born in County Down but the family moved to Dublin when he was six — fortunate for Dublin, Down's loss. His father played football with Down and his mother played camogie at local level. Gaelic games were in the blood. Des's brother Liam played at right-half-back for Dublin in the 1961 hurling final. When Des and his family moved to County Meath it was Meath's gain. His son Terry won two senior football titles with Meath at left-full-back in 1987 and 1988; Conor and Barry also played at county level.

Football was kinder to Des. He won four Leinster titles and two All-Ireland medals. It began in 1955. Dublin's previous Leinster title and All-Ireland success was in 1942. In the Leinster final of 1955 they routed Meath, 5:12 to 0:7. They seemed invincible — a forward line of devastating passing movements. The semi-finals of that year produced unique results: Kerry v. Cavan, a draw; Dublin v. Mayo, a draw. Both replays took place on 11 September.

Dublin and Kerry emerged. It promised a classic confrontation on final day. 'We were inexperienced really — not mentally right. The papers blew us up and we believed them. It all went to our heads. We all came together around the same age — no veteran to guide us. When things are going wrong you need a leader to hold young fellows together. We were red-hot favourites but failed to cope with Kerry's experience. We had a thing about Kerry. They were our bogey team.'

Des Ferguson in action

And so to 1958 and Des's first All-Ireland victory. The bogey team, Kerry, were despatched by Derry in the semi-final; Dublin's prospects looked brighter. 'As a team we were going over the top but we had the experience and it saw us through.' 1963 brought Des his second All-Ireland football medal. It is fairy-tale stuff. 'I hadn't played inter-county for two years. The travelling from Oldcastle for training and club matches was too much. So I quit. I can remember occasions when I played two games on the same Sunday — it could be hurling or football or both. There were even a few times when I played three games. Never felt it physically. You'd never refuse to play for St Vincent's: you felt a duty to play when called upon.

'Anyway, about 1963, Dublin played Meath in the first round and were fortunate to win. They had injury problems. The second round was against Kildare. I was cutting the grass when Kevin Heffernan arrived. "What are you doing down here?" I said. "Just came for a bit of a run," said Kevin. We chatted away, and after a while he said, "You'll come up tomorrow to play." Jokingly I said, "Why not?" But Kevin was serious, and after further discussion I agreed. The players didn't even know about it.

'I lined out at full-forward. Early on I got a clip in the back of the head. That settled me; after that everything went like a dream. In the next game we scraped home over Laois and beat Down fairly well in the semi-final. It was a very committed and determined team that faced Galway in the final.' That game was won and lost when Dublin took a sideline kick around the 14-yard line on the Cusack Stand side near Hill 16. With backs having time to concentrate, it wasn't the type of situation that would normally trouble a defence. 'But two or three of our forwards were lined up to put the ball in the net. That goal won the game. It finished 1:9 to 0:10.'

Despite the many football honours that came the way of the Ferguson family, 'hurling has always been the first love in our house: a dry ball, a firm sod, and sweat in your eyes — sure you couldn't ask for anything better!' Des is still active in GAA affairs at local level in Kells. He remembers the day in 1972 they travelled to Croke Park for discussions with Seán Ó Síocháin about their development programme. They spotted a plaque depicting an enlarged All-Ireland medal that was originally on the front of the old Hogan Stand but had been cast aside. It is now proudly displayed in the GAA Centre in Kells.

He has great admiration for the Wexford team of his era. He mentioned in particular the gentlemanly approach to the game of Tim Flood and Bobbie Rackard. 'I was fortunate in my playing days. I never marked a dirty hurler.'

As a dual player Des has much to reflect on: county and provincial titles in both codes, with St Vincent's and Dublin, respectively; two All-Ireland football titles. Railway Cup honours eluded him in football, but he was part of the hurling successes of 1956 and 1962. 'I regret now that I didn't spend more time at the hurling skills — at ball play. Concentration was mostly on football. I know there was scope to improve my hurling, and I now wish I had done that.'

He would recommend three changes to hurling. 'I'd do away with the full-back and full-forward — make it thirteen a side: it would make a great open game. Any score should be from the stick: that's the name of the game. Prohibit the use of one-handed overhead swinging of the hurley: it's deadly dangerous; there's little control over the hurley. It should be banned and seen as dangerous play.'

He also has dreams — just two. 'I'd love to see Meath in division 1 hurling and matching the best. I'd like to see the Sky Blue [Dublin] back in Croke Park on All-Ireland hurling final day.'

Des, we all hope your dreams come true.

Born 1931

"

During my days in Thurles CBS I played at centre-back in a Dean Ryan final against Castlemartyr at Mitchelstown. At full-time the scores were level and we won in extra time by 1:1. The Dean Ryan cup was an under-16 competition. John O'Grady played with Thurles CBS that day. I had left the CBS before they won a Harty Cup. I spent a short time in Mungret College in Limerick before returning home.

Lorrha beat us in the North Tipp final of 1948. I suppose I should say Tony Reddan beat us. He made his name that day. We couldn't score on him. As a goalie he was unbelievable. He was uncanny. He certainly had no equal in my time. That day, a very wet day, I was playing wing-forward.

In 1949 I won an All-Ireland minor medal with Tipp playing at centre-back. John O'Grady was in goal and in 1958 we both won a Senior All-Ireland

with Tipp. John was still in goal and I was right-half-back.

I suppose the highlight of my career had to be my call-up for the All-Ireland final of 1950 against Kilkenny. Paddy Leahy came to me at Thurles Sportsfield and said — 'We want to have you on in the final. What do you think?' 'No problem, Paddy, we'll give it a go,' I said. As I look back now I couldn't possibly have played in that final but for the experience I had gained playing on the Borrisoleigh senior team with great players and against great players in a very competitive championship that included teams like Holycross, Boherlahan and Lorrha. I suppose I didn't realise at the time how big it was to face into an All-Ireland final but having played in the Tipp championship, and with Tipp minors, gave me confidence. In actual fact I was only six weeks over-age in 1950 to be eligible for the county minor team.

My first trip to America in 1950 was special. We landed in Gander — what I remember most about it was that it was a very cold place. Some of the great opponents from my hurling days include Seán Clohosey, Christy Ring, Jimmy Duggan and Willie John Daly. Paddy Kenny had no equal as a goal getter. He was a *ciotóg* who played at corner-forward. Jimmy Smyth who hurled right-hand under was also a great corner-forward.

As a youngster I used admire John Keane of Waterford. He could play anywhere. He was special. In later years it was a treat to chat with Keane. I got to know Mick Mackey through the Railway Cup competitions. He was involved with the Munster team. Mick was a great character. Everybody loved Mick.

I miss the overhead hurling — you see so little of it now. You never see a dropper being hit now. 'Twas a great skill. I often did it in practice but I only did it once during my hurling career in a minor game against Limerick. You could get great length into your drive — great satisfaction to meet a ball on the drop and clear it upfield.

Players train very hard nowadays but we used train pretty hard too.

Jimmy Finn "

On my way to meet Jimmy Finn I drove through the town of Urlingford and across the county boundary into Tipperary. On the left-hand side of the road was a sign that declared: 'Welcome to Tipperary — Home of hurling — 2 All-Ireland championships.' Non-hurling passers-by probably wouldn't give the sign a second thought; but the knowing ones would smile, having noticed that some wag — probably a Kilkenny wag — had erased the 4, thus altering Tipperary's proud total of twenty-four titles to a mere two.

Anyway, on to Jimmy Finn — smiling. He hails from the parish of Borrisoleigh — a club with a proud hurling tradition, a club that gave great names to Tipperary senior hurling: Liam Devaney, Philly Ryan, Seán Kenny ('a man for whom I had great regard — a great captain and leader — he was powerfully strong — in Borrisoleigh he was known as "The Bulldozer"'), Paddy Kenny, Ned Ryan, Phil Kenny, Tim Ryan, Richard Stakelum, Bobby Ryan, Aidan Ryan, John McGrath, Conor Stakelum, and Noel O'Dwyer. The modern club really emerged in 1948 when, following skilled negotiations and sterling efforts on the part of the late Fr John Ryan, the two districts of the parish united under the new name of Borrisoleigh.

As Jimmy talked about the history of the club he reminded me that in 1910 teams from Tipperary and Cork captained by the renowned Tom Semple and Jim Kelliher, respectively, went on a historic tour and played exhibition matches of the ancient game in Belgium, at Malines, Brussels, and Fontenoy. It was the occasion of the Pan-Celtic Congress, held in Brussels. The game at Fontenoy was played on the historic battlefield and recalled those stirring lines from the poem 'Fontenoy' by Thomas Davis:

'On Fontenoy, on Fontenoy, like eagles in the sun,
With bloody plumes the Irish stand — the field is fought, and won!'

The hurling game at Fontenoy was won by Cork on the score 2:4 to 2:3. On the tour the Borrisoleigh club was represented by Jack Ryan-Lanigan and Eddie Finn.

Jimmy's earliest hurling memories go back to 1944 when he watched the two epic Munster final games between Limerick and Cork at Thurles. And in his mind's eye he can still see Christy Ring soloing down the right wing towards the Killinan goal in the dying moments of the replay and sending in a low ground ball that finished in the back of the net to give Cork a dramatic victory. He saw Mick Mackey too in those days — the autumn of his great career. 'Sure Mick was the daddy of them all. He'd go on a solo run, and fellows tackling him would just bounce off him and fall.'

His heroes in those young impressionable years were Mick Mackey and Timmy Ryan of Limerick, Christy Ring of Cork, and John Maher of Tipperary. Later he was to play with Ring on Munster Railway Cup teams when he saw at first hand 'the will he had to win and how fanatical he was about achieving victory.' But even the greatest have their lesser moments, and Jimmy remembers 1955 when a Combined Universities and Rest side played an Ireland selection. 'Johnny O'Connor of Waterford, at centre-back, played a blinder on Ring on the Ireland side and completely outclassed the maestro.'

Jimmy's career in the big time began at an early age. He played in the North Tipperary senior final at the age of sixteen. He remembers the first round of the championship of 1949, when

Borrisoleigh faced the previous year's champions, Holycross. 'We were underdogs, complete outsiders — not given a chance. Before taking the field my Uncle Tommy Ryan wished us the best of luck and added, "Myself and Father White will say the rosary for you."' Well, the game was a draw; the replay was won; and Borrisoleigh went on to win its first county senior hurling title — a reminder, perhaps, that, as Tennyson wrote, 'more things are wrought by prayer than this world dreams of.' That year Jimmy was on the Tipperary team that brought the county its sixth All-Ireland minor title with a victory over Kilkenny.

He came on as a sub in the league final of 1950 and played his first inter-county championship senior game when he was called up for the All-Ireland final against Kilkenny to a half-back line that read Jimmy Finn, Pat Stakelum, Tommy Doyle. A newspaper photograph (reproduced here) carried the caption 'Séamus Finn should get a "baptism of fire" to championship fare. He is wearing the jersey his father wore when he played rugby for Mungret College, Limerick.' He had the task of marking the Kilkenny stylist Jimmy Langton and he acquitted himself well. It was the beginning of an illustrious career at county level.

'We hit Kilkenny fierce hard that day. They had a good team. It was close all through. Towards the end we got a goal that seemed to clinch it, and then Jimmy Kelly from seventy yards sent in a ball that dropped into the corner of the net. We held on to win by one point. It was the second of Tipp's three in a row. You need a good team to win three in a row. You need luck too.'

In 1951 Jimmy, playing at right-half-back, captained Tipperary as they paraded around Croke Park for the final against Wexford. It was a great honour, in which fate and fortune played a big part. 'Seán Kenny, who would have been captain, was injured, and it was decided to toss between myself and Ned Ryan — a beautiful stick man,

something special — both of us hoping to lose.' The toss favoured Jimmy, and he led his county to victory before he had reached his twentieth birthday — probably the youngest to captain a senior team to All-Ireland hurling honours. By a coincidence Pat Stakelum had played in the same position two years earlier when he captained Tipperary to victory in 1949.

The All-Ireland success of 1950 and his captaincy in 1951 had fairy-tale dimensions. After those his most memorable recollection is the trip to America in 1950 to play the league final against New York. Two further trips followed, in 1957 and 1959, but it was the first one that left the most lasting impression. 'We gathered in Shannon Airport on the fifteenth of September. The plane, having taxied down the runway, failed to take off, so we were all put up overnight. The next day the take-off was successful. We were twelve hours in the air; landed in Gander, Newfoundland, after eight hours; a short stop; on to New York, which took four hours. We had three unbelievable weeks in the US. In that time we were taken on a tour of the US Military Academy at West Point; saw lacrosse being played; saw the Joe Louis v. Ezzard Charles world title fight at Madison Square Garden; saw a Danny Kaye show; were taken on a tour of Broadway; visited City Hall; and of course won the league final, but only just — 1:12 to 3:4.' New York, of course, had plenty of hurling talent in their line-out, including Terry Leahy of Kilkenny, Phil Grimes of Waterford, and Steve Gallagher of Galway.

Following the 1957 trip Jimmy spent three months in America and passed some of that time on a horse farm. He also hurled with the Tipperary New York team. That made him illegal for the 1958 championship, in which Tipperary had victories over Limerick, Cork, Waterford, Kilkenny, and Galway, who had a bye into the final. Paddy Leahy wavered about playing Jimmy but in the end took the gamble. It paid off. Lines of communication across the Atlantic wouldn't have been as efficient as nowadays.

All the honours that eluded many a fine hurler came Jimmy's way — with club, county, province and Rest of Ireland selections and in recent times by popular vote the right-half-back position on the Team of the Century selected in the Centenary year of the GAA, 1984. His only regrets centre around the losses to Cork in the tight, tense encounters of the Munster finals of 1952, '53, and '54. Nor was his career without its lighter and boisterous moments. He recalls being in Barry's Hotel on the night before a league game with Kilkenny — 'a fierce stormy night — we thought the game would be called off.

A pillow fight broke out; feathers drifted out the window; people outside thought it was snowing.' Energy and exuberance!

Jimmy's hurling career came to an abrupt and premature ending on 13 June 1959. In the second round of the North Tipperary championship against Roscrea he received a serious eye injury from an accidental stroke as he tussled for possession near the sideline. He wasn't yet twenty-eight. He had played his last inter-county game in the league final of 1959 when Tipp defeated Waterford by 0:15 to 0:7. 'I had a hard time on Tom Cheasty that day.' In his parting, hurling lost one of its immortals, one of its finest defenders.

Born 1964

by beating them again in the All-Ireland final.

"

Pete Finnerty

" During my years in the maroon and white I have had many great days and nights. The first day I played senior in 1985 against Cork in the downpour at headquarters, the two All-Ireland victories in 1987 and 1988, the All-Star awards, the trips to the States and the general convivial atmosphere that surrounded those ten years were brilliant. The one occasion that stands out above all the rest was in 1986, the All-Ireland semi-final against the Cats. With fifteen minutes remaining in the game I looked at the scoreboard, and we were leading by nine points. We had outhurled the Cats in all areas and we had also outfoxed them.

The reason that this victory was so sweet was, when I was a young lad I played hurling in the field behind our home from evening till dusk. I imagined myself as Brian Cody, Fran Larkin, Eddie Keher, or Billy Fitz — these were the great heroes, and they were all Cats. On that day in August 1986 we gave the youth of Galway their own home-grown heroes: Cooney, Ryan, Keady, Lane. Could this be true? Was it a once-off? No, we confirmed the result in 1987

Having greeted Pete, I went on to tell him that he was at that point the baby of this book and that at the other end of the scale Tom McInerney would be ninety that year (1996). I reminded Pete that he had retired at thirty and that now, at thirty-two, he could still be playing. He went early. Why?

He paused, smiled, and reflected for a moment. 'When I was in my early twenties I often heard of the great three-in-a-row Galway football team of the sixties. Nearly all of those retired on or before the thirty mark. I couldn't understand it — that is, not until I reached that age myself. Then I understood. It was easier to get injured; took longer to recuperate; the demands on energy seemed greater. In my young days, training was effortless; as you headed for thirty it became more demanding. It was five nights a week. As well as that there was the job and the family. I'd love to have continued, but I knew the speed wasn't there any more. All considered, it was time to go.'

When Pete was six his mother died. There were three other boys: John, Paddy, and Tom, aged ten, eight, and four, respectively. His father, also Pete, a farmer and psychiatric nurse, reared them all. 'He would pack nine or ten of us into his estate car and drive us to play the national school competition games. Our teacher, Seán Glynn, was an enthusiast, and we won three national school titles and went on to win the county under-14 title. Then the *Connacht Tribune* put up a set of bicycles — a Connacht championship. There must have been over fifty teams competing.

'When it came to the final we faced Killimordaly — Éanna Ryan's team, the team we had beaten in the under-14 County Galway final. This time the result was reversed. We had won the county medals; Éanna and his colleagues won the bikes.'

Pete's father loved going to matches. 'It gave him a new lease of life' after the shattering blow of losing his wife. Knowing he was on the sideline made Pete want to play better and to excel. Performance assessment from his father was always positive and supportive. A lovely relationship developed between father and son and has continued to this day. They go for a pint together, reminisce, and discuss the matches.

Pete played in all grades for his native Galway. At minor level he lost an All-Ireland semi-final to Wexford after a replay in 1980. The following year Kilkenny beat them in the final, and defeat was their lot again in 1982, this time at the hands of Tipperary.

He was good enough in those years to play junior for his county, but the 1983 final was lost to Cork by just two points. He spent three years on the under-21 team. Fate was more kind when he won his first All-Ireland medal in 1983 with a three-point win over Tipperary.

Now to senior level. In 1985 Galway faced the reigning All-Ireland champions, Cork, in the semi-final on a very wet and miserable day in Croke Park. 'We had several newcomers: we were complete outsiders. Fortunately for us, Jimmy Barry-Murphy wasn't playing with Cork. When it was all over I found it hard to believe we had beaten Cork.' Well, beat Cork they did, by the convincing score of 4:12 to 5:5. The springboard of that success was the Galway half-back line: Pete Finnerty, Tony Keady, Tony Kilkenny. They were magnificent, driving back time and time again determined Cork onslaughts. Their covering and understanding was a revelation. But it wasn't their first time together. The knowing ones knew, that that same half-back line

had played a major role in the under-21 triumph of 1983. In the final, Galway fell to their neighbours Offaly. They looked with hope to 1986.

Few could have anticipated the events that would unfold in Thurles in the All-Ireland semi-final of 1986 between Galway and Kilkenny. From the word go Galway were sheer magic. 'I will never forget that day. I always admired the Cats — was sceptical about our chances; but we outfoxed them. Everything went so well; we all hurled so well. I looked at the scoreboard at one stage and saw we were nine points ahead — imagine, nine points ahead against the Cats in a championship game! I felt brilliant.

'My mind went back to the league final in May — same venue — when they beat us 2:10 to 2:6. Joe Hennessy offered words of consolation after the game, saying, "You have a good little team: you'll win a league yet."' The final score made followers rub their eyes — hard to believe: Galway 4:12, Kilkenny 0:13. The Galway ploy of playing two in the full-forward line worked a dream; but it backfired when they played against Cork in the final, when hurried and misdirected clearances were going in to the unmarked Johnny Crowley. Coupled with that they conceded two early goals to Cork. It all added up to an uphill battle, a four-point defeat, and much discussion about what might have been.

As so often in the past, Galway looked with hope to the future. It was a young team. It needed the lucky break. They had demonstrated their ability, what they were capable of, the grandeur of their hurling in the 1985 semi-final win over Cork and the 1986 semi-final win over Kilkenny. Now they needed to do it in a final.

And do it they did — and twice in a row for good measure.

The nagging frustrations of 1985 and 1986 were buried following the two-in-a-row All-Ireland triumphs of 1987 and 1988. Both campaigns were tough and gruelling. Galway displayed courage,

Pete Finnerty (right) with Peter Quinn Uachtarán C.L.G.

character, and grit. There was steel in their hurling.

'In 1987 against Tipperary in the semi-final we lived dangerously at times, but I always felt we would win. The final against Kilkenny on a wet day was a tough, hard, physical game. I didn't realise until the game was over that Kilkenny had led us at one stage early in the second half by a point. Even though we won by six points I felt Kilkenny adapted better to the conditions. There were occasions when I used to feel we didn't tactically approach and handle a game properly. We let finals slip, but we never stole one.'

The following year Galway beat their old rivals Offaly in the semi-final and faced Tipperary in the final. It was ding-dong stuff — hard and uncompromising, not without moments of controversy; and it hung in the balance until the final moments, when Noel Lane, a substitute, rounded Conor O'Donovan for the only goal of the game and the clincher. 'We won those two finals against Kilkenny and Tipperary without conceding one goal: nine points to Kilkenny, fourteen points to Tipperary.' Galway looked good for 1989 — for three in a row, for Conor Hayes to be the first man to captain a team to three successive senior hurling titles. But there's many a slip ...

1989 is a hurling year in the Galway calendar that Pete would wish had never happened. It will be remembered as the year of the 'Keady affair'. In brief, Tony played a game in America; was reported; suspended — harshly, some would say. "89 is a very sore point with me. Tony did something many others were doing: going to the US to play in the championship there — a grey area in the GAA. The players going to the US gave huge entertainment to the exiles.' The suspension developed into a controversy. The sympathy of almost the entire country lay with Galway. The affair became an obsession in Galway and certainly deflected their minds from the impending hurling semi-final against Tipperary.

'Then we shot ourselves in the foot. About a week before the match an article appeared in the *Irish Press* stating that Galway wouldn't play without Keady. The public mood changed, and from being perceived as the afflicted we were now seen as an aggressor. Much energy that should have been directed towards the match was now being used in dealing with the Keady affair and the press. The sixth of August 1989 represents my lowest day in hurling. A game that was lost by three points was there to be won. We had a chance to do what our footballers had done in the sixties. It could have been our greatest day. As I said, it was my lowest day.'

Pete Finnerty was an outstanding right-half-back, a position where he gave many a superb display of classic defensive hurling. He was always very fit. Concentration, tenacity, timing, positional sense and well-honed skills were his hallmarks. His display against Cork in the All-Ireland semi-final of 1985, when he reached great heights, was arguably his greatest. It earned him the RTÉ Man of the Match award and also a B&I award. He won his first of five All-Star awards that year. Indeed, it might well have been a record-breaking six in a row if the controversy of 1989 had been avoided. All the awards were in the right-half-back position, and five in the space of six years reflect a series of consistently high performances — a sure mark of greatness. He won Railway Cup medals in 1986, '89, and '91. He was absent for the victories of 1987 and '88, when he was in America in a temporary capacity with his colleague Gerry McInerney.

Pete packed a lot of hurling into an inter-county career that began in minor ranks in 1980 and continued for fifteen years until the All-Ireland semi-final defeat by Offaly in 1994, after which he called it a day. As the years pass and great wing-backs of modern hurling are recalled and discussed, the name Pete Finnerty will certainly be among them.

Johnny Flaherty (on the left) with a club mate.

Born 1947

one needs in everyday life and if used properly can be a tremendous bonus to any player, and my wishes are that every young fellow should have a hurley and go through a career of hurling. I think it would leave us with a much better society today.

There were so many happy occasions — too numerous to mention here, because every match would have been an All-Ireland in itself. If I had one regret it would have been that when Offaly did reach its first All-Ireland in 1981 — well past my prime — that it would have been ten years sooner.

"

``

Hurling was always a big part of my life. I can never remember the time that I was without a hurley. I got more enjoyment out of hurling than anything in my lifetime.

In Kinnitty, where I come from, hurling was the only game played. We had it for dinner, breakfast, and tea. After that we went to the hurling field at night to develop us as young boys and men. Little would I have thought in my early career that hurling would have been so good to me and that one day I would end up playing in an All-Ireland for the county.

I have no doubt that hurling is the greatest game, both for player and spectator. And it is a great pity that it is not as popular as football. The lessons, discipline and education that a player has to learn on a training field to be a top-class hurler are the same lessons that

Johnny exudes animation as he talks about the game of hurling, which has played a great part in his life since his juvenile days. And as he talks with feelings of intensity he makes hand movements and on occasions stands up as he goes through the litany of skills that constitute the game of hurling — 'for hurling is an art form.' He is certainly one of its most ardent adherents.

He had his first great day in 1957 at the age of ten when he won a juvenile title with Kinnitty. 'I was on for about only ten minutes but in that time I scored 1:2.' And he was still scoring thirty-seven years later when he helped Kinnitty to win a county junior final in 1994.

Johnny played minor for Offaly in 1964 and 1965 before progressing to senior ranks in 1966. As a half-forward he came up against the great half-back lines of Tipperary, Kilkenny and Wexford. He names them: Mick Burns, Tony Wall, Len Gaynor, Séamus Cleere, Pat Henderson, Martin Coogan, Vinny Staples, Dan Quigley, Willie Murphy. He remembers them well — and no wonder.

It was the beginning of his learning process, learning what it was like to play at top level and how difficult it could be to make the breakthrough. He recalls games against Waterford and Tipperary in 1966 that were won; confidence was growing in Offaly. Aided by Brother Denis, they faced Westmeath in the championship of 1967. 'We lost what became known as the Battle of Birr.'

They looked forward to 1968 with confidence. 'Snitchy Ferguson gave us a few pep talks in training as we prepared to meet the All-Ireland title holders, Kilkenny. Well, who was appointed referee for the game but Snitchy Ferguson!

'Early in the first quarter John Kirwan was sent off. It was a terrible blow. Late in the second half I had an opportunity to possibly win the game. I got possession and, having avoided Séamus Cleere and Ted Carroll, the way to goal was open. I said to myself, "I'll burst the net — we'll lift the stand." I threw up the ball and was about to bury it when Jim Treacy hooked me. The ball fell against my knee and went wide.' Offaly lost in the end by four points. Johnny was still learning. He stood up and re-enacted for me his assault on the Kilkenny goal.

In the Leinster championship of 1969 Offaly showed they had the potential to be a hurling force when they defeated the All-Ireland title holders, Wexford, in the semi-final. 'It was a game in which Paddy Molloy gave an outstanding display.' So for the first time in forty-one years an Offaly senior hurling team was in the Leinster final; their opponents, Kilkenny. The question was, could they reverse the narrow defeat of the previous year? Well, they performed gallantly and lost by two points, 3:9 to 0:16; and those sixteen scores showed how much they dominated outfield. Unfortunately, it was an aging team. The breakthrough was a decade away; only Damien Martin and Johnny Flaherty would survive from the squad of 1969, and they would both emerge with added craft, cunning, and skill.

Johnny spent from 1971 to 1977 in the United States, although he did come home to play against Wexford in 1973 and Kilkenny in 1974, but without success. He found hurling in New York to be extremely competitive and of a very high standard. This was brought home to him forcefully in 1973. 'We brought out Pádraig Horan, Mick Cleere, Kieran Purcell, Francis Loughnane, Tommy Ring and Eugene Hannon to play for the Offaly team against Galway, who had all New York players. They beat us. The same happened Galway the previous year when they brought out several players only to be beaten by Clare.'

Johnny had the honour in 1973 of being on a ten-day South Pacific tour. 'This was arranged by John "Kerry" O'Donnell — Mr GAA in New York. We were joined by Ollie Walsh, Mick O'Connell, Christy Ring, and Niall Sheehy. We toured Australia and New Zealand and visited Hawaii on the way back. I remember a hurling game we played in Auckland. I was centre-back and Ring was corner-back. On one occasion I wasn't clearing fast enough for Ring's liking so he lashed on the ball and in the process belted me across the knees. As I limped away I could hear him say, "Are you all right, boy? Are you all right, boy?"'

In 1976 Johnny and several colleagues left New York and headed for Alaska. 'A major pipeline construction was being undertaken. It was an incredible culture change; it took a lot of adjusting. This was Arctic Circle country. At its most westerly point Siberia was only fifty miles away. In the winter months you had little more than two hours' daylight; in summertime you had eighteen to twenty hours of daylight. The money was great. The oil company treated us very well. The menus were unbelievable. There was no hurling. When I decided to go after about a year I was one-and-a-half stone above my normal weight.'

Johnny was undecided about his next destination. Anywhere in the world

Johnny Flaherty and John Bohane (Laois). (Photo: Jim Connolly)

could be a good place: Ireland, New Zealand, Australia, Hawaii, America. His friend Brendan Moynihan suggested that he go to San Francisco, where the All-Stars were. Johnny declined, saying, 'I'll be one of them in two years' time.' Only a small miscalculation: he was left-full-forward, one of five Offaly men, on the 1981 All-Star team.

Back in Ireland after his sojourn in North America he found himself among the substitutes when Kinnitty lined out for the county final. Then fate took a hand. Pat Delaney got injured in the pre-match puck-about. Enter Johnny Flaherty. 'The Kinnitty score was 1:8. I scored the eight points and made the goal.' Johnny collected his second county senior medal.

On the pitch this extrovert personality was a bundle of energy: fast, fiercely competitive, opportunist. We didn't really see him, and his vast range of hurling skills, in his heyday. Offaly were out of the limelight and Johnny was playing most of his hurling in America. We saw him in his twilight years; he shone brightly. Let's recall thosse years.

A semi-final victory over their neighbours Laois in the Leinster championship of 1980 gave Offaly a place in the final for the first time since 1969 against the All-Ireland champions, Kilkenny, who disposed of Wexford in the other semi-final, and a thrilling one it was too — the real final, many thought. But they reckoned wrongly. Showing grit, courage, resolve, and stamina, mingled with much quality hurling, Offaly went in at half time two points behind — a little unluckily perhaps — 3:6 to 1:10. The second half was thrill-packed. When Joachim Kelly departed the midfield scene injured, Johnny Flaherty moved out from corner-forward. By then he had secured two goals at crucial stages of the game for Offaly and contributed to other scores. Entering the closing stages Offaly were hanging on grimly in a cliff-hanger to a one-point lead. A last desperate typical Kilkenny assault was made on the Offaly goal. Anything could have ensued from the schemozzle

in front of goal; but back there was Johnny Flaherty. He gathered and raced outwards. The final whistle blew. Delirious pandemonium. Offaly, Leinster senior hurling champions for the first time. Johnny, one of many heroes.

And so to 1981. After a nine-month stint in America, Johnny returned in May. It was championship time again. Offaly retained their Leinster crown with a 3:12 to 2:13 victory over Wexford. Awarding Johnny Sports Star of the Week, the *Irish Independent* wrote:

'The cheer which greeted that Johnny Flaherty point near the end of the Leinster senior hurling championship final in Croke Park last Sunday was not so much a victory roar as a tribute to the veteran Offaly corner-forward. His contribution of a goal and two points in the downfall of Wexford capped an all-round quality display of class hurling which helped steer Offaly to their first All-Ireland final next September. Many believe that Flaherty's part was a vital one and it certainly earns our award Sports Star of the Week.'

Now to the All-Ireland final of 1981 against Galway. Five minutes to go and Galway two points up — clinging on, yet not looking like losing. Offaly attack; Brendan Birmingham passes to Johnny Flaherty in front of goal. The learning process that Johnny dedicated himself to since the late sixties was now put to good use. This time he wouldn't think about 'bursting the net.' The experience of a long career was about to pay a rich dividend. 'I was going to palm the ball onwards as Éamon Cregan had done the previous year against Galway to score a great goal. But instant second thoughts said don't. I grabbed it and palmed it over my left shoulder to the net.' It won the game for Offaly — victory in their first All-Ireland final.

On Friday 11 September the *Westmeath-Offaly Independent* wrote:

'All-seventeen players who participated in the game will be fêted as heroes, which is only right and proper. Naturally, however, there were some whose contribution was that little bit more than others and I

would put forward the names of Pat Delaney, Ger Coughlan and Johnny Flaherty as being the triumvirate who did most to ensure victory ... Johnny Flaherty's contribution was probably more positive for in the years ahead nobody will forget the man who scored the winning goal. However, his reputation should not be based on that score alone for throughout the game he was easily Offaly's most dangerous forward and obviously the man whom Galway most feared.'

Vintage stuff from a veteran thirty-four years of age.

Johnny has special words of praise for the great work done by Brother Denis for Offaly hurling and also the immense contribution from the Kilkenny man Dermot Healy. 'He changed our training programme; got us thinking about the game; discouraged fouling; and had a great calming influence on us.'

An admiring bard wrote these lines of praise:

Fleet of foot and full of gut
Just like a mountain hare
You wouldn't find the likes of him
In Galway, Cork, or Clare.
Perpetual motion at its best
That's Johnny Flaherty
A credit to his native heath
Dear, lovely Kinnitty.

Johnny selected his team from players from other counties, players he had observed, players he had played against.

Noel Skehan (*Kilkenny*)

Tom Neville (*Wexford*)	Pat Hartigan (*Limerick*)	John Horgan (*Cork*)
Sylvie Linnane (*Galway*)	Mick Roche (Tipperary)	Martin Coogan (*Kilkenny*)

Frank Cummins (*Kilkenny*)   John Connolly (*Galway*)

Johnny Flaherty (*Offaly*)	Ray Cummins (*Cork*)	Christy O'Brien (*Laois*)
Francis Loughnane (*Tipperary*)	Tony Doran (*Wexford*)	Eddie Keher (*Kilkenny*)

Born 1958

❝

In my hurling career a few people stand out for their comments, opinions, and influence.

The first person I encountered at an early age was a man known locally as 'Green Flag'. Jimmy Kelly was a man, then in his sixties, who used to lean against the gate of the sports field in Banagher watching all the hurlers train. He was there every evening there was hurling practice. He could tell you the strengths and weaknesses of the hurlers, and in those days of the great Rynagh teams that won ten out of twelve county championships, there was always a topic of conversation. His comments and observations on how Barney [Moylan] controlled the ball, how Pat Joe [Whelehan] could bat a ball so far one-handed, how Damien [Martin] could take a ball out of the air with his hurl or hand and how the backs knew where that ball would go were all titbits of advice that young willing hurlers could study and put into practice in their own game.

Then there was Jimmy's opinion of the younger players: 'He'll make it' or 'He won't make it.' As a young lad any praise or encouragement from an older person or player was always received with great enthusiasm and encouraged one to practise even more. If Jimmy said, 'You'll make it,' hopes of playing on a Rynagh's senior team or maybe an Offaly team, or even playing in Croke Park, could be achieved in the future. If Jimmy continued to reassure you, then you knew (or thought you knew) that you were on the right road.

The most important and significant influence on me was that of my family. All our family were involved in the game, with my late father [Tom] the mainstay. The encouragement, advice, travelling to see county matches were all factors in my hurling development. The interest shown by my father, who regularly took half-days off work to attend college matches — my mother always travelled to keep him company — the long journeys undertaken to underage county games, motivated one to work harder to fulfil ambitions. Throughout this development my father had a subtle way of keeping one in touch with reality. After games where things went well there was always a discreet 'Well done' or 'You did okay,' and then the punch line: 'What happened with the ball that ...' or 'Why didn't you do that ...?' On the other hand, if the performance was not up to scratch there was never unnecessary criticism, only an objective assessment of what went wrong.

All my brothers — Gerard, Declan, Frank, and Andrew — played hurling for the club and county at various levels, with Declan featuring with the Offaly seniors in the eighties, including the All-Ireland years of '84 and '85. My wife, Theresa, was always a keen follower and travelled to all the games. The support and encouragement of everyone made it much easier for me to concentrate on fulfilling many of my hurling ambitions.

In the mid-seventies I attended the NIHE in Limerick. Around that time I joined the Offaly senior panel and I travelled to training sessions and games with Pádraig Horan, who was then teaching in the city. Our conversations often centred on the future of Offaly hurling. Could Offaly make a breakthrough? Could we follow on from the Leinster club successes of St Rynagh's and transfer that to the county team? If an Offaly club could win a Leinster title, could the county team not do the same?

We talked often of the Limerick team of the seventies: Grimes, Cregan, Hartigan, McKenna. How did they achieve All-Ireland success? What did it take to achieve that success? We wondered what it would be like to play in a Leinster final, never mind an All-Ireland. On these thoughts and dreams we shortened many a journey. Little did we know how close we were to a breakthrough.

'For the next few weeks I'll be concentrating on keeping the crows out of the barley.' A comment passed by Damien Martin in an interview after the '82 Leinster final put hurling into perspective for me. It was a comment passed in the emotional aftermath of a match many thought Offaly should have won. Damien, a veteran of many championship campaigns, saw beyond all the debates and arguments that would ensue following a controversial Kilkenny goal and left no-one in any doubt that hurling, like all amateur sports, was only a game, and life outside of it continues whether you win or lose. Defeats in the years that followed always brought me back to Damien's comments, and no matter how disappointing the loss, in the greater game of life all was not lost.

99

Aidan Fogarty

In the years that lie ahead, irrespective of what direction Offaly hurling takes, Aidan will be able to look back and say that he was there at the dawn-ing of a great spring — a spring that bore much fruit and yielded rich harvests all through his career.

An under-21 Leinster hurling title in 1978 in which Aidan participated, together with players like Liam Currams, Brendan Keeshan, and Tom Conneely, was the harbinger of things to come.

He first donned the ever-so-attractive green, white and gold jersey of the Faithful County in a challenge game against Tipperary at Birr in 1976. And he recalled with a tinge of sadness that his opponent at wing-back that day, Phil Fanning of Moneygall, was later tragically killed in a car crash.

The last inter-county game played by this forceful and competitive hurler was against Dublin in the Leinster semi-final of 1991. 'I only played because one of the lads was injured. At thirty-three I was finding it hard to stay there. In training you found yourself marking younger fellows; you go for the break of the ball; he passes you out; you know you are gone. Time to go.'

In between those games there were highs and lows — zeniths and nadirs: the joys of victory; the disappointments of defeat. And of course the might-have-beens.

He excelled as a defender, operating mainly at right-full-back and right-half-back, although in 1988 he captained Leinster to his only Railway Cup success, playing at full-back. His approach to the game was a studied one — influenced in this respect to a large degree by their great coach and motivator, the Kilkennyman Dermot Healy. Aidan's style was tight and first-time, his covering highly effective.

After the Centenary Cup senior hurling quarter-final, in which Offaly defeated Kilkenny 1:17 to 2:11, Seán Kilfeather wrote: 'Significant too was the fact that after being five points behind in the first minute of the second half and trailing by the same margin after fifteen minutes, they battled back with great fire, determination and fitness and managed to deny Kilkenny a score in the last nine minutes of the

match. Nobody could pretend in those circumstances that Offaly were depending on only one man for their survival, but it is fair to say that their inspiration came mostly from Aidan Fogarty, who had a superb second half. He continually broke up Kilkenny attacks with timely interceptions, and his clearances, whether short or long, from the hurley or from the hand, invariably found a strategically placed colleague and lifted siege after siege as Kilkenny swept forward in search of a goal which would have given them the initiative.'

The hero of his youth was that classical and great left-half-back from Kilkenny, Martin Coogan. From his schooldays his father and mother were great supporters; they went to every game. It meant so much to Aidan. And his father was at all times an honest critic, positive and constructive, always encouraging. 'I always found that no matter how well you played, you could always look back and focus on one or two things that went wrong or were mishandled.'

The many honours that came his way were spread evenly throughout his career: seven Leinster titles between 1980 and 1990; two All-Ireland titles, 1981 and 1985; two All-Star awards, 1982 and 1989; Railway Cup, 1988; National League, 1991; eight county titles between 1975 and 1993; Leinster club titles in 1982 and 1993. 'Failure to convert the Leinster club victory into an All-Ireland title in 1983 was one of my big disappointments. We met Loughguile Shamrocks of Antrim in the final at Croke Park in April. It was a draw, 1:8 to 2:5 for us. We had the winning of it that day — also missed an easy free. We lost the replay in Casement Park a week later, 2:12 to 1:12.'

Let's now look at the great breakthrough by Offaly. It came in 1980 and it caught hurling followers and journalists by surprise. They faced Kilkenny in the Leinster final. The magazine *Sports World* carried a front-page heading, 'Easy for Kilkenny'. Hurling followers seemed to agree; only 9,613 turned up for the game, the smallest attendance of modern times. The final score was Of-

faly 3:17, Kilkenny 5:10. Those who came witnessed a piece of hurling history: Offaly's first Leinster senior hurling title, achieved against the odds, opposed by one of the superpowers of hurling, Kilkenny, the reigning All-Ireland champions. It was a triumph for courage. It was an example for the lesser counties to follow. It was a great moment for hurling.

Surprisingly, it doesn't rank with Aidan's great moments. 'Matt Ruth was causing problems for our full-back line, and I was switched from the half-back line to corner-back to mark him. A minor flare-up between the two of us led to my name being taken. Following this Dermot Healy took me off. I saw him walking down the sideline giving me the signal; I was disappointed. I think he thought I was going to lose the head.'

One can immediately see the wisdom of Dermot's decision in the circumstances. Here was a tense occasion: Kilkenny in trouble and facing defeat. A loss of concentration by any player could be disastrous — so would a sending off. Dermot was taking no chances. Aidan was replaced by Eugene Coughlan. Later, at the hotel, a phone call came, bringing the sad news that Pádraig Horan's father had died while listening to the match. Aidan departed with his friend Pádraig. Both events tended to blunt the historical victory. 'In the All-Ireland semi-final we met a very talented Galway team — a team that should have won more All-Irelands. We weren't good enough to beat them in 1980. There were only two points in it at the end, but the better team won.'

A year later Offaly reversed that result in the All-Ireland final — their first victory in their first appearance. For Aidan, the 1981 success was his greatest sporting moment and most abiding memory. I wondered what his thoughts were before that game. 'When Dermot Healy came to us he set about building our confidence. He had us believing it was only man versus man — the colour of the jersey shouldn't matter. It was fifteen against fifteen, and each opponent had only two hands, two legs, and one head — just like ourselves. We started to believe we could do ourselves justice against anyone. After beating Wexford in the Leinster final we had seven weeks to think about the final. Pat Delaney, Ger Coughlan and myself went off to Spain for two weeks; then it was back to All-Ireland training. The lead-up was all unknown to us. Dermot, who guided us through the pressure of interviews and publicity, kept emphasising that we should try to imagine it as just another game — a game against our neighbours. I reminded myself I went to school for a year with Galway's centre-back, Seán Silke — anything to play down the hype factor.

'In the dressing-room before the game everyone was nervous — didn't know what to expect; trying to concentrate on the game. Then the speech before you go out. I always found it hard to take in what was being said. I would be concentrating on my own game; the person I would be playing on — saying to myself it was just another game, telling myself not to let the occasion get to me.'

They returned to the dressing-room at half time six points in arrears. 'We were extremely nervous. It was a first half in which no player could feel he had done himself justice. We had given away thirteen points but no goal. We had scored the only goal. We were hanging in.'

And hang in they did too in the second half, and with five minutes to go they were within two points of wasteful Gal-way, 1:10 to 0:15. Two minutes later came the winning move involving Joachim Kelly, Pat Delaney, and Brendan Bermingham, who parted to Johnny Flaherty, who expertly engineered a palmed goal. It finished 2:12 to 0:15. The journey home, like all victorious journeys, would seem very short; the celebrations to follow would be protracted.

In 1984, the centenary year of the GAA, Offaly faced Cork at Semple Stadium, Thurles. It was Offaly's second final, Cork's fortieth — a unique hurling occasion. Aidan's memories? 'I don't like to talk too much about it. It sticks in the craw. It was one of those days when little went right. We were confident — had beaten Galway by fourteen points; had played in the '81 final; knew what it was like to be in a final. Thurles didn't have the same sense of tradition for us that it did for Cork. Croke Park would have seemed like a home venue to us. There are always nerves on the big day, but the awe barrier had been broken down.

'I felt we had a reasonable first half. The drawn-out ceremonies before the game got everyone edgy — didn't help either team. Cork got a run in the second half and we couldn't cope. We had first-half chances for goals that didn't come off — like Joe Dooley, who was looking good for an All-Star, going through for what looked a certain palmed goal, only to have his arm tapped by Johnny Crowley. I don't like talking about 1984.'

His team is selected from the men of his era with particular emphasis on the men he played against. Much thought went into the selection: the blend and balance had to be right in each line. He sought out players whose talents, qualities and characteristics would be complementary.

Noel Skehan *(Kilkenny)*

Joe Hennessy *(Kilkenny)*   Leonard Enright *(Limerick)*   Sylvie Linnane *(Galway)*

Aidan Fogarty *(Offaly)*   Ger Henderson *(Kilkenny)*   John Taylor *(Laois)*

Frank Cummins *(Kilkenny)*   Joe Cooney *(Galway)*

Billy Fitzpatrick *(Kilkenny)*   Martin Quigley *(Wexford)*   P.J. Molloy *(Galway)*

Pat Fox. *(Tipperary)*   Joe McKenna *(Limerick)*   Liam Fennelly *(Kilkenny)*

There was compensation, however, the following year, when Offaly again defeated their neighbours Galway with two points to spare. 'It was good to have won a second title. It added to the credibility of the team — basically the same players that made the breakthrough in 1980 and won the All-Ireland in 1981.'

Pat Fox (centre) with Ken Doherty (left) and Michael Carruth (right).

Born 1961

"

As far back as I can remember I had a love for hurling. With six boys in my family there were always hurleys behind the kitchen door. At the age of eight I went to every training session with my club, Éire Óg, Annacarty. I would stand behind the goal and puck the ball in to them, hoping my day would come.

Bill O'Donnell, who played for Tipp in the early forties, taught me in national school, and he was a man I admired. Thanks to my brother Séamus for starting me off. I went to Cappawhite Vocational School at secondary level; I played county vocational schools with Tipperary. I started playing with Éire Óg senior team at the age of fifteen, and intend to play for another fifteen!

My first big thrill was getting called to play minor county in 1978 and '79 and then winning three under-21 All-Ireland medals, '79, '80, and '81. Everything looked rosy until late '82. When I tore my knee ligament it looked all over. With a lot of hard work I built my knee up again, and in '85 I got back on the county senior team. The big breakthrough came in '87 — was one of my greatest memories. Winning the All-Ireland in '89 was great, but I knew that we must win another one to be remembered, as people considered beating Antrim was no big deal! 1991 was the icing on the cake, beating Kilkenny in the All-Ireland final. For me that night, receiving the Man of the Match live on television, was one of my proudest moments. I knew I couldn't achieve anything higher.

"

Pat Fox

We would have seen and heard much more of Pat Fox at senior level — a man who held his hurley right-hand-under to deadly effect — but for a knee injury sustained in 1982. It kept him out of the 1983 campaign, and he worked his way back through the junior county team in '84 — beaten by Cork in the Munster final. He was corner-back on the senior team that lost to Cork in a disappointing 1985 Munster final. In '86, when Tipp made an unexpected exit at the hands of Clare, he was on the subs' bench. From '87 onwards he established himself at right-full-forward and carved a niche for himself in that position. He developed into one of hurling's great corner-forwards and would have stood out in any decade.

He was a spirited, quick-thinking and whole-hearted performer, a tenacious forager who could turn on a sixpence and when in possession had the skill to produce scores, even when his options were limited and he had little room to manoeuvre.

Pat's inter-county career began at minor level in 1978, and he was still young enough for that grade the following year. He played at under-21 level for Tipperary for four years, picking up three All-Ireland titles in a row: '79 at the expense of Galway, when he played at centrefield, '80, and '81, with victories over Kilkenny when he lined out at left-full-back. He was versatile; 'I could play anywhere at that time.' He certainly could, but in the early eighties Michael Maher, who was then a selector, expressed the view that Pat's best position was corner-forward. And that's where he was when Tipperary faced Cork in the Munster final replay at Killarney in '87. It was an occasion of atmosphere, thrills, and high drama.

The game ended in a draw and went into extra time. Tipperary only took the lead for the first time four minutes into the second half of extra time. They kept coming from behind in a game that Cork seemed capable of winning and in which they seemed in general the more composed. The final score of 4:22 to 1:22 belies the closeness of a bruising, epic contest, full of drama, changing fortune, fierce excitement, and for those with weak hearts a shortening of their life-span.

For Tipperary, Pat Fox was outstanding — a constant worry to the Cork defence. He scored eleven points, seven from frees. 'In some ways it was a frustrating game for me. I drove the first three frees I took wide. I was pulled down in the square and the ref blew the whistle when all I had to do was tip the ball into the net. In the second half a shot I sent in rebounded off the stanchion at the back of the goal. It was a goal which we didn't get. There were times in the first half when it looked as if Cork would destroy us. Martin McGrath came on as a sub that day and got some great scores to give us heart. He was a big influence on our comeback. We never gave up, and our hunger wore Cork down at the finish.'

If ever hunger won a game it was this Munster final replay. Hurling-wise Tipp were ravenous. They hadn't won a Munster title since the 1971 epic contest with Limerick at Killarney; Cork, on the other hand, had won eleven. 'The win was unbelievable. Some of us were there for quite a while and it looked like we would never win. At times we looked very bad. Westmeath beat us twice in league games. We must have been bad — but we didn't think we were that bad.'

Pat's wife, Marita, was in Fitzgerald Stadium to share in the jubilation. 'What a win! They were back in the big time after so long. The excitement was unbearable. The jumping for joy could never be the same again after '87. I thought Pat was something else that day.' He won his first of three All-Stars in 1987. On display in his bar in Cashel is a clock superimposed on a lovely night picture of Boston, presented to him by the Tipperary Association in Boston 'in appreciation of his dedication to hurling and in honour of being selected an All-Star.'

1991 brought a repeat of '87, except that the replay — a battle royal, intense and uncompromising, full of fury and played in intense heat — didn't go into extra time. Cork again, on both days, looked the more composed and complete unit, and when they went nine points up fifteen minutes into the second half it seemed to be all over. But when the final whistle blew it was Tipperary 4:19, Cork 4:15. Pat had given a regal display in the blue-and-gold jersey, and Tipperary had won a contest that for long periods seemed beyond their grasp. They went on to defeat Kilkenny in the All-Ireland final.

Without a doubt it was Pat's greatest hurling year. He gave brilliant displays all through. 'I probably had one of my best hours in the replay in Thurles. I got 1:5 from play marking Denis Walsh. It was one of the best games Tipp were ever involved in for excitement. The All-Ireland final of that year against Kilkenny was the game that gave me the greatest pleasure. It mightn't have been the greatest hurling, but when you win an All-Ireland — that's the ultimate.'

All kinds of awards and honours flowed Pat's way in 1991. He received his third All-Star at right-full-forward; he was nominated Texaco Hurler of the Year; he was awarded RTÉ Man of the Match after his display against Kilkenny — for Marita, 'my proudest moment'; he was voted most consistent player of the year; he was chosen by the Tipperary Association in Dublin as Tipperary Person of the Year, 1991. And then came a signal accolade: Supreme Sportsman of the Year, 1991, at the Texaco awards — the first GAA man so honoured.

Pat recalled some of his many opponents. 'Martin Hanamy and Pat Fleury of Offaly were hard competitors. I had some fierce battles in Munster with Denis Walsh of Cork, whom I admired greatly. Ollie Kilkenny of Galway was a tough corner-back — hard to shake off. I found it difficult to get anything off John Henderson — in league matches mostly. Seánie O'Gorman and Pat Hartnett of Cork were also tough opponents who gave little away. I was often beaten by an opponent, but it was rare enough for me to be beaten two times in a row by the same opponent. I remember one day playing on Brian Corcoran of Cork when he was only coming on the scene. He gave me the run-around. I paid the piper for not knowing who he was; but I didn't get caught the second time.'

Some of the great players of his time? 'I'd have to say Ger Cunningham — brilliant. Nicky [English] would have to be one of the greatest of my time. Also Tony O'Sullivan and Joe Hennessy, who came a little before my time.'

Pat made his last appearance in the blue-and-gold jersey when he came on as a sub in the closing stages of the Munster final replay of 1996 against Limerick, but even his presence failed to swing the game in favour of the Premier County. Yet Munster finals will always conjure up for Pat great moments of hurling drama, grandeur, and excitement, as the 1913 did for 'Sliabh Ruadh' when he wrote the following stirring lines after the Tipperary-Cork encounter at Dungarvan in August that year.

> 'Twas an Autumn day and the sun shone down
> With a cheerful ray o'er the seaside town,
> And dense the crowds that thronged them there
> And joyous the shouts that rent the air;
> For there were gathered our country's pride
> From Lee, Suir, Nore and Shannon side;
> And came they too from Sarsfield's town,
> And forth from the shadow of Knockmealdown:
> E'en from the west were gathered there
> Young men comely and maidens fair;
> And with anxious step and eager pace
> Hurried they on to the trysting place,
> For here today, in contest fleet,
> Tipperary's best and Cork will meet —
> Here beneath the Comeraghs' frown
> They'll cross camáns for the Munster crown.
> Thus for an hour the battle raged,
> Hotter and fiercer they each engaged;
> Those stalwarts bold, unknowing fear,
> Their county's honour alone held dear,
> Seeking no gain or paltry pelf,
> Reckless of limb and life itself;
> Each heart true and stout and brave,
> No spirit there of serf or slave!

Born 1947

I played in two All-Ireland minor finals, 1963 and 1965. I came on as a sub in '63 when Wexford beat us and Dublin beat us in '65. I played in five National Leagues, winning one, in 1971, three Railway Cup medals, two Munster senior and one All-Ireland, in 1973.

"

"

I started with my club, South Liberties, in the late fifties at under-age. Only club success was to reach minor county final. During these years I was at CBS, Limerick, and we played Dean Ryan and Harty Cup. I was successful with Dean Ryan in 1963. 1964, '65 and '66 played in three Harty Cup finals and three All-Ireland colleges. During this period my club was playing junior hurling in East Limerick, with little success. A group of young players which included Pat Hartigan, Joe McKenna and my three brothers emerged, and in 1967 we became a senior team, and in our first year we reached Limerick county final, to be beaten in a replay by Kilmallock. We proceeded to compete in the next eleven East Limerick senior championships, winning ten, and about six county finals, winning four. As a result of county final wins we reached two Munster club finals and were beaten in both by Mount Sion and Glen Rovers.

At ten years of age Éamon Grimes got his first 'real' hurley, from Santa Claus; before that he used an assortment of home-made ones. His hurling brilliance quickly manifested itself. He played Harty Cup hurling for four years at Limerick CBS, and when he won his first of three Harty Cup medals in 1964 he was one of the youngest winners ever in this intensely competitive and prestigious competition. In 1966 he was proud to captain the team to its third-in-a-row success.

The triumph of 1964 led to All-Ireland success with a win over St Peter's College, Wexford. He was magnificent in that game. An article in the *Limerick Yearbook* of 1972 gave the following description: 'It was in Croke Park in April 1964 and all over the field one could hear people asking — who is number 12, that blonde lad on the Limerick team? It was of course Éamon Grimes, and I doubt very much that any forward display from a college lad at Croke Park for a long time could possibly measure up to his showing, which was superb, for on top of scoring two great goals against the breeze, young Grimes never lost a tussle for possession; for his solo running was a treat, and his first-time pulling too set an example for his colleagues.'

In 1965 they lost the final to St Kieran's, Kilkenny, on the score 6:9 to

Sexton Street, Limerick C.B.S. — 1964 Colleges' All-Ireland winners
Front row (left to right): *T. Crowe, M. O'Brien, T. Clohessy, E. Power.* Second row: *Rev. Bro. Burke, J. Kennedy, B Cobbe, D. Manning, E. Cregan, S. Shinners, P. Nash, P. Doherty, Rev. Bro. Hennessy.* Third row: *T. O'Brien, N. O'Gorman, L. Moloney, N. O'Neill, D. Russell, G. Boland, J. Leonard, E. Grimes.* Back row: *J. J. Fitzpatrick, Rev. Bro. White (Superior), J. Finucane.*

6:1. But they got revenge the following year when they defeated St Kieran's in the semi-final, 8:9 to 3:9, before going on to beat St Mary's, Galway, in the final.

1966 was the year he got his call-up to the Limerick senior hurling team. 'It was the first round against Tipperary, who had won the All-Ireland title in 1964 and '65. They were favourites to win three in a row. Well, we surprised them. Éamon Cregan had a super game, scoring 3:5 out of a winning score of 4:12 to 2:9. There were three Éamons in the half-forward line: Cregan, Carey, and Grimes. It was a great win — the first time Limerick had beaten Tipperary in the championship since 1948. It was the day before the Leaving Cert. I took an awful chance.'

Éamon's county senior career stretched from that first-round game of 1966 to when he came on as a sub for Willie Fitzmaurice in the All-Ireland final of 1980. The best Limerick team he played on? 'The 1966 team was by far the best. We lost the semi-final to Cork in Killarney by two points in rather controversial circumstances when the referee failed to apply the advantage rule and we had a goal disallowed.'

The victory Éamon got most enjoyment from was the 1973 Munster final defeat of Tipperary. 'I'd say that gave me more enjoyment than any other win. To beat Tipperary on their home ground on a terrible warm day in a final — great. Mícheál Ó Muircheartaigh says it was one of the best games he has seen.' It was certainly full of drama and excitement and finished with a suspense that would do justice to any Hitchcock thriller. After about ten minutes Limerick had gone seven points up. At half time they trailed by four points — 2:9 to 3:2. A quarter of an hour into the second half Limerick had forged ahead by four points — 6:3 to 2:11. The tension was terrible. The heat was intense.

With a little over five minutes to go Tipperary go one point up. Limerick draw level and forge one point ahead. Three minutes to go; the atmosphere is electric. A point, and Tipp draw level. A little over a minute remaining; then a seventy to Limerick, and the referee, Mick Slattery of Clare, tells Richie Bennis he must score direct. Cool as a cucumber, Richie bends, lifts, and strikes, and the white flag waving sends Limerick fans delirious — the first Munster title since 1955. Seán Foley has Richie Bennis on the ground in a bear-hug of enthusiastic congratulations.

That victory paved the way to Croke Park, and Limerick faced Kilkenny in the final on the first Sunday in September. 'What can you say about it? Nothing was going to beat us that day — no team in Ireland: we knew we would win the All-Ireland title when we beat Tipperary in Thurles. The 1973 final was the first time the teams were presented to the President. It was President Childers. He kept us waiting — it was probably only a few minutes but it seemed ages. Rain was pouring down.' The final whistle brought Limerick a seven-point victory, and Éamon, as captain, who had given a quality midfield display, proudly collected the McCarthy Cup amid scenes of rare excitement and jubilation. President Childers, watching his first final in his capacity as President, said, 'This was the greatest game I have seen in my lifetime, and I am speaking of all games.' It was a great year for Éamon and was further enhanced when he was nominated Hurler of the Year to win the Texaco award.

He played with and against many great hurlers during a long and distinguished career, and he talked about some of them. 'No doubt whatsoever but the hardest opponent I met was Len Gaynor of Tipperary. After that I would name Con Roche of Cork, Pat Lalor of Kilkenny, and Noel O'Dwyer of Tipperary. Within the county it would be Éamon Cregan and Phil Bennis. Pat Hartigan was a colossal man and a wonderful full-back. He had a great relieving clearance. Jim O'Brien I always compared to John Egan of Kerry football fame — both most under-rated players. I never once saw Jim hooked. It was the way he swung the hurley. He was as strong as a horse; his weight never changed, no matter what he ate. I used envy him.

'Éamon Cregan was one of the most talented and all-round hurlers you could find — my number 1. Seán Foley was a great wing-back and a good centre-back too. He played many great games but was fantastic in the All-Ireland final of 1973. Richie Bennis was one of the most valuable players any team could have, and he proved it many times. Liam O'Donoghue was like lightning — could play half-back and half-forward; was one of the outstanding half-backs of his time. I always thought Frankie Nolan didn't get the recognition he deserved as a forward: he was very effective. Joe McKenna for his scoring accuracy was remarkable — sure he only had to stand on the edge of the square. Andy Dunworth, who went to America, was another forward I greatly admired.'

And talking of America, Éamon had three memorable trips there, twice with the All-Stars and once as an All-Ireland champion. 'The hospitality was incredible. Families volunteered to put up players. I stayed each time with Gerry and Winnie Moore in Castro Valley outside San Francisco. In 1984 didn't their daughter Eileen represent San Francisco in the Rose of Tralee festival!'

The most exciting moment of his career? 'Oh, God, without a doubt I would have to go to the club — our first county championship win in 1972, beating Patrickswell. The game had everything.' His own greatest day? 'I'd have to say the county final of 1971, when we were beaten by Claughaun. I played my best hurling that day by far.'

In the early days of his working life Éamon used to travel, and in the course of his rounds he would call to the pub of the late Mick Hickey of Castleconnell. There was no end to the stories. Mick, who was a member of the Limerick team of the thirties, used tell of when he was based in Longford and he'd cycle down on Friday to home; rest on Saturday; play the match on Sunday; and then cycle back to Longford. And then there was Tommy Casey, the hackneyman, who first drove the Limerick players in the thirties — and continued to do so into the early nineties, 'and he's still driving today.' Well, into the car would get Mick Mackey, John Mackey, Jackie Power, Paddy Scanlon, and Timmy Ryan. Off they would go to Thurles to play a match. They would call to various pubs on the way back — would be received as heroes; never had to buy a drink; never got home the same day. It all reminded Éamon of when his father used to head for Thurles early on the Sunday morning of the match and wouldn't get back until Monday evening.

Éamon was also a first-class athlete. He represented his school in the 100 yards and 220 yards. Those were his favourite distances. He won many county events, which also included distances of 440 yards and 880 yards. He is particularly proud of the fact that the time record in Ireland for the junior relay race consisting of laps of 220, 220, 440 and 880 yards (one-mile relay) established in the late sixties by himself, Joe Laffan, Noel Spellesy and Dick Power, while representing Limerick, still stands.

Éamon won two All-Star awards, and the narrations associated with those awards tell us much about the man.

'1973. For his seemingly limitless energy; his desire to work all over the field, qualities which have made him a natural leader and a high scorer.'

'1975. For his seemingly unlimited energy, his incisive running and sharpness in picking off scores.'

Éamon was undoubtedly one of the outstanding hurlers of his day. So taken was J.P. McManus by the spirit of the indefatigable Éamon that he felt compelled to name one of his horses 'Grimes' as a gesture to the memory of a great hurler and athlete.

Born 1903

G alway, represented by Meelick, contested the first All-Ireland final of 1887 with Tipperary, represented by a Thurles selection — a 21-a-side affair, played in Birr on 1 April 1888 — and lost on the score Tipperary 1:1 plus 1 forfeit point, Galway no score. In the home final of 1900 Galway again fell to Tipperary on the score 5:7 to 0:1.

They didn't appear in an All-Ireland final again until 1923. That was the first time in the history of the GAA that two All-Ireland semi-finals took place. Limerick beat Donegal 7:4 to 0:1 — a game in which numbers were worn by players for the first time — and Galway beat Kilkenny 5:4 to 2:0. On the road to Croke Park, Galway had to face Roscommon in the Connacht final but emerged very easy winners.

Galway faced Limerick in the final at Croke Park on 14 September 1924. In their ranks was Ignatius Harney, one of five men from the Tynagh club, the others being Andy Kelly, Mick Derivan, Mick Kenny, and Jim Power, who as I write (September 1997) is still hale and hearty and is due to celebrate his 102nd birthday this coming November.

Ignatius was a key member of the Galway team all through the twenties. His début on the county team was unplanned, as his son Michael explained when I spoke to him. 'He went to a match as a spectator. Galway were short. He was told to tog out and play. He did well enough that day to win a permanent place on the team for himself.' He was one of the foremost players of his era and was selected on the Tailteann Games panel of 1924. He played the game with style and made hurling look simple, for he was a master of all the basic skills. He lived in an era of first-time hurling, and he was adept at lifting and striking the ball in the one movement, even when moving at speed. He preferred not to handle the ball if at all possible, and preached this to younger players.

For the 1923 final Galway went into collective training and took the field a very fit team. The political circumstances of the time were such that Galway had been offered a walkover by Limerick. This was refused by Galway. It all arose out of the issue of prisoners in the aftermath of the Civil War, with Limerick declining to fulfil an earlier fixture of June 1924. An emergency meeting of the Central Council awarded the match to Galway, but they declined such a bloodless victory. Fortunately the prisoner situation moved towards solution in July, and the match was re-fixed.

Galway won a fast, exciting game on a glorious sunny day on the score 7:3 to 4:5. It was Galway's first success and a great moment for hurling. Ignatius saw

Galway All-Ireland Team of 1923
Top Inset: *Ned Gilmartin, Mick Gill, Junior Mahony.* Top Standing: *Joe Kenny, Rev. J. Larkin, C.C. (Tynagh), Tom Kenny.* Top Seated: *Pat Harney, Barney Gibbs, Mick Dervan (Tynagh), Dick Morrissey, Steve Garvey, Jim Power (Tynagh).* Seated: *Andy Kelly (Tynagh), Jimmie Morris, Mick Kenny (Capt. Tynagh), Martin King, Tom Flemming.* On Ground: *Leonard McGrath,* Ignatius Harney *(Tynagh).*

his captain and club colleague Mick Kenny proudly take the McCarthy Cup across the Shannon to scenes of great jubilation.

It is interesting to look at the other All-Ireland finals in which Ignatius played. In 1924 Galway confirmed their rise to power in the hurling world by beating Tipperary in the semi-final, 3:1 to 2:3. A feature of that game was the great display of Jim Power at full-back on Martin Kennedy. The final against Dublin had two interesting features. It was played on 14 December — inconceivable nowadays that an All-Ireland could be played on such a date — and Galway had lost the services of the ace midfielder Mick Gill, now a member of the famous Garda team and resident in Dublin. No declaration facility existed in those days for players living outside their native county; so Mick, not being

in a position to play with Galway, threw in his lot with Dublin, and he played a major part in the 5:3 to 2:6 defeat of his native county. The result created the unique situation of Ignatius Harney and his colleagues winning and losing an All-Ireland title in the space of exactly three months, and for Mick Gill the unique honour of winning two All-Ireland medals with different counties in the same year.

In the semi-final of 1925 Galway defeated Kilkenny on the unusual score of 9:4 to 6:0. It was the day Kilkenny recalled that great goalkeeper of much earlier years, John T. Power — he was born in 1883 — but 1925 was not a happy semi-final for him. So for the third year in a row Galway contested the All-Ireland final but went under to a very strong Tipperary team on the score 5:6 to 1:5.

The twenties drew to a close with Galway playing Cork in the finals of 1928 and 1929. Even allowing for the fact that Cork were going through a brilliant phase, the results were humiliating for Galway. 1928: 6:12 to 1:0, the final in which that wonderful Galway hurler Mick King was seriously injured, the final in which Michael 'Gah' Aherne scored 5:4 for Cork and his brother Paddy 'Balty' Aherne scored one goal, between them scoring all of Cork's goals. 1929: 4:9 to 1:3. Galway wouldn't appear again in an All-Ireland final until 1953.

For Ignatius, however, there were many worthwhile memories to recall — games with club, county, province, and UCG. And of course there was that All-Ireland medal to add to his county titles of those years, together with his own wonderful contribution to the promotion of hurling west of the Shannon, of which he could be justly proud.

My article on John Killeen reveals the esteem in which he held Ignatius and confirms his status as an outstanding hurler who impressed not only his contemporaries but also a younger generation, who looked up to him with admiration and listened attentively to his hurling counsel.

For a personal glimpse of Ignatius I got in touch with his contemporary Jim Power. 'Ignatius was one of the greatest hurlers that ever took a hurley in his hand. It was a pleasure to watch him in action. He had speed and skill. I played many times with him at different levels. In those days UCG were allowed to pick three outsiders for their Fitzgibbon Cup matches. Ignatius and myself played with them.'

He died on 1 September 1954, aged fifty-one.

Born 1921

"

My dearest wish for the future would be to see the GAA make arrangements whereby former hurlers would obtain a ticket for All-Ireland hurling final day. It is so sad to hear of so many of these men who thrilled and entertained tens of thousands, and helped to make hurling the great spectacle that it is, unable to get a ticket for hurling's greatest day.

Michael Hayes **"**

There is a field at the entrance to Mick's farm. 'That used to be our hurling field. The Foleys and a few others would gather there in the evenings and hurl with my brother and myself. There was no team in Butlerstown, so a few of us played a minor match with Dunhill.' A neighbour, Seán Nolan, wasn't impressed with this, and the following evening he took a ten-shilling note from his pocket and told Mick to register Butlerstown with the county board. That was 1937. Two years later they won the minor title. 'But we lost it on an objection. By a mistake one fellow's

name was written down twice. We lost our medals on my birthday, the sixth of November 1939. The hearing of the case was like going to court in Hell with the Devil.'

Mick is very attached to the land. He loves the land, the crops it bears, the animals it nurtures. He knows its history. 'My grandfather was evicted in the 1890s. My granduncle gave them his house and a few acres; he then took the boat and was never heard of again. Difficult times. I was born in dangerous times: 1921, the year of the Troubles. My father was born in 1886. He won a county junior medal with Butlerstown in the early days of the century.'

Disappointment on the hurling field was nothing new to Mick Hayes: at county level it was part and parcel of life. Many a time Mick remembers trooping off the pitch with his county colleagues, dejected and dispirited. They used to wonder if there would ever be a dawning followed by a glorious sunset.

On occasions there was a real hard-luck story. Such a day was Munster final day, 1943. 'We were playing Cork. I hated playing Cork. It was so difficult to beat them. They were so skilful — so good at the game. I can remember a tussle between Connie Curley, our full-back, and Ted Sullivan. Ted couldn't get a stroke at the ball, but he kind of chopped down on it. It rolled barely over the goal line and stopped — what a goal to give away. At another time one of our backs got his hurley to an incoming ball and deflected it past Jim Ware in goal. Jack Lynch was scoring every free he took for Cork. Towards the end we got a 21-yard free. Cork packed the goal. John Keane came up to take it. 'Years afterwards I was travelling with a friend, who called into a monastery between Lismore and Fermoy. I was introduced to the bursar as Mick

Hayes, the Waterford hurler. "Oh," said the bursar, "we have another of your type here." "What do you mean?" I asked. "One of those fellows that's foolish enough to be hurling." He was referring to Con Cottrell, who had joined the Rosminian order.' Mick and Con had a great chat. "'I was so sorry for Waterford in 1943," said Con to me. "I can still see John Keane standing over the ball. I only remember him striking it. It hit me on the forehead. I was dazed and didn't fully come to, until back in the dressing-room. If my head wasn't in the way you would have won the All-Ireland.'"

Mick has mixed feelings about an All-Ireland win in 1943. It was the year Antrim beat Kilkenny to reach their first All-Ireland final and fail heavily to Cork. 'Our neighbours across the river in Kilkenny would have said it's the only way we could ever win an All-Ireland. Sure they say it's no wonder Hayes is such a fine hurler — didn't his mother come from Glenmore.' Mick chuckles as he relates it. 'I hurled on Mick Kennefick that day — a flyer; a beautiful hurler.'

Using 1947 as a guide, four teams appeared to have the necessary credentials to capture the McCarthy Cup in 1948. They were Cork, Limerick, Galway, and Kilkenny.

Galway, representing Connacht, had defeated both Leinster and Munster to win their first Railway Cup title on 6 April 1947. Later that year, at Birr on 27 July, they failed in a thrilling All-Ireland semi-final to Kilkenny by one point, defeat coming in 'lost' time. They had a very good team and some wonderful hurlers: Seán Duggan, Willie Fahy, John Killeen, Paddy Gantly, Josie Gallagher, and Hubert Gordon. They were All-Ireland material.

Kilkenny had defeated Cork by one point, 0:14 to 2:7, in a nail-biting All-Ireland final in 1947. They had also contested the league final of that year. The players were seasoned and experienced: great names like Jimmy Langton, Paddy Hayden, Mark Marnell, Jimmy Kelly, Jack Mulcahy, Dan Kennedy, Shem Downey, and Jimmy Heffernan. They would take beating.

Cork were on the crest of a hurling wave. They had won four in a row from 1941 to 1944; they won again in 1946 with what many consider one of the finest teams ever to leave the county. They had battle-hardened and vastly experienced players available: Tom Mulcahy, Willie Murphy, Con Murphy, Paddy O'Donovan, Jim Young, Christy Ring, Mossy O'Riordan, and Jack Lynch. They would be difficult to beat.

Limerick were still a major hurling force, capable of matching and beating the best. In 1947 they faced Cork in the Munster final; it finished 2:6 to 2:3. One sports journalist wrote: 'If ever a better team lost it was Limerick.' In the National League final of that year Limerick and Kilkenny played a thrilling draw, and the replay, which took place in March 1948 — 'a magnificent game that really thrilled a splendid crowd' — was won by Limerick, 3:8 to 1:7, over a Kilkenny team that showed only two changes from their wonderful All-Ireland line-out. Big names on the Limerick team were Paddy Collopy, Dick Stokes, Jackie Power, Tom Cregan, Jim Sadlier, and Seán and Mick Herbert.

Now to 1948 — and the unexpected.

A closing-minutes flourish saw Cork defeat Limerick in the Munster semi-final and book a place against Waterford in the final. Waterford won by one point in a dramatic finish to capture their second Munster crown. In Leinster, Laois created a shock by defeating Kilkenny but failed in the Leinster final to Dublin.

At All-Ireland semi-final level, Waterford disposed of Galway, and Dublin overwhelmed Antrim. The unforeseen had occurred. It was a repeat of 1938: Waterford v. Dublin.

'Best of luck, and don't make a hash of it this time,' said Jack Lynch to Mick after the final whistle in Thurles. Jack was referring to 1938. Waterford, through a combination of factors, including missed opportunities, had failed to Dublin in the 1938 final. It was close: 2:5 to 1:6. Now at last they had escaped the clutches of Cork. Only just, though. One point in it at the final whistle, and Christy Ring with the last puck of the game shaved the upright on the wrong side.

'More than a dozen years later I was at Clonmel agricultural show with my wife, Mary, and family. I spotted Ring on a stand and said to the youngsters — Eugene, Philomena, and Michael — "That's Christy Ring over there. You'll probably hear people talking about him today." As I spoke he spotted us and came down to us. He relived for me the entire action of the closing seconds of the '48 Munster final and the near miss he had at the end. "You might remember," said he, "Waterford got a cut in. Vin Baston went out to take it. I thought it was stupid. Jim Barry would never allow a centre-back to do that — leave the centre open. I lined up for the cut in. As the ball left the hurley I had it in my sights. I was going for it when Connie Murphy got his hurley to it. It ricocheted off his hurley and went over my head and into a ruck of players. I got possession, and when I threw up the ball to hit it, some fellow hit me with a shoulder." I hadn't the courage to tell him it was me.'

Mick believed in first-time hurling. When at midfield he never lost an opportunity to connect overhead on the dropping ball. 'Of course part of the art of hurling is to size up your opponent — to size up the opposition. I met Mickey Byrne one day going into Páirc Uí Chaoimh. "God be with the hurling in your time," said Mickey to me — "doubling on the balls from the sky. Nowadays they're putting their hands

Waterford All-Ireland hurling champions 1948
Back row: Mick Hayes, *Mick Healy (sub)*, Mick Hickey, Eddie Carew, Andy Fleming, *Jimmy Allen (sub)*, *Vin Baston*, John Keane, *Davy Power (sub)*, Tom Curran, *Josie Murphy (sub)*, *Patrick Neville (sub)*, W. Galvin, *Jas Galvin (sub)*. Front row: John Cusack, Jackie Goode, E. Daly, Kevin O'Connor, Jim Ware (capt.), C. Moylan, *M.Feeney (sub)*, *P. Waters (sub)*, J. O'Connor, *L. Fanning (sub)*.

up to catch it; the opponent who pulls is blown for dangerous play. The hurley is for playing the ball, not the hand." I reminded Mick of the advice Éamon Cregan's father used give him: never put your hand up where you can put the hurley up.

A player's performance in the championship played a key role in having him considered for the Railway Cup team in those days — but he had to be pushed from his own county: competition for places was fierce. Mick was on the Munster panel from 1946 to 1950. 'Johnny Leahy of Tipperary played a major part in my selection.' Mick's failure to make the team in 1944 after a magnificent display in the championship of 1943 caused eyebrows to be raised in some quarters. Again in 1949 when he was listed among the subs, 'Moltóir' in his column carried the heading, 'Omission of M. Hayes a big surprise.'

Dreams turned to reality when the final whistle blew on the first Sunday in September 1948. The accumulated doubts and disappointments of years were buried. Waterford were All-Ireland champions for the first time. The victory was clear-cut: Waterford 6:7, Dublin 4:2. 'I had the ball in my hand for the last three puck-outs from the Dublin goal. I wanted it as a souvenir. I thought Con Murphy would never blow the final whistle. I had the ball when he did, and as he advanced to collect it I was smothered by well-wishers.'

Mick left the room and returned with the sliotar and the hurley. I held them both and surveyed them. Fascinating to think they were an integral part of Waterford's success and Mick Hayes's greatest hurling moment, almost fifty years ago.

He called it a day in 1953. He had had a good innings. More importantly, he enjoyed it. 'I played my first and last minor game with Waterford against Cork in Fermoy in 1939. We lost. Éamon Young was on the Cork team. The Sunday after the 1939 All-Ireland semi-final I played a senior game against Cork. The Cork jerseys were a light pink: the

dye had run following the torrential rain on final day. I was at that final. I spent more time looking up at the sky watching out for German planes than I did watching the match: I had heard about the declaration of war and was afraid. In 1940, '41 and '42 I played junior. In 1943 I established myself on the senior team.'

Mick did all his club hurling with the local junior team. It was a reflection of his exceptional ability that he could make the county senior team from a junior club. A deep sense of loyalty and dedication is embedded in Mick's make-up. It was there for the land he loved; the hurling he played; the parish he served. Understandable therefore that he should have turned down overtures from Mount Sion and Erin's Own to join their ranks.

Regarding his successes — an All-Ireland medal, a Munster medal, Railway Cup honours — he said: 'Not bad for a country chap.'

His choice of team spans five decades:

Seán Duggan *(Galway)*

Andy Fleming *(Waterford)*   Nick O'Donnell *(Wexford)*   Din Joe Buckley *(Cork)*

Pat Stakelum *(Tipperary)*   John Keane *(Waterford)*   Paddy Phelan *(Kilkenny)*

Mick Hayes *(Waterford)*   Mick Roche *(Tipperary)*

Christy Ring *(Cork)*   Mick Mackey *(Limerick)*   Eddie Keher *(Kilkenny)*

Jackie Power *(Limerick)*   Locky Byrne *(Waterford)*   Tim Flood *(Wexford)*

Born 1902

Cork Munster Football Champions, 1928 (Original picture caption)
Top: Lt. J.J. Hogan, D. O'Donoghue, B.A.; Dr. J. Kearney (capt), M. Donegan, B.A., Ml. Murphy,
M. Comm; S. Vaughan, N.T.; T. Carroll, Dr. F. Callanan, T. Long. Bottom: J. O'Regan, N.T., J. Murphy,
Mat Murphy, J. Brennan, J. O'Callaghan, J. Hurley, Ml. Walsh.

He was a big man and was affectionately known as 'Big Jim'. A native of Clonakilty, he played hurling and football with his native parish in his young days. He was also active in the struggle for independence in the 1919–21 era and was commandant of the Clonakilty Battalion of the Volunteers.

He was a leading dual player in his day, but his prowess with the camán has tended to overshadow his ability as a footballer. It isn't widely known that he won a Munster senior football medal with Cork in 1928, to which he added a provincial and All-Ireland hurling medal. As a soldier of the independence movement, 1928 would certainly have been of special interest to Jim: it was the year of the death of John Devoy, the Fenian veteran, their longest-surviving leader, who died in October at Atlantic City, New Jersey, aged eighty-six. His remains were brought back to Ireland, where he was accorded a public funeral.

But back to Jim. He also holds the distinction of winning Cork county senior football medals with UCC in 1927 and 1928. On the 1928 team was Jack Russell, who went on to win nineteen caps in rugby for Ireland between 1931 and 1937. After Jim had finished his football with UCC he returned to his native Clonakilty and won a junior county football medal in 1930. He was a selector on the Cork senior football team that won the All-Ireland title in 1945 and also on the defeated teams of 1956 and '57 at the hands of Galway and Louth, respectively.

In 1925 he transferred to Blackrock hurling club — Clonakilty's loss, the Rockies' gain — a club famous since the early days of the association, one that gave great hurlers to Cork in every decade. With them he won four county senior hurling titles, in 1925, '27, '29, and '30. He added to this in the mid-thirties when he won a Meath senior hurling title with Kilmessan.

Cork 1931 All-Ireland champions. Jim Hurley is in the back row third from left.

Jim developed into one of the leading hurling midfielders of his day and gave great service to his native Cork in that position. He was a superb hurler, a powerful striker of a ball — could hit left and right and played with gusto and determination, which he maintained to the end of his days.

He played during a golden Cork era. It began with victory in a junior All-Ireland in 1925, followed by victory in a splendid game of hurling in the National League final against Dublin in May 1926 — the inaugural final of the National League competition; it ended with the Munster final of 1932, when Clare beat Cork, 5:2 to 4:1. In between those years Cork struck gold in the hurling world: Munster titles, 1926, '27, '28, '29, and '31; All-Ireland titles, 1926, '28, '29, and '31; two National league titles, 1926 and '30. Jim was a key figure, admittedly among a host of stars, in all those victories.

Aspects of the 1926 and 1931 campaigns are worth recalling. In the Munster final of 1926 it took three meetings before Cork disposed of the reigning All-Ireland champions, Tipperary. The first game had to be abandoned after about twenty minutes, because of encroachment by the crowd, with Tipperary leading, 1:2 to nil. A goal in the closing stages of the replay saved the day for Cork. And so to a third game, in which the domi-nance of Jim Hurley at midfield was a big factor in a five-point Cork win, 3:6 to 2:4.

A radio broadcast of the second game by 'Carbery' (P.D. Mehigan) took place from Thurles; this is believed to have been the first broadcast anywhere in the world of a game between two teams.

The 1931 campaign was demanding and gruelling. It would appear to have been the only time a team had to play seven games before being crowned All-Ireland senior hurling champions. It began with a narrow four-point win over Clare, 3:4 to 1:6; there followed a five-point victory over Tipperary, 3:5 to 2:3, at Thurles. Then came the Munster final against Waterford. When Waterford led by 3:0 to 0:5 at half time, a big upset seemed to be on the cards; but Jim Hurley saved the day eight minutes into extra time with an equalising point from a prodigious drive from well beyond midfield — the last puck of the game — leaving the score 4:0 to 1:9 for Cork. Controversy surrounded the game because of the length of extra time played and the fact that Waterford had a goal disallowed. The replay, however, was clear-cut, with Cork winning well. The three games against Kilkenny in the All-Ireland hurling final are part of hurling history, with Jim Hurley among the heroes, particularly in the first game.

The sixteen Cork players who took part in those games were all heroes at one time or another: George Garrett (who came on as a sub in both replays), Eudi Coughlan, Jim Hurley, John Coughlan, E. 'Marie' O'Connell, Paddy Delea, Mick 'Gah' Aherne, Paddy 'Fox' Collins, Paddy 'Balty' Aherne, 'Hawker' Grady (all from the Blackrock club), Bill Clancy, Dinny Barry Murphy, Jim O'Regan, Tom Barry, Morgan Madden, and Mick O'Connell. Sadly, none survives. The last of that great team, Paddy 'Fox' Collins of Glen Rovers, who figured in *Giants of the Ash*, died in February 1995.

Apart from the honour and glory of victory on such a historic occasion, each of the players received, in addition to his All-Ireland medal, a wrist watch and a miniature gold hurley.

Jim was selected for the Munster Railway Cup team in the inaugural year of the competition, 1927. Leinster won a wonderful game of hurling by two points, but Jim was back in 1928, '30 and '31 to claim the spoils of victory. He was also selected on the Tailteann Games team of 1932 — the third and last of a four-year series that began in 1924 when an All-Ireland selection played a team from the United States.

Jim was a great friend of Dr Pat O'Callaghan, the noted athlete and Olympic gold medallist.

His interest in and love of the game of hurling were immense. In 1944, with cars off the road because of wartime conditions, thousands converged on Thurles on bicycles — 'like ants on the move,' wrote Carbery — for the Munster final between Cork and Limerick, one of the epics of hurling history. Jim cycled from Cork on the eve of the game — a testament to his enthusiasm. He spent the night with the famous Leahy family of Boherlahan, evidence of the brotherhood of hurling men. No doubt they replayed many a match, reminisced into the early hours, talked of 'battles long ago' — and eagerly awaited many more.

Jim died in 1965 at the relatively young age of sixty-three.

Born 1946

'76, and '77; while the biggest disappointment was losing three All-Ireland finals in the seventies.

On the club scene the greatest day for Oulart-the Ballagh was the sixteenth of October 1994, when we won the county senior hurling title for the first time, having been defeated in five finals in twenty-five years. I was proud to be a selector with that team, which made the breakthrough for our parish. This year [1996] will be my forty-first playing hurling, as boy and man, and I have to say that I made great friends through the GAA.

My advice to boys would be to practise the skills and to try and eliminate the weaknesses from their game. I spend many hours every week passing on the skills to boys who, I hope, will get the same pleasure from playing as I did.

I would like to see clubs and the GAA make it compulsory for players to wear helmets with face guards, in order to reduce facial injuries and to allay any fears that parents might have about their children playing the greatest game in the world.

"

michael Jacob

"

I have always loved hurling, and I still get great enjoyment from playing it, as well as from coaching youngsters and managing teams.

The great Wexford team of the fifties inspired many boys to emulate their deeds, and I can recall waving to fans as they drove by our house on the way to the All-Ireland finals of '55 and '56.

In primary school in Oulart, Father Frank Staples was our coach and mentor, who did so much to promote hurling in our parish. I began my adult playing career at sixteen years of age as a goalkeeper on our junior team, a position I was to occupy for four years on the county under-21 team, finishing up with them as a midfielder in 1967. During my senior inter-county career I played first as a midfielder and then as a defender, while nowadays I usually wear the number 14 jersey for Oulart junior team. The highlight of my senior inter-county career was being picked as centre-back on the All-Star teams of '72,

It was a good and auspicious time to meet and talk to one of hurling's finest centre-half-backs. His club, Oulart-the Ballagh, had just won their second senior county hurling title (in September 1995), making it two in a row. Mick was one of the mentors and selectors. It was a proud moment for the parish. These victories were a reward for the dedicated work and endeavours of over a quarter of a century, a reward for the commitment and enthusiasm of those who encouraged and nurtured

Mick Jacob in typical defensive pose. (Photo: Jim Connolly)

under-age players in a small rural parish with a small population.

Mick is proud of the little parish's contribution to Gaelic games. In modern times it produced county players of the calibre of Tom Byrne, Christy Jacob (Mick's brother), Martin Storey, Liam Dunne, and Tomás Dunne. Back in 1910 Mick's granduncle, Jim Mythen, was a member of the Wexford team that brought the county its first senior hurling title. In more distant days Jack Royce, another revered son of the parish, toured America with the Irish athletes on the occasion of the 'US Invasion' of 1888.

Five times a county senior hurling title eluded the stout-hearted Mick — some defeats more painful than others. 'We lost to Rathnure in 1974. We had plenty of possession and opportunities but didn't take our chances.' In 1982 they lost by three points to Buffer's Alley. It is still remembered by those who saw it as the 'Mick Jacob final' — a day when his display at centre-half-back was majestic, a display that brought him the Man of the Match award, despite being on the losing team.

No All-Ireland senior medal came his way, although he did have the consolation of a medal as a sub in 1968 when Wexford, for the second time in a decade, surprised and shocked the favourites, Tipperary. Defeat was Wexford's lot in 1970, '76, and '77, each time at the hands of Cork, their bogey team. In particular 1976 was a bitter disappointment. 'We beat Kilkenny by seventeen points in the Leinster final. They were going for three in a row and had a great team. No-one gave us a chance: we were written off. That's what made the win so satisfying. We hurled like tigers that day. It was probably the best team display during my time with Wexford. We then had two great games with Galway at Páirc Uí Chaoimh — won the replay by a goal. Both games were terrible fast, and the heat was intense. They were played within a week of each other and were really energy-sapping.'

That brought Wexford to the final against Cork; and after the victories over teams of the quality of Kilkenny and Galway they had every right to feel confident. And that confidence seemed well founded when after six minutes they led Cork by 2:2 to nil and seemed rampant. But Cork steadied and were level at half time. When the final whistle blew, Cork were ahead, 2:21 to 4:11 — their twenty-second title. 'It was a game we could have won. We missed a number of good chances; we failed to score in the last quarter of an hour. It was my biggest disappointment in the purple and gold. The entire team were shattered — sick for months afterwards. We let it slip. Cork brought on John Horgan in defence and made switches that settled them.'

Those who were at the game will remember the splendour and magnificence of Mick Jacob's hurling at centre-back, and in the course of the game he was opposed by four different Cork players: Brendan Cummins, Mick Malone, Ray Cummins, and finally Jimmy Barry Murphy. He was equally superb three years earlier when Wexford beat Limerick in a thrilling National League final that gave Mick his only league medal. He was honoured with three All-Stars: in 1972, '76, and '77. In 1975 as a replacement All-Star he was nominated Player of the Series in the American tour.

In the period 1970–79 Wexford and Kilkenny contested every Leinster final and in so doing provided spectators with hurling thrills and some of the finest exhibitions of the skills of the ancient game — games in which Mick was always to the fore. He remembers the 1972 drawn game, which, over the eighty-minute period, produced the remarkable score of 6:13 each. More remarkable still was the 1974 final, a game of rare splendour, when Kilkenny at the height of their glory were fortunate to survive by one point, 6:13 to 2:24. 'I can still see those final seconds. We were playing with fourteen men — lost Phil Wilson in rather controversial circumstances just at half time. The scores were level, and I felt it would be a draw. A clearance from the Kilkenny half-back Pat Lawlor brought a free to Kilkenny. Eddie Keher came up to take it; time ticking away. He's in no hurry — he decides to tie his lace; goes through the routine of steadying, measuring, and looking — then sends over the winner. Heartbreak!'

'How do you do it, Mick?' I asked with incredibility as he told me he had played junior A hurling with his club that year (1995) at corner-forward, and scored 2:1 in one of those games, and he in his fiftieth year. He was of course a member of the Wexford team that won the All-Ireland Masters (over-40) title in 1991. That took our discussion back to Mick's early years. For four years, 1964–67, he played at under-21 level for Wexford, in goal for the first three and at midfield in 1967. They won the All-Ireland title in 1965 — a victory over Tipperary that avenged the previous year's defeat. In 1966 it took three games before Cork eventually won through in the second replay. Mick was called to senior ranks against Kilkenny in a league game in 1967 but didn't establish himself permanently until 1969.

His style was tidy and economical. His concentration made him ever alert. Countless hours of diligent practice produced a clean striker with great positional sense. Above all he was a ball player — yet there was no flinching in hip-to-hip and shoulder-to-shoulder exchanges, all within the canons of good sportsmanship. It all added up to a centre-half-back in the classical mould. Mick's approach to hurling was one of total dedication and commitment. He was always superbly fit. 'Training with the panel isn't enough: you must put in that bit extra yourself. I always did plenty of running on my own — through the fields, over the ditches, up the hills. You build up stamina and then work on speed. If you want to last the pace at top level you must have strength in the legs and wind in the lungs.' His slight, sinewy figure had hidden within it strands of steel and vast quantities of energy.

Mick is an ardent advocate of the wearing of the helmet — not just the head cover: the helmet with the facial guard. And he came to the conclusion the hard way — ciall cheannaithe. In a practice match against Gorey in the autumn of 1984 he got an accidental blow of the sliotar in the eye, hit full force from four yards' range. His wife, Breda, said she used to think that if you were fit and skilful you would always avoid such an injury; but freak circumstances do arise, and that is what happened to Mick, who now maintains that 'anyone who plays hurling without the facial-guarded helmet is mad.'

The household is immersed in GAA affairs. Everything seems to revolve around hurling and football. Hurleys and boots are clearly visible. Breda, a native of historic Boolavogue, played camogie at junior level with Wexford and is as enthusiastic and involved as Mick in the local club and its under-age players. Over the past five or six years their schedule would start in February and run right through to October. They would be involved with other dedicated people with at least one team every evening: under-10 football, under-12 hurling and football, under-14, under-16 hurling and football, minor and under-21 when they can field such teams. And of course Mick has his training with the junior A team.

The enthusiasm of Mick and Breda has proved highly infectious and has rubbed off on all the family. Mick junior represented Wexford in the Poc Fada and captained the local under-14 team to victory in the Féile na nGael competition. Helena also represented the county in the Poc Fada and played at corner-back on the county under-14 camogie team. Rory and Ursula look like following in their footsteps, at present playing at under-12 and under-10, respectively. All four joined enthusiastically in the discussions, showed an avid interest in what the other players had written in the large journal, and were to the fore in debating who would be selected in the various positions on that year's (1995) All-Star team, whether or not kicked goals should be allowed, and what legitimate counter there is to the act of kicking the sliotar. Fascinating to observe and behold! Discussions went on well past bedtime, and little Ursula finished up asleep on the floor.

On our way home my wife, Mary, and I couldn't help reflecting on the great unifying force hurling was within the household: the bond it created between parents and children, the depth and range of the youngsters' grasp of so many aspects of the game, debate on equal terms, and the lifelong benefit and sense of fulfilment their love and devotion to the game must surely bring them.

---

*This is Mick's team from the men of his time that he played against —
'chosen after much deliberation.'*

Noel Skehan *(Kilkenny)*

Fan Larkin *(Kilkenny)*   Pat Hartigan *(Limerick)*   John Horgan *(Cork)*

Ger Loughnane *(Clare)*   Mick Jacob *(Wexford)*   Martin Coogan *(Kilkenny)*

Frank Cummins *(Kilkenny)*   John Connolly *(Galway)*

Jimmy Barry Murphy *(Cork)*   Pat Delaney *(Kilkenny)*   Eddie Keher *(Kilkenny)*

Charlie McCarthy *(Cork)*   Ray Cummins *(Cork)*   Johnny Flaherty *(Offaly)*

Born 1922

Paddy Kehoe (left) *with Nick O'Donnell (Capt.) and Doctor Staunton, Bishop of Ferns, chatting after Wexford's 1955 All-Ireland win.*

"

These memories will always be special to me.

The rise of Wexford hurlers and the good fortune I had at the time to be in the prime of my career and to have been a member of the great team of the fifties — great sportsmen and great hurlers.

Football was my first love, and we were most unlucky not to have won an All-Ireland title in 1945.

Sad to say, only four of us now survive: Mick Kehoe (goal), Tom Doyle (left-full-back), Dermot Clancy (midfield), Paddy Kehoe (half-forward).

I enjoyed the army days, winning two All-Army titles, 25th Battalion (football); also played with the 5th Brigade. Great men I played with and against: Joe Keohane, John Joe O'Reilly, Mick Mackey, Brendan Lynch, Mick Daniels, Éamon Young.

Paddy Kehoe "

W hat an amazing man he is. At thirty four years, and around the fifteen-stone mark, he is still among the country's best forwards in both codes. He has retained that dash and enthusiasm which one associates more with fellows fifteen years his junior, and

139

25th Battalion football team. Paddy Kehoe *is fourth on on the left in front row.*

after all his years of playing activity, can still enjoy a game as much as any youngster.' Thus wrote one reporter after Wexford footballers had created a shock by defeating Dublin — Leinster champions and All-Ireland finalists — in the Leinster semi-final at Carlow, 2:7 to 0:7. Paddy Kehoe was their star performer, and with ten minutes remaining he had to leave the pitch with an injury that required fourteen stitches in the forehead. It was the summer of 1956. It was also the year he retired. He had much on which to look back, much on which to reflect.

He was one of the great dual performers. Indeed, you could call him a triple performer, for in his army days he played a lot of rugby, and he recalled a weekend when he played rugby at Lansdowne Road with the Curragh army team on Saturday and lined out for a Gaelic match at Croke Park the following day. Paddy played in all grades of hurling and football for his native Wexford. He won many honours, including All-Ireland, National League, Oireachtas and Leinster titles in hurling; in football he won a Leinster title in 1945. He was chosen for Leinster in the Railway Cup in both codes.

It all began in 1938, the first of three years as a minor. Paddy still vividly remembers the drawn game against Dublin at Gorey, when he was marking Seán Óg Ó Ceallacháin. 'I broke the bos of my hurley, leaving me with half a bos. I was too shy to ask for a replacement and afraid I might be taken off; so I played on, and even scored a point with it. We lost the replay at Kilkenny. It was the day Nicky Rackard made his début in the purple and gold.' After his minor days, Paddy moved on to junior level and progressed from there to senior ranks in 1943.

Because of the war, the army began a recruiting campaign in 1940, and in

September of that year, much to his mother's dismay, Paddy enlisted and remained in the army until June 1944. He was attached to the 25th Battalion. Life in the army appealed to Paddy. After an initial induction course, those who were proficient at games spent the bulk of the day on the playing fields. 'I never soldiered except for a few months, and after that I never had to have a rifle in my hand.'

The army provided food and clothing. Pay at first was 13s 2d (66p) a week. 'We were paid on Wednesday, and there was usually a fellow waiting in the passage to collect 10s (50p) you owed him.' In a word, money was a very scarce commodity — as the following story will show.

In the summer of 1941 Paddy received a letter at the Curragh from Stephen Roche, secretary of Wexford County Board, informing him that he and three colleagues — Jim Cody, Ger Kavanagh, and 'Cherry' Hawkins — had been selected to play for Wexford junior footballers in a Leinster championship game at Portarlington. Paddy was also a sub on the hurling team, playing at the same venue. Enclosed with the letter was a cheque for £3 to cover taxi hire. They held a meeting — you could call it a financial meeting. It was decided that to spend such a sum in such a manner would be irresponsible — perhaps even sinful. Fifteen shillings each had other uses.

'We got two large army bicycles and set off. Ger and myself shared one — he on the crossbar, me pedalling. I think he was asleep most of the time. It was a round journey of forty miles — the Curragh, Kildare, Monasterevin, Portarlington — a hot summer's day. We stopped along the way at a river to bathe our feet. We left the bicycles on the outskirts of Portarlington — couldn't let the selectors see how we travelled. I had intended getting a bit to eat before the football match, but the moment we arrived Paddy Breen told me to get up quick to the field, as they were short of subs on the hurling team.

Just as I arrived a player called Clancy went down injured — only five minutes of the game gone. In I went — played the rest of the game; then played the football game; set off on the return journey to the Curragh; stopped occasionally for refreshments. We arrived back around midnight.'

Such an endurance test would be unthinkable nowadays. But Paddy was a man of bronze, a man of stamina, inured to hardship by the circumstances of the times, the life-style of those days, and the physical fitness of army life. There were no comforts.

At 5 foot 9, Paddy weighed 12 stone 9 pounds. But more anon about his weight.

He played hurling right-hand-under. He had a tremendous burst of speed, great ball control, was fearless in action. He has been described as 'a natural performer — the effortless stylist — the football and hurling enchanter.' He was all that and more. He had strength, stamina and skill in abundance. It enabled him to play both codes at top level for a span of fourteen years.

Paddy had no hesitation in naming Mick Mackey as his hurling hero and the player he most admired. 'I loved his style and approach to the game. He got the ball and headed straight through. He would go through a wall.' I reminded Paddy that it was said that when he soloed through in the second half of the All-Ireland semi-final against Limerick in 1955 to score a great goal, he had the sliotar in his hand while pretending to solo, just as Mick was alleged to have done on occasions. 'I might have carried it a few extra steps,' and then he laughed, just as Mick would have.

Paddy always saw the humorous side of things; to interview him is to be entertained. His reminiscences were interspersed with much laughter. Among his anecdotes was the story of a colleague he knew who told him he always went to Confession and Communion when he discovered he was playing on a particular opponent.

Paddy preferred football to hurling. He would have loved to win a football medal — to have seen the Sam Maguire Cup rest by the Slaneyside. And so he talks about 1945 — the year of the football might-have-beens. 'When we met Kildare in the second round few gave us a chance. They had beaten the provincial champions, Carlow, in the first round. Well, we beat them by fourteen points. Laois had a very good football team in those days, and we beat them in the semi-final at Carlow, 4:5 to 1:11. Next came the final against Offaly at Portlaoise — a hard, bone-crushing game that we won, 1:9 to 1:4. I scored five points from frees that day. I often spent up to an hour in training taking frees from all angles.

'We were through to the All-Ireland semi-final against Cavan. Then came the well-intentioned but fateful decision. It was decided to take the entire team on two weeks' collective training to Rosslare Harbour. Two weeks was too long. It became monotonous. Players were removed from their natural routine. We were stuck to the ground when we met Cavan. It was an awful mistake. We lost by two points, 1:4 to 0:5. Later that year we met Cork, the All-Ireland champions, in the league and beat them. We lost the league final to Meath, 2:2 to 0:6.' So no major football title came Paddy's way. Let's therefore turn to hurling.

In 1949 Paddy left his job in the railway and went to Dublin. There, through the good offices of the publican Tommy Moore — the Kilkennyman who looked after countless hurlers who came to Dublin — he got a job as a rep for a mineral water company. He joined the Faughs hurling club and played in the company of Tony Herbert, Alfie O'Brien, Billy Rackard, Harry Gray, and Jim Prior. 'I was stood many a drink by GAA enthusiasts. My weight rocketed to 16 stone 10 pounds. That, coupled with a knee injury which was to recur from time to time, cost me my place for a while on the Wexford hurling team.' But Paddy was back for the 1951 campaign, and when Wexford stepped out onto Croke Park on the first Sunday in September for their first All-Ireland appearance in thirty-three years they got a tremendous reception. Paddy says he got a special ovation — all 16 stone 4 pounds of him, easily the heaviest man on the field.

Defeat was Wexford's lot, but they endeared themselves to Gaeldom — glamour, flair, sportsmanship, giant figures in purple and gold, novel exponents of the ancient game. They looked with hope and expectations to 1952, and many hurling followers felt they were All-Ireland material. And so to the Leinster final at Nowlan Park against Dublin. It seemed a mere formality, even more so when it was learned that not all the Dublin team had travelled.

Paddy had an outstanding game at wing-half-back, and it seemed to him in the first half that the Wexford forwards were toying with the Dublin backs — but not scoring enough. Yet at half time it looked safe — 2:5 to 2:1. The victory speech was ready. Then disaster. Three second-half goals to Dublin in quick succession, and Wexford couldn't respond. It finished 7:2 to 3:6. Supporters were stunned and silenced and travelled home shattered.

When the final whistle blew in 1954 and Cork had defeated Wexford by 1:9 to 1:6, Paddy began to wonder if his hurling career would finish like his football one: no All-Ireland medal. It's the one game Paddy would dearly love to play all over again, for he is convinced it should never have been lost. 'The forwards didn't click — in scoring terms, that is. We had so much possession, lost so many scores. In our anxiety we didn't always see better-placed colleagues.'

It is easy to understand why Wexford saw it as one they let slip; easy to understand too why players began to feel concerned about ultimate success and All-Ireland glory. They had contested five successive Leinster finals, won two, and failed in two All-Ireland finals. The psychological barrier was building up.

Wexford 1955. Paddy Kehoe is fifth from the left in the front row.

Success must come soon, or else ... Cold analysis reveals that individually Wexford had many outstanding hurlers, backed up by excellent physique and admirable temperament. What was lacking was the craft and cunning, the cohesion and combination, the confidence and composure, that comes with tradition and victory.

Paddy looked forward to 1955 and hoped that fortune would favour them. It would be his third All-Ireland final. Kilkenny fell in the Leinster final after a replay; Limerick had to give way in the All-Ireland semi-final; Galway were the victims in the final. 'I will always remember the time of the full-time whistle, blown by Bob Stakelum of Tipperary, 4:31 p.m., Sunday the fourth of September. Wexford All-Ireland champions — first time in forty-five years.' For Paddy a dream come true: a cherished All-Ireland medal. At thirty-three years of age, they don't come much later.

Confidence and composure — by-products of success — were now present in Wexford hurling. More glory and laurels followed for Paddy and Wexford in 1956. There was the defeat of Tipperary in the unforgettable comeback in the league final; a Leinster title at the expense of Kilkenny in a cliffhanger; defeat for Cork in a pulsating final, watched by over 83,000 spectators. Wexford were now supreme: all the great hurling powers — Galway, Limerick, Kilkenny, Cork, and Tipperary — had fallen to them. It was a good year to retire.

He weighs 16 stone and never forget
He has the heart of a tiger and the speed of
* a jet,*
Better keep your distance if you want to
* grow*
When you're playing on a man called
* Paddy Kehoe.*

Paddy chose the following team:

Tony Reddan *(Tipperary)*

Andy Fleming *(Waterford)*   Nick O'Donnell *(Wexford)*   Bobbie Rackard *(Wexford)*

Matt Fouhy *(Cork)*   Pat Stakelum *(Tipperary)*   Vin Baston *(Waterford)*

Harry Gray *(Laois)*   Jack Lynch *(Cork)*

Paddy Kehoe *(Wexford)*   Mick Mackey *(Limerick)*   Christy Ring *(Cork)*

Josie Gallagher *(Galway)*   Nicky Rackard *(Wexford)*   Eddie Keher *(Kilkenny)*

Hurlers and All

He gently tugs his father's coat, Mam
said, 'Keep close now, Pat,'
You're goin' to a hurling match, your
first — remember that.
Don't get lost in that big crowd, bless
yourself when goin' out,
And after, in the pub, be quiet — let
Daddy drink his stout.'
And so I saw the mighty game and traced
the sliotar's flight,
The flashing ash, the roaring crowd, the
colours all about.
I pinched myself, looked up at Dad, so
proud that I was there.
Such drama, action, music, laughter —
splendour everywhere.
The years rolled on and, oh, the joy of
balancing the ball
On the bos, and then a toss, against the
gable wall.
My first day on the Claughaun team — a
boy, but I was proud
To be a hurler — I could have cried or
shouted it aloud.
Then to the Brothers, Harty Cup — the
Brother's name was Tynan,
A Tipperary man for sure and one you
could rely on.
At physics, maths and Latin, a genius at
his station,

Born 1932

But hurling was his burning love, an
Irish celebration.
The county team then beckoned on, an
honourable promotion.
With hurling games in Munster, such
passion and emotion.
Limerick, Cork, Tipperary, Clare — the
proud men of the Decies,
The ebb and flow of luck and woe — the
hope one never reaches.
And through the crowd the calls come
loud, some good and many strange
sounds,
'Get the lead out of your arses, boys,'
'Come on, ye Mackey greyhounds.'
'Doubt ya boy' — there goes the cry,
Ringey has awoken,
He's won the match with lightning dash,
all Limerick hearts are broken.
And so the hurlers come and go, today's
lads are much faster,
With helmets, shin guards, rubs and pills
that make the ball go farther.
Names come tumbling through my mind:
Mick Mackey, Power, and Ringey,
The Rackards, Bobbie, Nick, and Bill, and
who'd forget bould Youngie,
The 'Rattler', 'Diamond', 'Goggles',
'Fox', Con Murphy, Connolly brothers,
Smyth, Hayes of Clare, McKenna, Keher,
Doyle, Stakelum, and others.
The writers John D., Raymond Smyth,
Fullam, Paddy Downey,
Norman Allen, Austin Flynn, and
singing Joe McDonagh,
O'Hehir, Ó Muircheartaigh, Ó Síocháin,
Ó Dúlaing, Tynan, Cregan,
Herbert, Hartigan — I could go on, but
you'd be here all evenin'.
The shadows stalk the gable wall —
there's no-one left to shout,
Pull the door as you cross the floor, and
bless when goin' out.

D. J. Carey, the Kilkenny hurler, in action (1996).

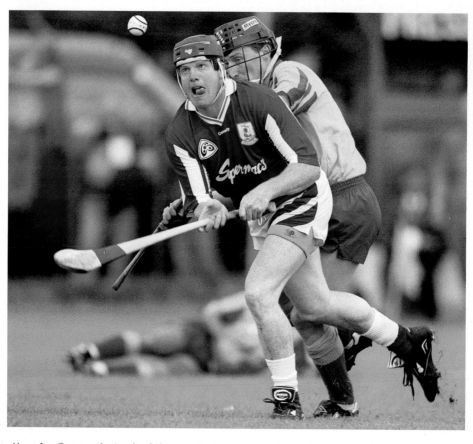

Above: Joe Cooney playing for Galway against Roscommon in the Connacht final of 1997.

Right top: Ciarán Carey of Limerick playing against Tipperary (1997).

Right bottom: Ciarán Carey racing away from Rory McCarthy (Wexford) in the All-Ireland final (1996).

Above: Cork goalkeeper Ger Cunningham (1997).

Left: Pete Finnerty (Galway) in action in the 1993 All-Ireland final.

Many years after he had retired from the game of hurling, Dermot travelled with his friend Séamus MacCrossan to Africa. Séamus was selling the lottery concept to the Gambian government in Banjul, and Dermot travelled with him to give financial advice. 'In the course of our journey we travelled through some rough territory, and at one point our guide pointed out a Catholic school. We stopped and strolled around. There were kids everywhere, all dressed in lovely uniforms. We went in a door at the side and down along a corridor. I saw a white guy on a bench overseeing pupils. "Hello," I said. "How are you?" he replied in the friendliest of tones, and followed up immediately saying, "1955 — 1:12, Munster final, Limerick v. Clare — Dermot Kelly." I couldn't believe it. I was dumbfounded. The man turned out to be a Holy Ghost father, a north Kerry man, and he was at the Gaelic grounds in Limerick on that Munster final day. We stayed on, and that night we all attended a wonderful celebration, which included the local bishop.'

1955 was a rather remarkable year in Munster hurling. Cork, All-Ireland champions, lost to Clare in the first round at Thurles. Any thoughts that it might have been a fluke were dispelled when Clare followed up with a second-round victory over the league title holders, Tipperary, at Limerick Gaelic grounds. They were playing the kind of hurling they served up when defeating Wexford in an Oireachtas final replay in 1954 — 3:6 to 0:12 — both games thrillers. They had the look of potential All-Ireland champions about them: physically strong and well balanced throughout the field. Meanwhile Limerick, without seeming impressive, defeated Waterford and qualified for a Munster final showdown with Clare — their second such meeting.

It was a scorching July day. Clare were firm favourites. The great Mick Mackey had trained Limerick. A Nigerian bishop threw in the ball. The scene was set. The final whistle produced a shock

Dermot Kelly with Christy Ring (1978) at the Cork Guinness reception for the Hurlers' Association

result: Limerick 2:16, Clare 2:6; and of the Limerick total Dermot registered 1:12. He was fed by a forward line — Ralph Prendergast, Liam Ryan, Vivian Cobbe, Gerry Fitzgerald, and Seán Leonard — that used the open spaces to the maximum and combined speed and first-time hurling to almost the point of perfection. That may well have been Dermot's greatest hour; but in the semifinal that followed, Billy Rackard, the Wexford centre-back, will tell you that for the first thirty minutes of that game Dermot was the best he ever encountered.

It was a novel pairing, Limerick v. Wexford — the first time the counties faced each other in a semi-final. It really gripped the imagination of hurling followers. Almost 60,000 thronged Croke Park — a record for a semi-final. After a first half of delightful hurling the teams retired at the interval, Limerick with a slender lead.

In the second half the Wexford half-forward line took over and in the end had a comfortable nine-point win. Wexford's experience — they had been building it up gradually over a six-year period since the Leinster final of 1950 — and their familiarity with Croke Park, proved to be a trump card. But they also made a few shrewd and telling second-half switches, and this, coupled with their physique, gradually wore down the Limerickmen, who were young and inexperienced and had just emerged from nowhere to take the Munster crown.

When the sports writer John D. Hickey picked his Ireland team in the *Irish Independent* on 19 January 1956 he selected Dermot at centre-forward. 'I accept Dermot Kelly's [Limerick] display in this year's Munster final for what it was, the best exhibition of centre-forward play we have seen in years, and he goes in unchallenged.'

Dermot played his colleges hurling with Limerick (Sexton Street) CBS and was selected on the Munster colleges team in 1950 and '51, winning the '51 title with a victory over Connacht. Team-mates in that victory were Austin Flynn of Waterford and Tony Wall of Tipperary.

He got his baptism of fire in Munster championship hurling in Thurles in 1951, when he was selected at right-half-forward on the Limerick team to play Tipperary, reigning All-Ireland champions; his opponent, the renowned and vastly experienced Tommy Doyle. He knew what it could be like to face an opponent of intimidating reputation. 'I was playing for City Gaels against Ahane in 1950. Mick Mackey, who was playing with Ahane, used in the course of his work sometimes drop in to our house. Naturally I was rather in awe of him. We got a 21-yard free — a crucial one. I was bending over the ball when Mick walked behind me and said, "Young Kelly, you have a lot to learn about this game yet." This was Mick Mackey the playboy. Yes, you guessed right. I missed the free.'

The three greatest hurling personalities Dermot met in his time were Jim Young, Mickey Byrne, and Jackie Power. 'Humour, fun and banter was central to all three.

Dermot Kelly with Mick Mackey (1980) at the All-Stars' Banquet.

'The most exciting team I ever saw was Wexford. I say that as a spectator — manly, fine-looking, clean and sporting; so strong; so dramatic. The Cork-Tipperary games of the early fifties were the best I saw.'

Dermot's wife, Breda, comes from a Tipperary family steeped in GAA history. Her uncle Jim played at centre-field on the Tipperary football team on Bloody Sunday. Her father, Mick, won a county football medal with Templemore in the mid-twenties. It is a beautiful medal and is worn by Breda as a cherished possession. While holidaying in America she missed it after playing a game of golf. Frantic searches and much retracing of steps failed to find it. With a sense of despair she put notices up in the golf club and elsewhere. Three months after returning home, and to her great delight, it arrived in the post. It was found in a sand bunker. Given the security measures now in place, a repeat loss is unlikely.

Dermot retired at a young age. So many defeats influenced his decision. 'Anyway, I wasn't training, and I was playing county football and hurling and club football and hurling — no point in fooling yourself: I felt it was time to go. The early fifties were lean, troubled and difficult days in Limerick hurling. I remember one championship match when we scored only one point against Waterford. In another game Clare trounced us when Jimmy Smyth scored, I think, six goals and a number of points. Hope began to dawn when we won the Munster title in 1955. Earlier that year we played Kilkenny in a challenge, following which I was convinced we had the makings of a good team. We looked like repeating the '55 success the following year, when we led Cork by two goals coming to the closing stages of the Munster final. Then came what was probably one of Ring's most dramatic turnarounds in an extraordinary match.

'Years later I asked him how he got those three goals. "I changed my hurley," he said, "and then I knew we had it." I reminded him that he threw one of them into the net and waved the green flag himself, and when I asked him who was marking him in those last ten minutes he said, "No-one." Ring, of course, would drift away from an opponent if it suited him. He would decide for himself what to do: he wouldn't necessarily wait for the mentors to make a decision.'

Limerick lost another superb game of hurling in the National League final of 1958 against Wexford, 5:7 to 4:8. That day they were captained by Dermot, who lined out at corner-back. He was captain of Munster in 1956 when they failed to Leinster in the Railway Cup final. All in all his decade in the top time yielded few rewards in the form of major trophies: a Munster title in 1955, Railway Cup honours in 1957 and '60, two county titles in 1957 and '58. Yet he made a lasting impact.

Abandoning the playing fields left him with more time for other activities. In 1972 he conceived the idea of a Hurlers' Association The first meeting was held in Hayes's Hotel in Thurles that year and was attended by Séamus Ryan, Pat Stakelum, Timmy Maher, Mick Hayes, P.J. Garvan, Jim Young, John McGrath, Denis Murphy, Jimmy Duggan, and Matt Nugent. Dermot was Secretary from 1972 until 1984.

There was of course his singing and music. And a right good song he can sing too, specialising in Percy French and compositions of his own. He became the first minstrel in Bunratty Castle in 1963. The hurling days are long past, but the singing days endure, and his many fine renderings — I can guarantee that they shorten the longest of car journeys — are available on tape for the benefit of music lovers, with a CD in the offing.

Born 1926

1948. However, he lost out on a medal, as only twenty-one medals are awarded. His county career — a brilliant one — ended in 1962 when Waterford lost heavily to Tipperary in the Munster championship, 5:14 to 2:3.

In a long innings, the major honours were relatively few, but the satisfaction derived from just playing the game and the friendships that followed richly rewarded John. When he closes his eyes and reflects on his hurling days, 'the honour of having seen Mick Mackey, Christy Ring, John Keane and Vin Baston in action, with all their hurling skills — four of the greatest — is second only to the thrill of the All-Ireland win of 1959 over Kilkenny after a replay.' And then John named with affection those forward colleagues of the '57 and '59 finals: Larry Guinan, Frankie Walsh, Tom Cheasty, Mick Flannelly, Dónal Whelan, and Tom Cunningham — a set of forwards who whipped the sliotar thither and yon, in sweeping ground movements, stretching the best of defences and creating openings for many a fine score. And then he drifted back in time to recall great names of an earlier era: Jim and Charlie Ware, Mick Hickey, Johnny O'Connor, Willie Barron, and Andy Fleming.

He played with Munster in the Railway Cup finals of 1952 and '54. 'I was partnered at midfield by two great Tipperary players, Phil Shanahan in '52 and John Hough in '54. We beat Connacht in '52 but lost to Leinster in '54' — the first Leinster win in the competition since 1941. He played in the semi-final against Connacht in '57 and was a sub in the final, when he won his second Railway Cup medal.

'Suit-length competitions' were a great attraction in the early days of John's career — and a much-coveted prize it was. ' I remember we played

66

It was a great honour to have played for Waterford and to have made so many friends.

John Kiely 99

J ohn grew up listening to his uncle, that great dual player Christy Moylan, 'who was always talking about the deeds of Jackie Power, Paddy Clohessy, Paddy Scanlon, and Dick Stokes.' John also played both codes; but as a sub against Kerry in the early fifties he watched Diarmuid Hannafin, who was well over six feet, soar into the air for the dropping ball and thought to himself, 'I'd need a ladder to get up with the likes of him; I'm too small for football; I'll stick with hurling.'

He was part of a panel of twenty-five when Waterford won the All-Ireland in

Waterford 1959. John Kiely is in the back row, fourth from the left.

Cork in Cork in 1953 — imagine it: a suit length. Well, for over fifty minutes Jackie Goode held Ring. We were winning. Then in the closing minutes Ring got two goals and we lost. I remember the first of those goals. The ball came to the left side of Ring; he went to pull but instead tapped the ball to his right, then pulled and stuck the ball in the net.' And John rose to his feet as he recounted the event in detail and demonstrated Ring's actions on the ball. 'We should have beaten Cork in the Munster championship of '56, but again late goals by Ring and a great display by Gerald Murphy beat us.'

During his days in London, John played with Seán McDermotts and won a London senior hurling title in the early sixties. 'I met many fine hurlers: Paddy Egan, Fintan Spillane and Billy Duffy from Galway, Phil Wilson and John King Redmond from Wexford, Mick and Paul Carmody and Billy Hayes from Limerick. Hurling was hard and physical in London.' He pointed to a nose scar as if to confirm it. John played in an intermediate final with London against Wexford but lost.

In later life he took up handball and performed with distinction. In 1983 he won the Golden Masters singles title. In 1989 and '90 he won the Golden Masters doubles, his partner Déaglán Mulcahy. In 1993 he won the Diamond Masters singles. He has won the Munster title for the past four years, 1993–96, but failed at All-Ireland semi-final and final level. In all, between Golden Masters and Diamond Masters he has won eighteen Munster titles. Seventy years of age and still winning handball titles — absolutely magnificent. No wonder his club, Kilgobnet, is immensely proud of him and has granted him life membership.

Father M.J. Ryan, now parish priest in Stradbally, County Waterford, played with John at club and county level until the mid-fifties. Here is an excerpt from a tribute he paid to John in an article in *An Déiseach* in 1974: 'Looking back on his playing days every man has golden memories, and indeed, my most enjoyable years hurling was the 1952/53 season when I played junior hurling with Éire Óg (Dungarvan). I had the unique experience of playing at centrefield with John Kiely. His enthusiasm for that year's junior championship, which we won easily, was as great as for any of his major tournaments.

'What can one say of John Kiely ... but that he was the complete hurler. He had all the gifts, intelligence, speed, power, unselfishness and an abundance of skill. One can look at a player from the sideline and not appreciate his qualities, even form strange ideas of him. But, if you partner John Kiely at midfield, as I did, you could have nothing but admiration for him, his style and his benefit to the team.

'Before the game John was always tense. No useless talk. From the moment he got togged out he concentrated. His mental approach to the game was admirable. As play began, the human dynamo just exploded into action. He never stopped. He ran, he jigged, he zigzagged, he literally distracted his opponent. The opponent was constantly looking for him and following *him*.

'The crowd enjoyed his play. They appreciated his skill. But, he was still detached from them. No-one could ever say he was a showman. No. But he was one of our really great players. He played a hard, non-stop, skilful game. He concentrated on the success of the team, and he wanted little of the glory himself.

'I shall never forget the clash between himself and Christy Ring in the Munster championship in Thurles in July 1954. They had a similar style and approach to the game, equal energy and, to me, an equality in skill. The consequence of such a clash was inevitable — no game. They just neutralised each other.

'To me it was a great experience and great fun to have played with him. His short expressions of encouragement during the game were invaluable. You had to share the rough and tough of centrefield with him to appreciate the man and estimate his hurling ability.'

John is one of hurling's quiet and retiring personalities. However, as you lead him deep into the territory of hurling memories and colleagues of bygone days the veil of shyness slowly lifts like a morning mist, and as he relaxes and recalls moments from the past there comes a smile that conveys to you how much hurling enriched his life, how much there was in that wonderful game for him, not only at home in Ireland but also during his days spent in England.

Born 1920

we would go to the bog to save the turf, together with some neighbours. We would bring the hurleys with us in the pony and cart. Callaghy's house was beside the bog. Mrs Callaghy would boil the kettle at lunch hour; after eating we would get the hurleys and spend half an hour practising. Everything was grand until my father heard about it. He put a stop to hurling in the bog. **"**

Joe Killeen

It was the afternoon of Sunday 27 July 1947. I was with friends in the Roches' house in the village of Ardagh. We were all glued to the radio. Micheál O'Hehir was transferring the excitement that was unfolding at Birr in the All-Ireland hurling semi-final between Galway and Kilkenny into the kitchen where we were gathered. The atmosphere was electric. Our young hearts were with the underdog — Galway. Normal time up, and Galway two points ahead. Surely they were heading for their first All-Ireland final since 1929! Then disaster: a point by Langton; a point from a free by Leahy; with the last puck of the game a point by Langton and victory, 2:9 to 1:11. We felt for Galway: so near and yet so far.

" In my young days in Tynagh the hurling was done on our lawn. The players left their hurleys in our house. Names I remember include Father Connie Boyle (RIP), Hubert Gordon, Ailbe (RIP) and Father Declan, the Keighery brothers, Keily brothers, Casey brothers, Regans, and Hobans. There were four of us: James (RIP), who played for Galway several times, including the 1947 semi-final against Kilkenny, Matt and Michael, who played a few times for Galway, and myself.

I always remember when we would be going to play for the club. My mother would be at the door with the holy water, telling us, "No fighting." We did our best, but sometimes failed. She always wanted us to play the game as it should be played.

The only mode of conveyance in our young days was a horse and dray. It would carry about fifteen of us; the rest of us would travel on bikes. Often we togged out by the side of the fence, and in Loughrea we togged in McNamee's loft. I remember when we were young

John Killeen, 'who never did anything but hurl day and night,' remembers it well. 'It's the one game I would love to play all over again. I felt we were robbed of victory: we let it slip. Paddy Gantly gave an exhibition of hurling that day in the last quarter as good as I ever saw — left and right.' It was a game in which John Killeen and Paddy Gantly held sway at midfield. They had a great understanding and were a wonderful partnership — could match the best of their day, could outplay most. 'It was the best team I played on. Earlier that year we beat Munster in a delayed Railway Cup final on the sixth of April — full of stars: Tommy Doyle of Tipp, Jackie Power and Peter Cregan of Limerick, Christy Ring and Jack Lynch of Cork, John Keane, Andy Fleming, Mick Hayes and Vin Baston of Waterford.

'I remember in that game Mick Ryan of Limerick came on for the injured Mick Hayes of Waterford. When he came on he said to me, "Did you do much training for this game?" "A fair bit," I said. "I'm not fit at all," said Mick. I believe we would have won the All-Ireland in '47 if we had beaten Kilkenny at Birr. It was a very well-balanced team; we were fierce unlucky.'

John hails from Tynagh, a parish that gave great names to Galway hurling. 'Ignatius Harney, my hero — a lovely hurler who always played wearing a hat. I played with him one day in a club tournament. The ball came my way. I blocked, lifted, handled, struck. "Don't handle it," said Ignatius to me — "lift and strike in the one movement; block and strike in the one movement." Speed of action on the ball was his motto. He was on the 1923 winning team, together with Mick Kenny, Anthony Kelly, Mick Derivan — a great corner-back; Jim Power — who celebrated his hundredth birthday on the seventh of November last [1995]; didn't look big in his clothes but he togged out a fierce man." Hubert Gordon, a lovely clean hurler, was there in my time. There was also Father Connie Boyle, a gifted hurler who played some games for Galway, but after ordination church rules barred him from playing. He was ordained in 1945 for the missions in Canada, then he was struck ill. He never got to the missions. I used visit him in hospital — a lovely big man. I saw him gradually fade away; he died in 1947.'

Among his most special memories of games is a club encounter against the army in a county semi-final. He was opposed by Vin Baston of Waterford, who was partnered by Tommy Moroney — both county players. A newspaper report stated: 'At midfield Army stars Baston and Moroney caught a tartar in Killeen and newcomer Hough.' It seems that the exchanges between, and the individual performances of, John Killeen and Vin Baston were a hurling treat.

Special too was the 1953 All-Ireland semi-final victory over Kilkenny. 'Hurrah for the men of the West,' wrote one reporter, who went on to say: 'Biggest successes of the winning side were John Killeen and Hubert Gordon, and their power play during Galway's devastating dash to snatch victory from Kilkenny on Sunday will be etched in the minds and hearts of all who were privileged to witness it.' It was a game in which John scored two vital and brilliant goals. His display won for him Sports Star of the Week.

Earlier that year — it was the twilight of his career — he was outstanding in a

---

This is John's team:

	Seán Duggan *(Galway)*	
Bobbie Rackard *(Wexford)*	Nick O'Donnell *(Wexford)*	Willie Fahy *(Galway)*
Tommy Doyle *(Tipperary)*	Pat Stakelum *(Tipperary)*	Vin Baston *(Waterford)*
Paddy Gantly *(Galway)*	John Killeen *(Galway)*	
Josie Gallagher *(Galway)*	Mick Mackey *(Limerick)*	Jim Langton *(Kilkenny)*
Jimmy Smyth *(Clare)*	Nicky Rackard *(Wexford)*	Christy Ring *(Cork)*

And having picked the team, he did what many of those who valiantly ventured to select a great fifteen did: paused; got an attack of the scruples; wondered where he had left Joe Salmon, Paddy Phelan, Jackie Power, Jimmy Finn and Jack Lynch. He stopped at that — no point in adding further to the scruples!

Railway Cup semi-final lost to Leinster. One newspaper report said: 'Joe Salmon and John Killeen ruled the roost at midfield and plied the Galway forwards with numerous opportunities ... Killeen at centrefield and later in the half-forward line was Man of the Match for Galway. Age did not appear to cramp this veteran's style.'

The All-Ireland final against Cork was lost, 3:3 to 0:8, Cork's third goal coming in injury time. 'It was an All-Ireland we might have won. The defence should have been left intact. Letting Mickey Burke follow Ring to midfield was a blunder. The further away Ring was from goal, the less a threat he was.'

His worst experience was losing to Laois in the 1949 All-Ireland semi-final. 'We gave it less thought than we should. Our eyes were focused on Tipp. It poured out of the heavens. We took the game for granted. It went wrong after about fifteen minutes and we couldn't put it right. For regrets, nothing comes near that.' The following year John came to live in Laois and won two county senior titles with Clonad in 1953 and '54.

He recalled an amusing story from a game against Cork at the official opening of Casement Park, Belfast, in 1953. 'Before the game I said to Joe Salmon, "I bet a pound I'll score the first one ever scored in Casement Park." "You're on," said Joe. The game began, and early on Joe got an easy chance to score a point. As he got possession I shouted for a pass, which he delivered without thinking. I took my easy point, ran past Joe smiling and said, "You owe me a pound."'

The victory over Wexford in the home final of the 1951 National League, 6:7 to 3:4, was a tremendous boost to Galway hurling. When John joined the Galway panel in 1944 he could look to a past in the county that produced excellent individual hurlers, many good teams, club hurling of a high standard, but few county successes. The rewards and achievements were meagre: a senior All-Ireland title in 1923, a National League title in 1932, and a junior All-

John Killeen and his wife Chris.

Ireland crown in 1939. The National League success in 1932 was snatched from the jaws of defeat in the final moments when a well-taken goal left the final score reading Galway 4:5, Tipperary 4:4.

Now in 1951 another psychological barrier had been pierced, following the Railway Cup success in 1947. The prize was a trip to America to play New York in the final. 'It was the trip of a lifetime. We flew out; were treated royally; beat New York 2:11 to 2:8; came home by boat, the *New Amsterdam*. The boat trip took four-and-a-half days; it was great.' No wonder it was! Just take a look at the breakfast menu (*see next page*).

It's interesting to recall that the New York goalkeeper in that 1951 League final was Pat Leamy, who emigrated from Tipperary. He was fifty-three years of age when he played in that game against Galway. He made brilliant saves but was beaten for one soft goal. In 1932 he had hurled with the American team in the Tailteann Games at Croke Park.

In the course of conversation the following names and comments surfaced. 'Bobbie Rackard — he was class. What a wonderful defender! Will I ever forget his display at full-back in the last quarter of the All-Ireland final against Cork in 1954! Seánie Duggan — his goalkeeping displays in the Oireachtas finals against Wexford in 1950 and 1952 were among the best I have seen. Phil Shanahan — he was always very fit and strong; the hardest I got to handle; one of the best I met. Christy Ring — well, he was the master, wasn't he? Joe Salmon — he was a first-class player, a fine midfielder and overhead striker; a gentleman and a very clean player. Paddy Gantly — it was a pleasure to play beside him. We had a great understanding. He was a strong player with all the skills, and he could hit left and right. Josie Gallagher — he was one of the game's greatest forwards. Willie Fahy — one of the best ever cornerbacks.'

John left me with this thought: 'After a game, having played the ball, it's great to be able to meet your opponent face to face and shake hands.'

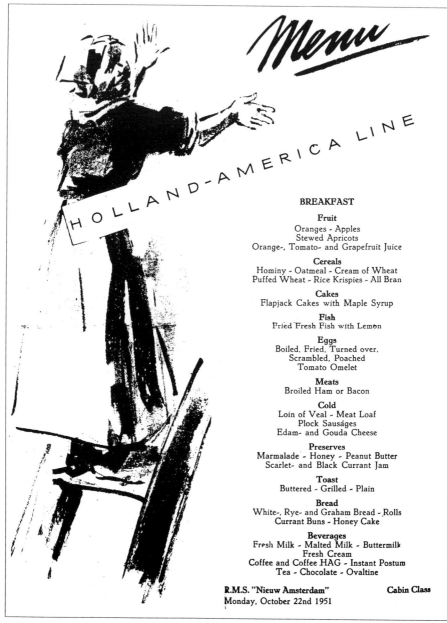

Menu

HOLLAND-AMERICA LINE

BREAKFAST

Fruit
Oranges - Apples
Stewed Apricots
Orange-, Tomato- and Grapefruit Juice

Cereals
Hominy - Oatmeal - Cream of Wheat
Puffed Wheat - Rice Krispies - All Bran

Cakes
Flapjack Cakes with Maple Syrup

Fish
Fried Fresh Fish with Lemon

Eggs
Boiled, Fried, Turned over,
Scrambled, Poached
Tomato Omelet

Meats
Broiled Ham or Bacon

Cold
Loin of Veal - Meat Loaf
Plock Sausages
Edam- and Gouda Cheese

Preserves
Marmalade - Honey - Peanut Butter
Scarlet- and Black Currant Jam

Toast
Buttered - Grilled - Plain

Bread
White-, Rye- and Graham Bread - Rolls
Currant Buns - Honey Cake

Beverages
Fresh Milk - Malted Milk - Buttermilk
Fresh Cream
Coffee and Coffee HAG - Instant Postum
Tea - Chocolate - Ovaltine

R.M.S. "Nieuw Amsterdam" Cabin Class
Monday, October 22nd 1951

Born 1967

"

For me the greatest gift in life was when my mother and father gave me a hurley and ball. Since then my life has always been around a game of hurling. Having watched my uncles playing for my parish, Patrickswell, and then for Limerick, the thrill I got from putting on the 'Well' jersey was so special and made me so proud to play for the parish. As a young fellow the minute I came in from school I would go up to the field with my good friend Patrick Carey and we would play away until we were called home. We would practise all the skills until we got them right. I never won anything with the club until I was fifteen, but the enjoyment was everything.

In 1984 — it was a year I'll never forget — everything seemed to go right for me, in that (1) I got picked to play for Limerick minors and ended up winning an All-Ireland, (2) a dream had come true, in that I made the Patrickswell seniors and in the process played with my great-uncle Richard Bennis and went on to win the county.

In 1986 I made my Limerick senior

début, and from there everything has gone well. Won an under-21 All-Ireland in '87 but had my greatest disappointment in '91, when we lost the All-Ireland club. I will never forget the feeling coming into the station in Limerick and to see the number of Patrickswell people taking over the station. It was one regret I have so far in my hurling life, not having the cup for a fantastic parish. The year ended on a high for me in that I won my first All-Star.

Hurling with Limerick has had its ups and downs, but I've really enjoyed every bit of it. The people I have met and have become great friends with could only have happened because of hurling. My greatest and fondest memory would have to be in 1994, looking down on the Thurles field, seeing it full with Limerick people waving their green and white, and here I am about to lift the Munster Cup after beating Clare. It is a moment I'll never forget. Also leading the Limerick team out onto the field on All-Ireland day was a great honour. The disappointment of losing that game was forgotten when we saw the crowd on our homecoming. It just told us what enjoyment we gave to these people.

Hurling has been very good to me and is a game that I would wish every young fellow would play — the enjoyment you get, the exercise you get, the thrill of the game, the social side of it, but best of all the people you meet. One man who I can thank a lot for my success would be Phil Bennis. He taught me everything I know and was always helping me.

"

'Sport is one of life's pleasures,' wrote Con Houlihan. Someone also wrote that it is full of beauty, drama, tragedy, and disappointment. Gary can identify with all of this. It is now more than ten years since he first proudly donned the green and white of Limerick in the league campaign of 1986/87. Many honours, much drama and lots of memories have been packed into that decade. And in that time he came to admire two opponents in particular: Bobby Ryan of Tipperary and Jim Cashman of Cork. And regarding D.J. Carey of Kilkenny he said: 'Who wouldn't admire his incredible level of skills!'

Indeed, before his senior days the drama and excitement began. It was the minor final of 1984, the Centenary year of the GAA, the venue Thurles. Semple Stadium was packed to capacity for the senior final between Cork and Offaly. In the minor game, Limerick, with Gary at centre-forward and leading by twelve points, were heading for an easy win when suddenly, well into the last quarter, Kilkenny staged a typical rally, and a succession of goals put them a point ahead. It was literally with the last stroke of the match that Limerick snatched the equaliser.

The replay at the same venue was a classic. Paddy Downey in his match report had this to say: 'Hurling at its best is a beautifully balanced blend of silken skills and fierce man-to-man combat, a spectacle of sport that almost beggars description. The replay of the All-Ireland minor final between Limerick and Kilkenny at Semple Stadium yesterday was such a spectacle ... no better hurling match has been played in any grade this year.' With seven minutes to go, Limerick were two points in arrears. Then Colm Coughlan, a substitute, took a pass from Gary Kirby and scored the winning goal with a powerful shot from an acute angle at the right of the town end. Gary's first All-Ireland medal; Limerick's third minor title.

As a forward he has been one of the game's most prolific scorers. A few samples will illustrate. In the county championship of 1996 he scored 2:6 against Doon, 1:7 against Claughaun, 2:10 against Na Piarsaigh, and 3:9 against Adare. In 1994 against Cork in the Munster championship he scored 2:5 out of a total of 4:14, and in the Munster final against Clare he scored eleven of Limerick's twenty-five points. When Limerick met Clare in the Munster semi-final of 1996 Gary put his name on 1:7 of Limerick's total of 1:13, and when they drew with Tipperary in the Munster final he scored ten of Limerick's nineteen points.

In that game Limerick were two points down and time was running out when they won a seventy. I wondered if Gary had been tempted to lob it in and hope for a winning goal. 'No. I asked the referee about the time and he said there were two minutes to go. I pointed it, and Frankie Carroll added the equaliser.' Many of Gary's scores have carried the mark of class — the touch of a master.

He is intensely proud of his club, Patrickswell, with whom he has so far won six county senior titles. He will always remember the immense pride felt by everyone when the club won its first Munster senior title in 1988. In many ways, however, it was dwarfed by the win in 1990. 'This was something else. We beat Éire Óg of Ennis by 8 points to 6 in a fiercely contested final; and we did it without Ciarán [Carey]. His absence through suspension was a bit controversial and it bothered us. Not only were we missing him but we finished the game with fourteen men — one of our proudest days.' Over the years this scrupulously clean performer has put a lot into the club through training and coaching the under-age players. At present he manages the senior camogie team and trains the camogie players of all grades. This includes his wife, Carmel, from Kinsale, who is an enthusiastic member of the senior team.

Only two unfulfilled dreams remain. 'Everything I could win in Munster has been won, and that includes an under-16 title with Limerick City.' He cap-

Gary Kirby in action against Antrim.

tained a winning Munster Railway Cup team in '95 and has won three medals in all. In 1987 he had the honour of being captain of the Irish under-21 shinty team. His National League medal came after a most dramatic game with Tipperary in 1992, played in atrocious weather. Aided by the breeze in the second half, they gradually chipped away at an eight-point deficit to draw level; and then, with the game in injury time, Declan Nash soloed out of defence and sent a clearance down towards the right corner. From there a cross by Joe O'Connor was met by the in-running Ray Sampson, who, without handling, batted the sliotar over the bar for the lead for Limerick for the first time in the game — and the winner.

Gary's class and consistency are reflected in four All-Star awards, the first in 1991 and then three in a row, '94, '95, and '96. 'There are only two gaps: an All-Ireland club title with Patrickswell; an All-Ireland senior title with Limerick.'

He knows what it is like to have the summit in sight — to be within a whisker of victory, to know that it was achievable — only to see the prize snatched, the hopes dashed. Regarding the 1991 club final against Glenmore he says: 'I'd like to have got a second shot at it. They won by four points. Personally, I didn't have a good game. Even though I lost two All-Irelands, losing for the club against Glenmore was my worst memory. You never know beforehand how a game is going to go for you. This year [1996] in the Munster semi-final against Wolfe Tones I felt great as I took the field. Out there I wasn't able to move — wanted to, but wasn't able.'

At county level there was the All-Ireland defeat of 1994 at the hands of Offaly when he was captain, followed by another defeat two years later by the men of Wexford. 'Even though we lost the All-Ireland of '94 I'll always remember the atmosphere of the day. It was something else. Something happened that day in the last five minutes. You can't analyse it: it was a huge disappointment — a feeling you wouldn't wish on anyone. Seven minutes to go and you felt you would be going up to collect the cup; then all of a sudden the Offaly players are milling around and ...

'In '96 I got a broken finger in the first five minutes. I remember going over towards the Cusack Stand to take a free from near midfield. I was trying to stop the bleeding before I took it — it was pouring from the finger. As I took the free I felt the searing pain go up my hand.' The question has been posed whether it would have been wise then to move Gary to full-forward. 'Well, I'd play anywhere. I'm playing full-forward with my club at the moment. In a way I regret I didn't go in full-forward, but I wouldn't go without being told. A lot of ball bypassed the centre-forward position that day.' So what about the two unfulfilled dreams? Despite the disappointment, Gary, true sportsman that he is, simply said, 'I'll be trying.'

We know he will, and if there is such a thing as deserving an All-Ireland medal, Gary surely does. We all wish him well.

> Take this honey for your bitterest cup;
> There is no failure save in giving up;
> There's no real fall so long as one still tries
> For seeming setbacks make the strong man wise.

Born 1941

Leinster team to win this highly valued championship. Receiving the cup that day for my club was probably the highlight of my sporting career.

Later that year we went on to win again our own county championship, beating the Rower-Inistioge in the final. This meant a lot to us, as no other reigning All-Ireland club champions had succeeded in retaining their own county championship.

Before retiring I had the pleasure of tasting success at local and national level again. In 1981 we beat the Fenians in the county final and went on to contest the All-Ireland again, against renowned Mount Sion. The final was once more played in Thurles, and we had a thrilling victory over very difficult opponents. It was great to win this final so late in my career, and I look back on my years playing with James Stephens with great pride and sense of achievement.

" The years 1969–1982 were very successful ones for my club, James Stephens. During that time we contested seven county championship finals, winning four.

One of the real highlights of my career was our championship victory over the Fenians in 1969. This was our first success since 1937, so naturally there was great excitement and celebration in the 'Village'.

Our next big year was 1975, when I had the honour of captaining James Stephens. We beat Galmoy in the county final and thus qualified to represent Kilkenny in the All-Ireland club championship for the first time. After a great Leinster campaign, including a thrilling victory over Buffer's Alley in Wexford Park, we won our semi-final and qualified to meet famed Blackrock in the All-Ireland final at Semple Stadium. After a terrific game against powerful opponents we emerged victorious and became the first Kilkenny and

F an's father, Paddy, small in stature and sporting a peaked cap, was an outstanding hurling stalwart of the thirties. He had a career to be proud of. When I mentioned this to Fan he dismissed it in light-hearted, mischievous tones, saying, 'Sure he had nothing else to do.' Paddy's career began in 1931, and he took part in the two famous drawn All-Ireland finals of that year. A broken collar bone sustained in the replay kept him out of the third game, but his brother Mick played at full-forward in all three games. Interestingly, Cork fielded the very same team in all three games, with the defender George Garret coming on as a sub in both replays. Kilkenny, on the other hand — mainly

'Fan' Larkin's father, Paddy.

through injury — were without Lory Meagher, Paddy Larkin, Dick Morrissey, Billy Dalton and Martin White for the third game.

In a career that continued until 1943, Paddy won all the hurling honours on offer in his day. 1933 brought him his only National League medal. He won nine Leinster titles, played in eight All-Ireland finals and was victorious on four occasions and was captain in 1936 when they went under to Limerick. He was an automatic choice on Leinster Railway Cup selections for eight successive seasons, from 1932 to 1939, and after a gap was back again in 1942. Three medals came his way in 1932, '33, and '36, when he was captain. An uncompromising defender who excelled at right-full-back and full-back, he would have been described in the terminology of his day as 'a hardy piece of stuff.' The stout-hearted Paddy died in 1977.

Fan (christened Philip Francis, becoming known as 'Fran' or 'Fan' to distinguish him from his first cousin, also called Phil Larkin) inherited the hurling skills, the physical attributes and the grim resolve associated with his father. He had an equally successful and outstanding hurling career, even though he had to watch the finals of 1966, '67 and '69 from Hill 16. 'I was blamed for the '64 defeat by Tipp. I was picked that day at left-full-back instead of right-full-back, because the selectors thought Seán McLoughlin was too tall for me to handle. So I found myself playing on Donie Nealon. He scored three goals. I was at fault for one but not the other two. I must say that Donie was the best forward I ever hurled on. I'd love to have got another chance to play on him. He was a most complete hurler: he had everything.'

After winning an All-Ireland medal in 1963 and then being dropped after 1964 and remaining in the hurling wilderness for about half a dozen years, it took a lot of character, ability and determination to work one's way back onto the county team in Kilkenny, where talent is so plentiful and competition for places on the team extremely keen. But back Fan came to a glorious career in the seventies.

The break came for him when his club, James Stephens, won the county title in 1969. 'Kilkenny won the All-Ireland title that year and we had no-one on the panel. Three years later, in 1972, we had nearly one-third of the team. Cork conceded two terrible soft goals in that final, one from a long way out from Eddie Keher and the other when they gave Frank Cummins a clear run up the middle.' Fan was back on the county panel in 1970. Rich harvests lay ahead.

'I grew up in a household where hurling was like religion. My mother played camogie with Kilkenny in the thirties. I remember my father often talking about Mick Mackey, Paddy Clohessy and Paddy Scanlon from Limerick. He played many times against them. He talked a lot too about Paddy Phelan and his lifetime friends Paddy Grace and Jimmy Langton. I think his favourite hurler was Peter Blanchfield; they were

Phil 'Fan' Larkin in the 1963 All-Ireland final against Waterford. (Photo: Jim Connolly)

great friends. My father won county titles with Tullaroan in 1933 and '34, James Stephens in '37, and Éire Óg in '39. In those days there was no parish rule in Kilkenny, and once you played senior you wouldn't be regraded to play junior.

'He took me to the All-Ireland final of 1947. I don't remember anything at all about it. I was only six. All I remember is getting sick on O'Connell Bridge after the game! He took me again in 1956, when he had a ticket for the Cusack Stand. I had none, and an official wouldn't let us in on the one ticket. My father asked to see Pádraig Ó Caoimh — they were both very friendly. He came down and got us in.' It was around this time too that Fan, in the company of his father, met Mícheál O'Hehir one Sunday in Wexford Park. He cherishes the memory, even more so now that Mícheál is no longer with us. 'He used to come into the dressing-room before a game and talk with new players and have a word with Paddy Grace. He knew everything about the players.'

Fan won his first Leinster title of the seventies in 1971, and from then until he retired after the All-Ireland success of 1979, hurling honours of all descriptions flowed his way. He was one of the outstanding full-back line defenders of the decade, and due recognition for this came his way through four All-Star awards and annual selection on the Railway Cup panel from 1972 onwards. Following proudly in the footsteps of his father, he played in all in nine All-Ireland finals and won five. He was an extremely tight defender whose forte was first-time hurling. He was one of the few who successfully coped with the elusive Ray Cummins of Cork. 'I had a good teacher: my father. He played on a big man in the '39 final — Ted Sullivan — and he knew how to handle him. When I played on Ray Cummins in the All-Ireland club final in Thurles in '76 I was thirty-two years of age and wiser towards when I was a young player. I knew Ray Cummins loved to reach to the sky and get the ball in his hand, and I didn't let him. I saw Ray give very good full-backs a terrible roasting.'

Thurles pitch and the year 1976 call to mind some of Fan's most memorable moments. 'In the space of three years I came away from Thurles with three major cups. I captained Kilkenny to a National League win over Clare after a replay in 1976. I captained my club, James Stephens, when we beat Blackrock in the All-Ireland club final of 1976

'Fan' Larkin's son, Philip.

at Thurles. We were the first team outside of Munster to win the club title. That is probably my most memorable hurling win. It was a wet day in Thurles. There is something special about a win with your club. When you play with the county and win, you don't meet the players again until training. With a club you are always meeting. A club is like a family. We won a second All-Ireland club title in 1982 when we beat Mount Sion. On the first of April 1979 I captained Leinster to a Railway Cup title over Connacht at Thurles. Thurles was a lucky place for me.'

Fan's son, Philip, is now carrying on

His team was selected, followed by the comment,
'You could pick another team just as good.'

	Noel Skehan *(Kilkenny)*	
Fan Larkin *(Kilkenny)*	Brian Cody *(Kilkenny)*	John Doyle *(Tipperary)*
Séamus Cleere *(Kilkenny)*	Billy Rackard *(Wexford)*	Denis Coughlan *(Cork)*
	Mick Roche *(Tipperary)*	Frank Cummins *(Kilkenny)*	
Jimmy Doyle *(Tipperary)*	Tony Doran *(Wexford)*	Mick Crotty *(Kilkenny)*
Donie Nealon *(Tipperary)*	Ray Cummins *(Cork)*	Eddie Keher *(Kilkenny)*

the proud family hurling tradition and seems set for a bright career. A talented and sporting performer, he won an All-Ireland minor medal in 1990 and captained Kilkenny to an under-21 All-Ireland success in 1994. He captained his club, James Stephens, in the county final of 1996. In a thrilling draw and equally enjoyable replay his team lost to Éire Óg (Gowran) by two points. Captain marked captain that day, D.J. Carey v. Philip Larkin, both giving a most sporting display; and after D.J. received the cup he complimented Philip for the extent to which he had minimised his (D.J.'s) contribution from general play. A bright future looms for a third generation of the Larkin family in the black and amber of Kilkenny.

Since retiring from the playing-fields Fan has remained in regular contact with hurling at club and county level: trainer, coach, and selector. Yes, hurling is a way of life in the Larkin household — 'nearly more important in our house than religion.'

Born 1939

"

I started playing camogie when I was fourteen. I played on the road at first and continued to play when I went to the Holy Faith, Dominic Street. I played for the Dublin colleges twice against Cork. We were well beaten in the first game. I was captain for the second one, and I scored the only point of the game — it was that close.

I always played outfield, but when I joined Celtic after school, when we used to practise on the greens in Marino, I went into goal. No-one else wanted to and I loved it, so when Eileen Duffy retired I took over. I was first picked for Dublin in 1959, and I went on to win eight All-Irelands, nine Leinster, and four Gael-Linn.

Eithne Leech **"**

When Eithne arrived on the county camogie scene in 1959 and took up position in goal she found herself in the company of some of the greatest camogie players of all time — among them Kathleen Mills, the leading All-Ireland medallist, with fifteen to her credit; Una O'Connor, following close

on Kathleen's heels with thirteen; Kay Ryder and Gerry Hughes, with nine each; and Kay Lyons, who won eight titles.

Dublin had been experiencing extraordinary success in the camogie world. Since 1948 — apart from 1956, when Antrim played Cork in the final — Dublin had contested and won every final, most of them decisively.

During Eithne's era, Dublin continued to contest the final each year. The only defeat was in 1967, when they failed in a replay to Antrim on the score 3:9 to 4:2. That ended the Dublin reign of supremacy, and since then they were successful on only one occasion, 1984 — the Centenary year of the GAA. Their first All-Ireland success — indeed the first year a camogie final took place — was 1932.

Eithne played in goal during her entire career. She wore spectacles — breakable ones early on, and then she got unbreakable ones. Unlike the great John Joe Doyle of Clare, she didn't cover them with goggles. She never had a mishap. She won eight successive All-Ireland medals between 1959 and 1966. For two of those years, 1963 and 1964, she was sub goalie, having lost her place after the 1963 drawn semi-final against Cork. 'I let in an easy goal. I went through a bad patch. It was a nightmare game for me. The paper on Monday said "Dublin show one change." That was how I found out. Before I read the article I knew I was gone.'

It all began for Eithne in her early teens when she played hurling on the road. 'I was a tomboy.' Her brothers had no interest in games, and she can recall her parents attending matches on only two occasions. 'The club training took place in Coolock. The Celtic club hired out a pitch from a farmer — it's all built up now. I used to cycle five miles each way to train. We trained for the county team at the Phoenix Park. We would spend a few hours hurling and then some physical training. Nell McCarthy from Cork was our trainer. She would take no nonsense. She had us under her thumb — just like kids. It was great when you were picked. Even to get a trial was great. In my eleven years on the Dublin panel I never missed training. Now it's difficult to get a full panel.'

She has retired five times from club activity — always with a presentation. Comebacks were made out of loyalty to the club and love for the game. She played as recently as 1995, in goal, senior B level, at the age of fifty-six.

When I met Eithne, in the company of her friend and former team-mate Una O'Connor, she was wearing the All-Ireland medal she won in 1965. Very attractive it was too: gold, bearing the arms of the four provinces. They beat Tipperary convincingly in that final. 'All games against Tipperary were hard. I remember in particular the All-Ireland semi-final of 1966 at Cahir. It was a desperate match — terrible tension all through. Scores were disputed. The crowd was on the pitch around the goal. I was afraid. I used to move out from goal for the puck-out. Kitty Murphy, a native of Tipp, was playing with us. She got a rough time. At full time we didn't know who had won — Una was going for her thirteenth medal. We were told go quickly to the hotel. At dinner we were wondering did we win or not. What tension! Then it was announced we had won by a point.' And hurling followers thought that events like that only happened at the Munster hurling final in 1950 at Killarney between Cork and Tipperary! I got a distinct feeling that Eithne enjoys wearing that 1965 medal.

The 1964 All-Ireland club victory conjures up an assortment of memories. 'It was the first club championship and it was wonderful to win it. It was our only success in that competition. A lot of teams entered. We must have played five or six matches before we got out of Leinster. We met Glen Rovers in the semi-final in Cork. The game was played on a full-length hurling pitch. We were lucky to get a draw. I remember Kit Kehoe came on for us as a sub in the replay at Parnell Park. Well, the first ball she got, she lashed it in the wrong direction. It came at me like a bullet, at a time when we were hanging on to a point lead. Luckily I saved it. Kit was very good, and so were all her sisters. She won All-Irelands with Dublin in 1965 and 1966 and with her native Wexford in 1975. We beat Deirdre of Belfast in the final in a very close-marking game. Our speed won it for us in the second half, with a final score of 5:2 to 1 goal.' A press report stated: 'Eithne Leech in goal for the winners, played a very big part in her side's victory and brought off some very good saves in the second half.'

'We always enjoyed our games against Antrim. They were so sporting and very nice. We often felt sorry for them. Year after year we would meet either in the semi-final or final. Only for us they would have won several titles. As it was they only won in 1966 and in 1967 after a replay, when they scored 3:9 to our 4:2. The most enjoyable and best game of camogie I ever played in was the 1965 semi-final against Antrim in the beautiful and heavenly surroundings of Glenariff. It was an incredible game — almost non-stop scoring.' Here is an excerpt from a report on the game: 'Dublin are through to yet another camogie final but it took them all their time to overcome the Antrim challenge at the pleasant little pitch in Glenariff last Sunday, after what must have been one of the most brilliant camogie matches ever played. Dublin won by five points 10:1 to 7:5 in what was a remarkably high scoring game but much of the honour of the day went to an Antrim side that included a couple of newcomers to inter-county camogie ... And were it not for some great saves by Eithne Leech, in goal, even those ten goals by Dublin forwards might not have been enough for victory.'

back Gerry Hughes. 'When a high ball was coming in she would look around and shout "Yours." We had a great understanding. For the puck-outs Kathleen Mills used say to me, "Put it ahead of me."' Eithne always marvelled at the skill and scoring power of her friend Una O'Connor.

She remembers with affection the late Seán O'Duffy, after whom the camogie cup is called. It has the same magic and yearning for camogie players as the McCarthy Cup has for hurlers. Seán taught them standards. He imbued in them a pride in the game they played. He liked discipline. 'He would tell us all to parade on the pitch carrying the hurley in similar fashion — and no waving to friends on the stand.' We all respected him.

And the game that got away? 'That was against Eoghan Ruadh in a final. We were leading by a point or two. They got a free — were told they had to score direct. It hit off my foot and went in; the goal was given; they won. It deprived me of a ninth county title.'

Eithne loved playing behind the full-

Camogie has given Eithne a lifetime of enjoyment. For her it was a pastime and interest that was both absorbing and rewarding. It has enriched her life in so many ways: friendships, memories, fulfilment and many rewards, both team and personal.

This is Eithne's team:

Eithne Leech *(Dublin)*
Gerry Hughes *(Dublin)*

Kay Lyons *(Dublin)*	Margaret O'Leary *(Wexford)*	Bridget Doyle *(Wexford)*
Sue Cashman *(Antrim)*	Mairéad McAtamney *(Antrim)*	Kathleen Mills *(Dublin)*
Judi Doyle *(Dublin)*	Deirdre Lane *(Tipperary)*	Angela Downey *(Kilkenny)*

Una O'Connor *(Dublin)*

Born 1971

Wolfe Tone na Sionainne was beginning to blossom in the early eighties. There was a fantastic under-age structure in the club, which developed as a result of the tremendous effort and work done by the national school teachers. Gradually Wolfe Tones started to become a force in Clare hurling, winning our first A title in the early eighties to winning every A title in hurling and football in 1988. The success at under-age level gradually matured to under-21 and later to the situation at present where we have in the past year won the county senior title combined with the Munster club.

I struggled to make the county teams at under-age level, failing to make the county minor or 21s except in my last year. In 1992, when I made my inter-county début in the under-21 championship, we lost the Munster final to Waterford, who later went on to win the All-Ireland. The following years of '93 and '94 were not much better on the county scene. In '93 we were destroyed, ruthlessly so, by a Tipperary team which hurled very well on the day. In '94 we were well beaten by Limerick, probably the most disappointing performance by any Clare team which I've been associated with. There is no doubt that defeat focuses the mind much more than victory.

In 1995 Clare won the All-Ireland. There was no magic formula which led to victory. We trained very hard. There was a fantastic work ethic within the team and the individuals associated with us.

1996 was a fantastic year for hurling. There is no doubt in my mind that it is the greatest game in the world. Each year it seems to be getting better, and the approach is becoming more and more professional. Most inter-county players are training five nights a week over a twelve-month period, building up to possibly six and seven nights a

❝

I was born into a hurling family in November 1971. My earliest memories of hurling started when I was bought a yellow plastic hurley when I was about four. It didn't take me long to graduate on to the ash variety, saving the plastic stick for my brother Frank, who was to arrive three years after me in 1974.

As I developed and reached the ages of nine and ten, the highlight of my week was training on a Tuesday, Wednesday and Thursday with my brother in Newmarket-on-Fergus. At that time the clubs from Newmarket were coming towards the end of a very successful hurling period, in which they won hurling championships almost yearly. 1981 was the year in which my father won his eleventh or twelfth senior hurling championship medal. On reflection, it strikes me now that my interest in training and hurling developed directly as a result of those nights inside in Newmarket.

week between club and county. It is a huge commitment but one which I've made without giving it a second thought.

Brian Lohan ."

Dreams bothered many characters in the Old Testament. They feared the portents. So it was with Brian Lohan of Clare. On the Saturday night before the 1996 Munster semi-final against Limerick he went to bed and in the course of the night had a dream in which he woke up on the Monday morning and reflected pleasingly on their victory over Limerick. It was a load off his mind. Then he woke up to realise that it was only Sunday morning and that the Limerick challenge still faced them. He was bothered — not sure what way to interpret the dream; not sure what was at work in his subconscious. Well, around five o'clock on Sunday evening he knew the reality. Clare, reigning All-Ireland champions and favourites in many quarters to retain the crown, led by 0:15 to 1:9 with five minutes remaining — and looking good for victory. But missed opportunities by Clare and four remarkable points by Limerick from play snatched victory from the Banner men on the call of time. It was a nightmare ending. 'If you don't take your chances you don't deserve to win.' For Brian, the award of RTÉ Man of the Match was poor consolation.

But Clare had been great champions, and Brian had moments to reflect on from their nail-biting victory over Offaly in the All-Ireland of 1995. 'Three weeks before the game I was confident we would win the game. I took up position at full-back, faced by Pat O'Connor. You know the way you want to occupy the best position in front of goal. Of course two people can't occupy the one position; so we are jostling. Then there is the sound of breaking ash, heard by the referee, Dickie Murphy, who turns around, sees Pat O'Connor with the handle of a broken hurley in his hand — free out, and Joe Dooley had the ball in his hand ready to shoot.' It is now well into the last quarter, and the game continues to hang in the balance. 'John Troy had moved to full-forward and got possession at the sideline. I shouldered him over the line, but the ball in his hand didn't cross the line. No flag went up. I cursed Willie Barrett, the sideline man. My legs were gone. But John Troy must have felt the same. He was unable to get away from me. If he had he would have scored.'

Brian reflected on the two 'soft' goals they gave away — especially the second in the second half. 'I and the other backs had four opportunities to clear the ball but we failed, and Johnny Pilkington stuck it in the net to put Offaly a goal up and about a quarter of an hour to go.' The final whistle was the sound every Clare hurling ear had longed for for eighty-one years. They were now All-Ireland champions — Clare 1:13, Offaly 2:8.

Writing after the game in *The Irish Times*, Jimmy Barry Murphy commented: 'I do remember being marked by a very good centre-back in the 1977 Munster final. His name was Gus Lohan. Yesterday his two sons Brian and Frank were brilliant. There is no other word to describe their performances.' And talking of Gus, Brian reminded me that his father played with Clare and his native Galway and won a variety of county hurling titles in an era spanning four decades, from the fifties to the eighties — and found time as well to play senior football for Monaghan and junior football for Clare. His was a career that took him into his early forties.

Victory in the Fitzgibbon Cup in 1994 — a competition that started in 1912 — 'was definitely one of my greatest moments in hurling. It was University of Limerick's second title — the first in 1989. It was my last year in college. For three years we had played in the competition and won nothing. Then came '94. We had a good team. We were physically strong, especially in the backs. We beat UCG, UCC and Waterford RTC in the final. All three games went to extra time. In the game against UCG we got a goal in the last two minutes to beat them by one point. It was a fantastic game — had a few incidents. Weather conditions caused the game to be postponed from a Saturday to the following Wednesday. A huge crowd attended — fierce excitement. In the game against UCC two sets of brothers were on opposite sides, the Maguires and ourselves.' Victory in the final over Waterford RTC was reward for a dedicated training schedule. 'It went on from September to March — a huge mental and physical commitment.'

In years to come, when many other games will have been confined to the limbo of forgotten things, Brian will still talk with vivid recollection and immense satisfaction of the 1994 Fitzgibbon Cup campaign, a campaign he enjoyed immensely; it will be for ever vernal. 'Every time Dara O'Neill — he was the captain — and myself meet we end up talking about the Fitzgibbon Cup win.'

The question is often asked whether the game of hurling and the men who play it nowadays match the standard of days of yore. The question of course has been asked in every decade of the GAA since its foundation; the answer has nearly always carried a yearning for the past. And yet when you think of the many exciting and thrilling games of the past decade — in particular the many 1996 produced — and reflect on the majestic performances of players of the calibre of Brian Lohan and his brother Frank, and others too, you begin to feel that our present does match our past and that the future of our game — despite the challenges it faces — seems assured.

Born 1953

"

It is a great honour for me to be included in this book recalling great games and marvellous players. When I first started playing hurling at national school in Feakle I never anticipated that I could get such great pleasure, meet so many people, play in so many famous venues or achieve success in a game which is such a large part of the fabric of rural life in Ireland.

I suppose listening to the commentaries of the late Mícheál O'Hehir was the first inkling I got of the excitement and passion which the game of hurling arouses. Watching the expressions on the faces of our neighbours as they followed every puck of the ball and commented on every score filled me with a desire to be part of such a great game. I remember when I was very young hoping that Mícheál O'Hehir would still be commentating when I was playing and that he would mention my name on the radio.

I started in an era when there was no formal coaching. We had just one ball, which was fought over, often using a rulebook which we invented ourselves. Of course when I entered St Flannan's College in 1966 everything changed. I soon realised that the sporting heroes of the college were the players on the Harty team, and if you didn't play hurling you were left in the shadows. I was most fortunate that at that time two of the priests who had just commenced coaching in the school were Father Séamus Gardiner and Father Willie Walsh, now Bishop Walsh. I was on the first under-15 team coached by the two of them, and they remained with our team right up to fifth year, when we lost the Harty Cup final. My skills in playing the game and my ideas in coaching were all formed by these two. Indeed, I was delighted to meet Father Gardiner in the Hogan Stand after the All-Ireland in '95 and to thank him for the influence he had on me many years before.

I played for the Clare minors for two years and for the Clare under-21s for three years, reaching Munster finals in both codes, all without success. The defeats of Clare in the Munster senior finals of the seventies and eighties have been well documented, but when I look back over my career my main memories are of the thrill of putting on the Clare jersey in every game, the marvellous players I played with and against, the travel all over the country to venues big and small, but above all the thrill of just playing the great game of hurling.

My ambition when I set out was to win a county championship with Feakle and to win an All-Ireland with Clare. It is ironic that we would win the county championship in my last game for Feakle, in 1988, after a lapse of about forty-three years and that finally Clare should win an All-Ireland with me as manager rather than as a player. I couldn't have asked for anything better!

"

A smile of elation covers Ger's face as he recalls the day he received the postcard informing him that he was selected to play for his native Clare against Tipperary in the Munster minor hurling championship. 'I remember that day well. I remember where I was standing the very moment I got the postcard. I kept it — I still have it somewhere in the house. It was a great moment for me. I couldn't wait to put on the Clare jersey.' The passing years have failed to dim that magic moment, which is now gathering around it a generous coating of nostalgia.

Ger loves the game of hurling. He exudes enthusiasm as he talks about every facet of it. Every time he donned the blue and gold of Clare a deep sense of pride gripped him; he felt as honoured the last time as the first time. Wearing the county jersey meant as much to him as his Railway Cup and National League triumphs and his All-Star award. Incidentally, his All-Star award of 1974 — his first of two — was Clare's first.

Growing up in Feakle, 'hurling wasn't hugely important' in Ger's house. The parish wasn't any longer the hurling force it had been in the thirties and forties. Ger's father never hurled — he ran cross-country — though Bill Loughnane, who was a first cousin of his father, won an All-Ireland medal with Dublin in 1938. So instead of hurling, Ger spent many a Sunday hunting with beagles in the company of the legendary Garrett Howard. 'Garrett was a fantastic character. He was so pleasant and positive about everything. He was an outstanding hurler and knew the game well. On the morning of the Munster final of 1955 he met a Clare player who was beating a ball against the gable end. 'We'll beat you [Limerick] well,' he told Garrett, adding that some of the players weren't that good. Garrett shook his head and said, 'I never met a bad one in a Munster final yet.' The result bore out his wisdom.

Ger was a member of a quite exceptional Clare team during the seventies and eighties, a team worthy of Munster and All-Ireland honours. But these coveted prizes eluded them. Four occasions in particular stand out. In 1977, '78 and '86 they failed very narrowly to Cork in the Munster final, and on each occasion Cork went on to win the All-Ireland. In 1981 they ran up against Limerick and Joe McKenna (he scored 3:3). But they did contest three successive National League finals, winning in 1977 and '78 at the expense of talented Kilkenny teams.

'Those league victories were like All-Irelands for us. The whole county was behind the team. I can remember the home matches at Tulla. The place would be thronged — standing on the hill. You would have to park your car and walk about two miles to the pitch. Those games were a huge influence on young lads, a legacy that led to our All-Ireland win in Croke Park in '95.'

He was an outstanding defender and formed a great half-back line with two other superb hurlers, Seán Stack and Seán Hehir. For seven years in a row, from 1975 onwards, he was a regular on the Munster Railway Cup teams. In a playing career that spanned sixteen years at county senior level he selected three opponents that stood out. 'Gerald McCarthy of Cork was brilliant in the air. He could strike left and right — had great hands and wrists; very hard to mark. Éamon Grimes of Limerick was very fast; covered an amount of ground; was very skilful; very difficult to hold. In my later years I encountered Nicholas English of Tipperary. He had a fantastic level of skill; great sharpness of mind. I think he played better hurling prior to the Tipperary breakthrough in 1987.'

Ger had the ideal temperament for the big occasion. He admits to loving it and never getting flustered, whether as player or manager. But he does remember one big occasion in particular when things were difficult. 'It was the 1978 Munster final against Cork in Thurles. The crowd was huge — one of the biggest for a Munster final; many were

locked out. There was a tension in the air that I never felt before or since. It was a very hot day: it was electric on the field — so tense.' In the eyes of many, Clare were favourites. It added to their burden. Well prepared they were physically; the mental preparation didn't match it. The score tells its own tale. At half time Cork led by 5 points to 3 and faced the breeze in the second half. It looked good for Clare. But the tension continued in the second half. 'A goal might have relieved it but it never came.' It ended 13 points to 11.

In September 1994 Ger became manager of the Clare senior hurling team. 'I had managed the under-21 team of '92 but was sacked after we lost the Munster final to Waterford, who subsequently won the All-Ireland title.' He immediately set about building the team's morale. 'They were down so low after the heavy defeats of '93 and '94 at the hands of Tipperary and Limerick, respectively, in the Munster finals that there was only one way they could go: up. The league became our testing-ground. We beat Tipp in a tremendous game, and when we lost the final to Kilkenny there were people who said we would never win anything. After the league we hurled and hurled. One of our main faults was the speed at which we played the game. We needed to up the pace: play the game at speed; hurl with real passion and drive; overcome skill deficiencies.'

His exuberance and infectious enthusiasm spilled over onto the players. His approach, befitting his teaching profession, was hortative. He urged and encouraged; he praised and drove. He was a generator of confidence, a moulder of spirit. A man of unshakable faith in the potential of his panel and players, he imbued in them a deep pride in the jersey they wore, in the county they represented, in the game they played. He bred a winning mentality. Came the Munster semi-final against Cork. 'It was a bit of a nightmare. I think we shot twenty-two wides — overanxious. We were the better team on the day but lucky to win — felt it had to be our year.' And so it proved.

Limerick fell in the Munster final. Clare celebrations knew no bounds. The barrier that had haunted Clare since 1932 was now no more. Galway fell at the semi-final stage. Clare, on a roll, looked forward to All-Ireland day and a date with Offaly.

Ger prepared well. Attention to every detail was vital. Success in most All-Irelands comes down to detail. He had noticed that Croke Park looked narrower than Cusack Park, where Clare trained; he measured it and found it to be six yards narrower. Cusack Park was marked out accordingly, and the players adjusted to the narrower measurements.

The atmosphere on final day was carnival-like. Glorious sunshine, a wonderful array of colour and the uniqueness of the pairing all added extra glamour to the occasion. The presence in the attendance of John Joe Doyle and Tom McInerney, who played in 1932, when Clare lost to Kilkenny — both heading for the ninety mark — brought a touch of nostalgia to the day .

It is now history that Clare won their second title and their first since 1914. Their captain, Anthony Daly, delivered a wonderful winning speech, one of the finest ever heard on final day. It was comprehensive, dignified, and thoughtful — a credit to him and the team he represented. Referring to Ger, he said, 'His obsession has become a reality.'

At our meeting I told Ger that I felt two lines from Wordsworth aptly summed up the victory for all of Clare:

'Bliss was it in that dawn to be alive,
But to be young was very heaven!'

In reply, Ger said, 'We were all young that day.'

It was after school hours when my wife and myself left his office. As we reached the car in the school grounds we spotted him close at hand in the school pitch, surrounded by young hurling enthusiasts. Lucky them!

The B&I Award 1979.

Born 1944

"

My first introduction to the game of camogie was at Portstewart convent in 1956. There had been no camogie in my home town, but my five brothers all played Gaelic for the local club (Portglenone), and my parents were very interested in the game.

At Portstewart the coaching was done mainly by one of the senior girls, and when I reached fourth year I took over the role. In 1961 and '62 I was the captain-trainer when we won the Ulster Colleges final, beating St Dominic's and St Louis, Kilkeel. Unfortunately there was no All-Ireland colleges competition at that time.

In my home town of Portglenone a camogie club was formed in 1944, but by the early fifties it had fallen away. Around '55 or '56 the club reorganised and competed in the Antrim Junior Championship and won in 1958. My

sister Frances was the captain of the team, and that was our first medal. The club then contested their first senior championship in 1963 but were defeated by Deirdre. It was not until the seventies that we came into prominence. By this stage my other two sisters, Theresa and Sheena, were playing for the team. I was player-coach for many years, and we had some very good players, which brought us a lot of success in the seventies. Portglenone won the Antrim senior championship in 1971, '72, '74, '75, '77, '78, '79, '81, '82, '88, and '92. I played until 1988, winning ten senior championship medals and eight Ulster club championship medals.

All-Ireland club semi-finals:

We lost seven: '71, Austin Stacks at home; '74, Ahane, Limerick, at home; '75, St Paul's, Kilkenny, at Kilkenny; '78, Ballyagran, Limerick, at home; '79, Athenry, away; '83, Athenry, at Carrickmacross; '93, Glen Rovers, at home.

All-Ireland club finals:

We played in two and lost both: Austin Stacks, 1972; Athenry, 1977.

I coached the under-age players as well as the seniors, and our minor team won seven championships in a row, from 1976 to '82. Many of those young players played on our senior team at that same time. Our club won three championships on the one day in 1979: minor, junior, and senior.

County career, 1958—83:

I missed out in 1980. I was captain of the county team in 1973 when we were narrowly beaten by Cork, 2:5 to 3:1; captain of county, 1979; captain of Ulster, 1979. Ulster championship titles with Antrim: 15. I played on the inter-provincial team for the same number of years. All-Ireland medals: 1967 and 1979. Inter-

Máiréad McAtamney-Magill in action during her last match, the 1988 County final against Loughgiel.

provincial medal: 1967 (Gael-Linn).

Individual awards:

First Antrim Sports Star award, sponsored by St John's, 1965; Cú Chulainn Award, 1965; Player of the Year, 1975, in Antrim; B&I Award, 1979.

I was teaching in St Rose's, Belfast, in 1965, where I coached the team to an Ulster intermediate colleges title.

Great Antrim players:

Sue Cashman, Moya Forde, Theresa Cassidy, Maeve Gilroy, Lily Scullion, Marian Kearns, Josephine McClements, Jackie McAtamney, Siobhán McAtamney, Chris O'Boyle, Mary McMullan, and Rita McAteer.

Opponents from other counties:

Marian McCarthy, Betty Sugrue (Cork), Órla Ní Shíocháin, Judi Doyle, Una O'Connor, Alice Hussey (Dublin), Twin Downeys, Ann Carroll, Helena O'Neill, Liz Neary, Bridie Martin (Kilkenny), Margaret O'Leary, Elsie Walsh (Wexford), Sarah Ann Quinn (Derry), Stephanie Kelly, Maura Caldwell (Down)

Most memorable inter-county game:

All-Ireland replay against Dublin in 1967: first All-Ireland. My father died on the evening of the first match. The replay was two weeks later, on the day of the Oireachtas final. I decided this game would be for my father, and it was one of the best I ever played. Nancy Murray was the Antrim trainer.

Most memorable club game:

Ulster final against Eglish, 1982. Eglish had beaten us the year before in the Ulster semi-final; we were out for revenge. This was an excellent game of camogie played at very fast pace at Newbridge, County Derry. Eventually we won by about six points.

The might-have-beens:

The 1978 All-Ireland club championship semi-final against Ballyagran, Limerick, at Randalstown. Portglenone were leading by eleven points at half time. Turn round, strong wind, they scored four goals on the trot and beat us by two points. They went on to beat Buffer's Alley, Wexford, in the final.

Leading Athenry, 1982 — second half, three long pucks dropped into square and converted into goals.

All-Ireland final against Cork in 1973; I was captain of the team. Beaten by one point.

Greatest moments:

Antrim and Ulster club championship wins. Individual awards. All-Ireland and inter-provincial wins. The day my club won the three championships on the one day in 1979. Myself and my sister and six nieces were all playing. My niece Jackie McAtamney played on all three teams. I coached the minor and the senior team. In 1979 Jackie and Siobhán, my two nieces, lining out with me in the All-Ireland final.

Amusing moments:

The 1978 Ulster final in Swatragh against Swatragh. My sixteen-year-old niece Siobhán McAtamney, who was playing on the wing alongside me, shouted, "Pass me the ball, Mammy." Everybody thought it was hilarious. I could see the funny side afterwards.

Sad moments:

Death of my father on All-Ireland final day, 1967; subsequent replay. Death of sister Theresa Grant on All-Ireland final day, 1977. She played full-back on our club team and had a few outings for the county.

People who influenced me in my career:

I was never really taught the skills but was obviously influenced by the late Jamesie Kearns, who used to come to Portstewart convent on a Saturday in my early years there. He was a great advocate of pulling on the ball on the ground. My parents gave me great support throughout my career by their interest.

People I admired:

Antrim's three ex-presidents of the Camogie Association, Rosina

McManus, Lily Spence, and Nancy Murray, for their dedication to the game as officials of the county board. I had great admiration for Phyllis Breslin (Dublin) as a referee.

Players I now admire:
Linda Mellerick, Sandra Fitzgibbon (Cork), Madge Hobbin (Galway), and Maureen McAleenan (Down).

"

Maireod Magill

Máiréad McAtamney ranks among the élite of camogie players. For over a quarter of a century she gave outstanding service to her native Antrim and had few peers as a midfielder. Her contemporaries who feature in this book testify to this, all selecting her for their chosen teams. I can remember hearing broadcasts of games she played in; the sound of her name seemed to ring in one's ears and she so dominated the scene that her name was constantly being repeated. Her interest in the game has continued to the present day. 'I started a new club in my adopted town of Randalstown. We are now in our third year and have about seventy members, from seven to sixteen. This year I have been appointed manager of the under-14 county team.'

She came from a family where her parents were highly supportive and Gaelic games were encouraged. Her sister Theresa played for Antrim but lost her life in a tragic road accident in 1977. 'That's a sad memory, as indeed was 1967, when my father died.' Three brothers played football for Antrim: John played at minor level; Aeneas played at senior level in the fifties and played his first county game at the opening of Casement Park; Tony played for fifteen years — won a Dr McKenna Cup medal and a Railway Cup medal with Ulster in 1970; in 1984 he was selected at midfield on the Antrim Centenary team.

In 1963 and 1964 Antrim reached the All-Ireland camogie final but were defeated each time by a star-studded Dublin outfit, 7:3 to 2:5 and 7:4 to 3:1, Dublin with household names like Gerry Hughes, Una O'Connor, Kay Ryder, Órla Ní Shíocháin, Judi Doyle, and Alice Hussey.

By 1966 Antrim had narrowed the gap in standards and gave Dublin a close call: it was 2:2 to 0:6. Six scores to four suggests a certain superiority, but Dublin got two vital goals — and goals win matches. 1967 brought a change of fortune. A very exciting final ended all square with Dublin, 4:2 each. Her father, who wasn't enjoying the best of health at the time, listened to the broadcast and, sadly, died shortly after the game ended. The joy of a great Antrim performance was overshadowed by this family loss.

In the replay Antrim dominated. They won 3:9 to 4:2 and were captained by another great camogie artist, Sue Cashman. That Antrim victory halted the Dublin dominance of the camogie scene. They had won ten titles in a row and were seeking their eleventh, while the ace forward Una O'Connor was chasing a fourteenth All-Ireland medal. Máiréad was brilliant in that final and played a large part in bringing the title to Antrim. 'It was one of those days when everything went my way. No matter where I was, the ball seemed to be there. It was one of my greatest days.' Her father would have been very proud. It was Antrim's fifth title, Máiréad's first All-Ireland medal.

Antrim camogie was now of a high standard, and people talked about the three-in-a-row team of 1945, '46, and '47. Narrow defeats left them pondering the might-have-beens in 1969, when Wexford beat them 4:4 to 4:2, and again in 1973 when, captained by Máiréad, they went under to Cork by the narrowest of margins, 2:5 to 3:1.

Then came 1979. It was the year Máiréad married Liam Magill; it was also the year she proudly captained Antrim to All-Ireland victory with a great win over Tipperary, 2:3 to 1:3 — her second All-Ireland medal after over twenty years of wonderful service to camogie and county. 'I absolutely adored the game and lived for it.' Sharing that victory with Máiréad were her two nieces, Jackie and Siobhán McAtamney. Jackie emigrated to America in 1981 and remained there; Siobhán played with Antrim into the nineties.

At club level no All-Ireland title came Máiréad's way, although Portglenone did contest the finals of 1972 and 1977.

The exhilarating glory-days of playing camogie are now a thing of the past, but the memories and nostalgia endure. Golf clubs have replaced the camogie stick; the handicap is 13.

Máiréad's All-Ireland selection is as follows:

Marian McCarthy *(Cork)*

Marie Costine *(Cork)*

Bridie Martin *(Kilkenny)*	Margaret O'Leary *(Wexford)*	Jackie McAtamney *(Antrim)*
Órla Ní Shíocháin *(Dublin)*	Sue Cashman *(Antrim)*	Máiréad McAtamney *(Antrim)*
Angela Downey *(Kilkenny)*	Ann Carroll *(Kilkenny)*	Judi Doyle *(Dublin)*

Una O'Connor *(Dublin)*

Subs: Betty Sugrue *(Cork)*, Elsie Walsh *(Wexford)*, Liz Neary *(Kilkenny)*, Sarah Ann Quinn *(Derry)*.

Born 1945

66

My whole life is centred around hurling, and I'm told by my parents that at eleven months old I had a hurley in my hand. Fifty-two years later I still have that hurley in my hand and get as excited now as I probably did then. It's really a love affair, and I can safely say I have never fallen out with hurling and I am still learning about it.

My dream was always to play in the red and white of Cork, and that vision never left me. When I was growing up I got the opportunity to play minor in '63 and then in '64 played under-21, intermediate and senior on the championship teams. Thankfully we made the big breakthrough in 1966, and it was a special year bringing the McCarthy Cup back to the city by the Lee after twelve years out of the limelight. We also won the under-21 title for the first time, and to cap it all I was chosen as Caltex Hurler of the Year.

My hurling world fell apart in 1969 when on my way to training for the All-Ireland final I was involved in a motorbike accident and broke my leg in

three places and was out of the game for over two years, missing the '69 and '70 finals.

My new goal was to win back my place, and I can remember my first game against Dublin in the National League. It was great to be back. Winning a National League medal in '72 gave me great satisfaction, and a Munster medal that year, but losing the '72 All-Ireland was a nightmare. My last game was against Waterford in the '74 Munster championship, when the Decies beat us.

I was always interested in the coaching side of the game and in 1970 went to Antrim, where there was great interest in the game, and they won their first All-Ireland hurling title and it was great to be part of it.

My journey to Clare came in late '76 and a new world opened up to me, and it was so pleasing to be part of a great Clare team that won two National Leagues, in '77 and '78, beating famed Kilkenny in both games.

Back to Cork as a selector in '82, but this time the Cats showed us how it should be done. But being coach in the Centenary year, 1984, and winning that famous title in Thurles was a great satisfaction.

Going back to Tipperary with Cashel King Cormacs to coach them for six years was another highlight, and they winning their first county title against Holycross and the Munster championship against Midleton were days to remember.

As my playing days are over, I love to go for a few pucks, and as long as I can will help out in the coaching and development of this great game. Ring once said the best years are yet to come and the best players are in the future. I believe we have not seen the best hurling yet or the best games. The game has not been fully

Justin McCarthy with the famous Cork trainer Jim Barry, 1967.

explored yet, and the future years will be great times for young people.

The friends that I made and the discipline that hurling has given me have moulded my life for the better. Thanks, Brendan, for allowing me to write these few lines, and thank God we have the GAA. Where would our lives be without it?

99

[signature: Justin McCarthy]

A distinguished hurling career, which seemed destined for greater heights, was abruptly interrupted before the All-Ireland final of 1969, and Justin watched the final from a wheelchair on the sideline, as our photograph shows. 'I tell you it wasn't nice sitting there. I felt it was my best year. We beat Wexford in the National League final. I was twenty-four — coming into my prime; getting stronger; more experienced and in really good form. The '69 team was one of the best I played with. For the final the selectors brought Willie Walsh from centre-forward to centre-back to fill my position. I think it was a mistake. Willie was the best centre-forward I ever saw hurling. The setback in the middle of my career was a terrible blow. I missed out on the campaigns of '70 and '71.'

Justin remembers when he was eight or nine being down in the College field, and Dan McInerney of Clare, who was involved in a construction job in Cork, was putting in some training. Justin spent his time hitting the ball back to Dan.

When Bord na nÓg was formed in Cork in the fifties, Justin took part in under-14, under-15 and under-16 competitions. 'Father Roch, a Kilkenny man, taught me a lot about hurling. "Play your own position," he would say — "know it: be in command."' The same hurling philosophy was preached by Billy Campbell, Jim O'Regan, Johnny Quirke, and Dinny Barry-Murphy.

All-Ireland final day at Croke Park, 1969.

In 1955 he wore the Cork jersey for the first time. It was a very proud moment. 'Father Roch arranged for the altar boys from Cork to play the altar boys from Kilkenny in Nowlan Park. Everything was laid on for us. We all felt so proud wearing the red jersey and marching behind the band. The Kilkenny boys wore the black-and-amber jersey. We won.'

Justin's hurling came from his mother's side. 'My father was a west Cork man. My mother's brothers, my uncles Batt O'Mahony and Ger O'Mahony, played with Young Irelands of Boston and won the American championship of 1934. Batt was captain.'

By 1966 Justin was a very accomplished hurler. He won All-Ireland under-21 and senior honours as a midfielder on teams captained by his namesake Gerald. His performance in the 1966 championship set him apart that year, and he was honoured with the Texaco Hurler of the Year award. The celebration took place in the Gresham Hotel on a Thursday night. Justin still has the menu.

'The following morning three of us had a big fry-up for breakfast. Then someone said, "What day is it?" "Friday." Friday — and we after eating meat. Horror: a mortal sin. We met Father Roch and explained. He said, "Don't worry, I'll give you absolution." An age of innocence.'

It took three games with Wexford to decide the under-21 final. 'The third meeting took place on the thirteenth of November. Jack Lynch threw in the ball. The final score read Cork 9:9, Wexford 5:9.' The *Free Press* reported on the game: 'Leading the way for the Southerners was Justin McCarthy, a player with a wonderful future before him in the game. He strode the midfield with such class and power that one at times wondered where the Wexfordman had gone. With him Gerald McCarthy joined in establishing a grip on midfield that could not be broken even by the spirited efforts of Con Dowdall.'

When Justin retired in 1974 he turned his attention to coaching. He first sampled this in 1969 when he was invited by Frank Smith and Niall Patterson senior to give coaching lessons to the Antrim hurlers. The following year Antrim won the intermediate title with a convincing win over Warwickshire.

'In 1975 I trained Cork for the first time, and we won a Munster title by defeating Limerick. I had learned a lot about coaching during the 1972 season. We beat Limerick in the National League final in Thurles by one goal; I was marking Seán Foley. The team was in great form. After that we were killed from training. That's why we fell away in the second half against Kilkenny in the All-Ireland final. As Father Tommy Maher said to me, "You left all your fitness behind in Cork." I learned that you have to be fresh in Croke Park. When you lose your freshness you lose your touch, and when your touch is out your confidence goes. Even though Galway beat us by two points in the All-Ireland semi-final I knew we had a good team, but I fell from favour after that defeat.'

Clare at this time had a very promising team and some excellent individual players. Justin was approached. 'They were looking for someone to lead them and mould them. It was a big decision for me in the autumn of '76 to decide to go to Clare. Father Harry Bohan gave me great leeway. All the players were deadly dedicated. It would be hard to surpass them in 1977 and '78. They were very unlucky in losing the Munster finals of those years to Cork; but they won the National League in those years with great wins over Kilkenny. I stayed with Clare until June 1980. I used travel three times a week to Tulla — a trip of ninety-eight miles each way. My last day with Clare was when they beat Galway at the opening of Cusack Park on the twenty-ninth of June. After that game Ger Loughnane gave me his jersey.'

Another challenge beckoned in 1990 when Justin took on the task of coaching Cashel. It was fifty years since they contested a county final. 'We were beaten by one point in the final of 1990. Many of the players were downhearted. They were pushing on and felt they wouldn't get the chance again. But they did. The following year we beat Holycross in the final.' That paved the way for a Munster club title and a place in the All-Ireland club semi-final against Kiltormer of Galway. It took three memorable games before victory went to the men of the west. 'I spent six years with Cashel. It was hard, being a Corkman in Tipp and coaching them about hurling. But I got to appreciate the Tipp people better. I learned about their deep interest in the game, their hurling culture, the background to it. I was honoured to be part of a great club and a great people. They had great players in the Bonnars and Pat Fitzelle — as brilliant a player as I have seen.'

When I phoned Justin to arrange our meeting he was 'out at the back pucking a ball around.' He had played his last competitive game with Passage in October 1991, when he won a City Divisional Junior League. On arrival I was able to identify his house by two hurleys shaped from wrought iron in the gate. In his scrapbook were two little plastic bags. One contained a sample of clay from the Bilboa Stadium in San Francisco, where he played at centre-back against Tipperary as an All-Star replacement in April 1972 and at the same time visited his sister out there. The second bag had a piece of the sod from Wembley, which Justin took as a souvenir after a Monaghan cup final there. These bear witness to a life, blessed with good health and energy, that has been immersed and engrossed in the game of hurling in one form or other from his juvenile days in the fifties right up to the present moment.

Regarding his team he said: 'In picking this team I am talking from experience as a player, coach, and selector. I have picked a panel to win. This team can't be beaten.'

Séamus Durack *(Clare)*

Fan Larkin *(Kilkenny)*   Pat Hartigan *(Limerick)*   Denis Murphy *(Cork)*

Séamus Cleere *(Kilkenny)*   Dan Quigley *(Wexford)*   Ger Loughnane *(Clare)*

Justin McCarthy *(Cork)*   Mick Roche *(Tipperary)*

Éamon Cregan *(Limerick)*   Willie Walsh *(Cork)*   Jimmy Doyle *(Tipperary)*

Charlie McCarthy *(Cork)*   Tony Doran *(Wexford)*   Eddie Keher *(Kilkenny)*

Remainder of panel: John O'Donoghue *(Tipperary)*, Willie Murphy *(Wexford)*, John Connolly *(Galway)*, Joe Hennessy *(Kilkenny)*, and Pat Fox *(Tipperary)*.

Born 1937

" "

It is more than thirty years now since I hurled with Limerick, but my memories go back to earlier days. I remember as a youngster standing behind the goals in Shelbourne Park, watching the Treaty Sarsfields players practising. There was one man who made a lasting impression on me: he was Timmy Murphy — God rest him now. He played at centre-back. He had a great pair of hands and was a wonderful hurler. No other back I ever saw after that, including the great county men, ever impressed me as much. He had everything.

" "

Tom McGarry (signature)

O nly a small number of sportsmen, relatively speaking, achieve a high level of proficiency in any particular field of sport. Fewer still become top-class dual performers. To meet a hurler, therefore, who had the distinction of turning in top-class displays in five different sports is rare indeed. It sets him apart — makes him unique. Such a man is Tom McGarry.

I met Tom on the evening of Thursday 25 July 1996. Michelle Smith had by then won her third gold medal for swimming at the Olympics; her bronze was yet to come. I knew Tom had excelled in many areas of sport, so with swimming the topic of the day I asked him, after our initial greeting, whether he had ever competed in swimming. 'No, I never won trophies at swimming. I swam just for training purposes. I used to cycle to Corbally Baths — often went in the dark at eleven o'clock at night. Swimming is great training for any sport. And I loved it.'

Let's now look at the sports in which he excelled.

Handball

'Handball was my favourite game. I played it seven days a week. I played it from my very young days — began off by playing against the gable wall of the house. It made you agile for all games — great training.' While at Limerick (Sexton Street) CBS he won the Munster colleges softball titles and went on to win the inter-provincial colleges, singles and doubles softball titles. Outside school he had the following All-Ireland successes: minor: softball singles champion, 1955; minor: softball doubles title with Martin Mullins, 1955; junior: softball doubles title with Martin Mullins, 1957; senior: softball doubles title with Martin Mullins, 1958 and '59.

'In 1956 Gael-Linn sponsored a new handball competition. It was open to players from all grades: minor, junior, senior. There must have been five hundred or six hundred entries. I won it two out of the three years I took part. The first time I won it I defeated the holder — the late Dr Des Dillon, a native of Clare, who also hurled with Clare and Dublin. I held it for two years and lost it to that great handballer from Louth, Joey Maher.'

The photograph (p. 185) shows Tom with the Gael-Linn Trophy, c, 1957 or '58, surrounded by admirers in his native parish.

The family success in the handball court didn't end with Tom. His brother Pat kept the flag flying with the following successes: junior: softball singles, 1967; senior: hardball singles, 1979 and '80; senior: softball doubles with M. Hogan, 1976; senior: hardball doubles with J. Bennis, 1978, '79, and '80. In 1980 Pat was nominated Player of the Year.

Hurling

'My love of hurling was second only to handball. I was a member of the Limerick CBS team that won the Dean Ryan Cup in 1955, and I was on the senior team beaten by North Mon in the final of the Harty Cup.'

In 1954 Tom came on as a sub on the Limerick minor team beaten by Tipperary in the Munster final, 3:5 to 2:3, and played in the same grade the following year. He made his senior hurling championship début against Clare at Thurles in 1956, and victory over the Banner County saw Limerick through to the Munster final against Cork to defend their title. 'It was the nearest we got in my time to winning something in the championship. We all gave of our best that day but came away losers. Cork looked beaten but came back; Limerick are doing it this year [1996].'

As hurling followers will recall, it was the day that Dónal Broderick at corner-back for Limerick was having the better of the exchanges with Ring and containing him in a vice-like grip. With the game in the last quarter, Limerick, hurling superbly, had increased their interval lead of three points to six points and looked in command — and winners. It was then that Ring struck and wrote another epic chapter into his hurling career. Opinions vary about whether he switched or merely moved outfield from Broderick; in any event, within the space of ten minutes he had scored 3:1 — two of those goals being of the fortuitous variety — and Cork as Munster champions were on their way to Croke Park.

'After that the nearest we came to glory was in the great National League final of 1958 against Wexford, when we lost by two points. In my playing days players were brought together for training for maybe two or three nights a week. Most of them would be physically fit but not necessarily mentally fit.'

Limerick hurling fell on lean times, but, fortunately for Tom, the Railway Cup competition and representative games gave him scope to display his brilliant hurling skills. The Munster hurling selectors recognised his hurling talents, and at right-half-back he won five Railway Cup medals: 1958, '59, '60, '61, and '63. The representative games were a contest between the All-Ireland champions of the previous year and a Rest of Ireland selection. Tom was chosen at right-half-back on the teams of 1959, '61, and '62.

Tom had a high level of physical and mental fitness, coupled with speed, strength, and stamina. These qualities, allied to a rich repertoire of hurling skills, made him one of the most outstanding and accomplished half-backs of his day.

It was around the mid-sixties that Tom fell foul of rule 27 of the GAA, the ban on foreign games, which barred players from attending or playing soccer, rugby, hockey, or cricket. Tom was suspended by the county board, and a great hurler was lost to our ancient and noble game at the age of twenty-seven.

Football

At Limerick CBS handball and hurling were Tom's preferences. 'If you were good enough you played football.' Well, good enough he certainly was. He was on the CBS senior team that won the Munster colleges title for the first time in 1956. He played minor football with Limerick and progressed from there to the county senior team. Unfortunately he was *persona non grata* in 1965, when Limerick won their way to a Munster final showdown with the football kingpins, Kerry. Limerick led at half time but Kerry rallied to be somewhat flattered by a 2:16 to 2:7 win. Tom's presence would certainly have narrowed the winning margin. He won three county titles with his club, Treaty Sarsfields, in 1956, '57, and '63.

Rugby

Tom's father was a rugby man — who in Limerick city wasn't? He played with Shannon before it became a senior power and in the days when the club fed the Garryowen senior team. It is not surprising, therefore, that Tom too played rugby, and with considerable distinction. He played in the centre and had the honour of captaining Young

Tom McGarry holding the Gael Linn Cup (in the centre) and friends c. 1957/1958

Munster in a Munster cup final against Garryowen, the victory going to Garryowen. Rugby pundits — and Limerick produces many of them — are said to have often expressed the view that if Tom had concentrated on rugby from his early days he would have been selected to play for Ireland.

Soccer

This was the beginning of his conflict with rule 27. Inter-firm soccer league competitions were common in many cities and towns. Tom, who loved all games, was first attracted to soccer through this route. After suspension by the GAA he took the game more seriously and

---

The Munster team with which he won his first Railway Cup medal in 1958 is lined out hereunder. It is full of household hurling names, remembered even to this day.

Mick Cashman *(Cork)*

Jimmy Finn *(Tipperary)*   John Lyons (Cork)   John Barron (Waterford)

Tom McGarry (Limerick) Martin Óg Morrissey (Waterford)   Tony Wall (Tipperary)

Séamus Power (Waterford)   Phil Grimes (Waterford)

Jimmy Smyth (Clare)   Liam Moloney (Limerick)   Jimmy Doyle (Tipperary)

Paddy Barry (Cork)   Christy Ring (Cork)   Dónal Whelan (Waterford)

Michael Maher of Tipperary and Tom Cheasty of Waterford came on as subs
in the final against Leinster.

185

reached a level of skill and proficiency that brought him to the attention of League of Ireland clubs. He spent a number of seasons playing with Limerick and Cork Celtic at centre-forward.

Tom is a retiring and self-effacing person, a most modest sportsman. His achievements as an all-round sportsman have been quite remarkable. He was a superb athlete — superb in ability and talent, superb in sportsmanship and example.

As we travelled back over the decades Tom spoke with reverence of those now imithe ar Shlí na Fírinne — Timmy Murphy, his childhood hero; Mick Tynan, schoolmate and county colleague; Des Dillon, handball opponent — and he bowed his head and made the Sign of the Cross to their memory as he spoke their names.

Still extremely fit and trim, he stands six feet tall, and in his playing days — a fit athlete — he tipped the scales at thirteen-and-a-half stone. A great one indeed was Tom — a sporting giant.

The good old days bring fond memories back to me in my aging years.

"

Thomas McInerney

*'It is known throughout the world
How the Mills and Tulla hurled.'*

66

There weren't any other games I liked better than hurling. I lived for it and went to every game within walking distance of my native parish, O'Callaghan's Mills. I played for a term with Young Irelands and played three matches one Sunday (with different clubs), for which I was called to Dublin County Board, but luckily for me Colonel Tom McGrath from the Mills was chairman and let me off with a warning not to repeat the offence.

My idols were Jim Hurley, Mick Gill, Tom McGrath, the Mackey brothers, Christy Ring, Jimmy Smyth, Lory Meagher, Paddy Grace, Matty Power, the Rackard brothers, Tony Reddan, and many others too numerous to mention.

Bhí mé luath agus tá mé mall. Níl fhios agam cad é do bhris sean-neart an chroí is lúth na mball. ('An gleann in ar tógadh mé' Douglas Hyde, An Craoibhín Aoibhinn)

As I write this article it is the early spring of 1995 and I have just returned from a most absorbing and interesting meeting with Tom McInerney, now in his eighty-ninth year, one of three surviving members of the Clare team of 1932. (The other two are John Joe 'Goggles' Doyle, who featured in *Giants of the Ash*, and Mick Falvey.)

A half-brother of the famous Pa 'Fowler' McInerney and thirteen years his junior, Tom is most modest about his own hurling prowess and describes himself as 'not in the same league as Fowler, who was a giant among giants. Fowler was a very controlled and sporting hurler. He never drew a rash stroke. If an opponent put up his hand to grab the sliotar, Fowler wouldn't pull the first time it happened. He would advise the opponent not to do it again, and after that Fowler would pull. He loved Gaelic games; no-one in Ireland went as often to Croke Park as he did.'

Tom was born in 1906, the year Michael Davitt died. Tom was a twin, and following his birth there were doubts whether he would survive. He told me that a neighbour was taking bets on whether he would live beyond a certain date. The optimists won.

He remembers his early years as 'among the most difficult in Irish history': political unrest, the First World War, War of Independence, Civil War, frugal living. In his lifetime he has witnessed social and economic progress and change beyond description.

My questions and promptings caused diversions and digressions from time to time and led us down Memory Lane, lush with nostalgia, to almost a century ago. 'I remember the War of Independence. The Tans often raided our house. One particular night they raided twice. They came up to the bedroom where we were sleeping, pulled back the clothes, and prodded the mattress with bayonets, searching for weapons. We were terrified and trembling but unharmed. You had to leave the door unlocked at night and leave a list on the back of the door of the number of people in the house. If you were leaving the district you had to get permission. Once my father went to Limerick and brought back a sack of flour. He wasn't authorised to go, and the authorities came and took the flour. They were difficult times. The potato was the staple food: we had potatoes for breakfast, dinner, and tea. And we had porridge for supper. The Glenwood ambush was the biggest in Clare. The neighbours called us out to see the fires on the Broadford hills that night — farmhouses burned by the Tans in revenge.

'My father was a very strict man. He didn't want any of us missing during the hay-saving or other busy times. So when Fowler was going off to train for the 1914 final he threw his bag out the top window; hid it in an outhouse; headed off; and came back when the training was finished. The team and mentors travelled to Dublin the Saturday before the match. It was only when Fowler returned at about 6 p.m. on Monday evening that we learned Clare had won.

'We never smoked in front of my father. He set off for Limerick one day in the side-trap with my brother Jack. A few miles out the road he put his hand in his pocket and exclaimed plaintively, "I forgot my pipe and tobacco, and my knife!" After a short pause he said to Jack, "You wouldn't by any chance have a pipe and bit of tobacco?" Jack produced a knife, a pipe, and tobacco. What we didn't do in front of my father and what he knew we did were two different things.'

Tom received his secondary education in St Flannan's College, Ennis. His father drove him there in a horse and side-trap. They passed by Ennis railway station; it was the first time Tom had seen a train, and the sight of it frightened him. He was a leading sportsman in St Flannan's: captained the school team, barred at the time from taking part in the Harty Cup because the school had introduced rugby, and won many trophies at running. When Tom hurled with Clare he described himself as 'the fastest runner in Clare — tall but not bulky.'

After Flannan's, a number of years were spent in Maynooth, and from there Tom moved to secondary teaching. He spent a year at that and then took up the profession that gave him much satisfaction and fulfilment: primary teaching. In the course of our discussion the 'Village Schoolmaster' in Tom would surface from time to time: a line of poetry; some words of prayer; a pronouncement; a recollection of the thundering words of missioners from the pulpit: 'Wherever the devil is by day he is at Clonloum crossroads by night' — all expressed by Tom with a rising voice and resonance that made great impact.

His hurling memories centred mainly around the 1932 campaign — and understandably so. Clare hadn't won the title since 1914, but from 1927 onwards they were threatening to make the breakthrough. That year they lost to Cork in the Munster final by five points. The following year they drew with Cork at the same stage but lost the replay. In the first round of the championship of 1930, Clare defeated Cork, the reigning All-Ireland champions, but failed to Tipperary in the Munster final. On the day Tommy O'Meara in the Tipperary goal was superb, and they went on to win the All-Ireland.

Tom McInerney (on the left) with his brother, Jack.

'Our four-point win over the All-Ireland champions, Cork, in the 1932 Munster final was something of a surprise and a sore point with Cork. They were still a great team, having won four All-Ireland titles since 1926. They had great men like Jim Hurley, Jim O'Regan, George Garret, and Gah Aherne. Seán Óg Murphy was no longer with them. He was regarded as the greatest full-back of his day — an uncompromising man to mark; he had strength, determination, and everything that goes to make a top hurler. We had great men in Tommy Daly, John Joe Doyle — who was as fast as a hare and had a very keen eye — Larry Blake, Mick Falvey, Fowler, Tull Considine, and Jim Holohan — known as "Dasher"; full of fire, fierce strong, and every part of his body disciplined.

'My happiest day in the Clare jersey was in the All-Ireland semi-final against Galway at Limerick on a calm, sunny afternoon. During training I said to Fowler that we would beat Galway, but his reply was, "You don't know Galway." Well, we were down thirteen points at half time and very down-

hearted. Galway retired to the dressing-room but we stayed on the field. Canon Murphy, who was in charge at the time, is supposed to have shaken a sprinkling of the Biddy Earley bottle on us to revive our spirits. We finished up winning by five points on the incredible score of 9:4 to 4:14. Mick King starred for Galway that day. Tull was the Clare hero. I was wing-forward and scored 1:2. Mick Gill cried bitter tears after that Galway defeat.

'Losing to Kilkenny in the All-Ireland final was my lowest moment and Clare's greatest disappointment. We went into special training for that game and spent two weeks at Mountshannon practising in McDermott's field. With many experienced players on our side, coupled with the wins over Cork and Galway, we felt confident of victory.' Tom is very critical of his own display — tends to shoulder much of the blame; feels he was *persona non grata* in the aftermath. But others blamed themselves too. 'Larry Blake, playing with a hurley that had the tip of the bos missing, stood in the line of vision of Fowler and Tommy Daly as Lory Meagher took

189

a sideline cut for Kilkenny. The sliotar deflected from its path, off the bos of Larry's hurley, and was finished to the net. If left to Fowler and the goalie it would have been cleared.

'John Joe Doyle, the captain, also felt a sense of blame. He took a sideline cut that went directly to a Kilkenny man; was sent into the Clare goalmouth; John Joe wasn't back to cover; a goal was scored.' But there were other disputed matters too. 'The goal-flag umpire flagged two goals for Kilkenny, despite square infringements. Fowler remonstrated, but to no avail. The referee blew full time with minutes remaining and at a time when Clare were pressing strongly and might at least have snatched a draw. Mick Falvey protested strongly to the referee after the game.

'I had a hurley in my hand for as far back as I can remember. But I had no childhood heroes from outside the parish. There was no broadcasting then, like now. There was one gramophone in the parish; no radio; and if you wanted a newspaper you had to go to Ennis. I played against Ahane in a church tournament in Newport. I was marking John Mackey. Mick was regarded as the best hurler of all time — he had everything. I'd rather mark John than Mick — although their father, Tyler, used to say that John was better.

'I remember when Clare and Tipp met in the championship of 1938 the eligibility of Jimmy Cooney to take his place in the Tipp line-out was seriously in question. Canon Hamilton begged and implored Johnny Leahy not to play him. Clare, who felt they were unlikely to win the game, were under instructions from the Leinster Council to object if Cooney played. Johnny's reply was, "We'll talk about that after the match." Tipp won by a street, and Clare's objection was upheld.'

Before I left we were looking at some photographs. 'We never took photo-graphs before a match — bad luck.' He had two in his hands and gazed at them in silence. The expression on his face was reflective and pensive. I knew he was drifting through an avenue now overgrown with the foliage of nostalgia. After a while he broke the silence and said, 'They were great old times. We lived from Sunday to Sunday to see a match — be it good or bad.'

Epilogue

Following my visit I got a phone call from Tom's daughter Treasa, telling me how much he enjoyed the three-hour chat, that 'it made him feel ten years younger.'

After Clare's great victory over Limerick in the Munster final, Tom felt further rejuvenated and sat down and wrote a letter to me. More great news was to follow for Clare followers and Tom. Galway were beaten in the semi-final, and that left us with an Offaly-Clare final and all the intrigue and drama that such a meeting could conjure up. Well, Clare won an absorbing contest in as dramatic a finish as was ever witnessed. And Tom was there to relish it all — a new dawn after eighty-one years of unceasing endeavour — in the company of his 1932 colleague John Joe Doyle.

'While here I stand, not only with the sense
Of present pleasure, but with pleasing thoughts
That in this moment there is food for future years.'

Rumour has it that some publicans in Ennis sold a quantity of Guinness for two pence a pint on the occasion of the victory — the same price as it was in 1914, when they last won. And talking of 1914, I came across a copy of the Clare team expenses for the All-Ireland final of that year. It is reproduced here and makes fascinating reading.

CLARE TEAM EXPENSES 1914

To the Central Council of The Gaelic Athletic Association
Dr. To the County Clare Hurling Team
Expenses of the All Ireland Final

	£ s. d.
October 10, 1914	
To car from Quin via Carrahan to Ennis	1 0 0
To car from Feakle via Tulla to Ennis	1 5 0
To car from Whitegate to Ennis	1 10 0
To car from O'Callaghan's Mills to Ennis	1 5 0
To car from Newmarket on Fergus to Ennis	7 6
To train from Ennis to Ennistymon	
twenty players @ 1/7 each	1 11 8
To car from Ennistymon to Lisdoonvarna	
for twenty players @ 1/6 each	1 10 0
October 17, 1914	
At conclusion of training, team was on this date	
motored to Ennis en route to Dublin	
Three motors @ £1 10 0 each	4 10 0
One motor at £1 15 0 and one free motor	1 15 0
Luncheon at Ennis 40/ and Gratuities to	
Waiters at Old Ground Hotel, 2/-	2 2 0
Tickets for twenty players @ 4/6 each	4 10 0
Two Char-a-bancs to convey team from	
Kingsbridge to Wynn's Hotel	1 5 0
Chauffeurs' Fees	1 0 0
Dinner for twenty players on arrival at Hotel	2 0 0
Beds for twenty	2 0 0
October 18, 1914	
Breakfasts for twenty	2 0 0
Luncheons for twenty	2 0 0
Two Char-a-bancs for day – to Croke Park	
and back to Hotel	3 0 0
Chauffeurs' Fees	1 0 0
Dinner for twenty players	2 0 0
Beds for twenty players	2 0 0
	——
	£36 11 0

'Sambo' McNaughton with his son, Shane.

Born 1964

66

My earliest memory is a Sunday afternoon in July 1977 when my manager, Alex Emerson, handed me the sliotar and told me to lead the under-12s onto the field for the championship final. As I won my first medal that day I had no way of knowing the unforgettable joys and sorrows, the memories and the passions but above all the wealth of friends that I would encounter from my love affair with hurling.

These friendships crisscrossed all counties, other countries and even continents. I've enjoyed a welcome from team-mates, opponents and supporters of all ages. Wherever I go I have been privileged to meet the famous and the not so famous in hurling and many other sports and enjoyed the acquaintance of many fine journalists and sports writers.

Like every other young hurler in Ireland I dreamt of playing in an

All-Ireland, and in 1989 that dream came true when Antrim faced Tipperary. The pride throughout the county was palpable, yet out of the desolation of defeat came a special sporting memory. We were astounded at the welcome we received from fans all over Ulster on our return. We went on a tour of the county to thank the fans for their support. At two o'clock one morning we arrived in the footballing village of Glenavy, where the fans had waited for us over four hours in the pouring rain. The incongruous sight of Ulster's beaten All-Ireland hurlers being cheered to the skies by hundreds of football supporters while Union Jacks fluttered over our heads will stay with me for ever.

As my county career wears, I find myself spending more and more time with Ruairí Óg juveniles. I get a great buzz from coaching and managing my young hopefuls. My wish is that I may be the influence on them that Alex Emerson was on me.

I hope they never feel the need to cash in commercially on any success that hurling may bring them but may give freely and willingly of their time and expertise to promote the game in all its glory to others. May they find in the GAA, as I did, the close comradeship of their team-mates, the ability to admire excellence in an opponent, the shared joy of success and the gracious acceptance of defeat but above all the fierce pride I felt wearing the maroon of Ruairí Óg and the saffron of Antrim.

99

Lawrence Mc Naughton
(SAMBO)

On Saturday 3 August 1996, before the All-Ireland semi-final between Antrim and Limerick, an article by Harry Greensmith appeared in the *Limerick Leader*, from which I have chosen the following extract.

> *'Is iomaí Nollaig a bhí me féin*
> *I mBun Abhann Dalla is mé gan*
> > *chéill*
> *Ag iomáin ar an trá bhán*
> *'S mo chamán bán i mo dhorn liom.*

The above verse from the beautiful song 'Aird Tí Chuain' written by John Mac-Cambridge gives an insight to the playing of hurling in the Glens of Antrim in the latter part of the eighteenth century ... The first Feis na nGleanna in 1904 at Cushendall featured a hurling match between Carey Faughs and Glenarm, a natural transition for the shinty players of both districts. And one of the umpires at the game was Roger Casement. And one of the speakers at the feis was Eoin Mac Néill, a professor of Gaelic, who, some twelve years later, addressed the Volunteers at Lough Gur, County Limerick.'

Sambo's every expression radiates his feelings as he talks about Antrim and Cushendall and hurling. 'I have a fierce pride, a fierce passion, a burning belief in the hurling played by my club, Cushendall, and my county, Antrim.' Pride and passion are words often tossed about, but in the case of Sambo he personifies them, both on and off the field. And he talks with pride about a beloved Cushendall supporter known to all as John Archey, 'who has seen forty-seven All-Ireland hurling finals and who follows Antrim everywhere.' Now ninety-four, 'he still walks the hills with his sheep but has to sit close to the sideline as he watches the matches' — the eyes are failing. And only a year or so ago his daughter drove him from Cushendall to Six Mile Bridge in County Clare to see Antrim play — pride, passion, spirit!

Seventeen years and plenty of defeats at top level haven't quenched Sambo's ardour for the game he deeply loves. Where that love came from is difficult to trace. 'There is no Antrim blood in me: my father came from County Cavan, my mother from County Derry.' Perhaps the hurling spirit of the Glens inspired him; or perhaps his natural aptitude urged him on; or perhaps it was his realisation that progress and prowess on the hurling-field were matched step by step with the elimination of a speech impediment that had afflicted him from childhood. Hurling bred confidence in Sambo.

When it came to playing a game of hurling, no sacrifice was too great, no distance too far. In 1982 he played a club match against Ballycran of County Down and was marking Hugh Gilmore. 'The following Sunday I was in Melbourne, Australia, to play with Sinn Féin against Young Irelands in the Australian states championship. Well, you won't believe who I saw running down to mark me when we lined out, but none other than Hugh Gilmore of Ballycran — the man I had played on a week earlier in Ireland. We won that Australian medal. Billy Fitzpatrick from Kilkenny also played in some of the games for Sinn Féin.'

And talking of Australia, I came across a passage relating to the game published several decades ago in *An Dord Féinne*, the organ of the Gaelic League in Australia, by 'Stocaire':

> *'Hurling is more than a game; it is a National institution, and par excellence the pastime of the Gael. It has survived through long centuries and has borne with it noble traditions. Its origin is shrouded in antiquity. In its own sphere it has as true an expression of Irish temperament and mentality as the Gaelic language, traditional music, or national dancing. The national character is written largely across it. It is the creation of the Irish mind and it has evolved and developed with the growth of the Irish nation.'*

In 1985 Sambo played with Harry Bolands of Chicago to win an All-American championship medal in Philadelphia. Add to the above his successes in Ireland and you have a player

Vanquished consoled by victor.
'Sambo' McNaughton and John Kennedy of
Tipperary at the end of the 1989 All-Ireland.

who won hurling honours on three continents.

On the home front there were many disappointments. In the All-Ireland semi-final of 1989 Antrim defeated a quite talented Offaly fifteen by 4:15 to 1:15. They then faced Tipperary in the final with a considerable degree of hope. For twenty minutes they matched Tipperary — who at times looked distinctly uneasy — in all sectors. Then, having missed a number of good opportunities, they conceded a fortuitous goal. Down eleven points at the interval, they lost in the end by eighteen points — evidence of that unconquered plague of some players, freezing in Croke Park! Our photograph shows Sambo walking from the pitch feeling utterly dejected, while John Kennedy, his friend and opponent, in his own great moment of victory finds time to offer a consoling arm and a word of consolation. 'Surely this photo shows what the game of hurling is all about.'

He was so upset after the semi-final of 1991 against Kilkenny that he left the pitch crying. Victory had come so close, and Antrim had played so well. 'We were leading by a point with time running out when Kilkenny got a winning goal to make it 2:18 to 1:19. Experience on the sideline would have won it that day: a substitution — something to slow the game down. We made no substitution at all during the entire game. I felt devastated. To beat Kilkenny would have been a great coup.'

But it wasn't all sadness in 1991; it was the year Sambo won an All-Star. 'It was a great honour, something you dream about. It will mean more to me as time goes on.' Chosen at midfield, he was following in the steps of Ciarán Barr (1988), Olcan McFetridge, and Dessie Donnelly (1989). It was a wonderful occasion for the consistent and popular Antrim man, voted Player of the Year in Ulster in 1991 and also Ulster Hurler of the Year in '91.

After his All-Star award a 'This is Your Life' presentation was made to him by his club. From many lovely tributes I have chosen the following extracts:

> *'The powerful rounded shoulders, the Henderson-like playing of the sliotar, the powerful determined striking, the courageous blocking, never pulling out of a tackle, combined to create his trademark.'*
> *"No frills and direct" has been his maxim ... Great players exhibit courage and class in the most adverse circumstances; that is what guarantees their place in the folklore of our national game'* (Peter Quinn).

> *'For some unknown reason he seems to attract the attention of kids, dogs and elderly women (Ursula does not fall into any of these categories) and of course is a big hit with the press. But there is a reason why and I believe it is because he has time for people. With all this goes responsibility, and I think Sambo will bear that responsibility well and successfully'* (All the players and Jim Nelson, team manager).

Sambo made his début in a league game on Iggy Clarke of Galway. 'My innocent childlike perception of the priesthood changed after that game.' He smiles as he reflects on it and recalls a story from his youth about a Father White who was a great hurling enthusiast and who

used to train them. 'He used to tell me it was wrong to steal anything but that if I ever happened to steal a few hurleys — well, that would be all right: God wouldn't burn me in Hell for that. Father White always said that there was no room for God in any dressing-room: he should be neutral.'

During his career he has given many brilliant displays in a variety of positions. 'I have programmes at home showing me playing in every position, from full-back to full-forward.' His most recent outstanding performance was in the All-Ireland semi-final of 1996, when he played at centre-back and was opposed by the ace Limerick forward Gary Kirby, whom he described as one of the gentlemen of hurling. As a youngster the player he admired most was Ger Henderson of Kilkenny. 'I'd love to have modelled myself on him. He was something else. And then when I got to play against him — just fantastic. He was a great centre-back. John Fenton of Cork was another hurler I admired — different from Henderson. He was a most graceful performer — showed hurling to be the art form it is; was like a ballet dancer on the field.'

Sambo has a soft spot for Cork and its people. 'Whenever we went down there they couldn't do enough for us. In my first All-Ireland I saw the great Cork three-in-a-row team of 1976–78. John Horgan sticks out from that game, also Ray Cummins and Jimmy Barry Murphy. I saw John come out from defence and drive the ball about a hundred yards. Eddie Keher caught my eye too. Hurlers over the border have always

seemed like gods: bigger, stronger, faster. This belief is still a problem in Antrim: some Antrim hurlers freeze when they see Jones's Road. But I honestly believe an Antrim hurling title is not far away. Look at the way Clare were devastated in the Munster final of 1993 — beaten by Tipperary by eighteen points — even worse than the score suggests — and yet they came back and won the All-Ireland title in 1995. Heart and passion: to me hurling is all about heart and passion. I was there that day. I love watching a game nearly as much as playing. To be sitting in Croke Park when Clare won — unbelievable. What an atmosphere! Whenever I watch a game I always play the role of manager — for both sides — plotting what I would do if I were in charge. As I watched Limerick against Offaly in the 1994 final there were things I would have done that would have won the title for Limerick.'

Sambo was the youngest of eleven children, six boys and five girls. (His wife, Ursula, is one of twenty-one.) In his family five of the boys played hurling, three of them assisting Antrim and Ulster. His mother never saw him play. 'She never saw me hit a ball in real life — she would watch the telly; but she always lights a candle for me when I go off to play.'

Nowadays Sambo gets tremendous enjoyment from putting something back into the game and its promotion. He travels countless miles to present medals and trophies. He enjoys in particular pucking the sliotar around with his young son, Shane, aged 9, 'who is very skilful and shows great promise,' and spending lots of time with children. 'They hang on every word you say.' Some day Sambo might manage an Antrim team; it would be his ambition.

The youngsters are lucky to have him, a man described as follows by Gerry McLoughlin in the *Sunday Press* on 4 August 1991: 'Sambo does not fear the dark places where timber tests the soul ... above all else you could hear Sambo's heart beating from the stand.' Yes, they are lucky to have him: a gentleman and outstanding sportsman; an ardent lover of the game of hurling. No finer exponent of the noble game has come out of Antrim since the days of the great Kevin Armstrong.

Paddy Molloy (right) *with Wexford stalwart defender Tom Neville at Gaelic Park, New York, 1965.*

"

I used to listen to Mícheál O'Hehir broadcasting the matches when I was a youngster. All the players he named were heroes to me. To this day I can still name the players of the great Cork four-in-a-row winning team. There were only two wirelesses in our neighbourhood. A crowd used to gather around Guinan's in the village of Killyon. Mícheál O'Hehir's description of the field painted a vivid picture for me as a youngster. He divided the field into sections and made it easy to follow the game. The first game I remember listening to was the 1944 Munster final, Limerick v. Cork. This was the Mackey and Ring era, and I remember the stunning silence when Mackey was about to take a 21-yard free for Limerick. He always seemed to score goals with every attempt. Then the great roar of approval from the crowded kitchen as he crashed the ball to the net. Similarly at the other

Born 1934

end, when Ring took his shots — it got the same response.

As a youngster Mícheál O'Hehir made a great impression on me, and I used to imitate him for days after with my own commentary, with the help of a bucket over my face. The excitement that O'Hehir could bring to the air waves was immense and made a great impression on my young mind. He brought the thrills of the game into the kitchen, and as a result I had a dream. It was this: that one day, when I grew up, he would sing my praises on the radio and I would be selling the dummies, side-stepping my man and crashing the ball to the net, and taking frees slap-bang in front of the goal, and sending them over the bar. How often did I hear him say, 'He bends, lifts, and strikes, and sends it over the bar'? It took me a long time to achieve my goal, but luckily I made it, near the end of my playing days. I think Mícheál O'Hehir was the greatest commentator of all time and is the unsung hero of hurling especially, and a deep debt of gratitude is owed to him.

My family was steeped in the GAA tradition. My father, Larry, won the first county title with Drumcullen in 1908. Previous to that he won a county title with Fortal. He also played for the famous Toomevara Greyhounds v. the also famous Nenagh-De Witts, as they were known at that time. In the early 1900s he also played with the county team. He was chairman of the Offaly County Board for a term and was succeeded by the late Seán Robbins. My uncle Mick also played for the county and won three county titles with Birr, where he worked at that time. Nowadays I am happy to see my own sons take such a keen interest in the game. Enda won an All-Ireland minor medal in 1987, and Paul and Pádraig won the Community Games All-Ireland under-14 in 1993. Daragh, who is now aged nine, practises pucking the ball into a bucket and is known to score six out of six and entices me out now and again to a puck-around.

As I write these lines my mind goes back to the past, and I recall with much sadness the names of four colleagues who are no longer with us: they are Nick O'Donnell, Des Foley, Ted Carroll, and Ollie Walsh. May their souls rest in peace.

In conclusion, I am deeply grateful to Brendan Fullam for allowing me the privilege of writing those few humble lines in such exalted company.

Paddy Molloy ''

P addy Molloy hails from Offaly — the Faithful County. It seems it was so named by that well-known Wexford Gael the late Martin O'Neill in one of his annual reports some time in the thirties.

Paddy made his county début in goal in 1952 on the Offaly minor team. He was a sub on the junior team that won the Leinster title in 1953 but failed to Tipperary in the home final. By 1955 he had progressed to the senior team and was a regular thereon for the next sixteen years.

He made his name early on as a goalie and defender, but as time passed his versatility was such that he played for Offaly in every position except full-back. So capable and accomplished was he that if called upon he would no doubt have acquitted himself with distinction at full-back too. 'I was a certain kind of disciplinarian — never said no: would play wherever the selectors wanted me.'

He was a gifted hurler with exceptional ability, one of Offaly's greatest. Imagine playing under-14 hurling with his club for six years! In defence he was resolute and played first-time, no-nonsense hurling. Breaking hurleys was a feature of his game. He always carried at least three, and sees it as vital to have a hurley with which you are familiar; he thinks little of players who don't equip themselves with several. As a forward he was lethal and capable of producing telling scores. Some of his scoring feats were extraordinary: in 1965 in two championship games he scored 4:12; in 1966 in twelve games he scored 11:63; in 1969 in three championship games he scored 8:15; in the Offaly senior hurling final of 1966 he was the top scorer, with 3:3. His performance in that championship won him the Offaly Sports Star of the Year award.

'The ferocity of club hurling in my time in Offaly was unbelievable. They used to come to the county final from the surrounding counties to see the action.' Paddy was further honoured in 1966 with an Ireland jersey — a forerunner of the All-Stars — at a reception in Dublin.

He was no mean footballer either. In 1963 he won a county senior football title with Tullamore. He scored 1:1 and got Sports Star of the Week for his performance. The *Midland Tribune* of 2 November said: 'Paddy in his unaccustomed role was one of Tullamore's heroes.'

Unfortunately during Paddy's hurling era the balance of power had not swung Offaly's way. Lack of success brings its own problems — financial and otherwise. He remembers a league game against Westmeath in St Brendan's Park in the early sixties when Offaly had only thirteen players and had to get two from the gate to make up the numbers. 'Be ready for Sunday' was the message players would receive the week of a match. And he remembers well a National League division 2 final when the only fare on offer was bread and raspberry jam. They asked whether they would 'have to hurl on that stuff' and were told, 'It'll have to do — it's not even paid for.' For Paddy it contrasted starkly with the Railway Cup games, when Martin O'Neill would ask, 'What will you have, Paddy, chicken, beef, or ham?'

Three games stand out above all others in Paddy's mind:

- — The county final of 1960, when he captained Drumcullen to victory and in so doing was the first man to receive the Seán Robbins Cup. 'We pipped Shinrone.' Seán Robbins was a well-known Offaly Gael. He refereed four All-Ireland finals: 1929, when Cork defeated Galway; the two drawn games of 1931 between Cork and Kilkenny; and 1932, when Kilkenny pipped Clare by one goal.

- — Beating Tipperary in a league game in 1966. 'I have great memories of that game, and good reason to remember it. It was played about the end of October. I had three acres of beet ready for drawing out. On the Friday night before the match my brother told me that if I wanted the tractor I could have it for Saturday; after that he needed it. Without any help I loaded and unloaded seven trailers — no heeling the load; all thrown in by hand and unloaded by hand. On Sunday morning I couldn't lift my hands. How can I face hurling Tipperary? I said to myself. I went to Mass; came home; felt a bit better. I went out and picked up an axe and swung it on a block several times; after that the hurley felt light in my hands. We hammered Tipp. It was a great thrill. I got a lot of congratulations after that game.'

- — Beating Wexford in 1969. 'Even though Wexford were All-Ireland champions I had a feeling we could beat them.' Well, Paddy's premonition was right. Offaly were 2:1 up after about six minutes; by half time they were five goals up, and at the final whistle they were five points to the good, 5:10 to 3:11. Paddy was Offaly's chief marksman, and Offaly were in their first Leinster final since 1928. In an earlier game against Laois he went on the rampage and scored 5:4 out of a total of 8:10.

It was a well-organised, strong and talented Offaly team that met Kilkenny in the Leinster final. They failed by only two points, 3:9 to 0:16, and Kilkenny went on to win the All-Ireland title. 'Pat Delaney murdered us that day — he got the goals for Kilkenny.'

That led us to a discussion on the Offaly team — an aging one in 1969 — and I wondered if they had missed opportunities to make a breakthrough in earlier years. 'After beating Tipp in 1966 I knew we were good enough to win at least a Leinster title and possibly an All-Ireland. The worst thing that ever happened to Offaly was to meet Westmeath in Birr in the 1967 championship. The game became known as the Battle of Birr. Joe Murphy was sent off after five minutes. Ten minutes later the referee, Jimmy Hatton from Wicklow, sent off Willie Gorman and Johnny Flaherty and one Westmeath man. We now had twelve playing fourteen, and lost. It was the worst thing that could have happened the team.'

In 1968 it was disaster again. 'Des Ferguson of Dublin was brought down to show us how. He told us the best thing we could do against Kilkenny was take all the points we could. Des was appointed to referee the game. Within ten minutes John Kirwan was sent off; we lost by four points.' Paddy is in no doubt that if the panel of 1966–70 could be assembled today, and managed with the expertise of today, they would win All-Ireland titles.

Was he ever sent off himself? 'I was. It was a game against Carlow. Moling Morrissey at centre-forward was catching every puck-out. I switched onto him. The exchanges were hard, and after one particular tussle I was both carried off and sent off. He was off too. I felt hard done by.'

Paddy's performances didn't go unnoticed by the Leinster Railway Cup selectors. For nine successive years he featured on the Leinster selections, beginning as a sub in 1963 and ending similarly in 1971. In between he gave outstanding performances in a variety of positions: centrefield, right-full-forward, left-full-forward, and left-half-back in 1965, the year he had the onerous and challenging task of marking Jimmy Doyle. He rose to the occasion in great style and demonstrated his class and potential, watched for the first time by a wider audience of hurling followers. He is full of praise for the

Paddy Molloy leads Offaly (N.Y.) in the parade at Gaelic Park New York prior to the game against Cork (N.Y.).

welcome, support and encouragement he got from his Kilkenny colleagues on the team, in particular his half-back colleagues, the late Ted Carroll and Séamus Cleere. The Railway Cup victory of 1965 over Munster, 3:11 to 0:9, was a very special day for Paddy and for Offaly: it was the first time an Offaly man had won a Railway Cup hurling medal.

Memory Lane tossed up snapshots and cameos stretching back over half a century. 'I was only three when I used to climb through a gap in the ditch, and a neighbour, Tom Dooley, carried me on the plough as he ploughed with his team of horses. I used to be afraid he would plough me into the ground. He was a giant of a man — my first hero. He played for years with Drumcullen.

'There was hurling every Sunday in Dooley's field. Mrs Dooley had a big yellow teapot with a red handle. She should be in the *Guinness Book of Records* for making tea. Everyone who came to the field on Sunday got tea from Mrs Dooley. She was a wonderful woman.

'I used always read the papers before and after the matches. I can still see the pictures of three Kilkennymen before the 1947 final: Tom Walton, Jimmy Kelly, and Jimmy Heffernan. Of course I can't say enough about Mícheál O'Hehir. The excitement he used create in me as I listened to his broadcasts was unbelievable. Every name he mentioned was a hero: John Mackey, Mick Mackey, Jackie Power, Din Joe Buckley, Willie Murphy, Christy Ring.

'I had the great honour of meeting Christy during the Cardinal Cushing games of 1965 in the US. Four hurlers were invited: Jimmy Duggan (Galway), Tom Neville (Wexford), Christy Ring (Cork), and myself. In the game between Offaly (New York) and Cork (New York) Tom Neville and myself were guest players with Offaly, and Jimmy Duggan and Christy Ring were guest players with Cork. Ring scored

3:2, at forty-five years of age. We then travelled to Boston to play a Tipperary team. I was marking a fellow called Joe Carey — wasn't taking the game too seriously; was chatting to him. Ring had scored a couple of points. He came over to me and said, "Lift your game; stop talking — you can talk to him all you like when it's finished. Don't you know we're playing Tipperary? We have to beat them." The ball hopped nicely in front of goal and I stuck it in the net. I looked at Ring. "Keep it up: put three or four more with it," he said. Every year after that I got a Christmas card from him. I regret now I didn't keep them. One day my daughter ran out to me in the yard and said, "Your friend is dead — your friend Christy Ring." I don't mind admitting I shed a few tears.

'My first visit to Croke Park was for the All-Ireland final of 1956 between Cork and Wexford. I was mesmerised by the speed of the game. I never realised it could be played at such a pace.

'One of the greatest displays I ever saw was given by Pat Henderson at centre-back for Kilkenny in the All-Ireland final of 1969 against Cork. I was at a Walsh Cup final between Wexford and Kilkenny in the fifties. I remember the first-time striking — overhead and on the ground — between Ned Wheeler and Willie Walsh as they contested every ball at midfield. There was nothing between them until near the end, when the strength of Ned began to tell.

'I quit inter-county hurling in 1971. After a league game I went to Pat Henderson and said, "I won't worry you again." "Hold on," he said, "and we'll win another Railway Cup." But I knew the legs wouldn't go. You don't give hurling up: it gives you up.'

As he picked his team he kept saying, 'Good God, I'm leaving off great men.'

Ollie Walsh (*Kilkenny*)

Ted Carroll (*Kilkenny*) Nick O'Donnell (*Wexford*) Paddy Spellman (*Offaly*)

Séamus Cleere (*Kilkenny*) Billy Rackard (*Wexford*) Willie Walsh (*Kilkenny*)

John Connolly (*Galway*) Mick Roche (*Tipperary*)

Jimmy Doyle (*Tipperary*) Pat Delaney (*Kilkenny*) Eddie Keher (*Kilkenny*)

Christy Ring (*Cork*) Nicky Rackard (*Wexford*) Paddy Molloy (*Offaly*)

Born 1928

1953. In the five years from 1952 to 1956 he played for the Combined Universities against an Ireland selection. His untimely death in 1978 at fifty years of age shocked Gaeldom.

I am indebted to Tom Morrison for his kind permission to reproduce the following article, which he published at the time of Gerard's death.

'The news of the death of Gerard Murphy, the former Cork All-Ireland hurler of the fifties, at the weekend caused sorrow and grief everywhere. A native of Midleton, he spent the last number of years in scenic Ballycotton, where he was widely known and respected. On numerous occasions I had the pleasure of chatting to Gerard and found him to be a quiet, modest gentleman who took a keen interest in sailing, but apart from liking it very much, his love was hurling.

'He first pulled a Cork minor jersey over his head in 1945 after playing a whale of a game for Midleton CBS against St Flannan's College in the Dr Harty Cup. The following year he was picked for Munster in the inter-provincial colleges series and won his first All-Ireland award when they defeated Leinster in the final. That same year he was again on the Cork minor team with little success, but the following season he went all the way with the Cork juniors, who won back the All-Ireland title by beating London in the final proper by 10 points.

'He made his senior début at left-full-forward in 1949 and scored a goal against Tipperary in the drawn Munster championship. He was then dropped for the replay and didn't play again until the opening round against Waterford in 1950. From 1952 onwards, Gerard's name became a household one whenever the game of hurling came up for discussion and with his powerful frame he earned his own special niche in Cork's three in a row.

'Looking back he liked recalling the

G erard's hurling skills manifested themselves in his schooldays. He stood out as a future star. He progressed steadily through all the hurling grades of his day: colleges, minor for Cork in 1945 and 1946, junior in 1947 and 1948, senior ranks in 1949. At the age of seventeen he won a Cork county junior hurling medal with his club, Midleton.

It took a player of talent and quality to gain and hold a place on the Cork panel from 1949 onwards. They had many star hurlers, among them Tom Mulcahy, Gerry O'Riordan, Willie John Daly, Matty Fouhy, Christy Ring, Con Murphy, Dave Creedon, Josie Hartnett, John Lyons, and Paddy Barry. They had some rousing games with Tipperary, Galway, and Wexford.

Gerard was a key figure and a tower of strength at midfield in the Munster and All-Ireland triumphs of the great three-in-a-row success of 1952 to 1954. They survived in close finishes, won games they might have lost — sure signs of a very good and talented team.

Gerard played Fitzgibbon Cup with UCD and UCC. He won National League and Railway Cup medals in

Cork team 1950. Cork v Waterford in the Munster semi-final at Thurles. Cork 1:4, Waterford 0:5.
Gerard Murphy, *Mossie O'Riordan, Gerry O'Riordan, Matt Fouhy, Joe Hartnett, Fr. John Thornhill, Tom Crotty, Tim Morrissey, Jim Barry, Willie John Daly, Con Murphy, Paddy O'Donovan, Christy Ring, Seán O'Brien, Willie Moore, Tom Mulcahy, Seán Twomey (sub).*

1952 season, not because it was winning his first All-Ireland medal but because of the quality of the games involved. "The Munster final against Tipperary was a fantastic affair — just a stroke of the ball between the teams. The semi-final against Galway was also a hectic game. The final with Dublin was an anti-climax, but winning my first medal made up for all that," he once said.

'A former UCC and UCD player in the Fitzgibbon Cup competition, Gerard named Christy Ring and Joe Salmon as the great players of his time. "In all honesty I must say that Ring was the best hurler I have ever seen. He had it every way, style, strength, fitness and a marvellous hurling brain. Galway's Joe Salmon was also admirable. I always enjoyed marking him and we seemed to bring the best out of each other."

'In his prime he won every honour the game can bestow — three All-Ireland medals, four Munster championships (all senior), a National League, Railway Cup as well as being a regular member of the Combined Universities sides for a number of years.

'When I once asked him was there any famous display that stood out in his memory he thought it doubtful if a player is conscious of giving a "display" during any game, as he would be too preoccupied with what might happen next. "This uncertainty is one of the glories of the game of hurling. However, it does seem that my displays in 1952 against Tipperary and in the 1956 opening championship round against Waterford in Fermoy were the highlight of my career in the red jersey."

'After playing another fine game in the '56 Munster final against Limerick he was again dropped for the All-Ireland final and he could never understand why. It was said that he did not prepare or train properly for this game, which was completely untrue. Though living in Dublin at the time, he trained and was as fit and prepared for that game as for any other. He did subsequently come on towards the end of the game but by then Wexford were well on their way to a second consecutive triumph.'

God rest him now.

Born 1897

A winning captain in his time of Blackrock, Cork, and Munster, Seán Óg Murphy made his name as an uncompromising and outstanding full-back, feared and fearless.

Cork were witnessing lean times in the hurling world when Seán Óg first appeared in the Cork jersey. He played in his first All-Ireland final in 1915, when the men of Laois proved superior on the score 6:2 to 4:1. Before that Cork had won six titles: in 1890, when an unfinished match against Wexford was awarded to Cork, then the first three-in-a-row by any county, 1892–94, and at the turn of the century two in a row, 1902–03.

A long sequence of losses was broken in 1919 when Dublin were defeated and Seán Óg won his first All-Ireland medal. Celebrating that victory with him were three other hurling sons of Blackrock: 'Balty' Aherne, who went on to win four further titles in 1926, '28, '29, and '31; Mick Murphy, also victorious in 1926; and Eudi Coughlan, who came on as a sub and shared the same subsequent successes with Balty Aherne. In the 1919 final Cork wore the red-and-white jerseys for the first time; up to then the county team had worn a saffron-and-blue jersey with a C on the chest. It seems that on the eve of the 1919 final British forces raided the Cork County Board premises and confiscated the jerseys — hence the change of colour.

The rich rewards and honours came for Seán Óg in the later stages of his illustrious career. Cork won four Munster hurling titles in a row in the period 1926–29. The 1926 final against Tipperary was unique: it took three meetings to decide the issue. The first game was abandoned at Cork Athletic Grounds after about twenty minutes following encroachment on the pitch from a capacity crowd of almost thirty thousand. The replay was at Thurles, and the organisation and stewarding under the generalship of that great captain of earlier years, Tom Semple, ensured that there were no crowd difficulties on this occasion. The game ended in a draw. The replay, again at Thurles, was won by Cork, 3:6 to 2:4. In defence Seán Óg was rocklike. Tipperary played three-quarters of the game with fourteen men after a defender was sidelined.

In the 1928 Munster final it took two games to dispose of Clare, and Seán Óg really excelled in the replay, clearing danger time and time again, playing a captain's part and leading by example.

In the four-year span 1926–29 Cork contested every All-Ireland final. They were captained by Seán Óg in 1926, '27, and '28, winning in 1926 and '28, losing in 1927 to a great Dublin outfit.

An injury in a game against Clare ended his hurling career before the 1929 championship. It was unfortunate: it deprived him of an All-Ireland honour that year, and he would also very probably have been there in 1931 to be part of the historic three final games against Kilkenny. Subsequently he displayed his talents as an administrator when he

Cork All-Ireland Hurling Championships 1928.
Back (left to right): *J. O'Regan, M. O'Connell, T. Barry, M. Aherne, J. Burke, P. O'Grady,*
Sean Óg Murphy (Capt.), *E. O'Connell.* Front (left to right): *P.Aherne, M. Leahy, P. Delea,*
D. Barry-Murphy, J. Hurley, E. Coughlan, M. Madden.

became secretary of the Cork County Board, a position in which he gave outstanding service and which he held until his death in 1956.

In the green and gold with his native Blackrock he was involved in many hectic and thrilling encounters in the Cork county championship. A great club won many honours; we will concentrate, however, on a remarkable game: a strange and unexpected defeat in the 1926 county final against their great rivals, St Finbarr's. Blackrock were county champions in 1924 and 1925. When Cork defeated Kilkenny in the 1926 All-Ireland final there were ten Blackrock men on the team; it was natural, therefore, that Blackrock should be firm favourites to defeat St Finbarr's in the county final, which took place on the first Sunday in November. But fate played a role in deciding the championship. In the early stages of the game two outstanding forwards and prolific scorers, Eudi Coughlan and Paddy Delea, were sent off. In addition to this misfortune, the records show that Blackrock had three goals disallowed. Yet in the end they lost by only one point.

Critics of the day contended that if

Seán Óg as captain had not adopted an all-out defensive policy towards the closing stages of the game the result might have been different — mere surmise: the wisdom of hindsight! Others felt that if the 1926 All-Ireland campaign hadn't been so demanding and gruelling Blackrock might have won despite the sendings off. Yet another view suggests that no matter how good a team is, it will, on a given day, because of a combination of circumstances, meet its match. It is a view that carries much substance.

Seán Óg's talents were not confined to the hurling field. In his young days he played football at inter-county level with Cork. He also won a Cork senior football medal with Nils.

Seán Óg and the full-back position were synonymous. His clashes with the ace Tipperary full-forward Martin Kennedy are legendary; when they opposed each other it was a meeting of two greats of the game. Martin regarded Seán Óg as the best full-back to have played the game, and in his aging years this self-effacing man would recall with modest pride his first Munster game, when Tipperary travelled to

Munster final, Thurles, 1928. Below is the original caption as it appeared at the time in the Tipperary Star. *The above group includes: Most Rev. Dr Harty, Archbishop of Cashel, Patron of the GAA (seated in centre); Mr Sean Ryan, Solicitor, President of the Association; Rev. J. J. Meagher, C.C., President, Tipperary County Board; Rev. Dr Doyle, C.C., Kilkenny; Rev. M. Maher, P.P., Killenaule; Rev. T. O'Connor, C.C., Thurles; Rev. M. J. Lee, Diocesan Inspector, Thurles; General Eoin O'Duffy; Major Fitzmaurice (famous Atlantic flyer); Chief Supt. Hannigan, Thurles; Mr W. Myles, Editor,* Tipperary Star; *Mr Con Browne, GAA, Limerick; Mr Dan Morrissey, Dungarvan, etc., etc.*

Cork and he scored four goals off Seán Óg.

Cork won the first National League title when they defeated Dublin at the Cork Athletic Grounds on 12 May 1926 under the captaincy of Seán Óg. He was captain too when he led Munster in the inaugural game of the Railway Cup competition — a real thriller — at Croke Park on St Patrick's Day 1927. Leinster won by two points. There was compensation, however, for Seán Óg in the victories that followed in 1928 and 1929.

With fellow-Corkmen Jim O'Regan and Eudi Coughlan he had the honour of being chosen on the Tailteann Games team of 1928.

In his playing days as a club man and county hurler he had as team-mates some of the greatest names in the hurling calendar, among them John Coughlan, Eudi Coughlan, 'Marie' O'Connell, Paddy Delea, Dinny Barry Murphy, Jim O'Regan, Jim Hurley, Tom Barry, 'Balty' Aherne, and 'Gah' Aherne.

Alan Lotty comes with a dash to cover Willie Murphy when the latter is tackled by J. O'Brien, Kilkenny's full-forward, in the 1939 All-Ireland final.

Born 1915

Limerick with a late goal on the score 4:3 to 3:4. Willie Murphy was playing at left-half-back. An injury to Paddy O'Donovan necessitated switches in the Cork team. Willie was moved to right-full-back for the final against Kilkenny — the thunder-and-lightning final — lost by Cork by one point.

From then until 1949 Willie Murphy hurled with distinction at right-full-back. He was one of the great defenders of his era and actually played at full-back in the 1945 Munster semi-final against Tipperary. As a youngster I formed the impression that he was a somewhat shy man, because in any team photograph in which I saw him he was always looking slightly away from the camera.

Cork had a great full-back line all through the forties. Manning the line with Willie were Batt Thornhill and Alan Lotty, Batt Thornhill and Con Murphy, Batt Thornhill and Din Joe Buckley, Con Murphy and Din Joe Buckley, and finally, in 1949, Con Murphy and Jim Young, who was captain. Willie had the signal honour of being part of the great Cork four-in-a-row All-Ireland wins of 1941–44. It created a record then; it has stood for over half a century; it may stand for a long time yet.

Willie lined out in the blue and white of Munster for the first time in 1940. Fellow-Corkmen on that team were Willie Campbell, Seán Barrett, Johnny Quirke, and Micka Brennan. Every year after that until 1948 he was in the Munster full-back line, mainly at right-full, but in 1942 and 1945 he filled left-full-back and full-back, respectively. It was a fine achievement: nine successive appearances. He was on the victorious side on seven occasions, losing only in 1941 to Leinster by one point and in 1947 to Connacht.

He played in nine Munster finals, losing only three — to Limerick in 1940, to Tipperary in 1941, and to Waterford in 1948. The year 1941 merits special attention,

He was known as Willie 'Long Puck' Murphy, because of the prodigious length he got into his deliveries from goal. And he did it consistently. He won his first (county) school shield medal with Ballincollig in 1926, at the age of eleven. At fifteen he played junior hurling for his club and played with the Cork minor hurlers for three seasons. In 1931 he had as colleagues on the county team Charlie Lynch and Micka Brennan. They beat Clare in the first round but lost the next round to Tipperary after a replay. Subsequently Willie played at junior level for Cork. His brother Charlie was also a player of note. Another well-known son of Ballincollig was Pat 'Hitler' Healy. He was on the Cork panel for a number of years in the forties and reappeared again for the Munster campaign of 1952.

Willie's senior career coincided with a wonderful era in Cork hurling. Out of the limelight and the big time right through the thirties, a glorious era ended in triumph in 1931. Cork by 1939 were blending together again a team comprising youth and experience. Their 1939 campaign began with a convincing win over the All-Ireland champions, Waterford. In a thrill-a-minute Munster final they beat

Cork 1942.
Back (left to right): J. Buckley, P. O'Donovan, C, Tobin, J. Lynch, C. Murphy, J. Barry (trainer). Centre: E. Porter, M. Kenefick, W. Murphy, S. Condon, J. Young, D. J. Buckley. Front: J. Quirke, D. Beckett, C. Ring, B. Thornhill, C. Cottrell. Missing from this picture of the Munster champions is A. Lotty who took part in the All-Ireland final.

the year Willie Murphy won his first All-Ireland medal but not a Munster one. It happened like this. Cork, by defeating Limerick, and Tipperary, with a victory over Waterford, qualified to meet in the Munster final. Then there was an outbreak of foot and mouth disease, particularly bad in Tipperary. There was no question of risking a game between Cork and Tipperary. Cork were nominated to play Dublin in the All-Ireland final. Victory came easily to the rebel county, 5:11 to 0:6. So with foot and mouth under control and Cork now All-Ireland champions, a delayed Munster final was played at Limerick on 26 October. The odds favoured Cork. In 1940 they had defeated Tipperary by eleven points. But a shock was in store; Tipperary won the Munster title by 5:4 to 2:5. It produced a unique situation: Cork were All-Ireland hurling champions of 1941 but not Munster champions of 1941.

Willie Murphy played in seven All-Ireland finals, losing two — both to Kilkenny, in 1939 and 1947, and, coincidentally, both lost by just one point, the winner on each occasion being scored with the last puck of the game. He also won three National League titles. No luck came his way at club level. Ballincollig reached the county final in 1942 and again in 1943. They lost each time to St Finbarr's, in '43 after a replay. Willie was a most loyal club man and gave long and dedicated service. He played his last game for Ballincollig in 1957, in his forty-second year.

He called it a day at county level after the two-and-a-half hour marathon first-round encounter with Tipperary in 1949 at Limerick. Cork had dominated the forties in Munster. For the next three years Tipperary would reign supreme. So his career ended as it began, with defeat. But in between there was much to relish and cherish. This fine hurling defender from Ballincollig had much to reflect on, a lot to be proud of.

Bhí sé in aois seasca a dó sa bhliain 1977 nuair a ghlaoigh Dia air.

Donie NEALON   1958–1969   Burgess-Youghalarra & UCD & Tipperary

North Tipp Champs 1964 Burgess Capt. Donie Nealon receives the cup from Seamus Ó'Riain

Born 1935

"
Looking back on my hurling life I know how fortunate I was to have been born into a very Gaelic-oriented family, as my father had won junior (1924) and senior (1925) All-Ireland medals with Tipperary, had played for Ireland in the Tailteann Games of 1924, and had travelled on a never-to-be-forgotten three-month trip to the USA with Tipp in 1926. My father spent many hours coaching my brothers Seán, Pat and myself in the basic skills of hurling and always placed great emphasis on developing both right and left sides and always striking on the ground or out of the hand when in full flight and at top speed. He ingrained a great love of hurling in me as a child that I cherish to this day. As youngsters we hurled at every opportunity, organised our own mini-games and 'three goals in', and spent hours pucking back the sliotar for the seniors when they trained in the local hurling-field, picking up new tips on the way.

My first major game attended was the Munster hurling final in Thurles, Tipp v. Limerick, in 1945 as a nine-year-old, travelling by bus with my father on the Saturday, and we were joined by my mother, who travelled by bus the next day to the game.

Strange to relate, I only played one competitive juvenile hurling grade, when as a twelve-year-old I played against our neighbours Kiladangan in the North Tipp under-15 hurling championship. We were well beaten; but is there a lesson to be learned?

I went to St Flannan's College, Ennis, at thirteen years of age in 1949, where hurling was a second religion, and while there won a memorable Harty Cup final v. Thurles CBS in 1954 and also played for Munster colleges that year. I owe a huge debt of gratitude to the St Flannan's trainer, Father Jimmy Madden, a master coach and expert tactician and probably the best coach I ever encountered, who did a lot for my confidence and hurling development. I also really enjoyed my hurling days with St Patrick's Training College in Drumcondra, whom I captained in 1956 to Kavanagh Cup (inter-faculty) and intermediate hurling league success. My later years with UCD were also very enjoyable and satisfying, winning three Fitzgibbon Cups, a Boland Cup and a Dublin SHC medal in 1961, along with my brother Pat, against famed St Vincent's. I loved college hurling and made numerous friendships that I have always treasured.

I won my first hurling medal at seventeen years with my native Burgess-Youghalarra, a championship I'll never forget, as it took three final games against Shannon Rovers to decide the issue. This was the first of my eight North Tipp intermediate hurling medals, leading on to two county junior hurling medals in 1964 and 1976. I always got great satisfaction and enjoyment from coaching my native Youghalarra National School teams, in both hurling and camogie, and my local Burgess team from juvenile to senior level. Our most recent success was a County Tipperary intermediate hurling title in 1993, when the team was captained by my son Seán. Incidentally, I was honoured to have been captain myself of the first Burgess team to win a county junior hurling championship, in 1964.

I always deeply appreciated the great support and encouragement I got from my wife and family, my parents, my club players, supporters and parishioners during my hurling career, as this meant a great deal to me, and I was always conscious that I was representing them whenever I lined out for my club or county. I later tried to repay them by training and coaching school and parish teams and acting as a club official in many capacities since 1963 to the present day.

My inter-county career started when I played junior for Tipp in 1956 and 1957 (without success), leading on to my first senior game in the National league v. Kerry in the spring of 1958 at Clonmel. I did not play minor county with Tipp, as I was born in December and was considered too light and too small for the team in 1953 at seventeen years of age; but plenty of farm work as a teenager during my summer holidays in the 1950s and hours of handball practice in the local Youghalarra handball alley built up my strength and toughened me up for my inter-county career later on. I got my chance with the Tipp seniors in 1958 and had the good fortune to realise my life's ambition of winning an All-Ireland senior hurling medal in my very first year; and the thrill of hearing the final whistle on the seventh of September 1958 will be for ever etched in my memory.

I had the pleasure of playing in eight senior All-Irelands altogether, fortunately winning on five occasions. It was marvellous to be a part of Tipp's greatest decade in hurling history, when seven Munster titles and four All-Irelands were won in the 1960s, along with five National Hurling Leagues and five Oireachtas titles for good measure. Losing the 1968 All-Ireland was especially painful, as we had an eight-point lead at half time, only to be demolished by a resurgent and powerful Wexford in the second half. I had intended retiring if we won in 1968, but when we didn't I continued on as a sub in 1969 and played my last game for Tipp when I came on a sub for the second half of the Munster final, which we lost to Cork.

Seriously ill with rheumatic fever in 1970, my hurling future looked bleak, but, thank God, I made a wonderful recovery to good health to continue playing with Burgess until the mid-eighties.

I became involved in the coaching and teaching of hurling skills and tactics on the summer courses in the mid-sixties in Gormanston College, County Meath, along with Father Tommy Maher, Kilkenny coach, and Dessie Ferguson, Dublin hurler. My first inter-county success as a selector-coach was with the Tipp intermediate team in 1966 and again with them in the same grade in 1971 and '72. Having ended my senior hurling career in 1969, I was approached to act as coach of the senior team in the spring of 1971, and although we lost the league final to Limerick by a point in Cork, I was proud to have trained and coached them to All-Ireland success later in the year, when we beat Kilkenny. At that time also I was involved with the Tipp under-21 hurlers, achieving Munster honours in 1973 but losing to Galway in the semi-final.

One of my greatest disappointments as coach was Tipp's last-minute defeat by Cork in the Centenary 1984 Munster final in Thurles, but I knew that day that Tipp were near a breakthrough once again. I was happy to play my part as selector-coach with Babs Keating, Theo English and John O'Donoghue (team-mates of the sixties) when All-Ireland senior honours were won in 1989 and 1991 as well as league and Oireachtas successes. It was a great pleasure to work with my former team-mates in those years, and Babs's new style of team management, physical preparation and sponsorship introduced a whole new dimension to the modern game. I have also enjoyed many successes as coach-selector to Munster Railway Cup hurling teams since the late seventies up to the present day, and I hold a special grá for this competition and would love to see it regain some of its former glory and public appeal.

I had the good luck to travel to the USA on five hurling trips, four times with Tipp for National Hurling League finals and once on the Cardinal Cushing games tour, and fully enjoyed the experiences of games in Gaelic Park, New York, Chicago, Boston, and Toronto (under lights), and I would love to see the American trips renewed for league winners. I also have fond memories of the Whit Sunday games in Wembley Stadium, London, in the sixties; and wouldn't it be great to see forty thousand patrons attend such games once more!

I started refereeing Bord na nÓg games at eighteen years of age and haven't officially retired from it yet. I had the honour of officiating at all grades of Munster championship games and National League games and refereed All-Ireland under-21 and intermediate hurling finals. On most occasions I enjoyed refereeing but see the recruitment of referees as a major problem for the association in the future, because very few are prepared to accept the abuse being dished out by players and mentors at the present time.

I have been involved as an administrator in my local Burgess club since 1964 and was very proud to have been part of a very hard-working club committee who purchased a playing field in 1975, which has since been developed into two excellent pitches, as well as building a magnificent club premises, including a spacious hall, dressing-rooms, a handball alley, a covered viewing-stand, and a committee room. I also enjoyed being involved as a competitor and an administrator in Scór competitions in the seventies and hope it returns to its former glory. I attended my first North Tipp convention in 1950 and my first county convention with my father in 1957 and caught the administration bug that saw me act as North Tipp Board secretary from 1968 to 1977 until I became Munster Council secretary in October of 1977.

Hurling has been my life and has brought me endless joy and entertainment, and I am delighted that all my own sons and daughters have become very involved in hurling, camogie, football and handball at county, college and club level, as this gives me a great sense of satisfaction to see the tradition continued on. At the present time I'm thrilled with the great profile that hurling has attained, and the public's enthusiastic response to the live televising of hurling is very reassuring for its future. The recent successes of Clare and Wexford have placed hurling on a new and exciting pedestal, and hopefully more and more young boys and girls will strive to excel at the world's greatest game.

I am privileged to have been given the talent to play hurling, a most enriching and fulfilling experience, and I thank God for the many hours of enjoyment it has brought to me and the great friends I made as a result.

Donie Nealon "

Donie's earliest memory is the Cork-Tipperary Munster semi-final of 1945. 'As was customary in our young days, we would set off around midday on Sunday and walk about two-and-a-half miles to Pallasmore to play hurling. We would have nothing to eat only a few apples we would steal from some orchard; to quench the thirst we would sip water from a nearby stream by cupping our hands together. It was on such a journey home we learned that Tipp had beaten Cork.'

This was a famous victory in Tipperary. They had halted Cork as they set off in search of an incredible five in a row. Hurling fever gripped Tipperary as they faced Limerick in the Munster final and thought of a first All-Ireland win since 1937. 'I went with my father to Thurles by bus on the Saturday and we stayed the night in Lambe's. It was my first match. All I remember of the game is Mick Mackey's solo runs, which came to nothing: he was at the end of his hurling days. Everything else is a blur.'

That was just over half a century ago, and since then hurling and the GAA have played and continue to play a major part in Donie's life. His roots on the paternal side are to be found in Croom, County Limerick. Daniel, his grandfather, having qualified as a teacher, left his native Croom and took up teaching in Youghalarra National School around 1880. When he retired in 1923 his son Rody succeeded him. Rody did his teacher training at De La Salle College, Waterford, and in 1918 played with Waterford in the first round of the Munster championship against Limer-ick. In 1922 he was teaching in Mullinavat, County Kilkenny, and played with Kilkenny against Laois. He then went on his summer holidays and wasn't subsequently called on by Kilkenny, who in a dramatic finish beat Tipperary in the All-Ireland final by two points. Perhaps Rody wouldn't have wished to play against his native Tipperary anyway. He became chairman of the North Tipperary Board at twenty-eight and represented Tipperary on the Munster Council. When he retired from teaching in 1963 his son Donie replaced him. So an unbroken line of three generations taught in Youghalarra National School for over a century, which must be a record!

'My father introduced us to hurling at a very young age. He was always very deeply involved and would come out playing with us. I grew up hearing of his exploits and from a very early age was deeply conscious of his great love for the game. When playing with us he placed great emphasis always on all aspects of first-time hurling.

'In my early teens my heroes were the men of the three-in-a-row All-Ireland wins of '49, '50, and '51, especially the North Tipp men Paddy and Seán Kenny, Jimmy Kennedy — ex-St Flannan's like myself — Tony Reddan, the Ryans of Roscrea — Dinny, Jack, and Mick — and Jimmy Finn. In the '45 lineout there was no-one from North Tipp. As a forward I was particularly interested in watching Jimmy Kennedy and Paddy Kenny in action. Tommy Doyle of course was a hero — he was a hero to everybody, he was so flamboyant.'

All Donie's family — Aideen, their late dearly beloved daughter, 'a great enthusiast, who travelled with me on one occasion to Belfast for a Railway Cup game', Declan, Seán, Dónal, Kevin, Emer, Sinéad, and Nuala — have been very involved in Gaelic games. Donie's lifelong commitment proved infectious. Declan, who is at present in America, played with Meath when employed there. Seán won two All-Ireland junior titles with Tipperary and was a

Twin daughters (Nuala and Sinéad)

sub on the senior team. Emer played 'a bit of camogie'. The twins, Nuala and Sinéad, who played for a Tipperary primary schools team against Dublin at Croke Park in the mid-eighties, have been very active on the camogie pitch; both have played at minor, junior and intermediate level for Tipperary. Sinéad captained the Tipperary minor camogie team in 1990 and led it to the county's first camogie title in any grade with a win over Kilkenny. Later, in 1992, she won a junior title and has played with Waterford RTC in the Ashbourne Cup. Donie bemoans the fact that Tipperary have never won a senior camogie title, despite contesting seven finals since the championship began in 1932. He looks with hope to better days.

During the sixties Donie won an array of honours that most hurlers only dream of. In 1962 he was chosen as Hurler of the Year. In that decade this richly talented, potent and opportunist forward played a leading role in a Tipp attack that ranked with the greatest, boasting in its ranks great players like Jimmy Doyle, Liam Devaney, Seán McLoughlin, John McKenna, Larry Kiely, and Michael Keating. 'Much of the credit for the success of the sixties goes to the Christian Brothers, who produced the raw material that brought eight Munster minor titles to Tipp in the fifties.'

Many memorable and diverse moments surfaced from his illustrious career as we chatted. 'My first big win was when St Flannan's defeated Thurles CBS in the Harty Cup final at Limerick in 1954. It was a tremendous game, played before a crowd of ten thousand. We beat a star-studded Thurles team by three points. They had seven or eight of the Tipp All-Ireland minor winning side of 1953. I was picked to play for Munster Colleges, but we lost to Leinster.

'The college days at UCD bring back

happy memories. As well as three Fitzgibbon Cup wins we won a Dublin county title by beating St Vincent's. That was a tremendous achievement. Vincent's had five of the backs that played against Tipp in the '61 All-Ireland final: Des Ferguson, Noel Drumgoole, Lar Foley, Liam Ferguson, and S. Lynch. They also had the midfielder Des Foley. We had Pat Hinchy of Clare, my brother Pat at centre-forward, Eoin Hurley, son of the great Jim, from Cork, Dick Dowling, and the late Ted Carroll from Kilkenny and Eugene O'Neill from Limerick. It was a great win, UCD 3:9, St Vincent's 1:9.

'You always remember your first All-Ireland win. It is something you dream about. Even though it wasn't a great contest against Galway in '58, the win was marvellous. On the way we beat Limerick, Cork, and Kilkenny. A most unusual thing happened in the final against Galway. I was wing-forward on Fergal Benson and having the better of the exchanges. Then Galway made a switch. They brought Mike Sweeney from goal out on me and sent Benson into goal, where he proceeded to play a blinder. I was switched to centrefield, but I was long enough on Mike Sweeney to know he was a very good player. Both performed splendidly in their new positions, and if Galway had started that way it might have been a much closer game than the final score of 4:9 to 2:5.

'I could never forget our '62 All-Ireland win. Our start was so dramatic: two goals in about ninety seconds. Wexford headed us afterwards in the second half but we pipped them in the finish by two points. I was physically and mentally drained after that match. It was so fast — very few frees in the entire hour. I remember, coming up to half time, I ran into Nick O'Donnell; both of us fell. I don't remember much about half time; I came to myself again after ten minutes of the second half. A switch took me to midfield. I particularly liked midfield: you had scope there. I got a vital point from my poor [left] side that put us ahead again in the closing stages.'

In a lifetime devoted to our games, Donie, always a great ambassador, has held many offices in the GAA world, between parish, county, and province: administrator, coach, trainer, selector, delegate, and referee, each with its own set of memories. He recalls in particular 1984, when 'we all cried after the defeat by Cork in the Munster final.'

At present (1997) he has the demanding role of secretary of the Munster Council — full-time for the past five years and part-time before that, going back to 1977.

I asked Donie how he viewed the present-day game in the context of the past and whether he would like any changes. 'I don't think the game has changed that much in the last forty or fifty years. One major change I see that is not good for hurling is the movement away from ground hurling and overhead striking. There is too much emphasis now on gaining possession and running with the ball, instead of striking it first time. I hate to see half-backs putting up the hand for the puck-out; the hand up is exposed to injury. They should use the hurley. I abhor kicked scores: all scores should be with the hurley. A change from my time that I like is the elimination of the third-man tackle: backs have to hurl now instead of holding off the man. And the protection afforded the goalie is welcome; he deserves it.

'I am concerned at the extent to which point-scoring is coming into the game to the exclusion of goals. Nothing lifts a match like goals — the green flag waving. I think it's a sign of a defect not to get a goal. When we beat Dublin in 1961 by 0:16 to 1:12 I felt the victory was a bit hollow. We never shook their net. I think a goal should be equal to four points; I intend putting that forward as a proposed change.'

Liz Neary (on right) *and others after the 1974
All-Ireland win*

"

I started playing camogie in the Presentation Convent school in Kilkenny about 1966, and being part of the first winning All-Ireland college team in 1968 even to this day gives me great satisfaction. One person in particular I have great memories of is Sister Monica (RIP), who was one of our best supporters.

My next great memory is being part of the St Paul's winning All-Ireland team in 1968 and going on to win six All-Ireland titles with St Paul's, but I would like to add that even to this day I regret playing with Austin Stack's against St Paul's in the Leinster club final, 1973.

I played with Kilkenny for quite a number of years, but I will always remember in particular the All-Ireland final of 1974 (our first win) and 1981,

Born 1951

when we drew with Cork, having been down by ten points. During that period we won many great games. One person in particular was mainly responsible: Tom Ryan. In my opinion he was the best trainer any team could ever have. Tom, even to this day, trains harder than most of the team himself.

In conclusion, looking back on my camogie career I have many great memories and made great friends. I had the pleasure of playing with and against great players, in particular Margaret O'Leary (Wexford) and Helena O'Neill and Angela Downey; but if I may give one little bit of advice, winning is not everything — and don't smoke.

Liz Neary **"**

Winner of major honours at college, club, county and provincial levels; one of the great ones — strong, forceful, determined; and, with apologies to Goldsmith, 'passing fit on forty fags a day.' She could handle victory with graciousness and defeat with equanimity. She puts amateur sport into its true context: sees it essentially as a healthy pastime, advocates that it be viewed thus. In brief that is Liz.

But let us probe a little deeper. 'I'm no good at remembering dates and years.' I promised I'd help refresh her memory.

There was nothing in her ancestry to suggest that she would be a first-class camogie player. In her early youth she had no heroes and showed no interest in either hurling or camogie; that is, until she went to Presentation Convent, Kilkenny, where it all began to happen. Two All-Ireland colleges titles were won. 'These were very special wins.

Kilkenny All-Ireland Champions 1974
Back row: *Ann Carroll, Carmel Doyle, Mary Conway, Teresa Brennan,* Liz Neary, *Peggy Carey, Annie Bowden, Mary Kennedy, Mary Purcell.* Front row: *Angela Downey, Marie Kavanagh, Bridie Martin, Teresa O'Neill (capt), Mary Fennelly, Helena O'Neill, Ursula Grace, Anne Downey.*
Mascots: *Bernadette Tracey, Maria Glendon.*

They remain so to this day. At college level you'll only get at best one or two chances.' And then she reflects and talks with affection and warmth about the late Sister Monica, one of their most avid supporters.

She became a member of the great St Paul's club. She shared in their first All-Ireland success in 1968, and the subsequent victories of 1969 and 1970 made it the first three in a row in the competition. Further successes followed in 1974, '76, and '87. In 1973 she was nursing in Dublin and there was a doubt whether she would get her place with St Paul's. So Liz threw in her lot with Austin Stack's of Dublin. Little did she think they would meet in the Leinster final; but, to her dismay, meet they did. 'Anyway, I felt we weren't going to win. Well, I played a great game — pulled on everything; cleared everything. I shouldn't have played against my former club.' Liz and Austin Stack's went on to win All-Ireland honours, her fourth club title.

Things looked bright at county level in 1968 when Kilkenny beat Dublin,

dominant for so long in the province. 'We thought we were sailing after that victory, but Wexford gave us a lesson in the game when they beat us by six or seven goals. I'll never forget the display of Margaret O'Leary for Wexford that day, or indeed many other days too. She got a goal from midfield. It was struck with power and accuracy; from the moment it left her hurley it wasn't going anywhere but to the back of the net. She was the main cause of our defeat. I used to hate the sight of her on the field — always meant trouble for us; broke my heart, I don't know how many times.'

The breakthrough for Kilkenny came in 1974. In a wonderful replay, Kilkenny defeated Cork 3:3 to 1:5 to capture their first All-Ireland title. Liz was to the fore with a great display at half-back. Further titles followed in 1976 and 1977. And then came the memorable final and replay of 1981 against Cork — for Liz a never-to-be-forgotten final. 'It was a day when I found it very hard to concentrate on the game. I can still see myself looking at five crows as they flew over the Hogan Stand. My opponent, Mary Geaney, was left-handed and also a hockey player. I couldn't manage her. At one stage we were down ten points and I had the referee worn out asking her the score. Then when we were six points down and less than ten minutes to go I was beckoned from the sideline. I was playing so badly I was sure I was being taken off. Instead, I was told to go to full-forward. Didn't I score two goals to draw the match! Cork were really upset. They had the game won. I felt sorry for them.'

For the replay Liz was restored to full-back, where she gave a quality performance as she captained Kilkenny to victory — their fourth All-Ireland title, Liz's fourth All-Ireland title. Her camogie talents were further honoured in 1981 when she was awarded the B&I Camogie Star of the Year award, and in Kilkenny she got the Camogie Sports Star of 1981 award.

During her long and illustrious career Liz never suffered serious injury. There was, however, one year when a run of bad luck gave her a black eye on four occasions in a short space of time. Given the nature of her job, she had to go on sick leave. Indeed, one of those black eyes cost her an interview with a Dublin hospital: 'We wouldn't consider employing someone who played such a physical sport,' she was told. How times have changed — unthinkable now.

That reminded Liz of an amusing incident. A camogie friend of hers received a black eye playing the game. It looked quite nasty. Some days later she was queuing in the post office with her husband. Two elderly women within earshot were heard to say, 'I'd say he did it.' Hubby immediately took to his heels. 'In a game against Antrim in the early seventies I was split on the nose. The doctor stitched it; I fainted. And every time I came through and saw him I fainted again.' She smiles at the thought of it.

Her final years brought three successive All-Ireland titles: 1985, '86, and '87. For Kilkenny it was the prelude to a great seven in a row.

In an honours-filled career Liz also won National League, provincial and inter-provincial titles. Her biggest disappointment was the semi-final defeat of 1980 at the hands of Limerick. 'They got a goal that day that went in at the outside between the upright and the side netting. It won the game for them. Of course these things tend to even out. In a game we played against Cork the ball rebounded off the steel bar at the back of the net and back out the pitch into play. That one cost Cork the game. I knew by the sound that it had hit the steel bar.'

The final curtain came down on Liz's camogie career after the club final of 1987 — victory over Glen Rovers. The previous year St Paul's had lost a thriller to the Glen, 4:11 to 5:7. 'So it was great to win in 1987 on the score 1:4 to 0:5. It made up for 1986. I felt it was going to be my last game. I wanted to win.' Well, it was her last game. She could look back with pride over twenty years — many achievements, including seven All-Ireland county titles and seven All-Ireland club titles. She gave up the camogie. She also gave up the fags.

This is Liz's team, followed by brief comments on each player.

Marian McCarthy *(Cork)*
Marie Costine *(Cork)*
Ann Holden *(Kilkenny)*   Bridget Doyle *(Wexford)*   Elsie Walsh-Coady *(Wexford)*
Liz Neary *(Kilkenny)*   Mairéad McAtamney *(Antrim)*   Margaret O'Leary *(Wexford)*
Angela Downey *(Kilkenny)*   Helena O'Neill *(Kilkenny)*   Linda Mellerick *(Cork)*
Mary Geaney *(Cork)*

Marian McCarthy: Marian was a great goalie; great puck-out and great clearance.

Marie Costine: a great full-back; played in this position for many years for Cork; very tough player.

Ann Holden: in my opinion Ann is the most under-rated camogie player ever; one of the best defenders I ever met; very close marker.

Bridget Doyle: excellent centre-back; great to read the game.

Elsie Coady: Elsie played in many positions for Wexford; very determined player; always gave of her best; I would love to have seen her win an All-Ireland medal.

Liz Neary: this is the position that I would like to have played in, but as I was not fit enough I spent most of my playing career in the backs.

Mairéad McAtamney: I only saw Mairéad playing a few times, but I can clearly remember her as a great player.

Margaret O'Leary: Margaret was always a very tough opponent but always a very sporting player; she terrified me many a time.

Angela Downey: skilful beyond belief; there will never be another player to equal Angela.

Helena O'Neill: Helena was a great team player; she will always be remembered in Kilkenny for the point she scored from a free in the All-Ireland final of '74 to earn Kilkenny a replay.

Linda Mellerick: very talented player; fast, and capable of taking scores from midfield or the forwards.

Mary Geaney: as a left-handed player I always found Mary a very difficult player to mark; she broke my heart many a time.

Born 1948

joyment as Jack and I get, we will feel we have done something right!

"

Órla Ní Shíocháin

Is treise dúchas ná oiliúint! As my wife and myself talked to Órla and her husband, Jack, a picture unfolded that must surely constitute a family sporting record. In 1993 Órla and her daughter, Naoise, played on the Portmarnock team and won a Dublin camogie league medal. Órla was in goal. In 1994 Jack, aged forty-eight, won a Dublin junior hurling medal with Portmarnock. On the same team was his son Shane, who in 1995 was on the Dublin minor panel. Jack played in the forwards. 'I just lined out,' he quipped.

So here we have the delightful picture of mother and daughter and father and son sharing the joys of victory on their camogie and hurling teams. Let's therefore look at the background that created this tremendous sporting enthusiasm. Let's trace the roots.

A GAA exhibition was held at the RDS in the Centenary year, 1984. Órla and Jack were present with their family. It was either a video or a display of pictures that led Shane, aged five, to proclaim aloud, 'That's my grandad,' when he saw Seán Ó Síocháin. A little later, when he saw Séamus Ryan, he again declared, 'That's my grandad.' A bystander who heard both remarks lightheartedly said to the child, 'They can't all be your grandad.' Couldn't they?

Swinging a hurley came naturally to Órla. She preferred this to playing with dolls. 'I was a real tomboy.' The skills of camogie were sown and found root at an early age. She played in matches while in national school, and when she went to the Holy Faith Convent in Clontarf she

"

I was the only girl allowed play with the boys on the road when I was very young, and that has to be my first memory of playing with a hurley. Camogie and the GAA (through the influence of my father) played a huge part in my life. My memories of going to Croke Park every Sunday with my father and, while waiting for him after the match, hitting a ball up against a wall for a long time are still strong in my mind. It was probably the best training I ever had at the skills — certainly the earliest — and I probably didn't even realise it at the time.

The friends I made, the influence of my family, the influence of Jack's family, have all helped to enrich my life. I remember wonderful matches I went to — camogie, hurling, and football — too many to single out any one in particular, but long may I have the health to continue.

Our children, Naoise, Shane, and Feargal, play camogie, hurling, and football, and if they can learn to be humble in victory, overcome the disappointments of defeat and, no matter what else, keep playing the games and get as much en-

progressed rapidly in the game under the watchful eye of a camogie enthusiast, Molly Murphy, and developed into a stylish player, adept and accurate off both the left and the right hand.

The glory and delight of victory came early to her. In 1964, the year she sat for her Inter Cert, she was picked on the Dublin senior camogie team. Her selection was a surprise, but the quality of her display was such that she was chosen later that year for the Leinster side and won an inter-provincial medal in the Gael-Linn competition. At that time Dublin camogie was on the crest of a wave, and the team recorded a 7:4 to 3:1 victory over Antrim in the final — the county's eighth successive win. 'It was fantastic.' The team was captained by Una O'Connor, who was to go on and win thirteen All-Ireland medals — 'a very good stick player.'

Órla remembers being an enthusiastic supporter at an earlier final won by Dublin. 'After the game I went up to Kathleen Mills and asked her for her hurley, which she gave me.' Kathleen was a camogie legend who won fifteen All-Ireland medals in a career that spanned over twenty years and ended in 1961.

Further All-Ireland successes came Órla's way in 1965 and '66 with wins over Tipperary and Antrim, respectively. The final of 1967 was lost to Antrim after a replay; it signalled the end of a great Dublin era. Órla was still playing in 1982 — having had her third baby in May of that year — but they lost to Cork in the final. It was probably Órla's greatest sporting disappointment. How she would love to play that game all over again! 'We can remember things we should have done that day. There were so many misses — so many wrong options. When you lose by a point you always bemoan the misses. The loss of our star midfielder, Mary Mernagh, through injury was a severe blow. It meant that the forwards got a lesser supply of the ball. We missed a lot of chances.' Órla was a midfielder and forward of exceptional quality.

Angela Downey, doyen of modern camogie players, placed her among the greats she played against.

Órla's first club was Austin Stack's, with whom she won two All-Ireland club titles, in 1971 and 1972. 'Winning the club titles was a huge thing.' When Austin Stack's disbanded, Órla moved to Celtic. In all she won eight county titles. She also won provincial and inter-provincial honours.

Her career with the county was briefly interrupted after she got married. A rule at the time excluded married women from playing. It appears to have had its origin when a camogie player was down injured and a man rushed onto the pitch shouting, 'What about the baby! What about the baby!' Even though the county selectors dropped Órla, the provincial selectors picked her on the Leinster team. Shortly afterwards the rule was deleted.

After the 1982 defeat by Cork, Órla retired from inter-county camogie but has continued up to the present day to be active at club level. The rules of camogie were designed with the purpose of making it a non-contact sport. 'When I started my playing career there was very little physical contact. Now it has got tougher — faster perhaps, but tougher. With men involved in training, shouldering has crept into the game. There is greater emphasis on fitness now, and I think more of the players have a wider range of skills. There is a very good under-age standard in Dublin, and the national playing population is increasing. I'd like to see it less physical. Otherwise, the game is fantastic.'

Órla's enthusiasm came from her father, who had a tremendous influence on her. 'GAA was huge in our house.' She remembers her father taking the school team for a fast walk around Clontarf as part of a training programme. 'And he would take me down to the field at the weekends and I would practise taking frees — left-handed and right-handed. I would start on one wing; work my way across the pitch to in front of goal; then onwards to the

Father, Seán Ó Siocháin and father-in-law, Séamus Ó Riain.

other wing.' She went to Croke Park regularly with him. 'The first big game I really remember was the 1961 All-Ireland hurling final between Dublin and Tipperary. I remember feeling shattered that day when the final whistle blew and Dublin lost by one point. I was at the football final in 1963 when Dublin beat Galway. That was a wonderful day. I remember too my father taking us to a Munster final specifically to see Christy Ring. It was towards the end of his career. There was a feeling of awe going to see Christy. It was really the purpose of the trip.'

Her father was, of course, Seán Ó Síocháin, a man whose name will always be synonymous with GAA affairs. He was born in Cill na Martra, near Macroom, County Cork, in 1914. His early days were enriched by the Gaelic traditions all around him: music, song, dances, games. He was particularly impressed by the spirit of co-operation he witnessed among the rural community, evidenced at its brilliant best through the meitheal system at harvest time. This moulded his character and helped him immeasurably in his adult life.

He qualified as a national teacher in 1935 and taught for eleven years. In 1946 there was a national teachers' strike, during which the post of assistant to Pádraig Ó Caoimh, general secretary of the GAA, became vacant. Seán's application — one of six — was successful, but he did not take up duty until the teachers' strike was over. In 1964 he was appointed successor to Pádraig Ó Caoimh, and in 1979 he retired from the post of director-general. From 1979 to 1982 he was ceannáras director, and in that three-year period he was involved in a fund-raising programme for the new headquarters that brought in over a million pounds. Seán looked on his work with the GAA as a labour of love. He loved meeting officers of the GAA at all levels and was always very conscious of the incalculable value of their unpaid contribution.

He was blessed with a fine singing voice. Success at local and national festivals led to his being selected on three popular radio programmes, 'Ireland is Singing' in the late thirties, 'Round the Fire' through much of the forties, and in the fifties 'Balladmaker's Saturday Night'. Radio exposure led to frequent requests to sing at concerts throughout Ireland and overseas. He did four concert tours in the United States, in 1957 as a member of a group from Belfast and in 1958, '59 and '61 as organiser of the tours, which got bigger each year and resulted in sixteen concerts in twenty-one days in 1961.

He also excelled on the sports field. He played minor, junior and senior football for his native Cork and had the unusual honour in the late thirties of captaining the Dublin senior football team when his club, Clanna Gael, won the Dublin county title. But the honour was short-lived — one game only, beaten by Kildare in the first round. In his time he played with and against many great names, and in a telephone conversation he recalled some of them for me: Paddy Moclair, Paul Russell, Henry Kenny, John Dunne, Jim O'Regan, Jack Lynch, Éamon Young, Paddy Whitty, Brendan Nestor, Alf Murray, and Jim McCullough. He played Railway Cup football for Munster in 1936. Seán was a tremendous ambassador wherever he went. He had a great speaking voice, a face with character etched on it, and a personality that merits that great indefinable term, charisma.

Now to Órla's husband, Jack. A native

The family

of Moneygall, County Tipperary, he played minor hurling for his county in 1963 and 1964; under-21 in 1965, '66, and '67; joined the senior panel in 1968; won a Dublin county hurling title with UCD in 1968; and was one of four brothers on the Moneygall team that won the Tipperary senior hurling title in 1975 and '76.

The Ryan household — five boys and five girls — was a hotbed of GAA activity and heated discussion. Órla remembers her visits there when she was going out with Jack. After a match on Sunday evening they would assemble for dinner. Jack's mother would make a pronouncement before the meal — a pronouncement based on experience: 'I don't want to hear anything about the match until the dinner is over. I'm leaving the house if there's talk about hurling.' Silence would be observed for about ten seconds. Then the father would start gently in low tones and work along until he would come to saying, 'And do you know each other at all on the field, do you?' Bedlam! Poor Mrs Ryan. But deep down she understood. She had her own hurling background; her uncle Darby Collison won an All-Ireland title with Tipperary in 1916.

Orla Ní Shíocháin's husband, Jack (Ryan)

And who is the father? None other than Séamus Ryan, president of the GAA from 1967 to 1970, an ardent lover of the GAA and its games. A teacher by profession, he won a Waterford county hurling medal with De La Salle in the mid-thirties when he was in training. He played inter-county with his native Tipperary in junior hurling and junior football. He was very involved in athletics, especially the 440 yards and the high jump. But he used to compete in everything. Those were the days when athletes cycled to the venues. Before competing they would look at the trophy board and conserve energy for the most worthwhile prizes.

Órla's team and her comments are as follows:

Sheila Murray (Dublin)

Margaret O'Leary *(Wexford)*

Bridie Martin *(Kilkenny)*   Allie Hussey *(Dublin)*   Kay Lyons *(Dublin)*

Kathleen Mills *(Dublin)*   Mairéad McAtamney *(Antrim)*   Órla Ní Shíocháin *(Dublin)*

Angela Downey *(Kilkenny)*   Ann Carroll *(Kilkenny)*   Judi Doyle *(Dublin)*

Una O'Connor *(Dublin)*

'Other players I would love to include in my team are: Eithne Leech, Mary Ryan, Mary Sherlock, Bridget Keenan, Marion Conroy *(Dublin)*, Deirdre Lane *(Tipperary)*, Marian McCarthy, Pat Moloney, Liz Garvan *(Cork)*, Liz Neary *(Kilkenny)*, Mary Sinnott, Elsie Cody *(Wexford)*, and Sue Cashman *(Antrim)*.

'It has been my privilege to play with and against all of these players except Kathleen Mills and indeed against many other players I would love to have included here.'

Ó scríobh mé an cuntas seo is trua liom a rá gur imigh Seán ar Shlí na Fírinne 2 Feabhra 1997. Solas na bhFlaitheas go bhfeice tú, agus glóire na n-aingeal go gcloise tú, a Sheáin.

Above: D.J. Carey (Kilkenny) keeps his eye on the ball in the All-Ireland quarter-final against Galway (1997).
Below: Pat Fox (Tipperary) and Brian Lohan (Clare) battle it out in the Munster final 1993.

Above: Aidan Fogarty (Offaly) and Tony O'Sullivan (Cork) chasing the ball in the 1984 All-Ireland final.
Below: Billy Dooley (Offaly) and Seán Flood (Wexford) in the Leinster semi-final, 1997.

Brian Lohan (Clare) sweeps in during the Munster final of 1997.

Top: Gary Kirby (Limerick) achieves a fine balance.

Right: George O'Connor (Wexford) at the Leinster final of 1993.

Top: Martin Storey of Wexford runs clear of Pat O'Neill of Kilkenny (1997).

Right: Wexford captain, Martin Storey lifts the Liam McCarthy cup in the All-Ireland hurling final, 1996.

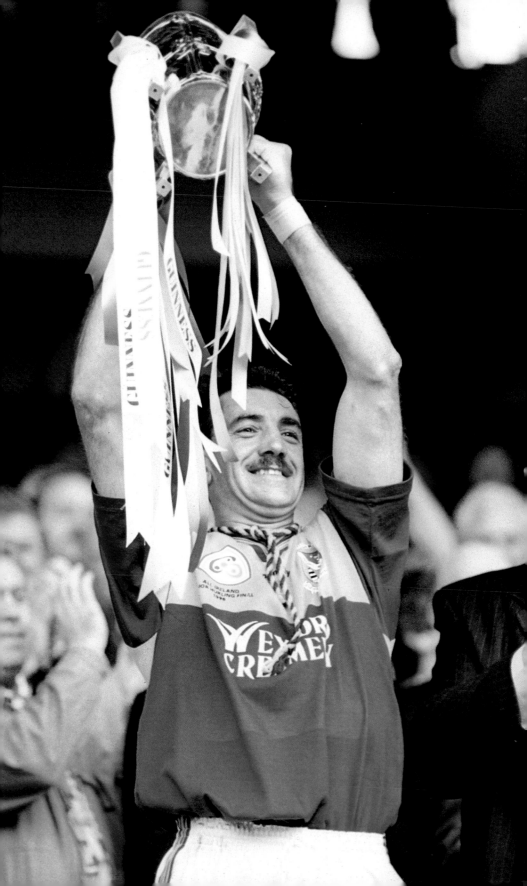

Above: Gary Kirby and Ciarán Carey (Limerick) have a close encounter with Colm Bonnar (Tipperary) in the Munster semi-final, 1997.

Left: Seán Silke (Galway) in 1984.

Born 1933

Christy O'Brien with county senior cup, 1956.

" My love for the game of hurling developed by listening to tales of great deeds on the hurling fields as we sat around the open fire. Later it went a step further by attending the Boys' School in Borris-in-Ossory, where my teacher was Bob O'Keeffe, president of the GAA, 1935–1938.

My first memory of holding a hurl was when my brothers Paddy, Jimmie, Nicky — who is now Brother Basil — and neighbours Joe Whelan and his brother Pat used to play at our home in the 'Liberty'. Later our sister Mary used to join in the games. The goalposts were two chestnut trees.

I went on to play with the school, where my first success was winning a medal by defeating Roscrea. Following this, minor and adult competition were next in line. Times have changed compared with the early years: no proper coaching, togging out under the ditches, and often hurling in the bare feet, as boots were scarce at the time. We hurled on our way to school and back again. Every chance we got we had a hurl in our hands. Hurls had to be cut by axe and saw, shaped out by hatchet, planed, spokeshaved, and finished off with a piece of broken glass.

The transport was by horse and trap or donkey and cart, bicycles, and an odd motor car. As the years went by the improvements in preparation improved, and I often think back and compare the past with the present. Good facilities, sponsorship and being well looked after by club and county are now available, and rightly so. I believe it is a step in the right direction to attract our youth to our games, as we have to compete with other attractions.

"

Christy O'Brien

Victory generates vibrancy. Unfortunately, the converse isn't always true. The great game of hurling is alive and well and vibrant in Laois; yet such vibrancy has failed to generate success. The only All-Ireland win the county has had in any grade was a senior title in 1915.

The great Christy O'Brien, one of the finest exponents of our ancient game and one of Laois's greatest hurling sons, played with his native county for eighteen seasons; and in all that time it is hard to believe that he never had the thrill and honour of playing even in a Leinster final. 'Sometimes you would lose heart, but the love of the game kept you going. Any win is a great thing, and you looked forward to the next game. We won division 2 National League titles in 1959 and 1965. It meant a lot to Laois. We felt we would learn from playing against the good teams. But somehow we lacked confidence when we faced them. Sometimes we would give the good teams a good game, but we seemed to lack that little bit extra. We needed someone to work on our mental approach. This was evident on a few occasions when we lost to Kilkenny and Wexford in Leinster semifinals, days when I felt we were as good as them, everywhere except on the scoreboard.'

As a youngster Christy remembers listening to the broadcasts of Mícheál O'Hehir. At half time they would all go out and be Mick Mackeys and Christy Rings and Jimmy Langtons and Harry Grays. Those were the days of fantasy and dreams. In his playing days he regarded Ned Wheeler, Billy Bohane, Tony Wall and 'Jobber' McGrath as the best he encountered.

Christy played minor for Laois for three years. His brother Paddy played at left-half-forward for Laois in the 1949 All-Ireland final against Tipperary and also played with Dublin. Jimmy played at intermediate level with Laois, and Nicky (now Brother Basil) played senior for Laois.

When Christy closes his eyes and travels back through Memory Lane, three occasions stand out above all others. They relate to parish, province, and an American trip. In 1956, as captain, he led his native Borris-in-Ossory to its first county senior hurling title. They beat Cullohill in the final; the photograph shows him being carried shoulder-high from the pitch bearing the Bob O'Keeffe trophy — bearing too the scars of battle. It was the club's greatest moment — a club that came into existence in the very early days of the association, a club that

Borris-in-Ossory County S.H. Champions, 1956.
Back row: *Joe Keesham (trainer), John Egan, Br Basil O'Brien, Jimmy Kelly, Fint Kealy, Murt O'Donnell, Jim Whelan, Joe Thompson, Paddy O'Brien, Liam White,* Christy O'Brien, *George Hanrahan, Donal Walsh, Fint Egan, Joe Sweeney, Joe Whelan (chairman).* Front row: *Jack Kealy, Kieran Bergin, John Kelly, Michael Guerin, D. Bergin, Joe Hanrahan, Dinny Kealy, Tom Kelly.*

acquired its pitch in 1937 from the Land Commission through the efforts of the late Bob O'Keeffe, in whose honour the grounds are named.

Further county titles followed in 1957, '60, and '61. In 1972 Christy made a comeback. 'All the old comrades were gone.' Christy was in his fortieth year. He lined out at full-forward and in the final against Ballyfin finished with a personal tally of 3:4 — a product of craft, guile, skill, and experience. 'We beat Camross in the semi-final. I felt sorry for Ballyfin. They had never won a title. It was their best try ever.' That victory brought to five Christy's county titles.

His talents as a hurler were spotted by the Railway Cup selectors, and he was chosen on the Leinster team in 1956. 'Injury kept me out of the final against Munster, but I did get a medal. Jobber McGrath of Westmeath was drafted in in my place.' From then until 1965 Christy rarely missed a game with Leinster. Three more Railway Cup medals were won in 1962, '64, and '65. 'It was an honour to play with the great ones: Des Foley — a brilliant mid-

fielder; Eddie Keher — a great forward; the Rackards — powerful men. I will always remember the support and encouragement I got from Ned Wheeler when I played for Leinster and the confidence that gave me. To win against Munster was great. They had such famous names: Christy Ring, Jimmy Smyth, Liam Devaney, Jimmy Doyle, John Doyle, Austin Flynn, Tony Wall, Phil Grimes, Séamus Power, and Mick Roche.' Those were the halcyon days of the Railway Cup competition. Christy was in the company of the élite.

In 1966 he was chosen to go to America to take part in the Cardinal Cushing Games. It was a signal honour for a great sportsman and wonderful hurler. 'Others in the company of five hurlers and twelve footballers were Pat Dunney, Austin Flynn, Christy Ring, John Doyle, and Bernie Hartigan. Ring was manager of the team. We played with Limerick (New York) against Galway (New York), the champions. Ring was playing on a big full-back called John Maher. He switched with me at centre-forward. The switch worked: we won. Ring was more competitive than any of us. He gave it everything. We played one game in Gaelic Park, New York, and one game in Boston before a crowd of about ten thousand. The proceeds went to the missions in Peru.

'The trip lasted two weeks. I lived like a king for those weeks. We stayed at Hotel Manhattan but dined at John Kerry O'Donnell's restaurant, which was about a ten-minute walk away. I didn't know Ring until I went out there. Even then you wouldn't meet him often. He was very disciplined and retiring. There was always someone looking for him, and sometimes he had to hide to get away.'

Canon Seán Collier, parish priest of Borris-in-Ossory, a great hurling enthusiast, played with Laois in 1948 and still relishes their championship victory over the reigning All-Ireland champions, Kilkenny. He regrets that the church rules of the day prohibited himself and another clerical student, Kevin Molloy, now a priest in England, from playing with their native Laois in 1949 and participating in the All-Ireland final of that year — corner-back and full-back, respectively, in 1948. Here is how he remembers Christy:

'When requested to put pen to paper with my impressions and memories of Christy O'Brien, the first thing that came to mind was — yes, here was a great hurler who had got everything it takes to gain the ultimate prize. Christy O'Brien was without doubt a Laois hurling giant. He reigned supreme for around twenty years and leaves behind a great record, the only missing link and the all-important one — an All-Ireland medal. He was captain of the Borris-in-Ossory team that brought the O'Keeffe Cup to the village for the first time in 1956. He led his team by example. He was totally committed and on the day he gave it everything. Powerfully built and with skill to match, I regard him as one of the finest centre-half-backs I ever saw. Naturally, as a parishioner of mine we regularly have a chat about the game of hurling and especially on the eve of big games, and then on the Monday mornings at about 7.30 a.m. we discuss where our predictions went wrong or were successful. Again and again it is the same old story — Croke Park dreams gone down the Liffey.

'The aim and ambition of every hurler is to parade around Croke Park on the first Sunday of September and after the final whistle to climb the steps of the Hogan Stand, amidst the cheers and excitement of well-wishers, to be acclaimed a member of a winning All-Ireland team. Like many other people I have watched the men from Wexford, Offaly, Kilkenny — most of those next-door neighbours of Laois — achieve this honour, but alas I am still waiting for the men from Laois to do likewise. You ask yourself why have they failed — is it lack of manpower or the ability to compete with the best?

'In more reflective mood the obvious is plain to be seen. With a shrug of those broad shoulders we both agree that we have not got a sufficient all-round team to do the job. It was the same in Christy's day — great displays but in the end pipped by a Kilkenny team due to their greater skill and craft. I can distinctly remember on many occasions during my years in Kilkenny

---

This is Christy's team — and having selected it he said,
'Sure you could pick a few, couldn't you?'

	Ollie Walsh *(Kilkenny)*	
Jimmy Brohan *(Cork)*	Nick O'Donnell *(Wexford)*	John Doyle *(Tipperary)*
Jim English *(Wexford)*	Bobbie Rackard *(Wexford)*	Jimmy Finn *(Tipperary)*
Ned Wheeler *(Wexford)*	Seán Clohessy *(Kilkenny)*	
Christy Ring *(Cork)*	Christy O'Brien *(Laois)*	Jimmy Doyle *(Tipperary)*
Tim Flood *(Wexford)*	Nicky Rackard *(Wexford)*	Eddie Keher *(Kilkenny)*

how hurling enthusiasts would praise and marvel at the magnificent performances of Christy for Laois or Leinster in Railway Cups — for which he proudly displays four successes in 1956, '62, '64, and '65. So popular and successful at this standard was he that he was chosen on the Rest of Ireland v. Tipperary in 1970. And of course one of his greatest occasions was the trip to America for the Cardinal Cushing Games in 1966.

'To me Christy is a very friendly, popular person and one who can look back with pride on his hurling days and feats. I know like myself his one wish is that Laois hurling will meet with success and I think it will, if sufficient care and thought is given to the schools and an ongoing programme properly organised with maximum emphasis on discipline, commitment and skills.

'Is é mo ghuí laethúil go leanfaidh sé mar sin go dtí go mbeidh an iománaíocht á h-imirt ag gach mac máthar sna contaetha uilig.'

Born 1959

66

1979 seems a long time ago now, but that was the first year I donned the Wexford jersey. It was against Offaly in the Oireachtas final. We were victorious that day, and little did I think on that day it would be seventeen years later that we would walk the steps of the Hogan Stand once again.

People sometimes ask how or why I kept going over those seventeen years. I suppose in the beginning it was an adventure, and the fact that Wexford were Leinster champions in '76 and '77 made expectations always high, that we would too. Further to that I suppose the love of the game was my incentive. To perform on the big stage was always an incentive thrill, coupled with the fact that I always enjoyed training and being part of the camaraderie of a team. My sincere belief that one day we would win was also a motivating factor. Throughout these years, while never achieving the ultimate we were always able to compete with the best, which was very encouraging.

I always felt too there was more at stake here than hurling — more of a culture or tradition, and the hopes of Wexford people in general. It meant keeping these tremendous values alive, none more so than when I travelled to Sligo recently with our local primary school principal (who is a Sligo man) and the McCarthy Cup in tow to meet a man by the name of John Hughes from Geevagh [a local club], which has no tradition in hurling, trying to sow the seeds of our great game. I was taken aback by his sheer enthusiasm for the game. It made me feel how lucky I am, or was, to be given the chance to play at top level. I also remember visiting a local pub by the name of Mickey Peters' and my friend Kevin [teacher] putting the McCarthy Cup on the counter, to be greeted with the question, 'Did you win that today or what?' I knew at that moment I was in a hurling wilderness.

In all the years of hurling and having played so many games and experienced so many defeats, 1996 was really a dream come true. It was an incredible year and one that no Wexford person will ever forget. Hurling is alive and thriving once again in Wexford.

The 'homecoming' was like nothing ever experienced in Wexford before — not since the people of 1798 marched together (I am led to believe). One of my greater memories on the night was spotting the famous Kilkennyman Christy Heffernan in the middle of the cheering crowd, and at that moment Liam Griffin turned to me and said, 'Christy has won many All-Irelands, some ordinary, but you have won one extraordinary one.'

99

George O'Connor

230

Sunday 5 September 1996 turned out to be Thanksgiving Day for George. The final whistle, just before five o'clock, heralded a moment of prayer — prayer before celebration. We can only speculate about what silent words passed through his mind, what thoughts, as he dropped to his knees on the sod of Croke Park, closed his eyes, and joined his hands in fervent prayer.

It had been a long career since that three-point Oireachtas final win over Offaly in 1979. A youthful George looked forward to hurling glory; he hoped to do better than his late father, Paddy, who captained a Wexford junior hurling team to Leinster honours in 1940. Many a spring promised an autumn harvest; but so many times a blight struck. Too often did the referee's final whistle spell nightmare and grief and disbelief. So many times in those seventeen years in the purple and gold were Wexford as good as the best — kept the hurling flag flying; did honour to the game — yet failed to reap tangible reward.

Before 1996 George saw Wexford fail in six Leinster finals at Croke Park — twice to Kilkenny and four times to Offaly — and nearly always it was a case of so near and yet so far. It was the same story in the National League. They lost five finals: to Limerick and Cork in Thurles, to Offaly and twice to Kilkenny in Croke Park.

As the years passed 'Croke Park became a monster' in George's mind. And it grew bigger with every defeat. There were so many occasions when Wexford seemed to possess a self-destruct element. Consider in particular the Leinster final of '93 against Kilkenny: four points ahead with about as many minutes remaining. They had played some wonderful hurling — looked the supe-rior team — yet had to settle for a draw, followed by a replay defeat. Earlier that year in Thurles we saw more of the same. They lost a league final to Cork after three games, despite having had ample opportunities to win the title.

So many defeats sowed seeds of doubt in George's mind, especially as regards Croke Park, and as time passed he became a prisoner of those doubts. Yet he never abandoned hope. He felt that given the breaks, combined with a disciplined approach, firm, positive management, and a proper mental outlook, Wexford could once again climb to the top of the hurling world.

The opportunity came in the person of Liam Griffin. Professional approach, attention to detail, individual analysis, dedication to the task on hand — all took on a new meaning. 'I was disciplined and dropped for a game when I opted to play for my club instead of a county selection. Others got similar treatment. Open discussion was encouraged. Statistics relating to each player's performance in every match were placed on computer. An analysis of the performance followed. The whole objective was to eliminate errors and improve performance. The opposition was studied in detail. A positive attitude was bred in every player.'

Centrefield, centre-back and centreforward, in that order of preference, were the positions George played in during a distinguished hurling year. And during that time he admired in particular the hurling qualities of Joe Cooney, Tony Doran, John Fenton, D.J. Carey, John Connolly, Mossie Walsh, and Joachim Kelly, 'with whom I had some great clashes. He would hurl like a tiger — a great sportsman; would never say a word during a game except to his colleagues.'

On the pitch, George — who also played senior football for Wexford from 1978 to '84 — cut a fine athletic figure. He was always very fit and mobile. He was conditioned to physical demands by his daily work on the farm, and, as a consequence, the hardships associated with close physical exchanges on the field of play were taken by him in his stride.

In his displays he combined flair and dash with the flamboyant and daring. He would soar into the air, oblivious of danger, to grab the sliotar with the left hand, a hand on which every finger has been broken at least once, where all the fingertips are damaged and bent. 'My problem if an opponent pulls on the ball and I haven't protected the hand.'

In the '96 campaign George was as enthusiastic and committed as ever. He was happy to be part of the panel and play whatever role was required. To many of the players he was a father figure, looked up to and revered.

He played against Kilkenny and Dublin. For the game against Offaly he came on in the closing stages. Against Galway he replaced his brother, John, who was injured early in the first half. Came All-Ireland day against Limerick, and Fate, unkind to Seán Flood — a sterling defender, injured in the game against Galway — smiled on George, who was drafted from the substitutes to line out for Wexford at midfield. A testing challenge it was at thirty-seven years of age, but the experienced George was endowed with the physical and mental resilience — now that he was no longer a prisoner of doubts about the 'Croke Park monster' after four memorable victories there in the '96 championship — to cope with the demands of Croke Park on All-Ireland day.

His All-Ireland medal at thirty-seven meant much more to George than if he had won it in his earlier years. At the celebration that night he savoured every moment, every detail, every smile and compliment. He wanted to be able to remember the occasion vividly in years to come and recall it clearly for family and friends. The privilege — which has eluded so many great hurlers — of winning an All-Ireland medal came George's way as the sun was setting and he took the stage for the last time. The final curtain came down in triumph amid a sea of purple and gold, and in that moment all the disappointments of a long career vanished from memory.

Born 1914

'God gave us our memory so that we might have roses in December.'

Over the doorway in iron letters was *Ua Floinn,* and in the doorway stood Dónal, holder of a leadership certificate in mountaineering and a member of Laune Rangers Mountain Rescue Team — a strong, hardy 83-year old, dressed in trousers and light singlet, despite typical March weather. The greeting was in Irish, and you immediately felt at home in the company of this gregarious extrovert.

Dónal had been a vocational teacher by profession, specialising in woodwork, a master of his craft with first place in Ireland. In his room was a large assortment of books, many of them now out of print. He had been perusing *Sloinnte Gael is Gall* by Woulfe. 'I can't find your name here,' he said to me. 'What's Mary's surname?' 'Kickham,' I replied. 'Ah, Kickham. The first prize I ever won was *Tales of Tipperary* by Charles Kickham. It was for a sprint.' You were reminded of the Village Schoolmaster, and as conversation unfolded you knew you were in the company of a captivating seanchaí.

'Galway played Tipperary in a senior hurling game at the opening of McDonagh Park in Nenagh. We won the set of medals that carried a bust of Thomas MacDonagh, one of the executed signatories of the 1916 Proclamation.'

A native of Castletownroche and now living in Ballyhea in north Cork, this Corkman, with hurling and football skills, went to County Galway to teach in 1936, and took the people of that county to his heart. 'I taught in Spiddal but also took classes in Athenry and in the summertime had classes in Ros Muc. I loved the people of Connemara. They were a wonderful people. I did fishing and shooting with them. I used

"
Brendan and Mary, it is a great pleasure to have met you and renewed all the memories of games and hurling events. The greatest pleasure from hurling was the friendships formed, not alone amongst your own team comrades but also with the opponents. I must pay tribute to Galway and Galwaymen: they were the best, and gentlemen to the bone. I learned more about hurling in Galway than any other place. God be good to Mick Gill and Ignatius Harney, our good mentors. And to Seánie Duggan — who, if Ring or Mackey went two paces from you, shouted, 'Flynn!'

Freisin do mhuintir Chonamara agus foireann Mhíchíl Bhreatnaigh agus an corn a ghnóthaíomar sa bhliain 1946. B'fhearr liom an bonn sin ná a bhfuil de bhoinn agam. Buíochas.
"

Dómnall ófloinn

233

to walk a lot. I cut turf with the sleán and saved it. And I played football with them as well. In 1946 Mícheál Breatnachs, a team selected from Connemara, won the county junior football title, the first time the trophy crossed the Corrib — a team of all Irish-speakers; my proudest medal.'

Many a time during his years in the west he cycled at Christmas and Easter from Spiddal to Castletownroche, a journey of 132 miles. 'It used take me eleven hours. I'd spend eleven hours in the saddle and pedal along at twelve miles an hour. I had very strong legs — I still have.' No wonder he is so agile and active. He still fishes and shoots and is a deadly shot. 'But I do no more hill-walking. I know my limitations.' He lived in an era of harsh economic circumstances. The people of those days were inured to hardship.

Victory celebrations were different from today. Recently there was a gathering in Ballinasloe to celebrate the Railway Cup hurling victory of Connacht in 1947, the first time the trophy went to the west. I remember it well, for it was among the first hurling broadcasts I listened to. I showed Dónal a photograph of himself that I cut from a newspaper fifty years ago. He looked at it, saying, 'I was a good-looking fellow then!' That win over a star-studded Munster team, while unexpected, wasn't surprising. Galway during the forties produced many outstanding hurlers and on a number of occasions came within an ace of major honours. 'The night before the game I went to the pictures and bought the papers. I was in the same room as Paddy Gantly. I looked at the names of both teams and said to Paddy, "That Munster team won't beat us." The final score was Connacht 2:5, Munster 1:1 — the lowest score ever recorded by a Munster team in the competition. And the Munster half-forward line read Christy Ring (Cork), Jackie Power (Limerick), Jim Young (Cork).

'The result was a study in containment. We didn't let them get into their stride. During the game I clashed with Jackie Power and broke his hurley. He threw the broken handle over the bar and said, "That's the only score I'll get today." After the game three of us went to Tommy Moore's pub to celebrate, but when we arrived it was closing time and we couldn't get in. In the end we got a bottle of wine and shared it between us; imagine, a bottle of wine between three to celebrate our first Railway Cup win. I remember on some of our trips to Dublin we'd sleep three to a bed — a big four-poster: Mick Nestor, Inky Flaherty, and myself. They were great days.'

The hurling memories are many and varied, covering playing days at club, county and provincial level. During his days in Galway he hurled with Liam Mellows and won a number of county titles. He had the unique distinction of playing full-back in front of Paddy Scanlon (Limerick), Tony Reddan (Tipperary), and Seánie Duggan (Galway) — three of the game's greatest goalkeepers. At club level he fronted Paddy and Seánie; at county junior level he played with Tony. His longest term was with Seánie Duggan, and he holds him in the highest regard. 'Duggan was great. He was always on the alert. He marshalled his defence and surveyed it. If you stepped two feet away from where you should be or weren't covering your man, he would shout, "Flynn!" You got the message, and the same would go for the rest of the backs.

'Paddy Scanlon worked in the timber department in McDonagh's. I used order timber from him for the school. He stayed in the Ivy Hotel and we often met. Sometimes he would send a message to Limerick that he wouldn't play on a particular Sunday. Mackey [Mick] and Timmy Ryan would arrive at the hotel on a Saturday night, have a few drinks with Scanlon, bundle him into the car at midnight, and take him away to play the match.

'I remember we played a tournament game for Shrule church: Liam Mellows, Galway champions, versus Ahane,

Limerick champions. The prize was a set of hurleys. I was marking Mackey. We broke twelve hurleys that day — sheer determination. In those days, no matter what happened you wouldn't go down: it was a dishonour to go down in my day. We didn't shake hands after the match, but later on when one of the Galway fellows wanted to be introduced to Mick, we shook hands.'

Galway were playing Cork in a championship game and a colleague of Dónal was debating how he would cope with the speed of his opponent. 'I think I'll bring him back to my own flight,' he said to Dónal. And he did — just a slight slowing down. And coming off the field after the game he walked up to Dónal and said, 'These growing feathers plucked from Caesar's wings / Will make him fly the ordinary heights of men.'

While the Railway Cup title of '47 was Dónal's greatest win, he feels he played his best game of hurling at full-back with UCG in a Fitzgibbon Cup final against a very talented UCD team, sprinkled with great hurling names: Dick Stokes of Limerick, Nicky Rackard of Wexford, Jimmy Kennedy of Tipperary, Mick Feeney and Ned Daly of Waterford. He missed two All-Ireland semi-finals against Kilkenny at Birr, each lost by one point. In 1945 he had an exam at Bolton Street the day after the match and couldn't risk a hand injury; in 1947 a feis was being held in Ros Muc and he was refused leave to play. We will never know what difference to those results the presence of Dónal might have made: the thirteen-stone-plus defender, strong and fit and talented, 'equal-handed left and right.'

One of his greatest days was the All-Ireland semi-final clash with Cork at Ennis in 1944 'when I captained Galway and we lost by one point. I was on Ring that day — first at half-back, and when he went out to centrefield I followed him. We were robbed that day. Willie Murphy pucked the ball out for Cork. I won possession, and as I struck, the referee blew full time, and the ball fell

on top of the net. It should have been a draw.'

His trophies and medals may be relatively few, but those distant memories enrich his life, and reminiscing animates him. Playing the game was his greatest reward, and in one particular year he played with thirteen different teams in five different counties. Five would have been legitimate: Galway, Connacht, UCG, Mícheál Breatnachs, and Liam Mellows. The remainder? Well, they required an alias.

The following is an excerpt from an article by his son Diarmuid published in February 1997 in the *Examiner* and reproduced with his kind permission. Dónal had marked Ring and Mackey about a dozen times each. Diarmuid questioned him on them, and indeed others too. First Mackey.

'One of his greatest strengths was his strength — he was like the pier of a gate. You couldn't shake him, couldn't knock him. But he also had speed and ingenuity — plenty of diversity. Take a ball off the air one time, knock you with a shoulder next time — seldom did the same thing twice in a row; a great man to inspire a team. He was full of old dodges too. If he got between referee and ball he would often

put the ball up under his jersey, go hopping along, pretend he was soloing.

'Weaknesses? "I don't think he had any. They say he was a dirty player. I never found him dirty. Any man that turns the bos of the hurley to hit you, you don't regard him as dirty. It's the man who turns the pole — he's a psycho. And though these were few and far between, they existed."

'What about Ring? "Ring was an opportunist. It wasn't so much what he'd do on you in his own position, but he was always ready to shoot across to the other side, always watching for the intercept — that was his game. He also had great strength, great speed and great accuracy. Once Ring got the ball in his hand, if he was within thirty or forty yards, you could chalk down a score — he was going to get it.

"Then there was the rhythmic factor. Everyone has a rhythm, as easily recognisable as their voice, and you can identify them just by listening to their movements. When you tuned in to a forward's rhythm it was easy then to mark him. But Ring had a tremendous burst of acceleration, could break his rhythm. It

made him much harder to mind, and he relied on it a lot. Mackey also had it, but not to the same extent."

'Weaknesses? "Like Mackey, I wouldn't say he had any — I never saw any, anyway. He was courageous, same as Mackey, put his head in anywhere for a ball ..."

'The big question: who was better? "I wouldn't like to venture. I couldn't say that one was better than the other. Ring was certainly the greatest opportunist — to see them and take them. But Mackey was the more inspirational — a great man to lift a team. Ring tended to do it on his own. And he could. He was the more skilful of the two. But more effective? I couldn't tell you."

But if you had to win, had to pick just one man, who would you have? "If going out against a very good team, needed a leader, inspiration — Mackey."

'But then here's the rub — were they the best you hurled on? "Jim Mullane of Clare gave me more problems than either. He was the best I played on."

'The best you saw? "It's complicated. First, you have to define the position. It's easier for forwards to come into the public eye — they're scoring. The prominent counties then have an added advantage. But what criteria do you use? Speed, skill, strength, anticipation, intelligence — especially brain work. Many backs might have more of these qualities than the forwards, but how do you judge them? No scores to show for it. Timmy Ryan of Limerick was up there, could play the ball in the air with his arms fully extended — one of the most difficult skills. If Josie Gallagher had played with Cork or Tipp they would be talking about him today. But the best I ever saw was Paddy Gantly of Galway — the Missioner. They should know that in Cork city. Gantly and Hannify — another Galwayman — won many a county for the Barrs back then. Gantly was the greatest hurler I ever saw, the most flamboyant. And Jaysus, he used to smoke eighty fags a day!"'

This is Dónal's team:

Seánie Duggan *(Galway)*

Willie Murphy *(Cork)*   Batt Thornhill *(Cork)*   Willie Fahy *(Galway)*

Dónal Flynn *(Galway)*   Jim Brophy *(Galway)*   Jim Young *(Cork)*

Timmy Ryan *(Limerick)*   Paddy Gantly *(Galway)*

Jim Mullane *(Clare)*   Mick Mackey *(Limerick)*   Bobby Forde *(Galway)*

Josie Gallagher *(Galway)*   Nicky Rackard *(Wexford)*   Christy Ring *(Cork)*

And having picked the team, he wondered about Jackie Power *(Limerick)*, John Keane *(Waterford)*, and in particular Willie Campbell *(Cork)*. 'Campbell was a great hurler — one of the best I saw; he was an outstanding forward.'

Mary O'Leary (and her brother Seánie)

Born 1955

"

I started my camogie career in 1968 with Glanworth where I won my first junior club medal. Then in 1974 I joined my present club — Watergrasshill. My inter-county started at under 18 level in 1971 and in 1973 I won my first All-Ireland at junior level. This was a great achievement for us, as we were the first team to win this title for Cork and the first time that both junior and senior had been achieved by any county. Then in 1975, I captained the Cork seniors, but we lost to Wexford in the All-Ireland final. I remember Kathleen Tonks in goal that day for Wexford — she was excellent.

1978 then was the year I won my first senior medal against Dublin and then 1980 against Limerick — after a replay and 1982 and '83 again against Dublin. My biggest disappointment was losing the 1981 All-Ireland against Kilkenny in a replay. But you have to accept these things and accept the good with the bad. One of the highlights of my inter-county career was with Munster in 1982 against Leinster which we won by a point. It was one of the best camogie games in my time for sheer guts and

determination from both sides and it was a pity that it was witnessed by so few people. Another of my sporting highlights was with my club, Watergrasshill in ladies football when we won the club senior All-Ireland final in 1981. For such a small club and with a limited amount of players to choose from, it was a fantastic achievement.

In most recent times I am delighted to see that RTÉ are giving the game more coverage and that it will be televised live this year. Maybe we could help, ourselves, as well, in using the players of high profile to help try to promote the game even to a higher level than it is. I thoroughly enjoyed my playing days, both with my clubs and county, on and off the field, because I feel that even though playing the game is all important, meeting and mixing with people after and being able to talk about the game, is just as important.

I am one of the lucky ones in that I achieved a lot at inter-county. But it's not easy. You have to put in the hard work to be able to get anywhere. As well as that I played with some of the best players around and also against them.

Play the game to enjoy it and accept that you can't win them all — but you can try.

Mary Leary   "

M ary came from a household steeped in hurling tradition. 'She takes after my father,' remarked her mother to me — a lovely hospitable lady, whose fond recollections vividly portrayed life and customs and events from the Ireland of her childhood. It was then I discovered she was referring to Tom Mahony who won an All-

Mary O'Leary's grandparents — Tom and Hannie Mahony

Ireland medal at half back with Cork in 1902 — a team captained by his first cousin, the legendary and in many respects, peerless Jim Kelliher. They overwhelmed London in the final — played 11 September 1904 — on the score 3:13 to nil, having beaten Dublin in a replay in the home final at Tipperary.

Tom and Jim also took part in the final of 1907 — played in Dungarvan on 21 June 1908 — one of hurling's classics — but they lost by one point to Kilkenny. Mary's mother wears on a gold chain the very attractive Munster medal won by her father Tom in 1907 — a most cherished possession. Inscribed on the reverse of the medal is 'Munster championship hurling won by Dungourney 1907' Mary cherishes a miniature gold hurley of her grandfather's one of which was presented to each of the panel of Cork players who won the 1903 All-Ireland title.

Mary's mother recalled that, 'he would take down the melodian at night and play some tunes and he would sing "Boulavogue" and "Down by the Glenside" and mean every word of it — and he would sing "Siúl Aroon" (My Mary of the Curling Hair) and I can still see the way he would run his fingers through his hair — and the neighbours would come in and they would play forty-five, sometimes all night. I would hear the murmuring when I'd wake up in the morning.'

Tom was tenacious as well as skilful. 'He would sometimes recall the occasion when he was given the job of keeping Tom Semple in check.' And did he? 'He did.' Enough said. Tom, born in 1876 — a victim of eviction in his young days during the Land League's struggle for Irish Tenant farmers — lived to the great age of 95. So the source of Mary's skills and those of her brother Seánie go back a long way.

The camogie career of Mary and the hurling career of Seánie run on parallel lines from the late sixties to the mid eighties with Seánie having a slight head start. Both were forwards. Both were prolific scorers. Both were masters of the ancient craft and had a competitive spirit and sense of position that placed them among the foremost forwards of their era.

Mary's playing days began with two Munster minor titles, before she won a junior All-Ireland with Cork in 1973. After that she played in six All-Ireland senior finals — losing in '75 and '81 after a replay to Wexford and Kilkenny respectively — winning '78, '82 and '83 at the expense of Dublin and '80 when Limerick were defeated by three points after a replay. It was the first time ever that it was an all-Munster final.

In 1978 the O'Leary family created a unique senior record with Mary winning an All-Ireland senior camogie title and Seánie winning an All-Ireland senior hurling title. The chances of it ever being repeated are very slim indeed.

1982 saw Mary at her devastating best. Cork faced Kilkenny at Nowlan Park in the All-Ireland semi-final and Mary contributed 1:7 in a game that ended in a draw. In the replay at Ballinlough she scored 1:8 and Cork advanced to the final against Dublin. That game hung on the balance until the last minute when Mary sent over the winning point from a forty yards free. Out of a winning score of 2:7 to 2:6 Mary accounted for 1:6.

Later in the year Munster met Leinster in the Gael-Linn cup inter-provincial final — a competition dominated by Leinster. Again Mary scored the winning point from a free in the closing minutes. It ended 3:10 to 2:12 and Mary scored the remarkable tally of 2:8 in a most exciting and uncompromising game. Here is a report on the match from the *Cork Examiner*:

> '*After an exciting and at times over robust final Munster took the Gael Linn inter-provincial senior camogie title by narrowly defeating Leinster at Na Fianna grounds in Dublin yesterday. It was Cork's Mary O'Leary, who after a quiet first half exploded into action in the second, snatching the winning point from an injury time free after an even first half in which a Leinster goal by Edel Murphy was immediately cancelled by a similar effort by Mary O'Leary. Leinster led at the interval by 1:6 to 1:4 thanks to a flurry of points by Angela Downey.*
>
> '*Goals by Marian Sweeney and Mary O'Leary midway through the second half left Munster four points ahead and seemingly on the way to victory. But once again Angela Downey came back to put Leinster ahead with one minute remaining. But Munster were not finished and following Marian Sweeney's levelling point, Mary O'Leary got the winning score.*'

It's a game that is high on the list of Mary's most satisfying achievements for in beating Leinster they had beaten the cream of the camogie world. She finished 1982 as Cork's top scorer that year with 7:39 to her credit.

She was awarded the Glen Abbey Women in Sport Award in November '82 and the following month she was nominated the B&I Camogie Player of the Year. It was a fitting and well deserved honour that placed this camogie artist in the ranks of such prominent previous winners as Bridget Doyle (Wexford), Angela Downey (Kilkenny), Máiréad McAtamney (Antrim), Marian McCarthy (Cork) and Liz Neary (Kilkenny).

In the All-Ireland semi-final of '84 against Dublin at Parnell Park — one of her last games — she was 'the only one with a score that day' for Cork.

Now for a few words on her brother Seánie — an equally legendary figure. While Mary was winning club, county, inter-provincial and personal awards, Seánie was having equal success in the hurling field. He operated at corner forward — mainly on the left. And despite injury and illness he was one of the deadliest and most outstanding of players to man that position. He would hang around the edge of the square and wait. It was that quality of patience, allied to his hurling skills, vision and opportunism, that made him such an effective corner forward. His mother told me that he broke his ankle playing football. 'He went up for a ball and whatever way he came down he broke his ankle. After that he lost his swerve — he never had the same swerve again.' She went to all the games and now enjoys watching Seánie's sons Tomás and Ciarán in action at underage level and hopes they will emulate their forebears.

She was in Thurles in '84 for the Centenary final and put down her head as she thought the movement that led to Seánie's superb first-half goal was about to break down. She didn't see the goal being scored but was lifted out of her seat by an exuberant Cork fan as the sliotar hit the net. She was in Croke Park for the three in a row wins of '76, '77 and '78. In the puck around before the '77 final Seánie broke his nose and when Ring, his mentor and childhood hero, was told about it, he simply retorted — 'forget about it, you don't hurl with your nose.' From seven All-Ireland appearances Seánie was victorious on four occasions. He also won

240

National League titles and was awarded three All-Stars. At underage level, he won All-Ireland minor titles in '69 and '70 and under-21 titles in '70, '71 and '73.

Mary's camogie days came to an abrupt ending. A back injury following an unfortunate car accident in 1985 prematurely ended the camogie career of this brilliant and potent left-handed forward. She has, however, continued to be involved with the game in an administrative capacity.

Her camogie team drawn from five counties is as follows:

Kathleen Tonks *(Wexford)*
Marie Costine *(Cork)*

Vera Mackey *(Limerick)*	Bridie Martin *(Kilkenny)*	Mary Canavan *(Kilkenny)*
Elsie Cody(Walsh) *(Wexford)*	Deirdre Lane *(Tipperary)*	Sandy Fitzgibbon *(Cork)*
Mary O'Leary *(Cork)*	Pat Moloney *(Cork)*	Angela Downey *(Kilkenny)*

Mary Geaney *(Cork)*

Margaret O'LEARY-LACEY 1961–1977 St Ibar's, Eoghan Ruadh, Buffer's Alley, Oulart-the Ballagh, & Wexford

Born 1947

Margaret O'Leary-Lacey after the All-Ireland win in 1968.

"

Camogie in my opinion is one of the greatest games for girls. It is part of our heritage. No other sport can match the skill, speed and intelligence needed to play the game well.

I have cherished memories when not knee-high of being brought off to the boys' hurling matches in Willie Doran's field by my late father. My brother was playing then — oh, how I wished it was myself! That was getting the opportunity to play. There was always a great hurling tradition in my home area around Monamolin. So most parents urged their children to participate in our national games.

Being involved in the game of camogie since the early sixties, I have witnessed many changes in the intervening years. The introduction of under-age competition and coaching in primary schools have contributed to many young players being able to master the skills and craft of the camán.

One of the biggest flaws in the game today is the lack of total commitment because of participation in other sports, such as hockey, football, and soccer.

Wexford All-Ireland champions in 1968. Margaret O'Leary-Lacey is first left in the back row.

Certainly there are greater demands on players today, as there is greater emphasis on physical fitness.

1968 was Wexford's greatest year, winning All-Irelands in minor, senior and colleges hurling. Then for the first time our senior camogie team made the breakthrough, winning the All-Ireland. 1968 was a great year for me personally, winning an All-Ireland with Wexford and also winning an All-Ireland club medal with Eoghan Ruadh of Dublin. Later in the year I captained Leinster to an inter-provincial medal.

My ambition is to continue playing for as long as I am able. I would like to impart some of my knowledge of the game to my two young daughters, Mary and Una, and also to the many promising players emerging in Oulart, where I now reside.

99

Margaret O'Leary Lacey

In 1995 Margaret played full-forward for Oulart-the Ballagh senior camogie team. They were beaten in the county final after a replay by Rathnure, who then went on to win the All-Ireland title. 'When you think that we led in the drawn game by five points, with five minutes to go, it makes you think of what might have been. It's always that bit more difficult for the team that's trying to make the breakthrough.' Margaret was then forty-eight; thirty-four years had passed since she first played for the county senior team in 1961 at the age of fourteen.

'I am exceptionally fit. I would run a mile no bother.' She has the figure of an athlete: tall and slender, lithe and lissom, packed with energy. She coaches the under-age teams, often three nights a week for three hours, before doing a training stint with the seniors — all of them nearly half her age. 'I take the youngsters on a couple of rounds of the pitch. They need that kind of training nowadays — too much travelling done in cars. I always cross the finishing-line first; most of them are winded by then.'

Her childhood days in national school evoke memories that compare with her greatest moments. 'There was training in the field at home every evening — often up to thirty or forty of us. There were four teams. My father was over one of them. We used to play every weekend — a league, like a mini-All-Ireland to us; full belt, give and take. He would sit in the ditch watching us. His presence made you try that bit harder.' Was he very proud of her? 'He was my hardest critic. No matter how well I played, he was never 100 per cent satisfied. He would always dwell on the things I did wrong. There was no way I could get a swelled head. I suppose when we won the All-Ireland he was proud, but inwardly: he was never able to express those thoughts to me. I'd like to have heard his words of praise.'

Her early years were spent with St Ibar's (Shelmaliers). Indeed, the day after she joined the club Séamus Keevans of Wexford football fame came looking for her to play with Oylegate. When she took up employment with the ESB and was posted to Dublin she joined the Eoghan Ruadh club. Later she played with Buffer's Alley of her native parish, and in recent years she threw in her lot with Oulart-the Ballagh, where she now lives.

Her achievements are many. During her time with Eoghan Ruadh she won three Dublin leagues, three county titles, and an All-Ireland club title in 1967. Buffer's Alley contested seven All-Ireland club finals in a row between 1978 and 1984. They were victorious in 1979, '81, '82, '83, and '84, with wins over Athenry, Killeagh, Athenry, Kilkerrin-Glenamaddy, and Glenamaddy, respectively. It brought to six Margaret's collection of All-Ireland club medals. She played in five All-Ireland finals with Wexford and was successful on three occasions: 1968, '69, and '75. She won honours at provincial and inter-provincial level and captained Leinster to victory in 1969.

Her talents as a player were widely recognised. She was an outstanding centre-back but also played at full-back and midfield. 'I loved the centre-back position. Whenever I went to hurling matches I always took up position around the forty-yard mark so as to observe the style and tactics of the centre-back. In this regard Ger Henderson of Kilkenny was my model. I liked his attacking style — the way he went forward to clear. Tony Doran was another hurling hero.'

There was rejoicing and pride in Buffer's Alley when the *Gaelic Weekly* award for camogie went to Margaret and for hurling to Tony. Other hurlers she admired were Henry and Mick Butler. And she had football heroes too, in the persons of Mick O'Connell of Kerry and Noel Tierney of Galway. In 1966 and '68 she won the John Power Award as Wexford's Camogie Sports Star, and it was in 1969, if memory serves her right, that she was voted Camogie Player of the Year.

Without a doubt, her greatest moment was the winning of the All-Ireland title with Wexford in 1968. Here is how she recalls it. 'Kilkenny beat Dublin, and we then beat Kilkenny. We had to travel to Antrim for the semi-final. No-one gave us a chance. Antrim were All-Ireland champions, having beaten Dublin in a replay in 1967. The game was played in Glenariff — a marvellous setting. That day I witnessed in action one of camogie's greatest players, Máiréad McAtamney, at midfield. I'll never forget our victory over Antrim. The players were phoning home; they couldn't believe it at home.

'We beat Cork in the final by 4:2 to 2:5. We had been striving for a few years. It was Wexford's first time appearing in a final, and to win after just making the breakthrough was marvellous. The following year we repeated our success over Antrim by beating them in the final, 4:4 to 4:2 — two in a row for Wexford.'

A lovely surprise awaited Margaret after the 1968 All-Ireland win. To show their appreciation of her success, her colleagues in the Eoghan Ruadh club presented her with a magnificent bronze statuette of the dying Cú Chulainn, legendary figure of hurling folklore. It occupies a place of prominence in her home.

The defeat by Kilkenny in the final of 1977 is the disappointment of her career. 'I was captain. I played full-back that day. It was one of those games that you look back on, analyse, and say it could have been won. However, games are about winning and losing, and it is important to be able to win and lose with dignity.'

Margaret doesn't wear the helmet but certainly advocates it for the under-age players. Only once did she receive a serious injury. It was in a club semi-final at Swatragh, County Derry, played in atrocious weather. 'The game would have been called off but for the fact that we had travelled so far. I was hit across the face, had stitches under the eye; my nose is crooked since. A complete accident; I blame the weather conditions.'

There is no sign of her enthusiasm and ardour abating. These characteristics have rubbed off on Mary and Una, who, at the ages of ten and eight, respectively, have already mastered many of the skills of the game. Hurling and camogie fever pervades and permeates the entire household, a topic for regular dialogue and discussion — a wonderful unifying bond.

Nor was Margaret contemplating retiring. She was looking forward to the 1996 championship. 'I wouldn't mind making way for a younger player, but as long as the selectors think I'm good enough I'll play.' Remember she can still run that mile — no bother.

Her team is selected from players that spanned her county era. 'It excludes Lily Parle, one of Wexford's greatest, who was before my time, and Angela Downey, who arrived towards the end of my career — the best I witnessed.'

	Eithne Leech *(Dublin)*	
	Liz Neary *(Kilkenny)*	
Elsie Walsh-Cody *(Wexford)*	Margaret O'Leary *(Wexford)*	Bridie Martin *(Kilkenny)*
Mairéad McAtamney *(Antrim)*	Bridget Doyle *(née Kehoe) (Wexford)*	Kay Lyons *(Dublin)*
Ann Carroll *(Tipperary)*	Sue Cashman *(Antrim)*	Judi Doyle *(Dublin)*
	Una O'Connor *(Dublin)*	

She cheers our team, her eyes aflame,
And after Sunday's final game
I'll meet her in a glen I'll name —
And ask her to the altar.
— 'The Lass that Loves a Hurler' (Carbery)

Nancy, Matty's widow, wrote to me on 10 January 1995 having read my first book, *Giants of the Ash*, and having noted the many references there to Matty. Here is an extract from a lovely letter: 'Matty (RIP) is dead now for almost thirty years — hence he is forgotten except by a few old-timers. I have often thought that his memory has been neglected by the powers that be ... that he should have featured in the Hall of Fame ... I couldn't recount all the trophies he accrued ... I'm sure that no-one expects that Matty's wife still survives ... There was a gap of sixteen years in our ages ... but for me he is for ever young.'

I decided to visit Nancy and talk to her about Matty, who started off in life as an employee of the Great Southern Railway. As a member of the Kilkenny Brigade during the struggle for independence he was suspended by the

Born 1899

GSR for refusing to take a trainload of Black and Tans from Kilkenny to Waterford. Afterwards he joined the Garda Síochána and their famous hurling team in Dublin.

It was a pleasure to meet this gracious and vivacious 79-year-old lady in 1995, whose support for hurling and Kilkenny is as strong as ever. 'I was only seven years old when Matty won his first All-Ireland in the 1922 championship.' That game was played on 9 September 1923. Entering the closing stages and with Tipperary leading and looking like winners, the large crowd began to leave Croke Park. It was then that Kilkenny rallied, and the crucial winning goal was scored by Matty following a fierce tussle in the Tipperary goalmouth after Kilkenny had taken a seventy.

'By 1931 my two older brothers were hurling mad — it was the only thing then. When Kilkenny reached the final they came to Father looking for the fare. He came from the Kilkenny-Carlow border, where there was little hurling, and he couldn't understand the euphoria. Money was scarce, but after the first draw Father again obliged with the fare for the second game. We had to wait until they came home to learn the result. Their excitement as they told about the second draw was indescribable. Even Father was getting interested. Matty always said it was the most exciting and best game he ever played in — and he never missed a game. No team after had the same effect on us: our generation never forgot it.'

The following prophetic words of Seán Ryan, president of the GAA, appeared in the *Irish Press* on Saturday 5 September 1931: 'Granted fine weather, we will have the best final and greatest gathering seen in Croke

Kilkenny 1937. Matty Power is first left in the front row.

Park since Kilkenny and Tipperary met in the 1922 final.'

Nancy and a neighbour went to work in the civil service in Dublin in 1933, and a garda arranged accommodation for them — in Power's Guesthouse, owned by Matty's people. It was the first time she came face to face with Matty. She became a regular attender of matches and remembers many of the great names of that era: 'Tull' Considine and 'Fowler' McInerney of Clare, Dinny Barry Murphy and Jim O'Regan of Cork, Mick Mackey, Jackie Power and Paddy Scanlon of Limerick. 'Paddy was the best goalkeeper I ever saw. All the Kilkenny players but especially Paddy Phelan — he used to enjoy his hurling so much — delighted in it: you'd see him laughing on the field. He died in England and is buried there. Sad.'

Nancy was at the 1933 final and remembers 'Lovely' Johnny Dunne's winning goal; also the frightening experience of being swept away with the crowd as it emerged from Croke Park. 'Following that victory the team got a trip to America — a wonderful treat in those days, and of course they travelled by ship and spent several weeks at sea.'

Kilkenny were beaten in the Leinster final of 1934 by Dublin after a replay, but Nancy and Kilkenny were back again in Croke Park for the 1935 final against Limerick. 'It was a fierce day — never stopped raining. All my relations came by coach from Kilkenny. They were drenched to the skin. They descended on my place after the match and took every stitch I had; when they were gone I kept saying to myself, what will I wear to work tomorrow? I thought Matty played his best game ever that day for Kilkenny. Limerick got revenge the following year, and in 1937 we travelled by train to Killarney for the final against Tipperary — more in hope than anything else: it was an aging team. It was a terrible disaster (3:11 to 0:3). It was Matty's last game.'

In 1939 Nancy and Matty married and went to Galway for the honeymoon. 'Well, who did we walk into in the street that evening but Paddy Scanlon. We invited him to the hotel. He came, accompanied by a number of friends. They sang until five in the morning. Those hurlers were great pals.'

Matty's career at senior county level stretched over a period of sixteen years. In that time he won all the honours in the game. He was one of a select band to have won All-Ireland titles with two counties: four with his native Kilkenny and one in 1927 with his adopted Dublin. He amassed the incredible total of twelve provincial titles: nine with Kilkenny and three with Dublin — surely a senior hurling record. He made his reputation as a corner-forward, one of the greats in that position. He could score and make scores for colleagues. His key attributes were speed, quick thinking, and a great sense of position.

He had the distinction of being selected on the Tailteann Games teams of 1928 and 1932. The initiative to revive the ancient Tailteann Games was taken by Dáil Éireann with a view to the games taking place in August 1922. However, because of the Civil War the games were not held until 1924. In 1928 Ireland won the game on the score 5:9 to 4:3. It was played at Croke Park on Sunday 12 August and refereed by Paddy O'Keeffe of Cork. The game was described as follows: 'From start to finish it was a clean game contested in a fine sporting spirit. The exiles played with grit and dash, and at no period and in no quarter could Ireland afford to take the opposition lightly.' The teams were:

Ireland: Dr T. Daly (goal), Jim Walsh, Mick Gill, Matty Power, Garrett Howard (Dublin); Seán Óg Murphy, Jim Regan, Eudi Coughlan (Cork); Phil Cahill, Martin Kennedy (Tipperary); Mick King, Mick Derivan (Galway); John Joe Kinnane, (Limerick); Ned Tobin (Laois); Tull Considine (Clare).

America: J. Dermody (goal), Jack Keoghan, Henry Meagher, P. Fitzpatrick (Kilkenny); J. Grey, T. Fitzgibbon, P. Delaney (Laois); C. Clehane, J. Galvin (Cork); J. Halligan, J. Horan, A. Cordial, W. Ryan (Offaly); J. Burke (Clare); T. Hickey (Tipperary).

Jack Keoghan on the American team, a native of Tullaroan, won an All-Ireland medal with Kilkenny against Cork in the 1907 final, played at Dungarvan in the summer of 1908 — a classic final, against which future games were measured for many years. The American team travelled to Ennis on Sunday 2 September and defeated Clare by 4:7 to 2:6.

Every year from its inauguration in 1927 until 1936 Matty was chosen on the Leinster Railway Cup teams. In a team of the decade 1925–35 this highly skilled and accomplished hurler — beloved for his gentleness, kindness, humility, and sportsmanship — would have been an automatic choice.

D'imigh Matty ar Shlí na Fírinne sa bhliain 1965.

Born 1900

The Tipperary team which won the All-Ireland S.H. Championship in 1937. Back row (left to right):
W. O'Donnell, J. Maher, Ger Cornally, J. Ryan, W. Wall, Phil Ryan, J. Lanigan, J. Cooney. Second row
(left to right): M. Maher, J. Gleeson, P. Purcell, Jimmy (Butler) Coffey, D. Murphy, T. Treacy, T. Kennedy.
Front row (left to right): D. Gorman, G. Doyle, T. Doyle, P. Ryan, T. Butler, W. Barry, P. Maher, D. Mackey,
Tom Semple, captain of the 'Old Blues', is seen at the back row (extreme left) and Capt. Johnny Leahy,
Tipperary Co. Secretary, is at the extreme right of the same row.

Phil was one of Tipperary's greatest hurling sons. He captained his native Tipperary in the early thirties and in his time gave brilliant displays at left-full-back, centre-back, and left-half-back. His prowess is reflected in his Railway Cup appearances — eight in all, the first in 1928, the last in 1936, in which he was victorious on five occasions: 1928, '29, '30, '31, and '34.

The Railway Cup championship began in 1927. Competition for places was intense: it was considered a tremendous honour to be chosen to play for your province. Selection carried with it the badge of prestige. Phil won his fifth and last Railway Cup medal in 1934. It was a team of star names, worth recalling: Larry Blake (Clare); George Garrett, Dinny Barry Murphy, J. Kennedy (Cork); Phil Purcell, Tommy Treacy,

Martin Kennedy (Tipperary); D. Wyse (Waterford); Paddy Scanlon, Ned Cregan, Tom McCarthy, Mickey Cross, Paddy Clohessy, Timmy Ryan, Mick Mackey (Limerick). They defeated Leinster on the score 6:3 to 3:2.

Phil was also an able administrator, as he proved when he occupied the position of county secretary. He was involved in refereeing too, and had charge of the memorable 1947 All-Ireland final between Cork and Kilkenny.

In his young days there was no All-Ireland minor championship: the first such campaign took place in 1928. So he first made his name at county level when he captained the Tipperary junior team to All-Ireland victory in 1924 with a comfortable win over Galway, 5:5 to 1:2. He hadn't progressed to senior ranks in 1925 when Tipperary seniors, led by the renowned and redoubtable Johnny Leahy, triumphed over Galway to bring the county its tenth senior success. However, he was on the panel that toured America in 1926 — a memorable tour that began on 11 May when the team and officials boarded the SS *Bremen*. They played games in New York, Chicago, Boston, Buffalo, and San Francisco. They were the first county team to tour America, and it was the first time an Irish team toured there since 1888.

Phil won his only All-Ireland medal in 1930 when John Joe Callanan captained Tipperary to victory over Dublin. Phil at centre-back that day gave an outstanding display. Other great names on that team were the goalkeeper, Tommy O'Meara, whose display in the Munster final of that year proved to be the undoing of a very formidable Clare team; Phil Cahill, a very effective and stylish forward who loved to run onto a ball that was played onto his path ahead of him — it revealed him at his deadliest; and three who figured in *Giants of the Ash*: Martin Kennedy, Tommy Treacy, and John Maher.

1930 was a great year for the Premier County. They won a treble of All-Ireland titles — senior, junior, and minor — the first time such an honour was achieved. The junior and minor victories were at the expense of Kilkenny.

> *It's not a crown of diamonds,*
> *Not yet a crown of gold,*
> *But a treble crown of laurels*
> *That speaks of fame untold.*

Five of the victorious 1930 team — Tommy O'Meara, Phil Purcell, Phil Cahill, Tommy Treacy, and Martin Kennedy — won further honours on St Patrick's Day 1931 when Munster defeated Leinster in the Railway Cup final, 1:12 to 2:6.

As with the 1925 All-Ireland win, the 1930 triumph was celebrated with another tour of America in 1931. The party — among them Johnny Leahy, manager, and Father J.J. Meagher, president of the county board — set sail from Cobh on 8 September and on arrival in New York were greeted at the City Hall by Deputy Mayor McKee. Games were played in New York, Boston, Detroit, Chicago, and San Francisco — all victorious. Tipperary were declared world champions and at a farewell supper were presented with a magnificent cup bearing the inscription *Trophy presented by Major James J. Walker for World's Hurling Championship, Ireland v. America, 1931*. The trophy is now a revered possession in Tipperary.

I paid a visit to Johnny Ryan, who featured in *Giants of the Ash,* to hear what he had to say about Phil Purcell, a fellow-clubman whom I knew he greatly admired. 'How are you, Johnny?' I enquired as I received a céad míle fáilte from one of hurling's finest gentlemen. 'It's lonely — my wife went to hospital a few days ago,' he told me. We chatted for a little while; it helped to ease the loneliness. Here is what he told me about Phil.

'I admired him greatly — died young, only sixty-three. He was a wonderful ground hurler — left and right. He captained Tipperary in the early thirties. He won county titles with Moycarkey in 1927, '32, '33, and '34, and I think he also won the 1937 one. You see, the knee went against him. He injured it in a Railway Cup game in a clash with Ned Wade — a Tipperary man playing with Dublin and Leinster. Surgery wasn't a complete success. Despite that he lined out against Limerick in the Munster final of 1936.

'I'll recall two incidents from that game for you that will show you the kind of hurler Phil was. In those days the forwards and centrefield men lined up for the throw-in: only the backs were in position. From the throw-in John Mackey tipped the ball to the wing, but it went further than he had intended. Phil met it first time on the ground, left-handed. It struck the upright and glanced wide. What a stroke — almost one hundred yards.

'Shortly after that the ball broke from a clash between Mick Mackey and John

Maher. It came between Jim Roche and myself. I flicked it on to the path of Phil. This time he met it right-handed — a first-time ground stroke; sent it wide. I'd love to have been able to hurl like that. I tried it once or twice but I couldn't drive it as far as Phil. Anyway, it wasn't my style of play. Soon after those incidents he was backing for possession with John Mackey. The knee went, and he had to be taken off. He was one of a large panel for the championship of 1937, but he didn't play in any of the matches. The left-half-back position went to Willie Wall. Phil's first cousin Tommy won an All-Ireland with Tipperary in 1945 at left-half-back, and he won Railway Cup medals in 1945 and 1949.'

'Moycarkey for a hurler!' was a great saying in Tipperary in bygone days. In Phil Purcell, Moycarkey and Tipperary certainly had one.

Born 1951

College and it was here under the watchful eye of Ned Power that my love of hurling flourished. As a school, we enjoyed great success in this period, winning numerous colleges titles at juvenile, junior and senior levels. The sixties was a great era for underage hurling in Wexford. We won All-Ireland minor titles in 1963, 1966 and 1968. I played on the minor teams of 1967, '68 and '69. One of my greatest memories is winning the '68 minor final, on a historic day for Wexford hurling.

I played my first senior championship match for Wexford in 1970 and my last outing was in 1989. In those twenty years of Leinster championships, I have many sad memories and only a few very good ones. The Leinster final victory of 1976 was perhaps the most satisfactory. Kilkenny had beaten us in the previous five finals and in '76 we beat them by seventeen points. We really should have won that All-Ireland, having been eight points up against Cork after ten minutes. We had really good teams in Wexford throughout the seventies and we were very unfortunate not to have won at least one All-Ireland title in this decade.

If the fifties, sixties and seventies were the good times of Wexford hurling, the eighties and early nineties were surely the worst of times. Some of the reason for this I believe, is the lack of success achieved at underage in the seventies. There was a long period in Wexford when there was not enough attention being paid to under-age hurling.

As well as playing for Wexford, I also had very many happy years playing in the black and amber of Rathnure. I was part of a very strong Rathnure team and I have ten senior championship medals.

For most of my club career I played as I did for Wexford, in the forwards. However, in latter years, I played at full-back and enjoyed many a great tussle

"

My first hurling memory goes back to 1960 when I was nine years old. I remember Mícheál O'Hehir broadcasting the 1960 All-Ireland final between Wexford and Tipperary. Tipperary were strong favourites in that final, but Wexford had a great win.

When the match was over, I went out on the farm to bring in the cows, with my hurl and ball and pretended to be both Billy Rackard and Tim Flood who had both just won their third All-Ireland medal.

In September 1963, I entered St Peter's

Only hurling photograph of the five Quigley brothers — taken at Croke Park, 7 May 1967 — the day St Peter's College, Wexford defeated Limerick CBS in the All-Ireland Colleges Final replay and Wexford defeated Limerick in the National League semi-final. Martin, John and Jim — St Peter's diagonal hoop jersey. Dan and Pat in the Wexford jersey.

with the one and only Tony Doran.

Because I was fortunate enough to play senior hurling for twenty years, I have hurled with a huge variety of players. People like the great Pat Nolan who had senior medals from the fifties, was still playing when I joined the Wexford team, as was Tom Neville.

Throughout the seventies there were so many, such as Tony Doran, Mick Jacob, Ned Buggy, Willie Murphy, Teddy O'Connor, Liam Bennett, 'Heffo' Walsh and then in the eighties the 'youngsters' such as George and John O'Connor, John Conran, Jimmy Holohan, Billy Byrne, Martin Storey, Tom Dempsey and Liam Dunne. I think I retired (or was retired) in 1986. There are those, however, who would say that I had more comebacks than Lazarus. In 1988 I was a spectator at the first round of the championship against Laois. Three weeks later I scored 2:2 in

the semi-final against Kilkenny. That is the stuff that dreams are made of! Twenty years — people often ask me what made me keep going? I can honestly say that it was a privilege for me to wear the purple and gold. In truth, I might be out there still only for a dodgy knee!

Martin Quigley

It was the afternoon of Monday 14 July 1997. A most fitting time indeed to meet with Martin Quigley, star of former years and one of Wexford's greatest hurling sons, now involved with the county under-21 team.

His native Wexford had on the previous day fashioned a remarkable Leinster title victory over Kilkenny in a tense, dour, physical, energy-sapping

253

Pre-match parade of 1970 All-Ireland final. Cork led by their captain Paddy Barry (right). Wexford led by their captain Mick Collins followed by four Quigley brothers: Dan, Martin, John and Pat.

contest that was laced with drama and excitement from start to finish.

In time, when the game will move into the realms of legend, Billy Byrne will head the heroes chart. The thirty-seven-year-old veteran was sent into the fray with about ten minutes remaining and the scoreboard reading Wexford 1:12 Kilkenny 1:11. Now for stuff of folklore and fairy tales and dreams. All the remaining scores came from Billy — a goal from the first ball that came his way, 'a my left foot' effort. Then a point and then another point and he nearly had another goal. Final whistle Wexford 2:14 Kilkenny 1:11. Truly a game for the gods.

The supporters spilled on to the pitch in huge numbers, cheering and flag waving and venerating in a delightful celebration of victory and spontaneous outpouring of reflected glory.

But back to Martin. A brilliant career began in his school days at St Peter's College, Wexford with whom he won Leinster and All-Ireland colleges titles in 1967 and '68. Both All-Irelands went

to replays. 'In 1967 we played Limerick CBS in Portlaoise. They were moving the ball fast — criss cross hurling — stretching us. With time almost up they were a goal ahead. Our wing-forward got the ball and for some strange reason the corner-back rushed out towards him leaving me all on my own. The ball was lobbed in to me and I palmed the equaliser. We won the replay in Croke Park by ten or eleven points. Again the following year we were lucky to draw the first day with Coláiste Chríost Rí at Clonmel but like the previous year, we won the replay at Croke Park by eight points.'

His career in competitive hurling ended twenty-three years later in 1990 when he won his last of ten county titles with Rathnure at corner forward at a time when he was troubled by a knee injury. It will come as news to many outside the county that Martin played a lot of his hurling in defence for his club — and with distinction too. 'I hurled a good few years at full-back for Rathnure. We were playing Buffers Alley —

we had many great battles with them — and Dan had to go off injured. I was brought back to mark Tony Doran. That's how it started. I did reasonably well.'

Rathnure, of Rackard fame, was further enhanced in the hurling world by the Quigley family. In 1972 John, Jim, Martin and Dan won a Leinster club title with Rathnure but failed by one point to Blackrock of Cork in the All-Ireland final. In 1974 they were joined by Pat and after success in Leinster failed again to Blackrock, after a replay, in the All-Ireland final. Martin is extremely proud of his native Rathnure. 'We won seven county titles in ten years and had hurlers who could play on any county team. The support within the parish was fantastic and there was a great positive attitude. Under-age players were very well catered for. Win or lose, the approach to the game in Rathnure was purist. The club was a model within the county — up there to be beaten.'

The family created a unique record in 1970 that may stand for a long long time. In the All-Ireland final of that year against Cork, the Wexford half-forward line was an all-Quigley one — Martin, Pat and John. The centre-back position was manned by Dan — Big Dan to hurling followers. It was the first eighty-minute final. Wexford were forced to line out without the services of Eddie Kelly, Willie Murphy, Phil Wilson, Ned Buggy and Christy Kehoe. It heralded an uphill struggle even before the ball was thrown in — and so it proved to be. Wexford scored 5:10 but Cork, exposing a defensive weakness, mercilessly exploited it and ran up a tally of 6:21 to take the honours.

Martin is Wexford's most decorated All-Star — being honoured on four successive occasions from 1973 onwards. The selectors' comments on three of those occasions reveal much about Martin, the hurling man.

- 1973 — For the wide range of his hurling skills, his constancy of purpose and his obvious versatility.

- 1975 — For his all-round ability and craft and the competence he showed in a variety of positions during the year.

- 1976 — For his intelligent hurling and clever distribution of the ball as much as for his great versatility.

He was Sportstar of the week — 'I think 'twas 1977' — following a league match against Clare at Tulla. 'Clare used play their home league matches there. 'Twas a graveyard for visiting teams. I think we were the first team to beat them there. They were good then — they won a couple of league titles. 'Twas a good day for us.'

Throughout his career Martin was a potent forward — an ever-present threat — a real problem for opposing defences. In 1988 he banged in two great goals against Kilkenny and the following year, with his thirty-eighth year completed, he came on as a sub — his last hurrah — against Kilkenny and was still sharp enough to find the net.

Martin won an All-Ireland minor medal in 1968 with a victory over Cork but he suffered at their hands for three years in a row at under-21 level with defeats in '69, '70 and '71.

Martin's mother had little or no interest in the game. 'I think she only went to one match ever and it wasn't an important one.' His father, however — 'who played a bit of football' — was a fanatical supporter. 'I remember as a kid going to a lot of matches with him. That's where we got our enthusiasm from. I remember one day he invited the referee to the line to fight. I was mortified as a child. In his later years he gave up going to matches. He used to get 100 per cent worked up and that wasn't good for him.'

Martin took some hard knocks during his playing days. He was stitched several times. There are marks on the face and around the eyes. He remembers a league game against Offaly. As he contested a dropping ball he was hit on the back of the head. 'At half time Dr Bowe looked at it and inserted nine stitches — no anaesthetic. You just clinched your teeth and braced yourself. The trainer asked if I was OK. Ah, he'll be all right, said Dr Bowe — he's a hardy young fellow — he'll be all right. Out I went for the second half. It was the last place in the world I should have gone.'

Martin's association with the game didn't end with retirement. From 1990 onwards he spent three years as Manager of the county senior team. As well as being a selector at present for the county under-21 team, he is also involved at under-age level with St Martin's where his sons now play. In retirement he takes an occasional mental glance at the hurling ledger and he sees in its pages some outstanding unsettled scores. At this stage, it is most likely they will be either written off, or go statute barred.

Martin's team from the men he played against is as follows:

Noel Skehan *(Kilkenny)*

Fan Larkin *(Kilkenny)*   Pat Hartigan *(Limerick)*   Eugene Coughlan *(Offaly)*

Ger Henderson *(Kilkenny)*   Seán Silke *(Galway)*   Iggy Clarke *(Galway)*

Frank Cummins *(Kilkenny)*   John Connolly *(Galway)*

Francis Loughnane *(Tipperary)*   Martin Quigley *(Wexford)*   Eddie Keher *(Kilkenny)*

Kieran Purcell *(Kilkenny)*   Ray Cummins *(Cork)*   Seánie O'Leary *(Cork)*

Presentation by club chairman Andy Jordan to Paddy Quirke

Born 1956

"

In Dunroe, the townland where I was born, on the outer fringes of Bagenalstown parish, adjoining Myshall parish, there was no tradition of hurling. My mother was an only child, and my father, a small farmer, never played the game; but I had two aunts, Minnie and Lill, who were fine camogie players. Camogie was strong in the area at the time, so I guess hurling must have been in the blood. My uncle Pakie also was a fine athlete.

There were seven of us in the family, five boys and two girls. I had two older brothers, Éamonn, the eldest, and then Seán, and two younger brothers, Séamus and Tom. My two younger sisters, Mary and Ann, played camogie with Myshall. First we attended a one-teacher primary school in Killoughter-nane, which was closed in 1966; then we cycled seven miles every day to the De La Salle boys' national school in Bagenal-stown. It was Pat Ryan, a Limerick man,

who introduced us to the game. He was living in Bagenalstown at the time. Éamonn was the first to start playing. We started pucking around at home, first in the farmyard and against the gable end of the house; then we got more organised and erected a goalpost in a field at the back of the house. We were playing with Bagenalstown school team and club at the time.

At this time Father Phil O'Shea organised a juvenile club in Myshall parish. There was no juvenile club in the area at the time, so the standard was very low. Father O'Shea got permission from Bord na nÓg to play anyone who had attended Killoughternane school. That included us. So we started playing with Myshall. I still remember one of Father Phil's chants: 'Keep pulling — it'll have to move.' At this stage at under-14 to be beaten by ten goals was a victory in our eyes. We were learning fast that losing wasn't always a defeat.

Any spare time we had at home we were out hurling. Some of our neighbours joined in, and a game would be organised. Those were great days. Éamonn was the best of the bunch. Seán and myself often tried to mark him. As we progressed to under-16 we were winning the odd game, but we had no real success; but still we always looked forward to the next game. The late Mick Tobin, who was secretary of the senior club at the time, brought us to a lot of the matches, driving many miles out of his way to collect us, and always treating us to an ice-cream after the game. The car would be loaded down with what he called 'brats of chaps'.

Andy Jordan, the master in Myshall national school, was the first chairman of our club when it was re-formed in 1968 — a true Gael if there ever was one. Andy was involved in all GAA activities in the club. Michael Davitt's, a parish team for Leighlin, was our main rival at minor level. Father Kennedy, feared by all under his command, was in charge of the 'All-Blacks', as they were called. We had the pleasure of beating Michael Davitt's in a league final in 1973. I was captain for our first victory and medal. I was marking my best friend and rival, Pat Foley. Many a good duel I had with Pat. Sadly, he was killed in a car accident in December '79.

I remember the last couple of minutes of that game. We were one point down and it looked like another defeat. I won the ball around midfield and hit a long, high ball into the square. Red Pat Nolan pulled and stuck the ball in the net. That was Pat's last game, but it was the start of something big for me.

Andy Jordan brought us to a minor seven-a-side competition in Dublin. We were narrowly beaten in the final. Mick Holden was one of the opposition that day.

Naomh Eoin won four under-21 championships in a row from '72 to '75. All Father O'Shea's and Andy Jordan's hard work had paid off.

Naomh Eoin joined the senior hurling ranks in 1969 after winning the junior hurling championship. I remember my first senior hurling game with Naomh Eoin against Bagenalstown. I was about sixteen at the time and playing in goal. I was afraid of my life, but all was well, because I had the three strongest men in Carlow in front of me: Pat Keogh, Brian Fox, and Ted Butler. Éamonn was midfield that day and marking the legendary Jim English. Pat Ryan, the man that started us off, was corner-forward for Bagenalstown.

In our first senior final in 1973 we were beaten by Ballinkillin. We turned the tide in '74 by winning the club's first senior hurling title. We went on to make it three in a row. Naomh Eoin was on the map as a hurling force. I didn't realise at the time what those victories meant to the Myshall people. It brought great excitement and life to the village. I was selected on the Carlow senior

team in '74, a place I held for the next sixteen years.

I was training Naomh Eoin in '75 and '76. In '75 we were going for the double, but Tinriland beat us in the football final. In '76 we beat Carnew Emmets in the first round of the Leinster club championship. St Rynagh's beat us in the second round, 2:16 to 3:9. This result put Naomh Eoin on the map as a hurling force in Leinster. In '77 we were beaten at the semi-final stage. That year I was picked on the Leinster Railway Cup team. I was thrilled; I never expected it. Leinster won the Railway Cup, but I did not make the first fifteen.

'78 was the best county final I was ever involved in — against those arch-rivals, St Mullin's. It was the first time we came head to head in a county final. It was always going to be a cracker. I was in Dublin at the time on a teacher training course, so I did a lot of training on my own out in Fairview Park. It took four-and-a-half hours of action-packed hurling before the final whistle blew — four games and one period of extra time. Éamonn was centre-forward and hard to stop. He scored thirteen points the second day. Seán was a no-nonsense full-back. You would think twice before attempting to pass him. I was midfield, along with Black Jimmy Doyle. Jimmy scored eight points from play the third day. We had a powerful half-back line: Ned Kavanagh, John O'Hara, and Michael Nolan.

The third day in extra time we went three points up and only minutes remaining. Peter Nolan, a brother of Michael, got cramps in his legs. He was corner-back. St Mullin's were on the attack; Peter on the ground; Pat Keogh, unmarked, got possession and rattled the net for the equalising goal. The fourth game was equally exciting. My brother Seán was sent off early in the game and things looked bleak, but we all played out of our skins and emerged two points to the good. Naomh Eoin used twenty-eight players in that four-and-a-half hours' hurling. This was a game which brought to a conclusion a

Paddy Quirke in action (right) *against Laois in the Keogh Cup, 1986.*

superb chapter in the history of Carlow hurling. I was picked on the Leinster team again.

In '79 we were beaten in the county semi-final, but I won my only Railway Cup medal on the field of play. The final was fixed for Thurles and the opposition, Connacht. I was playing in my favourite position, midfield. Fran Larkin was the captain. I was marking John Connolly. At that stage I feared no-one and I could mix it with the best. I was playing with the best in Leinster — Tony Doran, Ger Henderson, Martin Quigley, Pat Carroll, Mark Corrigan, Peadar Carton — and enjoying it.

I was selected as a dual replacement All-Star in 1980 and travelled to America. Kerry and Galway were the All-Ireland champions at the time. The late Mick Morrissey, a St Mullin's man who won All-Ireland hurling medals with Wexford in the fifties, was living in New York at the time. Mick looked after me while I was there. He presented me with a plaque as a mark of the first Carlow man on an All-Star trip. We travelled to Chicago and Los Angeles. I remember in Los Angeles the night before our final games I was walking out the front door of the Holiday Inn. I could see this man, Barry Jordan, eldest son of Andy the Master, walking towards me. He was in San Francisco for a few years. Barry and a couple of friends flew down to Los Angeles to support me. The next day I was playing midfield against Kerry, marking the Bomber [Eoin Liston]. I won the Man of the Match award for my efforts. I also played a hurling game against Galway the same day.

Seán Doyle, a Carnew man, was appointed trainer of Naomh Eoin in 1980, a position he held for the next four years. Seán had played for Carnew and Wicklow and was no stranger to most of our lads. Seán was a tough, hard hurler and a great GAA man.

We won the championship again in '81. My younger brother Tom was on the team, corner-forward. The four of us played with Naomh Eoin for the next decade. We beat St Mullin's again in '82. Championship count at this stage: St Mullin's 5, Naomh Eoin 6. My brother Éamonn was top scorer in the SHC in '73, '74, '76, '78, '79, '81, and '82.

I trained Naomh Eoin from '85 to '89. We won our second three-in-a-row, '85, '86, and '87. Winning our only football title in '86 and achieving a rare double was a career highlight for me. Osmond Bennett was our masseur at the time. Rathnure provided the opposition for the second round of the Leinster club championship in '87. We were beaten by one point after being eleven points up at half time. I will always remember Éamonn's duel with the great Martin Quigley. We were beaten in the next two county hurling finals of '88 and '89.

From 1990 to '93 I was chairman of the juvenile club. I had a great secretary in Des Murphy, the driving force behind the juveniles at the time. I coached the under-14 hurling and football teams for the next five years. We went on four Féile trips: twice to Tipperary (Portroe and Lorrha), Galway (Kilconierin), and Limerick (to a club called Blackrock). Séamus Murphy was appointed trainer in '90 — a Rathnure and Wexford hurler, a man who had great passion for the game. We enjoyed every minute of his training. We have won the championship every year since 1990 — six titles in a row. We beat St Mullin's in four consecutive finals, including two replays. Séamus has been appointed Rathnure trainer for the coming year.

In the early days we trained in a field called the Ranch — no dressing-rooms, but that was not a problem. I remember going to train on a motorbike, often straight from work, and looking up to see how high the sun was in the sky. This would be an indication of how long we had for training. Our senior team at the time was a very strong physical side: men like Brian and Liam Fox, John and Tom Foley (Danoli's trainer), Willie and James Eustace, Seán and Éamonn, Pat Keogh, Ted Butler, and Black Jimmy Doyle, just to mention a few.

Andy Jordan was there from the start and to this day, even though not actively involved, never misses a training session. I remember Andy saying to me around 1980, 'I hope I live to see the day that we will win a senior football title.' Andy was asked after the six in a row, 'Do you think we can make it seven?' 'Well,' said Andy, 'it's the next number after six.' Andy has two sons on the present team, Ciarán and Peadar, last year's captain.

Tommy Murphy was a dual player from the start. He was chairman for a couple of years and secretary for many years. He is now PRO for the club and county. Willie Eustace, a great club man, was a dual player and is chairman of Naomh Eoin for the last sixteen years, one of the driving forces behind our club.

On the county scene I started in the '74 championship against Meath. We had very little success. We won three National League medals and two Keogh Cups. I never enjoyed playing in the winter. We often travelled long journeys — Kerry, Derry, Down, Mayo, Armagh — in bad conditions and played tough games on poor pitches. I was very disappointed in '86: we lost to Kerry in Thurles, 2:14 to 1:16. This was the All-Ireland B home final. In '87 we beat Down in the home final in Trim. This was my best performance in the county jersey. I was centre-forward and training the team. There were seven Naomh Eoin men on the team: Ned Kavanagh, John O'Hara, Michael Nolan, Noel Smithers, Michael Slye, Tom Quirke, and myself. I was always a play-maker and I got a lot of possession that day and set up many scores. After the game the crowd came over to the players' exit and clapped us off the field.

We had some great trainers: Dan Harnedy, for example — he was a players' man; Moling Morrissey, brother of Mick — a great Carlow hurler himself; Moling has been appointed county trainer for the coming season [1996]; Ollie Walsh — a man apart; Christy Kehoe, of Wexford fame; Martin Fitzpatrick, brother of Billy — he brought the county team their first All-Ireland B title. John O'Hara was a selector along with that great hurling man from Carlow town Tommy Corcoran.

Patrick Quirke.

By geography and population Carlow is one of the smallest counties in Ireland. Within the county borders the games of hurling and football are alive and vibrant. Much dedication and effort is put in both by players and officials. Sad to relate, the rewards and spoils of victory that such commitment merits are not reflected on the trophy sideboard of the county.

Let's look briefly at their moments of glory. In 1944 Carlow won the Leinster senior football title by defeating Dublin, the All-Ireland champions in 1942, by 2:6 to 1:6. They failed in the All-Ireland semi-final by only two points, 3:3 to 0:10 — a points tally that would suggest many areas of supremacy outfield — to a powerful Kerry combination, who in turn lost the All-Ireland final to Roscommon by just two points. No All-Ireland football title in any grade has come Carlow's way, but in recent years, including 1996, Éire Óg of Carlow town has performed magnificently against the best in the All-Ireland club championship.

On the hurling front Carlow won the All-Ireland intermediate title in 1962, and on Sunday 28 April 1963 they made their first appearance in the senior hurling championship when they met Offaly in the first round at O'Moore Park, Portlaoise. It was a winning dbut, 5:5 to 3:7, in a really tough encounter where the exchanges were extremely hard. Many hurling lovers hoped at that time that they would do a Wexford on it and emerge as a force. Unfortunately, the talent wasn't there in sufficient depth. Their only other hurling success of significance was an All-Ireland senior B title in 1992.

So it is against this background of little reward that we look at the career of Paddy Quirke and his remarkable achievements. He had no special hurling heroes growing up, 'but there was great talk about Mick Mackey, Christy Ring, and John Doyle: they were talked about regularly, even though their careers went back decades.' Modern players he admires include D.J. Carey, Seán McMahon, Liam Dunne, Johnny Dooley, Brian Corcoran, Brian Whelehan, James O'Connor, and Brian and Frank Lohan.

Paddy was a dual player with club and county, and he so distinguished himself that he was honoured by the Railway Cup selectors and played inter-provincial for Leinster in hurling and football. At club level he has so far won fifteen senior hurling titles between 1974 and 1995. In 1986 he made it a double when his club won both hurling and football titles — an achievement unique in County Carlow GAA history.

Of all the county titles he won, the hurling victory of 1978 over St Mullin's stands out as special — a victory that time cannot dim; a victory that will be talked about for many years to come in the households of the parish. It took four draws and extra time to decide the issue — surely a record. The standard of hurling in the club is reflected in some of their performances in the Leinster club championship. In 1976 they met Carnew Emmets in the first round. 'It was one of the toughest games of hurling I ever played in. After that it was St Rynagh's of Offaly. We lost by only four points — another very hard game; tough days. In 1987 we met Rathnure of Wexford; lost by only one point, after being eleven points up at half time. It would have been great if we could have won a Leinster senior hurling title' — honour for Carlow; honour for hurling.

Paddy recalled a humorous incident in a club game with the Westmeath champions, Brownstown. 'It was a particularly wet day; the going was heavy, around the goalmouth was very muddy, difficult for hurling. My brother Seán was playing full-back, all fourteen-and-a-half stone of him. A difference of opinion arose between Seán and the full-forward, with play continuing outfield. Seán got him down on the ground; put his knee on his neck; put his hand on his head and began pushing it down into the mud. The full-forward looked up at Seán and said, "Do you skull cattle?" End of fracas: humour won.'

Paddy Johnson of Kilkenny refereed many of their games in the Carlow championship. He was respected. 'He would come into the dressing-room before the game with the ball in his hand; then he would say, "Lads, I won't put you off — you put yourself off." Holding up the ball he would say, "That's what counts. Best of luck." Off then to the other dressing-room with him.'

With his county, Paddy's senior hurling career spanned seventeen years: 1974 to 1990, and in senior football he played from 1974 to 1987. He played hurling and football for Leinster in the Railway Cup competition, a dual performer in 1979 and 1981. No football medal came his way, but he did have two hurling successes, the first as a substitute in 1977, and the great honour in 1979 of being the first Carlow man to line out with a winning Railway Cup hurling side. In 1964 a fellow-county man, Martin Hogan, came on as a sub for Des Foley of Dublin and won a hurling medal.

Paddy's talents also came to the notice of the All-Star selectors. In 1980 he was chosen as the dual All-Star replacement and travelled to America with the cream of Ireland's hurling and football men. In the football game against Kerry, Dermot Earley of Roscommon was injured in the early stages. Paddy took his place and faced Eoin 'Bomber' Liston at midfield — 'a very competitive player.' His performance won him the Man of the Match award. 'It was fantastic to get it. I didn't know there was such a thing. It was announced out of the blue at the banquet.' His selection as dual All-Star will always remain his greatest memory; it represented the pinnacle of personal achievement. In 1979 he had the honour of being selected on an Irish team to play against a Scottish shinty team.

Paddy recalls going to San Francisco to play some games. 'It was very tough hurling; hurling in America was very hard and physical. I put in my hurley, angled with the bos to the ground, to block an opponent; got a severe belt across the face; was taken off of course and rushed to hospital by colleagues. I had no social security cover, but my friends who were with me decided I was now Patrick Foley (a genuine holder of social security). So suddenly I was Patrick Foley. Still somewhat dazed, I heard the name Patrick Foley being called; I made no response. "That's you," said John Behan to me. In I went to the surgery. "Were you playing that crazy Irish game?" the doctor queried.'

On the occasion of the silver jubilee of the club a presentation was made to Paddy by the club chairman, Andy Jordan, the 'Master'. The inscription reads:

Iúbhaile cúig bliana fichead
1968–1992
Naomh Eoin
Ardghradam
ar
Phádraig Ó Cuirc
de bharr a ghaisce san iomáint is sa pheil
le club, le contae, le cúige is fiú le plúr
na hÉireann

Paddy has been described as 'a deadly dangerous centre-forward, stylish, accurate, makes play for the rest of his forwards.' He hasn't retired yet from club activity. He has no regrets, and looks back on his playing days with immense satisfaction. 'I gave 100 per cent from day 1. I was always fully fit and in tune for every game.'

May Carlow produce many more like him!

This is Paddy's team from the men of his era:

Noel Skehan *(Kilkenny)*

Aidan Fogarty *(Offaly)*   Pat Hartigan *(Limerick)*   John Horgan *(Cork)*
Mick Jacob *(Wexford)*   Ger Henderson *(Kilkenny)*   Iggy Clarke *(Galway)*

Frank Cummins *(Kilkenny)*   Paddy Quirke *(Carlow)*

Johnny Callinan *(Clare)*   Martin Quigley *(Wexford)*   John Fenton *(Cork)*
Éamon Cregan *(Limerick)*   Tony Doran *(Wexford)*   Eddie Keher *(Kilkenny)*

Born 1925

> " Just imagine what would my life have been without hurling. It would not have been life at all. It brought me so much enjoyment playing it — it brought me into contact with the very best of friends. It was kind to me in securing employment in the lean days and has been most generous in my business. I enjoy the games as much as ever, and I look forward to Tipp getting back on the winning trail. I would not mention any player in particular as being the best — I saw so many great players. "

Mick Ryan

Mick Ryan's club career is a fascinating one. At first he played with his native Roscrea. The highlight of that career was the county final of 1945, when Roscrea and Thurles Sarsfields clashed at Nenagh. Thurles had a very seasoned outfit: nearly all had county experience — men like the goalkeeper, Gerry Doyle, Tommy Doyle, and of course that great centre-back

John Maher, who was captain. But Roscrea, who were ten points down with little more than five minutes remaining, almost created a sensation by scoring 3:1 to force a draw. The replay, which was brought to Thurles, was lost on the score 1:4 to 1:0. Mick felt robbed of that title, because an umpire signalled wide when the sliotar went out through the net between the inside of the goalpost and the net. 'If the ball had been wide it would have hit the umpire.'

After that, employment took him to Kilkenny, where he hurled with Dicksboro' and in the company of men like Paddy Grace, Dan Kennedy and Dick Carroll won county honours in 1950 with victory over Éire Óg. For that county final replay he left Cork at one o'clock and was in the Dicksboro' colours for the throw-in at half past three.

By now he was working in Cork, and for the championships of 1951 and 1952 he played with Blackrock. In 1953, however, he transferred to St Finbarr's and for a dozen years gave many majestic and power-packed performances until his fortieth birthday, none greater than his display in the replay of the county final of 1955, when, before a crowd of 35,000 people, St Finbarr's dethroned the reigning champions, Glen Rovers. And in the second half of that game Mick, at centre-back, with a heavily bandaged head wound and wearing a cap, gave a performance on Christy Ring that even the Glen Rovers followers openly admired and applauded. That victory created the unique situation of a Tipperary man winning his two county medals in Kilkenny and Cork, both games going to a replay.

Mick was a class performer: tenacious, fast, graceful, and skilful. Whether at centrefield or centre-forward or, in the latter days of his career, at centre-back, his striking was sweet and his distribution accurate, and he could double on a ball whether on the ground or overhead. Spectators who saw him in the games against Cork in the six years from 1949 to 1954 will recall those qualities. In particular, they will remember his display in extra time in 1949 at Limerick Gaelic grounds when he crowned his performance with a great goal that ended Cork's hopes. Again in 1951 at the same venue he was switched from centre-forward to midfield in the second half, where he curbed a hitherto rampant Christy Ring and began the move that brought the goal that levelled matters for Tipperary and set them on the road to victory. It was close: 2:11 to 2:9.

Graphically etched in his memory are the early days of his hurling life. 'We marched three miles to play a match in a national school league, led by our teacher, Mrs Brown, and when we won she marched us back — proud as Punch. She was marvellous. My father used to make our hurleys. He was good at making hurleys. My brothers, Jack and Dinny, also played for the county.'

Mick marvelled at the hardihood of the human frame as he watched awestruck the intensity of the exchanges between the Limerick and Cork players in the Munster final of 1940. He saw at first hand that day the courage of spirit and body required of those who would aspire to play with the giants of the game. And it wasn't long until he was moving in that direction himself.

'I played senior hurling for Tipp in a four-county league on the 19 March 1942 — three months before I wore the county minor colours. Coming off the pitch after the game, John Maher asked me what age I was, and when I replied seventeen he said, "Good God, go home and come back in two years' time." We became great friends afterwards. I was only sixteen when I played with Roscrea against Boherlahan in 1941, and in the 1942 championship against Thurles Sarsfields I scored 2:3 in the first half, playing at right-half-forward.'

Mick established himself permanently on the county team after the 1945 All-Ireland victory. Three years of frustration lay ahead as they suffered first-round defeats at the hands of Limerick, with John Mackey at full-forward posing all kinds of problems for the Tipperary rearguard. But 1949 brought lots of changes in Tipperary and heralded a great era for their hurling followers. In the years that followed, indeed, the county was so rich in talent that Mick recalled a particular Sunday when Tipperary fielded two senior teams, to play Limerick in Nenagh and Cork in Mallow — and his recollection is that they won both. Holding your place, therefore, meant that you had to perform at a consistently high standard.

'We travelled to play Waterford in a National League game at Carrick-on-Suir, with a trip to America at stake. In the car Phil Purcell told me I'd have to pull my socks up or I wouldn't hold my place. "You picked a bad day to tell me," I told him, "what with me playing on Mick Hayes." No fellow ever blotted me out, but I could never get away from Hayes — and I liked to roam: that way you could exploit an opening. Well, with ten minutes to go, Waterford were hammering us — nine points ahead. Then Declan [Goode] made a series of switches that saw Mick Hayes move to a different position. Didn't I score three goals, and Stakelum got a point to win the game! You should have seen and heard Hayes after the match!'

Mick is proud of the three-in-a-row All-Ireland victories of 1949, '50, and '51. Relatively few players achieve such an honour. Tipperary accomplished it only once in the past, and that was away back in 1898, '99, and 1900. He would love to have made it four in a row in 1952, but Cork edged them out in the Munster final on the score 1:11 to 2:6. The result wasn't without controversy; but if they were unlucky in 1952, Mick sportingly admits that they were fortunate to survive in Killarney in 1950.

To his All-Ireland victories were added Munster, Railway Cup, National League and Oireachtas successes. In 1952 he was selected on the first All-Ireland hurling team to play the Combined Universities. It is worth recalling the line-out:

'Mick Mackey was being interviewed one time and a competition was held in the bar as to who he would say was the best player he had seen. We all wrote a name on a piece of paper and put it in a jar with half a crown. I wrote down Jackie Power. Mick was asked who was the best he had seen, excluding himself. Mick replied that, *including* himself,

	Tony Reddan *(Tipperary)*	
Jackie Goode *(Waterford)*	Paddy Hayden *(Kilkenny)*	Colm Corless *(Galway)*
Séamus Bannon *(Tipperary)*	Pat Stakelum *(Tipperary)*	Willie Walsh *(Kilkenny)*
Phil Shanahan *(Tipperary)*		Christy Ring *(Cork)*
Padge Kehoe *(Wexford)*	Mick Ryan *(Tipperary)*	Josie Gallagher *(Galway)*
Paddy Kenny *(Tipperary)*	Derry McCarthy *(Limerick)*	Willie John Daly *(Cork)*

In his playing days Mick 'hurled with and against many wonderful hurlers — too numerous to mention.' But he couldn't help recalling the feats of some. 'Tommy Doyle would never say a match was lost: he would try to the last — a never-say-die spirit. I'd have Tony Reddan and Nick O'Donnell on any team. Jimmy Finn was a supreme hurler, and Pat Stakelum was a very solid half-back. I played on Timmy Ryan, the Limerick midfielder, one day towards the end of his career. He was a fine player — big and strong; skin and bone — no surplus flesh. What amazed me about him was the height he could get up to, under a dropping ball, to double on it. Jimmy Langton was a very modest man, a great ball-player with a lot of skill. I loved playing beside Jimmy Kennedy. He had great anticipation. No matter what way I played the ball, Kennedy would be in position when it would land. He was great altogether — unbelievable. Johnny Ryan was an outstanding player — a great wholehearted defender.

Jackie Power was the best. He could play anywhere. He damn near beat us in the 1949 Munster final. He came in on a solo run — hurleys flying at him from all angles; scored a great goal — but it wasn't allowed. Phil Purcell used to say, "Stop Power and you'll stop Limerick."'

Mick also played football and won a county senior title in 1952 with Clonakilty. 'There was never a dull moment in that campaign. We were involved in five draws. It made some of the witty ones say that Clonakilty were a very sporting team: they always gave their opponents a second chance.'

We parted smiling as he related another story to me. 'Dinny Barry Murphy, Jack Barrett of Kinsale and Fox Collins used travel together to matches. For the entire journey Dinny Barry and Jack would talk, reminisce, tell stories and yarns, recount deeds and exploits from the past and enjoy it all. Fox Collins would sit silently, and he used to say, "They bring me along to do the listening."'

Paddy SCANLON   1932–1941   Ahane (Limerick), Liam Mellows (Galway), & Limerick

Born 1906

T his great son of Castleconnell first played with Limerick in the Thomond Feis competition of 1932. It was a four-county tournament in which Limerick beat Tipperary and Clare shocked the All-Ireland champions, Cork, in the semifinals. In a great game of hurling Limerick narrowly beat Clare in the final on 12 June. It heralded the beginning of a most glorious era in Limerick hurling and the career of Paddy Scanlon, whose dazzling performances between the posts in the decade that followed placed his name among the greatest of hurling goalkeepers.

In the twenties Tommy Daly of Clare was the prince of goalkeepers, and his name was synonymous with brilliance between the posts. His departure coincided with the arrival of Paddy Scanlon. For superb goalkeeping the thirties belonged to Paddy. Long before his retirement his name had become a metaphor for goalkeeping excellence and the benchmark by which all future goalkeeping performances would be measured. Paddy was superb — arguably equalled, never surpassed.

The following hurlers whom I met in the course of my writing selected Paddy as their number 1: Willie John Daly, Jack Lynch, Din Joe Buckley, all of Cork; Seán Herbert, John Mackey, Timmy Ryan and Paddy McMahon of Limerick, Paddy Buggy from Kilkenny, and Sam Thorpe from Wexford.

It is said that on one occasion Paddy pucked the ball from one end of the field and sent it over the bar at the other goal. According to a neighbour of Paddy's, this happened in his young days when he went off and played a game with neighbouring Newport in Borrisoleigh. The opposition wondered where they got him. Those were the days when it was more difficult than now to establish whether a man was illegal.

Paddy was lynx-eyed and fearless and possessed a cool temperament and the sharpest of reflexes, a combination of characteristics that made him great between the posts. And he needed all those qualities, for he played in the days when the rules allowed the forwards to thunder in on the goalkeeper and bundle him, ball and all, into the back of the net. To offset that threat Scanlon often lashed first time on the ball — be it lobbing from the air or travelling bullet-like between ground and crossbar — and cleared to safety. It was a great skill and it minimised the options of in-rushing forwards, who had to give second thoughts to their own safety.

Those who knew Paddy well have described him as a wonderful companion, a great storyteller, amiable and affable. Paddy worked for various firms, including McMahon's of Limerick, and when he moved to Galway to take up a position at McDonagh's he hurled with the local club, Liam Mellows.

Paddy Scanlon saves against Cork in the Munster final at Thurles, 1940.

Here is what 'Carbery' had to say about Paddy Scanlon in his column in the *Cork Weekly Examiner* after the Munster final of 1939:

'For a long part of the hour one man stood between them [Cork] and their long-sought place in the Munster sunlight. A quiet, pale-faced man this; he can sing a good song in company and is one of the pleasantest companions in the world. His name is Scanlon — Pat Scanlon of Ahane, for some years at business in Galway county. Five feet nine, well built all over; the most consistent goalkeeper in Ireland, this lynx-eyed man is cool as a polar bear under pressure. Holding his ash right hand down, he stands close to the left corner of his net and watches every attacking and defensive move. No keener judge of backs or forwards than Pat Scanlon. Whether the shots threaten right or left, on the sod or close under the rigging, he seems to command them all with unpremeditated art. Last Sunday at Thurles the Limerick goalkeeper was better than ever. When Cork's fearless forwards crashed balls in close to the half-hour, Scanlon's goal seemed to have

a charmed life. Cork's fifteen played against seventeen men at Thurles — fourteen through the field and three Scanlons in goal.

'There was "a small dark man" [Maurice Walsh, the novelist] hidden away among the forty-two thousand spectators. His hair is steel grey now. But "while rivers run" he says he will give "the key above the door" to Pat Scanlon.'

A year later, following the Munster final between the same counties, 'Carbery' wrote:

'Pat Scanlon got four times as many shots to stop as Buttimer, who made few mistakes. But it was the hurling fairies of Lough Gur that peopled Limerick's goal around Scanlon. Divil a doubt about it. No normal goalie could cover the shots that came from long range and short; right, left, and centre. Ted Sullivan pasted one at him in the second quarter from the seven yards line. Scanlon stopped it dead and shovelled it out before he was buried in the net. Not one hurley he had but a score of them shooting out at all angles. And his ash was a magnet.'

'Thomond', writing in the *Limerick Leader* after the 1939 Munster final between Limerick and Cork, had this to say:

'As Johnny Leahy stated after the match, I am a long time witnessing great games and great defences but never in my long career have I enjoyed such goalkeeping as kept by Paddy Scanlon during that first half. Again and again his stoppages were marvellous. It was amazing to everyone that he saved his net time and again. There has been great goalkeeping on that pitch since the days of "Hawk" O'Brien, Andy Fitzgerald, the late Dr Tommy Daly, Jackie Ryan, etc. etc., but never has there been displayed such a holding of the fort against such swift and clever attackers, favoured by a strong breeze and backed by a glaring sun, as displayed by Paddy Scanlon on the Thurles pitch on last Sunday.'

It is little wonder, therefore, with a man of the calibre of Paddy Scanlon between the posts that Limerick in the period

Limerick 1939. Paddy Scanlon is in the back row, third from left.

from October 1933 to April 1938 won fifty-eight of sixty-five games played in Ireland, England, and America, drawing four and losing only three. Of the team of that era and later, Mícheál O'Hehir once said in an interview, 'The word "great" is thrown about like snuff at a wake, but the Limerick team of the late 1930s and 1940s — they deserved it.'

Paddy won All-Irelands with Limerick in 1936 and 1940. He was there when Limerick drew with Dublin in the 1934 final. He missed the replay because of illness and his place was taken by Tommy Shinney of Fedamore — a former Limerick and Munster goalkeeper. Paddy took part in four of the five record-breaking successive National League victories of 1934–38, missing out in 1936, when Tommy Shinney was again called upon to man the goal. Paddy won five Munster titles: four in a row, 1933–36, and again in 1940. Apart from 1939, when the Waterford custodian Mick Curley was given the nod, Paddy Scanlon was the Munster selectors' choice from 1934 to 1941, and in that period he won five Railway Cup medals. He had the honour of captaining Ahane to their first county senior hurling success in 1931.

Paddy never married, and he died in 1977, aged seventy-one.

After Paddy's retirement a 'bard' signing himself T.B., Sligo, wrote a poem in his honour. Here is the second verse, which appealed to me:

> No more we'll see him walking back to
>   guard the net 'gainst fierce attack,
> While leather flew and ash did crack and
>   'fans' were loudly cheering;
> No more our throbbing hearts he'll thrill
>   by his uncanny science and skill,
> When forwards eager for the 'kill' were
>   thwarted by his clearing;
> No more we'll watch his long puck-out,
>   which dropped the 'forty-yards' about,
> And set our vanguard 'on the scout' for
>   scores that made us happy;
> No more we'll mark his flashing blade,
>   blocked and parried, flicked and flayed,
> And put all swordplay in the shade, so
>   deft it was, so snappy.

Born 1928

"

I was born in the parish of Toomevara on a January day in 1928, the son of a small farmer. There wasn't a hurling tradition in my family, but my father was very interested in going to the local matches and would bring us along, my two brothers and myself. It was during the Second World War years, so a pony and trap was our main mode of transport. As a result of my father's interest in the game I too developed a great love and passion for the game of hurling.

I learned the skills as I grew older and would listen carefully to the older people and try to put into practice any clever idea imparted to me. I played senior hurling with the Toomevara Greyhounds in 1945 at the age of seventeen and won a North Tipperary senior hurling championship the following year, 1946. The year 1946 was a good year for me, as I got my place at centrefield on a Tipperary minor hurling team.

We played Cork in the Munster minor hurling final at Thurles, and in the last few minutes of a very exciting game of hurling I got the break of the ball as a result of a mis-hit seventy-yard free to score a winning goal and win the match by a single point. Cork were deeply disappointed, and our joy seemed everlasting.

It was now time after those winning encounters in 1946 to develop my hurling skills further and try and reach senior county hurling status. My first entry into senior hurling ranks was to be selected on the 1948/49 Tipperary National Hurling League team at centrefield. We beat Clare at Thurles in early November 1948 and qualified to

270

meet Cork in February 1949, again at Thurles.

It was half time at the qualifying game against Clare at Thurles; a big tall man approached me and was interested in my play and gave me the following helpful tips. He was, of course, Timmy Ryan of Limerick and Ahane, one of the greatest. He looked me in the eye and said, 'I'll give you two useful tips now and see how you will respond in the second half. The first one is, don't run up or down the field: run across and so get the break of the ball. The other idea is most important: just nudge with your shoulder or arm your opponent simultaneously when striking the high ball.'

I implemented these two points to the full and played a 'blinder' in the second half.

In trying to win the 1948/49 National Hurling League final at Thurles against Cork we didn't do any collective training. I remember getting a letter from the Tipperary County Board secretary stating that they were not financially fit to train the senior hurling team. Although he suggested ways to train, we had to train ourselves. I used to get up at seven o'clock in the morning and run and sprint in our field at the back of the house in order to achieve the required standard of fitness to beat this great Cork team.

We won the National League senior hurling final at Thurles in February 1949, and it was a great victory, particularly as this Cork team was the best ever, as they had won four All-Irelands in a row, 1941–1944, inclusive.

Tipperary now had a youthful team made up of a number of ex-minors from the 1945, '46 and '47 teams. Dublin contested the three minor hurling finals 1945, '46 and '47 and won two: 1945 and 1946. Tipp were third-time lucky and won the 1947 minor hurling final.

It was now time for Tipp to move forward in search of provincial and All-Ireland honours. We achieved this end and won three Munster finals and three All-Irelands, 1949, 1950, and 1951. It took us two hours and a half to beat Cork at Limerick in the 1949 senior hurling Munster championship. Most spectators would love to relive this one, for sheer hurling fever and excitement. We never looked back after that experience, and I was privileged to play at centrefield in all those games.

We beat Limerick in Cork in the 1949 senior hurling Munster final and I was lucky to be in the right place at the right time to stop and clear Dick Stokes's 21-yard free. We were a goal in front at this point and so beat a great Limerick team; and the famous Jackie Power had played his last game.

In the fifties I was selected on the Rest of Ireland teams playing the Combined Universities selection each year and won Sports Star of the Week in 1952 playing on Joe Salmon of Galway. This was possibly the best hurling display of my entire career.

I decided early in 1950 to leave my father's farm in search of the bright lights and moved to Dublin to work in Johnson Mooney and O'Brien's bakery and play hurling for Young Irelands hurling club. I wasn't disappointed and enjoyed the years I spent there. Some great hurlers played for Young Irelands hurling club but were never in my time able to blend together with enough enthusiasm to win a Dublin county senior championship.

I was still playing for Tipperary and was fortunate to win four National League medals: 1948/49, 1949/50, 1951/52, and 1956/57. I was long puck champion of Ireland in 1951. The competition was held at the GAA grounds at Kilmacud, and lifting and striking the ball the maximum distance was the test involved. Included in a large entry were the Rackard brothers, and they were surely great exponents of the hurling game.

Concerning the National Hurling league victories in my time, the great incentive was to travel to America. I travelled with Tipperary to play at the Polo Grounds in 1950 and again in 1957.

I suppose next to playing for your county was to earn a place on the provincial hurling team. I kept up my interest and training and played with Munster four years in a row to win in 1950, '51, '52, and '53. The memories of rubbing shoulders with Christy Ring, Dick Stokes, Jimmy Smyth, Matt Nugent, Andy Fleming, Willie John Daly, Vin Baston, Mattie Fouhy, Mick Hayes, Seán Herbert, Jackie Goode and John Kiely and others will always live with me and control my thoughts whenever hurling or great players are discussed.

I played for Dublin in 1954 and 1955, and my partners at centrefield were Norman Allen in 1954 and Con Murphy in 1955. We reached the Leinster final (hurling) in 1954, to be beaten by Wexford, and were defeated in the Leinster hurling semi-final by Kilkenny in 1955. While we had good Dublin teams in both years, Wexford were stepping up the pressure to win All-Irelands and succeeded in 1955 and 1956 after long years of waiting.

In 1956 I changed jobs and joined Esso Ireland Ltd and went to Clonmel to work. I started playing for Tipp and Toomevara once again. Tipp won the 1956/57 National Hurling League, and we lost in the championship of 1957 to Cork.

While I was in Dublin I had a great interest in the Young Irelands hurling club. I turned out for every game in my six years there and so earned a good reputation with the club officials. The club was initiated in 1923, and thousands of players were involved over a long number of years. In 1953 I had the distinction of being selected as Player of the Club. This was indeed a great honour for me and one which I will always remember and never forget. We had players of the calibre of Bill Walsh (Kilkenny), Paddy Hogan (Laois), Willie Dargan (Laois), Mick Ryan (Limerick), Frank Duignan (Galway), Mick Daniels (Dublin), Philly Ryan (Tipperary and Dublin), and Charlie McMahon (Clare and Dublin). There was also, including myself, a large number of Tipp players who wore the Young Irelands colours:

Tommy Treacy, Jim Devitt, Seán Kenny, Paddy Kenny, and Séamus Bannon.

Faughs and St Vincent's were the dominant teams in my time, and so we didn't succeed in winning a Dublin county senior hurling championship.

When the Tipp team came back from America in 1957 I decided to retire from inter-county hurling. It was my second trip to the States, 1950 being the first, and I enjoyed both immensely. The Irish in New York and Boston really made us feel at home and couldn't do enough to make the trip a memorable one for all of us.

I continued to play for Toomevara at club level and captained a winning senior hurling team in 1958 to win a North Tipperary senior hurling championship. We won three in a row after that, 1960, 1961, and 1962, and won a county final medal in 1960 beating Thurles Blues at Templemore.

I continued to play with Toomevara until 1966, and towards the end of that year I made up my mind to retire from club hurling after a long and fruitful career, winning five North Tipp senior hurling championships: 1946, '58, '60, '61, and '62, and a county hurling final in 1960.

I attained a GAA coaching certificate in hurling in 1977 and trained and coached Laois and Portlaoise for a number of years. I was more successful with Portlaoise, winning five senior county football titles between 1966 and 1971. Since then Portlaoise have become a major force in Laois, winning several county senior hurling and football championships.

When I retired from Esso Ireland Ltd in 1982 I trained and coached Killenaule to win three South Tipperary intermediate championships in hurling, 1983, '85, and '86. The club have since won two South senior hurling championships and have become a force in South Tipperary hurling.

I played golf too for a few years and won the Esso Cup in 1960. I didn't continue, although I showed promise, but took up training and coaching the Portlaoise club in 1966.

I suppose as I am now getting older I tend to dream and in my dreams would like to be back in Thurles or Croke Park driving that ball relentlessly from the centrefield position into the forwards in search of scores. I have had wonderful years of enjoyment, me and my hurling stick, and I have met excellent people and players, which have helped in no small way to consolidate my view that here is an association — the GAA — which is first class, incorporating my favourite game, hurling, the best field game in the world.

99

Phil Shanahan

Phil grew up in rural Tipperary in the parish of Toomevara. His childhood heroes belonged to his native parish. Toomevara had a proud tradition, going back to the days of 'Wedger' Meagher, 'who had great interest in the game — was a great distributor of the ball — was made of steel,' and who wrote himself into legend as he led the famous Toomevara Greyhounds to many a hurling victory.

> *Hurrah for Toomevara*
> *May your banners never fall.*
> *You beat Galway and Queen's*
>   *County*
> *And you levelled Cork's stone wall.*
> *I never will forget the day*
> *Kilkenny's pride went down*
> *Before the skill of Wedger's men*
> *In sweet Dungarvan town.*

Men like Jack Harty and Stephen Hackett, who were on the losing side in the 1913 All-Ireland final, were revered. There was much talk too about Lory Meagher of Kilkenny, John Joe 'Goggles' Doyle of Clare, and the glamorous Limerick team of the thirties, particularly Timmy Ryan and Mick Mackey. Phil was nurtured in a culture and tradition that made him passionately aspire to wear the blue and gold of his native Tipperary. It came to pass.

1949 is for Phil the most memorable year of his career. He embarked on his first year in championship hurling with a National League medal to his credit, and it ended with an All-Ireland medal — something countless hurlers spend their hurling life dreaming about. The Munster campaign was a tough one. It took two-and-a-half hours of intense, uncompromising exchanges to put Cork away. Clare proved to be very stern opposition at the next hurdle. Then came the Munster final against Limerick. Phil remembers the game well. 'We were outplayed in the first half, and at half time it didn't look as if we would win. All through the game Jackie Power at full-forward for Limerick gave us hell. If Limerick had won that Munster title they would have had to erect a monument in the city to Jackie. And remember he was dealing with a very good Tipperary defence. It was of course Jimmy Kennedy's hour of glory, with ten points of Tipp's total of 1:16, one point from play and nine from frees, from all angles and distances.'

What Phil didn't say was that his own performance at midfield in the second half was a key factor in Tipp's three-point win. And he still vividly remembers those tension-packed closing moments, when 'Limerick got a close-in free, and Dick Stokes stood over the ball, and the Tipp backs swarmed around their goal in protective stance, and Dick went for the equalising goal.' It was saved, and Phil emerged with the ball and sent it to Séamus Bannon; the final whistle sounded; Tipp were Munster champions again. The rest of the All-Ireland campaign turned out to be a formality. Antrim were heavily defeated, and in the final Laois succumbed in the second half to the sheer power of Tipperary's hurling.

Phil was one of the leading midfielders of his day, and he was also a most dedicated club man. Having retired, somewhat prematurely, from the inter-county scene in 1957 he continued to play at club level until 1966 and gave some excellent performances on men of the calibre of Jimmy Finn, Mickey Byrne, and Tony Wall.

Here is a sample of what some sports writers have said about Phil. *Irish Independent*, 30 July 1951, after Tipperary had beaten Cork, 2:11 to 2:9, in the Munster final:

> *'It seems that some Tipp. man always comes to the rescue when things are looking bleak. One day it is Bannon, another Kenny, another Stakelum and so on but yesterday it was truly Phil Shanahan. As against Limerick two years ago he pulled out his best in the second half and was easily the outstanding midfielder.'*

Railway Cup semi-final against Leinster, 1952:

> *'This was really Shanahan's game and without detracting in the slightest from displays of the rest of the Munster men, it can be truthfully said that the Tipp. player was the hero and star of the hour.'*

Midland Tribune, 22 October 1960 (Toomevara 3:15, Thurles Sarsfields 2:7):

> *'Apart altogether from his staggeringly accurate free taking, Tom Ryan was one of the brightest stars of the day, distributing the ball with speed and effectiveness, learned no doubt from team mates*

> *such as Hough and Phil Shanahan. The latter as kingpin of the half forward line more than held his own with such redoubtable opponents as Tony Wall and Michael Murphy. His three points were beauties.'*

A game Phil recalled with a lot of satisfaction was the Rest of Ireland v. Combined Universities in 1952. It was the inaugural game of the series. He was partnered by Christy Ring at midfield, and they were opposed by Joe Salmon and Des Dillon, respectively. He remembers it as being his best display of overhead striking. It brought him a Sports Star of the Week award. Ring always took his hurling seriously, and this game was no exception. Before the game started he said, 'Never put frills on the first ball, Phil — get rid of it.' It was a maxim that formed part of Ring's hurling philosophy.

Phil had the honour of figuring in the three-in-a-row All-Ireland successes of 1949, '50, and '51. He had a different midfield partner each year: Seán Kenny in 1949, Séamus Bannon in 1950, John Hough in 1951. The panel changed very little over the three years, and in achieving the rare honour the Tipp men were emulating a similar success their forefathers had in 1898, '99, and 1900.

His team is a fascinating one, drawn from several decades of the GAA.

'Skinny' O'Meara *(Tipperary)*

John Keane *(Waterford)*   Bobbie Rackard *(Wexford)*   John Joe Doyle *(Clare)*

Tommy Doyle *(Tipperary)*   Tony Wall *(Tipperary)*   Jimmy Finn *(Tipperary)*

Timmy Ryan *(Limerick)*   Phil Shanahan *(Tipperary)*

Christy Ring *(Cork)*   Mick Mackey *(Limerick)*   Jimmy Doyle *(Tipperary)*

Eddie Keher *(Kilkenny)*   Martin Kennedy *(Tipperary)*   Jackie Power *(Limerick)*

We talked about the team.

'I picked Skinny O'Meara because I heard so much about his ability as I grew up in Toomevara. It is said that in one particular game in the dying moments, with his side ahead by one point, a piledriver came his way. If he grabbed or blocked it he would have been bundled, ball and all, into the net. Instead he angled the hurley in a manner that diverted the ball towards the sideline — a rare and skilful technique. The story is told that on threshing day the men would take a two-hour break for dinner and proceed to hurl in O'Meara's field.

'I picked John Keane because any man who could do well on Mick Mackey would have to be included.

'The performance I saw from Bobbie Rackard in the 1954 All-Ireland final when he switched to fullback was such that I would have to select him there. I never saw a man play as well.

'I never saw John Joe Doyle play, but there was an old man who used to cross our yard on the way to Mass and he used tell me about Goggles: the way he would block the ball above his head; run the sliotar down the hurley; grab it and advance to clear — an outstanding corner-back.

'I saw the Tipp half-backs, Finn, Wall and Doyle perform so valiantly so many times that I couldn't pass them over. Playing in front of them you wouldn't have to drop back too often.

'For my partner at midfield I have chosen that prince of midfielders, Timmy Ryan. He was a master of what is called sense of position.

'For sheer hurling artistry and brilliance you couldn't beat my half-forward line selection of Ring, Mackey, and Doyle.

'I couldn't pass over Martin Kennedy at full-forward; he used make life so difficult for Seán Óg Murphy of Cork.

'For crisp, hard, terrific shots I have chosen in the corners Eddie Keher and Jackie Power — marvellous men; skill personified.'

Born 1950

"

It was impossible not to become involved in hurling — as I was born into a house where sport was always discussed as hurling was played by Dad and uncles. Also and more importantly our house and farm was located in the parish of Meelick/Eyrecourt — who proudly remember their participation in the first All-Ireland final v Thurles of Tipperary in 1887. Memories of great games, and great hurlers, were shared, as neighbours, uncles or visitors paid a visit. Men like Joe Salmon, Billy Duffy, Fintan Spillane (all locals) were mentioned with reverence and put up as stars to emulate. Thus we were given targets to aim at. However, success didn't arrive easily. In fact my first memory of representing my club was as a sub for the under-14s — who received a great dressing down without calling on my services. The amount of taunting and criticism I received propelled me to try harder and practise more often — which I did at the gable end of our house which fronted the main road and this interfered with passing traffic — still, allowed me to know every car registration passing the road!! Throughout this time I realised how great it was to belong to our parish — in fact as I com-

menced to play for Meelick/Eyrecourt seniors at 16 I realised how special it was — this special feeling still remains as I now wear their junior B jersey. Hurling for me was a dream. Key to my success in those years was the encouragement received from locals, Michael Joyce N.T., and especially FrVincent Marren (RIP) and Kevin Thornton in Garbally where my hurling progressed alongside rugby, and especially athletics. Interestingly, this was the time of the GAA ban — and life provided the constant fear of suspension if the club became aware. Now I know they were always aware of my misdemeanours. But they understood my predicament. My coaches seemed such Giants, especially Kevin Thornton, who guided the Garbally hurling team to its first Connaught colleges hurling title in twenty years over rivals St Mary's Galway in 1968. While we later lost the All-Ireland semi final to eventual winners St Peter's Wexford, this Garbally team provided a number of players to the county team — Frs Iggy and Joe Clarke, Andy Fenton, Ciarán Fitzgerald (Irish rugby Captain), Michael Donohue and John Lyons. It also started a long relationship with my marker Martin Quigley whom I competed against until 1984, as he gave loyal service to Wexford.

As a minor I enjoyed the privilege of playing against Cork as Galway competed in Munster. Unfortunately, fulfilling the fixture was the limit of our contribution as team preparation and training were less methodical and more amateurish than current preparation.

After Garbally College I moved on to St Patrick's College, Maynooth, winning two Fitzgibbon Cup medals in 1973 and 1974 and two University Colleges League medals. It was there under the guidance of Fr Gerry Meagher (Tipperary RIP) and Fr Liam Ryan (Limerick) that my game and especially the importance of a team contribution, continued to develop. Hours spent in the ball alley or practising, especially ground hurling with Iggy and Joe Clarke, Andy Fenton, Paddy Barry, Paddy Boland, Seán Stack, Aidan Kerrigan, Henry Goff, Frs Willie and Paudie Fitzmaurice, Ollie Perkins, Jack O'Neill, Victor Blake, Séamus Fitzgerald, Gus O'Driscoll and many others, most of whom played successfully for their own counties, some of whom played in All-Ireland finals.

It was during those years I had the privilege to win county junior and intermediate medals with Meelick/Eyrecourt. What an occasion — and how our small parish celebrated and enjoyed our success. Gradually some of my clubmates received the county call with Jack Lucas starring at wingback for the seniors. It was during this time I received the call for Galway seniors also — and played, commencing initially in 1971, to continuously in '72 for the next twelve years, finishing after the Centenary Year in 1984.

Highlights of my career were our successes in making the breakthrough in 1974/75 league to eventually win — recording victories over Cork, Kilkenny and Tipperary on the way. That was an especially joyous occasion followed three months later with the All-Ireland semi-final victory over a well fancied Cork side. We floated on air for days until M.J."Inky" Flaherty sobered us up into the reality of what lay ahead. We were meeting the 'Cats' in our first All-Ireland final and unfortunately we played well below our best. They were the team of the early 1970s with Keher, Delaney, Purcell, Henderson, Coady, Brennan, O'Brien Crotty etc. It would have taken a good performance to deny them, which we were unable to give.

The following year in Cork, Wexford denied us after a replay. I always believe our drawn game was the best hurling game I played in and a point from Frank Burke — at least 100 metres out — is still vivid in that very hot, humid day.

After our failure, again, to Kilkenny in 1979 — victory twelve months later was both well overdue and well deserved. It was like being released from a prison. Many supporters had lost faith through our continuous defeats — the players through the encouragement of Babs Keating and Joe McGrath 1978–79 and Cyril Farrell and 'Inky' Flaherty in 1980 had infused a tremendous love, pride and determination which excluded throwing in any towel. More than anything else the victory provided great encouragement to mentors of club teams within the county and also a fitting reward to longer serving stars who experienced so many bad days — especially players like John Connolly who was a colossus on weak Galway teams a dozen years before. Essentially victory was attained from great displays from about twelve players with other three neutralising their opponents.

The following year provides the low point of any players career — losing a final as Captain. Unfortunately the 1981 final was played between two non-traditional counties — minnows of hurling as someone said, and Offaly gradually, gradually, stole away the Liam McCarthy as we missed many good scoring chances, while Pat Delaney and especially Johnny Flaherty ended our dream for two in a row. Their uncanny ability to stay in touch, while defending against our superior forwards in the first half contributed immensely to their victory.

In summary I'd like to thank the many great people mentioned who infused such a great love for the game — without them Brendan's book would not have my humble memories. Thanks for the opportunity.

99

In his young days Seán excelled at athletics and played schools rugby at inter-provincial level for Connaught in the positions of outhalf and centre. But the love of this versatile sportsman for the great game of hurling still remains and finds expression through his involvement with the youth and his participation with his club at Junior B level. A sliotar well struck in any one of the wide varieties of options available, still thrills and satisfies, just as much today as it did in his halcyon days.

While at college Seán worked in the States in the summertime and hurled with Harry Bolands in Chicago. There, his right arm, first broken in a minor championship game with Cork, was again broken. The setting was defective so the hand had to be rebroken and reset. A glance at the arm confirms the damage. Did it subsequently bother you if an opponent came in contact with that hand? 'I felt like giving him a lethal injection!'

Seán was in the States in 1973 when London surprisingly defeated Galway in the All-Ireland quarter final but the following year he was flown home for the semi-final against Kilkenny. "I arrived on a Friday evening — didn't cope well with jetlag — and played rubbish". Homer nodded. Even the great ones have an occasional off day.

The Fitzgibbon Cup titles won with St Patrick's College Maynooth in 1973 and '74 were very special. These were the only occasions to date that Maynooth won the title and in so doing at the time broke the stranglehold the other Universities had on the title, especially UCC and UCD.

His championship displays of 1975 and 1980 earned him two well-deserved All-Star Awards at centreback. The following narration accompanied his 1975 selection. 'For being the essence of shrewdness in his county's defence where he dominated so impressively throughout the year.'

He played in four All-Ireland finals and on each occasion was part of a great halfback line. In 1975 and '79 it read: Joe McDonagh Seán Silke Iggy Clarke.

In 1980 when Joe McDonagh and Iggy Clarke were absent through illness and injury respectively it read: Sylvie Linnane Seán Silke Seamus Coen

The 1981 line was: Sylvie Linnane Seán Silke Iggy Clarke.

Seán was Captain in 1981 when a classy and experienced Galway team failed to a tenacious and never-say-die Offaly combination — a most disappointing day for a skipper hoping to lead his county to two in a row at a time when many supporters and neutrals felt it could have been a third in a row — for in '79 they looked the form team but went under to Kilkenny.

1980 was a year to remember in Galway. On 17 February Connaught beat Leinster 1:13 to 1:10 after extra time in Ballinasloe in the Railway Cup. On St Patrick's Day Connaught beat Munster 1:5 to 0:7. That day, ten minutes into the game, Seán took a seventy that travelled all the way to the net. In what was a tight low-scoring game that goal proved to be vital at the final whistle. It was the second time only that the trophy crossed the Shannon but that victory paved the way for five further Railway Cup titles in the '80s — a reflection of the strength and quality of Galway hurling in that decade when the county also won a record eight in a row Vocational Schools titles 1980–87.

In the championship of 1980 Galway defeated Offaly in the semi-final 4:9 to 3:10 and had three points to spare over Limerick in the final. The breakthrough after countless frustrating failures since 1923 heralded an unleising of jubililation, celebration and emotion, rarely seen in Croke Park.

It was probably Seán Silke's greatest day in the maroon of Galway. He was majestic at centreback and in the course of the game faced three different opponents in John Flanagan, Joe McKenna and Willie Fitzmaurice. His contribution to Galway's win was incalculable. One small banner in the crowd proclaimed 'Silke is not a soft touch.' The surname — hurlingwise — was never more apt, for Seán's display was a silken one.

Peadar O'Brien in his report in the *Irish Press* on Monday 8 September voted him 'the outstanding player on the field — the immaculate Seán Silke' — immense praise indeed on a day when there were several brilliant individual performances.

He recalled some of the great forwards of his era — Pat Delaney, Kieran Purcell, Billy Fitzpatrick and Eddie Keher of Kilkenny; Ray Cummins and Jimmy Barry Murphy of Cork; Tony Doran of Wexford; Joe McKenna of Limerick and P.J.Molloy of Galway. 'One of the best hurlers I ever saw was Barney Moylan of Offaly who had a great game on Eddie Keher in the Leinster final of 1969 when Eddie was in his hurling prime.' Seán described Joe Henry of Mayo who played Railway Cup hurling with Connaught as 'an exceptionally great hurler' and he had special words of admiration for the late Pat Carroll of Offaly. Without hesitation he named Mícheál O'Hehir as the hero of his youth. He would like the current Guinness advertisement to gear itself towards placing emphasis on the many skills of the game.

Regarding the rules of the game he would make a change in scoring values with a view to encouraging more ground hurling, especially among the forwards. To this end he would give double value for any score registered from a ball, whipped on, on the ground. He believes this would add immensely to the development of the game and he would begin with the youth.

Seán, who was hurling Officer for Connaught for two years in the late seventies, and who will always rank with the hurling immortals of the centre-back position, called it a day at county level after the All-Ireland semi-final defeat at the hands of near neighbours Offaly in the Centenary Year 1984.

Born 1964

66

I grew up in the half-parish of the Ballagh, the other half being Oulart. From as long as I can remember, hurling played a very important part in my life. I am the youngest of eight children and started playing hurling at the age of six or five. I remember coming home from school and playing with my brother Tom in the field in front of the house for hours. Those days we were Mick Jacob, Tony Doran, John Connolly, and dreaming of playing in Croke Park some day.

There were four or five people who had a major influence on my hurling development. Firstly there was my father, John, who encouraged us all to keep playing. His motto was, you can never practise the skills enough. He also never held back on a bit of a tongue-lashing if you didn't play well. Then in national school there was Father Frank Staples CC, who put us through our paces. An uncle of George and John O'Connor, he believed in toughness and never 'crying'. Mick Jacob and Jimmy Prendergast also had

major influences on my hurling development.

My career with Wexford started with the under-14 team in 1977 and '78, winning a Leinster medal in 1977. This was my first time to play in Croke Park; all my birthdays had come that day. I never played minor hurling for Wexford but played under-21 for three years, being beaten in Leinster finals by Kilkenny. I played with the Wexford junior team in 1985, winning a Leinster and All-Ireland. I made my senior début in the National League in '85 against Roscommon in Enniscorthy. My dream was to be on a Wexford team in an All-Ireland final. Success was very hard to come by, with Wexford being beaten in four Leinster finals — '88, '92, '93, and '94 — and five league finals, counting replays — '90, '91, and '93 (three games against Cork).

My career was beginning to slip away from me and I thought I was not going to achieve my dream. When Wexford hurling was at a low ebb a man called Liam Griffin took over as manager in 1994. This man had a great love for, and belief in, Wexford hurling. The championship of '95 was like any other — beaten again. In September '95 things changed. We trained like never before. The championship of '96 was my dream come true and a year I will never forget. We beat Offaly in the Leinster final — my first. Then we beat Limerick in the final — All-Ireland medal at last.

The one thing that I will never forget about hurling is the great friends that I made over the years, and I can pick up the phone and ring any of these lads and go and visit and spend some time with them. I had the privilege of wearing the purple and gold of Wexford and enjoyed every second of it. Hurling is the greatest and fastest game in the world, and it is not all about winning —

but it is 'quare' nice to get one just the same!

Martin Storey

Wexford hurling lovers have now another episode of glory to add to great past deeds. However, before we talk about 1996 let us glance back briefly.

The hurling men of Wexford won fame about three hundred years ago, and it was at that time they were accorded the title 'Yellow Bellies'. Sir Caesar Colclough of Tintern in south Wexford, a descendant of one of the Norman settlers of 1169, is said to have been on friendly terms with King William III (of Battle of the Boyne fame) and often boasted of the hurling skills of his south Wexford tenants and neighbours. William eventually challenged him to bring over twenty-one Wexford men to play an equal number of Cornish men, whose skill, no doubt inherited because of their Celtic origin, made them famous as wielders of the camán.

Before the challenge game Colclough held a trial match between two local south Wexford teams, the Scarrogas (so called because they hailed from south of the River Scar, which flows into Bannow Bay) and the Beany Boys (men from the baronies of Forth and Bargy, where beans were once extensively grown). Following the trial game Colclough picked twenty-one of the best hurlers from both sides and set off with them for Cornwall.

The Cornish men looked with contempt on their Slaneyside opponents as they stripped. Colclough gave his men a glass of whiskey apiece and told them to tie yellow kerchiefs around their middle so that they would easily recognise each other on the field. They did this and trooped onto the Cornish pitch that day in the seventeenth century.

Of course they hurled their opponents off the field, exhibiting, in doing so,

such a degree of skill and craft that William and his wife were heard to shout, "Well done, Yellow Bellies! Fine fellows, Yellow Bellies!' The name has stuck, and Wexford men are proud of its origin.

In 1910 Wexford won its first All-Ireland title in any code when its senior hurlers defeated Limerick by 7:0 to 6:2. Great names associated with that historic occasion include Seán O'Kennedy, P.J. Mackey, Dick Fortune, Sim Donohue, Mick Neville, who survived into his late nineties, and Dick Doyle, their captain.

There followed a golden era in football, with six successive senior Leinster titles between 1913 and 1918. Four of these were translated into All-Ireland titles, 1915–18. Hurling went into decline.

Forty-five years were to pass before Wexford would win a second senior hurling title. They did that in 1955 under the captaincy of the late Nick O'Donnell and buried the many disappointments they had suffered since they rose to prominence in 1950 with a great Leinster final display against Kilkenny at Nowlan Park — a game lost by one goal but that might well have been won. The years from then until 1955 became a learning process — painful at times. Time and again the graph rose, only to dip agonisingly when expectations had reached a high pitch.

But the victory of 1955 bred and instilled confidence, and further All-Ireland honours followed in '56 and '60. Between 1950 and '62 Wexford won six Leinster titles and contested six All-Ireland finals. In those years the purple and gold spelt hurling glamour, a glamour that enhanced and enriched our ancient game. It was the era of the Rackards — Nicky, Bobbie, and Billy — of Tim Flood, Ned Wheeler, Jim Morrissey, Mick Morrissey, Padge Kehoe, Paddy Kehoe, Nick O'Donnell, 'Hopper' McGrath, Jim English, and Martin Codd, to name but some.

A new generation of hurling men — which included, under Dan Quigley's captaincy, Pat Nolan, Tom Neville, Eddie Kelly, Willie Murphy, Phil Wilson, Paul Lynch, Jimmy O'Brien, and Tony Doran — won a fifth All-Ireland title for Wexford in 1968.

The fifties and sixties gradually receded, and Wexford hurling, as measured by major honours, fell on lean days. Hurling followers found themselves turning increasingly to the past and speaking in idolising tones of their heroes of those days, each passing year adding to their aura of greatness. A whole new generation of Wexford people had grown up by 1996, and very few under forty years of age would have any recollection of the superb Wexford second-half resurgence that brought about the downfall of Tipperary in the final of '68.

Now in 1996 they had new heroes, captained by Martin Storey of Oulart-the Ballagh, a man dignified and gracious in victory. He was an inspiring captain and had a splendid season, which culminated in a well-deserved All-Star award, his second such honour. His leadership and experience had a settling and calming influence on his colleagues, especially the younger members of the panel. All in all, Martin probably had his best year ever in the purple-and-gold jersey, with speed and quick stickwork being the hallmark of his style as he strode with authority the terrain that a half-forward must strive to dominate if his team is to succeed.

Martin gets tremendous support from his wife, Rosaleen, a most avid and enthusiastic follower of the game. The following is an excerpt from her article 'The Other Side of the Storey' in the *Wexford GAA Yearbook, 1996*:

'Being a Donegal native, I was accustomed to the game of Gaelic football as opposed to hurling, and because I loved sport, supporting my local club and county was a regular week-end venture with my Dad, growing up. I proceeded to Dublin and became a registered general nurse where Martin and I had the good fortune of meeting each other. As our relationship developed I adapted quickly to this fast, most skilful, amazing game. When Martin and I got married, I knew hurling was part of the package. Now almost ten healthy, happy years and three children later, I can honestly say, when health and sickness is not an issue in our family, hurling is more than a game — it is our way of life. Our life has always revolved around hurling, so much so, that the births of all our children are associated before, on, or after a hurling game, be it club or county. Our family day out is a Sunday — Mass, an early dinner, a hurling game, a few drinks following the game and then a take-away on the way home.'

As a spectator Rosaleen says she stays 'very quiet' and adds, 'I don't know how many Memorares I say during a game.' The two best games of hurling she has seen are the drawn Leinster final of 1993, Wexford v. Kilkenny, and the Leinster final of '96, Wexford v. Offaly. She doesn't know what she will do when Martin gives up the hurling. 'Maybe the children will be playing by then.'

The first time Martin saw hope was when they beat Offaly in the quarter-final of the 1996 league, even though they subsequently lost the semi-final to Galway. 'We had trained very hard and built up a great closeness. We were working a thousand per cent in unison. Liam Griffin used say he hadn't the fifteen best hurlers in Wexford but he had the fifteen who wanted most to win. We all said we would give it one almighty go: there were no maybes. I could remember a few mornings when I woke up sick to the guts after losing a match we should have won, like the two drawn league finals of '93 v. Cork, the drawn Leinster final of '93 v. Kilkenny, the Leinster semi-final of '90 v. Dublin — bad mistakes and wrong options. That's hard to get out of your system. But if you lose to Offaly or Kilkenny by seven or eight points then you don't deserve to win and you can accept defeat. The thing that used really annoy me was to read in the papers that

Wexford were good losers. I was never a good loser — George [O'Connor] was never a good loser — when we should have won.'

As Martin held the McCarthy Cup aloft in the Hogan Stand, success-starved Wexford fans gave vent to their feelings of joy and jubilation. He had much to reflect on in a campaign where Wexford had to battle with intensity in each contest. There was no easy game. Courage, character, fitness, endeavour, composure and concentration were all tested at different times to the very limits. For it was, as their trainer, Liam Griffin, said, a game for warriors — the Riverdance of sport. But Wexford didn't want an easy game. After the Leinster final Liam Griffin said, 'If we're going to win the All-Ireland I want to do it in a year when we beat Kilkenny, Dublin, Offaly, Galway, and Limerick.' He had his wish.

It had been a memorable campaign, and I wondered how Martin had perceived each of the five hurdles that barred the road to success. 'In the early stages of the game against Kilkenny I couldn't believe I was getting so much freedom. I got an amount of possession but little scores. I had four wides on the trot, and then I got three points in quick succession. I had clear-cut chances, and suddenly things fell into place. We led at half time by 9 points to 4. We were hurling our hearts out, but in less than a quarter of an hour into the second half Kilkenny had cut our lead to one point. The doubts come at you. You can get as used to losing as you can to winning; it can be very hard to get rid of doubts. Then Billy Byrne scored a great goal. It then clicked with me that we could win this one. Towards the end Kilkenny were getting frees, and it was so unlike them, they were going for goals instead of points.'

When the final whistle blew, the score was a sweet sight to every Wexford eye: Wexford 1:14, Kilkenny 0:14. A bogey team had been despatched. Wexford set their sights on a Leinster title.

'Would you believe it, Dublin were the one team I was afraid of. I was nervous. You'll always be a little bit nervous, but it was the only day I was worried going to Croke Park. We were expected to beat them. We were eight points up at half time; then everybody seemed to take their foot off the pedal. We lost the momentum, didn't score for over a spell of twenty minutes, only got four points in the second half. The final whistle was a relief: it was like getting out of jail. I thought of the way they caught us in either '89 or '90. I got laid out that day.' Dublin had often proven to be a difficult team to beat. Old-timers will remember in particular 1952 and 1961, when Wexford appeared capable of winning an All-Ireland crown, only to be surprised by Dublin in the Leinster final.

'My one memory of the game against Offaly was the minute the final whistle went. It was the memory of the year for me. It sank in straight away: I was after winning something with Wexford. I had ten seconds to myself, and I thought to myself, Wexford will walk up the steps of the Hogan Stand today — not Kilkenny, not Dublin, not Offaly. It was a brilliant feeling for me. It gave me the greatest satisfaction. I have the ball from that game. I asked the referee when would time be up and he said, "Now." The goalkeeper pucked out the ball — away from me. I had to run nearly fifty yards to get it. Someone claimed it was the fastest I ran all day! I remember with about half a minute to go Tom Dempsey was trying to run Wexford supporters off the field. He was afraid the referee might call off the match, and we winning.

'Before the game Liam Griffin had said to us to believe in the game plan; believe in each other; keep working — even if fifteen points down. Liam believed that Wexford teams of the past had lost because of lack of belief. Liam was a great influence. Our training programme was phenomenal. Every angle was covered: psychological, emotional, fitness levels. It stood to us in the last ten minutes. We were mentally tougher.

'It took a year to develop the game plan. My style changed from carrying to laying off passes and picking out lads. I was probably the most sceptical man in Wexford about the game plan, but Liam brought me around. I was very happy with the way the year was going for me. My game had improved. I had a double hernia operation in December '95. It was troubling me for a long time. It was destroying my hurling, but I struggled on because the club was going well. I felt fitter in '96 than in any of the previous four years.'

The game was a classic — one of the great ones in the history of the association. Wexford were rank outsiders, Offaly red-hot favourites. The game had everything, including a surprise result. 'In the game against Galway you could say we got out of the fire. It was the game nobody wanted to lose. The hurling at times was scrappy, because so much was at stake. The pace was so fast and furious you hadn't time to settle on the ball. What surprised me was the poor quality of the Galway free-taking: it used to be their trade mark. But, being a Wexfordman, I could understand!'

The path was now clear for an All-Ireland clash with Limerick, the first such meeting since 1918. 'Both teams were very well prepared. We were calmer before the match, and it stood to us. It was always going to be a fifty-fifty game. At the beginning of the championship I would have settled for a Leinster title; but when we won that, we said we were going to win the All-Ireland, and that drove us on. For me the whole day was special. It was

nineteen years since Wexford hurled in September. I was captain. I was playing on the Limerick captain, Ciarán Carey, with whom I was friendly down the years.

'In the parade before the match, when Limerick broke away and we were walking on our own, I felt a weird sensation, a kind of — I don't know how to describe it. I wasn't sure what to do. I asked myself should I break; are we right; are the lads getting nervous? Then I said to myself, march to the end. We'd got inspiration that morning from Seánie [Flood]. He gave us a chat — then broke down. It spurred us on.

'The first five balls or so that came my way, Ciarán got all of them. He was hurling much better than me. I could feel my head sinking. How could I encourage the team if I wasn't producing the goods myself? On one occasion I went to chase Ciarán and tripped over myself. I pointed to Damien [Fitzhenry] to send me a high one. He waved his hand saying no, I'd missed too many. Then he sent me one. I caught it and got a free. My attitude changed.'

The final whistle saw Wexford capture their sixth All-Ireland crown: a three-point win over Kilkenny; six points to spare over Dublin; an eight-point defeat of Offaly; Galway headed by three points; a two-point win over Limerick.

Unlike defeat — and especially after so many of them — the realisation of victory sank in very slowly. 'I found it awful hard to grasp it. At times I found it hard to believe. I woke up the morning after the game in the hotel and saw the cup beside me near the bed. Jesus, I thought to myself, we're after winning it!' An rud is annamh is iontach!

Born 1934

Tony blossomed as a hurler in Thurles CBS and was on the Munster Colleges team that defeated Connacht in the final in 1951. Colleagues on that team included Austin Flynn and Dermot Kelly, who were later to achieve fame in the jerseys of Waterford and Limerick, respectively.

Soon he was under the watchful eye of the Tipperary senior selectors, and in 1953 he was chosen to man the centre-half-forward berth. He was still playing in the forwards when Tipperary failed somewhat unexpectedly to Clare in the Munster semi-final of 1955 at Limerick. Glory days for Tipperary; and indeed his own glory days were still in the future.

Following the retirement of Pat Stakelum, one of hurling's finest centre-half-backs and sportsmen, Tony Wall was given the centre-half-back position. Not only had he to prove himself there but he had to cope with the outstanding reputation of his predecessor. He did both admirably and with distinction.

As captain in 1958 he led Tipperary to All-Ireland honours with victory over Galway. The Tipperary half-back line read: Jimmy Finn, Tony Wall, John Doyle — one of the best in the history of hurling.

Tony's performances in the 1958 championship were of such a high quality that he received the Caltex (now Texaco) Hurler of the Year award. It was the first such honour. The decade ahead was an era of riches for Tipperary hurling, and it brought Tony an abundance of honours: Railway Cups, National Leagues, Oireachtas titles, Munster titles; seven All-Ireland finals contested, five victories. In 1964 and 1965 Tipperary had a double hat trick of victories, capturing the National League, the All-Ireland, and the

From left: *Jim English (Wexford), Tony Wall (Tipperary) and Ned Wheeler (Wexford), 1960. (Photo: Jim Connolly)*

Munster colleges' team 1951. Tony Wall is second from right in the front row. Dermot Kelly (Limerick) second on the left in the front row and Austin Flynn (Waterford) second on the right in the back row.

Oireachtas. At the same time Tony was playing outstanding games for his club, Thurles Sarsfields, and they too were going through a golden era. In the period from 1955 to 1965 the club won ten county titles, losing out only in 1960.

Tony was an army man and did duty in Cyprus in 1966; as I write he is second in command of the Defence Forces. He flew home from Cyprus for the league final against Kilkenny and was honoured with the captaincy. In a close, low-scoring game Kilkenny won, 0:9 to 0:7. It was a rare major triumph for the black and amber over the men in the blue and gold — a portent of what 1967 held, the superstitious might have contended.

It has been said of Tony that he was born to the centre-back position. He was certainly one of the greats to man that demanding berth. There was an efficiency and precision about his hurling that reflected the training and thinking of an army man. In his years at centre-half-back he was an inspirational performer. His approach was strategy-driven: tactical, clinical, and calculating, matched by a temperament that was phlegmatic and unflappable. He saw his first task as halting the advance, be it ground or aerial; then the clearance, which could be short, or long,

as circumstances would dictate, and placed in the path of a well-positioned colleague.

In 1967 Tipperary emerged from Munster with a convincing win over Clare, 4:12 to 2:6. In Leinster, Kilkenny proved too good for Wexford on the score 4:10 to 1:12. The All-Ireland scene was set for a confrontation between Tipperary and Kilkenny. It would be their eleventh such meeting. After Kilkenny's dramatic win over Tipperary in the dying moments of the 1922 final the score stood level at three wins each. But since that date, four consecutive meetings saw victory go to Tipperary. The most recent was 1964, and the score was rather unflattering to the Noresiders: Tipperary 5:13, Kilkenny 2:8. So all kinds of pride and honour were at stake on both sides in the 1967 final. A dour rather than classic game was expected — and so it proved to be.

The day came and went. It was Sunday 3 September. The final score was Kilkenny 3:8, Tipperary 2:7. The Tipperary jinx on Kilkenny had been broken. John Doyle was denied his ninth All-Ireland medal. Tony Wall called it a day. One of the giants of hurling departed the stage.

*And there goes Walton, the posts
assaulting,
The green flag rises for another score.*

Born 1880

Often referred to as 'Little Sim', his first All-Ireland home final was that of 1903 with Kilkenny at Dungarvan (played 16 July 1905), when they were trounced by Cork on the score 8:9 to 0:8.

For the 1904 championship Sim Walton, as secretary of Tullaroan club, had a significant say in the selection of the county team. He was a man who was capable of rising above parochialism in the interests of the county and demonstrated this by drawing on players from Mooncoin, Piltown and Threecastles to augment the Tullaroan selection. When the final was played at Carrick-on-Suir on 24 June 1906 Kilkenny avenged the humiliating defeat of 1903 with a one-point victory over Cork, on the score 1:9 to 1:8. Sim's selection policy was vindicated.

Thus was born a great Kilkenny era. Between 1904 and 1913 they annexed seven All-Ireland titles. Sim played in them all and was captain in 1912 when they recorded another one-point victory over their arch-rivals, Cork, 2:1 to 1:3. That game was played at Croke Park on 17 November. Three other great hurlers shared those seven All-Ireland victories with Sim: Jack Rochford (who figured in *Hurling Giants*), 'Drug' Walsh, and Dick Doyle.

Dick Doyle came from a remarkable Mooncoin hurling family. His brother Eddie won six All-Ireland medals, and a second brother, Mick, won five. Between them they created what must be a family record with eighteen All-Ireland senior hurling medals.

Sim was a man of medium height and weighed about eleven stone. He inherited his love of hurling from his father, John Walton, who pioneered the game in the days before the foundation of the GAA. Sim's speed, opportunism and repertoire of skills set him apart in his day and at centre-forward or full-forward enabled him to outwit many a bigger and heavier opponent. He had courage as well as brains, a combination that stood to him when he faced up to defenders of the renown and calibre of Jim Kelliher of Dungourney and Cork fame. Of farming stock, Sim's other great interest in life was greyhounds, and in his young days he kept many a good one. The most famous of those was called Captain Sim and it ran in the Waterloo Cup.

It is interesting to recall briefly the venues, dates and scores of his seven All-Ireland successes, together with comments from the press.

- 1904 (played 24 June 1906), Carrick-on-Suir: Kilkenny 1:9, Cork 1:8. 'At last Kilkenny can claim the championship of Ireland in hurling. Her veteran hurlers, sprinkled with the new blood which has

Kilkenny's famous hurling champions. All-Ireland winners, 1909.
Back row(left to right): Sim Walton, Bill Hennebery, Jim Dunphy, Jack Rochford, Paddy Lanigan, Jack Keoghan.
Middle row(left to right): Jim Ryan, Eddie Doyle, Joe Delahunty, Dick 'Drug' Walsh, Matt Gargan, Dan Kennedy, Mick Shortall. Front row (left to right): *Mick Doyle, Dick Doherty, Jim Kelly, Dick Doyle.*

latterly grown up in our midst, have achieved a veritable triumph which will long redound to their credit and skill; have come out best in a home final which will be made memorable for years to come by the dogged persistence which characterised the encounter, the close contest which it evoked and the brilliancy of play which it gave rise to. Following their notable victory over Dublin at Enniscorthy a fortnight before, Tullaroan on Sunday surprised their friends and confounded their opponents by their masterly display of hurling ... for three years past Cork has held the championship and defended it against all comers. They had almost come to be looked upon as invincible' (*Kilkenny People*).

- 1905 (played 30 June 1907), Dungarvan: Kilkenny 7:7, Cork 2:9. this was a replay following an objection to the game of 14 April 1907, which was won by Cork on the score 5:10 to 3:13, played in brilliant sunshine before an attendance of about ten thousand. 'For the second time in succession Kilkenny wrested on Sunday at Dungarvan the championship of Ireland from the famous Cork hurlers. It was a gallant victory — a victory well deserved, stubbornly fought for, and in the end easily gained, and stamped the Kilkenny wielders of the camán as undoubtedly the foremost hurlers in Ireland and that means the world. The match was the sensation of the year. Not withstanding the fact that Kilkenny gained a splendid victory over them last year at Carrick, Cork were looked upon this time as invincible. Their three point lead over Kilkenny in the match at Tipperary of which this was a replay, served to create a further feeling of confidence in their prowess and superiority. That they should go under by such a huge score on Sunday was therefore nothing short of sensational and makes Kilkenny's win all the more noteworthy. Cork's prestige was seriously damaged thereby and Kilkenny seems at last to be coming into its own' (*Kilkenny People*).

- 1907 (played 21 June 1908), Dungarvan: Kilkenny 3:12, Cork 4:8. played before an estimated attendance of fifteen thousand, this was one of the great finals — a lot of scores, excitement, thrills, nail-biting right through the hour. The last act of a dramatic occasion came when Jimmy Kelly of Mooncoin sent over the winning point on the call of time as he doubled, drop-puck style, on a clearance from John Anthony. 'Amidst scenes of the wildest enthusiasm, Kilkenny were declared the victors in the All-Ireland final at Dungarvan on Sunday last. This is the second time in recent years that they have won the event by the small majority of one point, but those who witnessed Sunday's contest with an impartial eye and studied carefully the different movements of the game were forced to the conclusion that even had they not won Kilkenny's was still the better team. The manner in which the successful ones acquitted themselves was a source of intense pleasure to their huge following of supporters, while at the same time it called forth the warmest encomiums from their opponents. It was truly a great match and the play on both sides was exceptionally brilliant. In the opinion of the oldest followers of the pastime, it was the most splendid exhibition that has ever been witnessed' (*Kilkenny People*).

- 1909 (played 12 December), Cork: Kilkenny 4:6, Tipperary 0:12.

- 1911. 'The All-Ireland final between Kilkenny & Limerick was fixed for Cork early in the year. The match was postponed on the field on account of the very bad weather conditions. Limerick disagreed with the adjournment, but the Central Council upheld the action of the officials and the match was refixed for Thurles. Limerick refused to travel on this occasion, and at a meeting of the Central Council held subsequently, Kilkenny were awarded the match. Limerick appealed to the GAA Convention against the decision of the executive body, but were defeated by a large majority. The matter was again under consideration at a subsequent meeting of the Central Council when Limerick was suspended indefinitely' (*Kilkenny People*). There was a goal rush in the Munster semi-final of that year at Tipperary when Limerick defeated Clare, 10:5 to 6:1. It is not widely known that Kilkenny won the Leinster senior football title in 1911 by defeating Meath, 2:4 to 1:1.

- 1912 (played 17 November), Croke Park: Kilkenny 2:1, Cork 1:3. No doubt the question on the lips of hurling followers when the 1912 championship began was whether Kilkenny could win their sixth title since 1904. There was evidence that challengers could come from several quarters; it is interesting, therefore, to look at the key games of the 1912 campaign. Wexford, the 1910 All-Ireland champions, were still a hurling force. On Sunday 11 August they faced Kilkenny at Jones's Road in the Leinster semi-final. It was a stirring contest. Kilkenny survived by the narrowest of margins, 4:4 to 4:3. In the Leinster final, played at Port Laoise on Sunday 15 September, Kilkenny faced Laois, who were to contest the All-Ireland finals of 1914 and 1915, being victorious in the latter year. However, at Port Laoise in 1912 Kilkenny were much superior and won, 6:6 to 2:4.

In Munster it was anyone's championship. On Sunday 18 August at Ennis, Tipperary (champions in 1908) faced Clare (who were to win the All-Ireland title in 1914). It was close and exciting and in doubt right up to the final whistle, Tipperary emerging winners on the score 3:3 to 2:3. At Waterford on Sunday 1 September, Limerick, Munster champions and All-Ireland finalists of 1910 and 1911, met Cork in the Munster semi-final. Here is how 'Sliabh Ruadh' described the game: 'One of the toughest and most terrible tussles ever waged for the Munster crown took place at Waterford on Sunday September 1st between Cork and Limerick. Interest on the issue was widespread and the Suirside city saw an immense hosting of Gaels. The match was stubbornly fought from start to finish with a slight advantage in favour of Limerick. Leading by a point coming on to time Limerick fought like demons. Then Byrne of Sarsfields pulled at a wing ball, up to Kinnefick, the latter crossed to Kennedy of Carrigtwohill and the Limerick citadel fell. Half time scores were even at 1:2 each — final score Cork 2:2 Limerick 1:3 ... Cork had defeated a great Limerick team.' Wrote 'Vigilant': 'When Cork secured the last and winning goal men seemed to have taken leave of their senses; hats, coats, and umbrellas were thrown into the air. Cork went mad for

A colleague is borne on his last journey. (Jack Rochford who died 17 October 1953, featured in Hurling Giants*). Clockwise from rere bearing the coffin: Pierce Grace, Dick Grace, Jack Anthony,* Sim Walton, *Jack Lennon, Paddy Grace.*

joy — the impossible had been accomplished.'

In a dogged and determined encounter Cork defeated Tipperary, 5:1 to 3:1, to regain the Munster crown, last held in 1907. Now to the All-Ireland final, played before a crowd of twenty thousand. Both Kilkenny goals had a touch of the unexpected about them. The second — the last score of the match, and the winner — was particularly 'soft'. They all count, however. Cork may well have been on top outfield, but Kilkenny were superior on the scoreboard. Here are some comments on the game. 'Kilkenny were more than lucky to win by the minimum margin' ('Sliabh Ruadh'). 'Kilkenny are the luckiest team in Ireland today or any other day. They are All-Ireland champions now and that is the thing that matters' (Tom Semple). 'We should have won easily. We had terrible bad luck. Kilkenny are not in the same street with us. The crowd [encroachment]

killed us. Tipperary and Limerick were both better teams than Kilkenny' (Barry Murphy, Cork captain). 'Kilkenny were certainly fortunate to win' (M.F. Crowe, referee). 'A stiff fight, but the final of the Munster Feis tournament with the same teams was a much better contest. I admit Cork's lead at the interval should have been larger' (Sim Walton, Kilkenny captain).

Here is how the news reached Kilkenny.

'Shortly after five o'clock a telegram announcing the result of the match was received in Kilkenny, through the kindness of the "Kilkenny People". As the specified time approached for the arrival of the wire intense excitement prevailed, and an enormous crowd gathered outside the Post Office and waited with undescribeable anxiety. When the telegram did arrive its contents were immediately announced to the impatient throng. The news of the victory was received with prolonged cheering. It spread like wild-fire, and for nearly four hours after the arrival of the telegram, crowds visited the "People Office", where all doubts were set to rest. From the coming of the welcome news, preparations were begun for the reception of the All-Ireland champions, and the streets were gaily illuminated and tar barrels were burned at every corner in the city' (*Kilkenny People*).

- 1913 (played 2 November), Croke Park: Kilkenny 2:4, Tipperary 1:2. 'It was the fastest hurling final that we have ever witnessed. It was a long way ahead of last year's final between Cork and Kilkenny. The ball travelled with lightning rapidity, and every man on the field seemed to be a sprinter of the first order. It was a hard game, but then it was a game of champions — and, more than that, it was between scientific Kilkenny and dashing Tipperary' (*Freeman's Journal*).

Those victorious teams were studded with great hurling names, among them 'Fox' Maher, the Doyles of Mooncoin, Jack Rochford, John Anthony, John T. Power, Dan Kennedy, 'Drug' Walsh, Jimmy Kelly, Matt Gargan, and the Graces of Tullaroan, Dick and Dr Pierce.

Sim was still in the Kilkenny colours, wearing the captain's jersey, when they lined out for the 1916 final at Croke Park on 21 January 1917 against Tipperary, led by the renowned Johnny Leahy. An absorbing game of hurling that seemed to be going Kilkenny's way at the three-quarter stage was rescued by Tipp with a frantic last-quarter effort that denied Sim Walton what would at that time have been a record-breaking eight All-Ireland medals. He came out of retirement in 1919 to play in the Leinster final against Dublin, but even his presence was unable to forge a Kilkenny victory, and Dublin won on the score 1:5 to 1:2.

Thus ended the career of one of hurling's greatest forwards, who started his career in the days of the seventeen-a-side and witnessed the transition to fifteen-a-side in 1913, the year he won his last All-Ireland medal. Sim ranks with the immortals of the game. He died in December 1966.

Oh look at Walton their posts assaulting,
At last he raises the final score;
Our shouts were heard on the Hills of
  Clara
When he beat O'Meara, the 'Barn Door'.

Phil WILSON   1961–1974   Ballyhogue, Oylegate-Glenbrien, Rapparees, & Wexford

Born 1939

"

Hurling for me was a way of life. I grew up on a farm in Ballyhogue during the late forties and early fifties. During those years my brothers and I played hurling and football every evening in our yard, as this was the only way of entertainment during those days. So apart from the enjoyment for ourselves I developed a great love for hurling, which I still have today.

I made my début with Davidstown-Ballyhogue at club level. When I was selected to play for Wexford in 1957 one of my greatest ambitions was fulfilled, especially having the distinction to play with some of Wexford's greats, like Jim Morrissey, the Rackards, Padge Kehoe, and Ned Wheeler. My determination to achieve the ultimate became a way of life. It came to fruition in 1968 when we brought home the All-Ireland cup. But you know, hurling is not just about All-Irelands. It's about schools, clubs, counties, and All-Irelands.

Even though my hurling days are over, I still get great pleasure from training and coaching at club level, which today is a different way of life. But nevertheless the love I have for

the game is still the same. It becomes part of you and stays part of you.

"

Phil Wilson

Phil grew up 'doing nothing else but hurling, and the names of Jimmy Langton and Nicky Rackard were mentioned more often than any others.'

The biggest thrill of his youth was the 1954 hurling final between his native Wexford and Cork before an attendance that exceeded 84,000. 'I'll never forget the crush going in. I watched the game from the Hill. That was something special. I was standing for hours: from before the minor game to the end of the senior game.'

In 1959 Phil emigrated to London. He was now a dual player, and a formidable one at that, having played at minor level in both codes for two years for Wexford and, while still a minor, played on the senior football team at the age of seventeen-and-a-half against the mighty men of Kerry. 'Football during my time was the poor relation. We never got together. You'd be told the match was in Croke Park at half three; if you want a lift the car will leave at such a time; if you're travelling yourself, tell us.' Both county careers lasted thirteen years, the football 1957–70, the hurling 1961–74.

In his two years in London he played with Father Murphy's, a team consisting entirely of Wexfordmen. 'There was a tremendous sense of loyalty — a right team spirit. Going to the field three times weekly to practise was a way of life. The field was at the back of Wormwood Scrubs prison.' In 1960 he was selected for the London junior hurling and football teams. The hurlers won the

All-Ireland title, beating Carlow after a replay, but the footballers lost to Dublin.

Phil worked on the buildings and lived with six colleagues in a rented house. Phil did the shopping, and all six took turns at the cooking. 'If I could hurl like you,' said a colleague to Phil, 'I'd go back home.' And that's what he did, in 1961. For a short while he worked with Power's distillery and hurled with New Irelands in Dublin; then he returned to Wexford, where he took up permanent employment with Esso. Since then GAA affairs have been central to Phil's life. His contribution to Gaelic games, both as player and coach, has been immense.

In his time Phil has played with Father Murphy's, New Ireland, Ballyhogue, Oilgate-Glenbrien, Rapparees, and Starlights. He has coached Askamore, Rapparees, Starlights, Claughbaun, and Ballyhogue. As a player his club successes include senior hurling titles with Oylegate in 1963 and Rapparees in 1978 and five senior football titles with Ballyhogue. In the field of coaching he guided Claughbaun to a senior hurling title in the early nineties and Starlights to a senior football title in 1983. 'I have spent as much time coaching and training as I did playing the game — that's forty years. I'm going to call it a day now.'

I met Phil some days after the memorable All-Ireland win of the Wexford senior hurlers in 1996. Celebrations were still in full swing, and purple-and-gold flags and pennants proudly decorated the county. It was twenty-eight years since the McCarthy Cup had come to Slaneyside. Phil was on the victorious team that won a historic victory in 1968 when conquering Tipperary, 5:8 to 3:12. 1968 was a wonderful year for Wexford. St Peter's College won the All-Ireland hurling title for the second year running, beating Coláiste Chríost Rí, 5:10 to 4:5, in a replay. The minor team beat Cork to take the All-Ireland title. In their first final appearance the senior camogie team beat Cork, 4:2 to 2:5. Four All-Ireland hurling crowns — much to cherish; much to be proud of.

What were Phil's memories of '68? 'I had written to my brother Jack, who was in England and who I hadn't seen for ten years, asking him to come home. He arrived two days before the match. On the Sunday we went to half nine Mass in the local church at Bellevue. People were saying, is that fellow going to hurl today? As it was I was making no change in my routine. I drove right up to Croke Park with Jack, and in. I watched some of the minor match standing in the Cusack Stand. The legs began to feel awful tired. Six months' training, I thought to myself, and the legs tired even before the game starts. I went into the dressing-room and lay down on a seat.'

Before a big game Phil liked a period of peace and solitude: time to reflect and relax and prepare mentally for the contest ahead, away from the euphoria of supporters, away from the well-intentioned but distracting admirers. 'Soon Dr Daly, the team doctor, came in and asked me where were the others. "Watching the minor game," I told him. "They should be in here lying down like you, relaxing," he said. I had great admiration for Dr Daly. He was an expert on fitness — knew every fellow's fitness level. Before a Leinster final or All-Ireland final I wouldn't hear what was going on in a dressing-room. I would be high as a kite in anticipation of the game ahead.'

This was Phil's third final — all against Tipp. He was on the losing side in '62 and '65. At half time in '68 things looked ominous — 1:11 to 1:3, eight points in arrears, and the team playing badly. 'During that half neither John O'Donoghue in the Tipp goal nor Pat Nolan in ours pucked a ball to my side. I got no play on P.J. Ryan. I was a disaster. I can give no reason. At half time I said to myself, it's now or never: shake yourself. I made up my mind it would be different in the second half, and it was.' A transformed team played inspired hurling. Phil won his first and

Phil Wilson in action.

only All-Ireland. He missed the 1970 final against the winners, Cork, having been injured in the semi-final against Galway.

The best Wexford team he played on was the 1962 line-out. They beat Kilkenny in the Leinster final, 3:9 to 2:10. He remembers the final against Tipp. 'Martin Lyng and myself were at mid-field and facing Liam Devaney and Theo English. It was my first final. I remember I was finishing up work one evening when I said to Jim Morrissey [a star midfielder of the fifties], "What will we do with these two on Sunday?" His reply set me back in my tracks. "What do you care about them? If you care, don't go." That was Jim: he always had a no-nonsense, positive mentality.

'I remember going for the first ball under the Cusack Stand and getting it. Devaney pulled high and hard. I thought of Morrissey. Shortly after, Devaney got possession and headed for the sticks. As I chased I knew he saw the green flag waving. I pulled hard from behind — broke my new hurley; my name went into the book. I had evened the score between Devaney and myself. Martin and myself won the midfield battle that day.'

It wasn't, however, enough to win a hurling thriller that saw Tipperary two goals up after ninety seconds and Wexford two points in arrears at the final whistle. 'In the course of the hour I faced three different opponents: Liam Devaney, Donie Nealon, and Tom Ryan — three brilliant hurlers. My biggest regret is losing that day and not chasing McKenna when he went on the solo that led to Tom Ryan's goal.'

Phil is one of hurling's unsung heroes. He was rarely missing from the Leinster Railway Cup selection in the decade ending 1972. He was All-Star material. A man of athletic build, he was a forceful hurler, and that, combined with speed, skill, strength, and stamina, made him a handful for any opponent. He had the style of play that always reminded me of Séamus Bannon, that great Tipp player of the early fifties. And interestingly, they played in the same positions: half-back, centrefield, half-forward. When they got possession they had the ability to lose their marker, surge forward in an attacking move, and draw opponents out of position.

Over forty years Phil has contributed much to Gaelic games as a dedicated mentor and trainer, as one of the all-time great dual players. While he agrees that it is good to win and that a win is essential at times to generate enthusiasm, nonetheless his maxim is that at the end of the day, 'playing the game is what counts most.'

Statistics

Name	Born	County	Club	Era	All Ireland medals	National League medals (1926–)	Railway Cup medals (1927–)	County Titles	Provincial Titles	All-Star awards (1971–)
Jimmy Brohan	1935	Cork	Blackrock	1954-64	–	–	5	2	1	–
Billy Burke	1912	Kilkenny	Tullaroan	1934-45	1	–	–	–	6	–
Micky Byrne	1923	Tipperary	Thurles Sarsfields	1945-60	4	7	–	14	4	–
Noel Campbell	1920	Antrim	Mitchel's	1942–c.54	–	–	–	1	–	–
Ciarán Carey	1970	Limerick	Patrickswell	1988–	–	1	3	5	2	3
D.J. Carey	1970	Kilkenny	Young Irelands	1989–	2	2	1	1	3	5
Mick Cashman	1931	Cork	Blackrock	1952-63	–	–	6	2	1	–
Tom Cheasty	1934	Waterford	Ballyduff & Portlaw/Portlaw	1955-67	1	–	4	5	3	–
Seamus Cleere	1940	Kilkenny	Bennettsbridge	1959-69	2	2	3	6	4	–
Paddy Clohessy	1910	Limerick	Fedamore	1928-40	3	4	6	1	5	–
Joe Cooney	1965	Galway	Sarsfields	1984–	2	3	4	4	–	5
Mickey Cross	c.1901	Limerick	Claughaun	1923-37	2	4	4	1	5	–
Martin Cuddy	1950	Laois	Camross	1976-86	–	–	–	10	–	–
Ray Cummins	1948	Cork	Blackrock	1969-82	4	5	2	6	9	3
Ger Cunningham	1961	Cork	St Finbarr's	1981–	3	2	3	6	7	4
Pa Dillon	1938	Kilkenny	St Lactain's	1960-73	3	1	2	2	6	–
Billy Dooley	1969	Offaly	Seir Kieran	1991–	1	1	–	3	2	2
Johnny Dunne	1905	Kilkenny	Mooncoin & Dicksboro'	c.1928-38	2	1	2	2	3	–
Pat Dunney	1945	Kildare	Éire Óg	1962-77	–	–	4	10	–	–
Des Ferguson	1931	Dublin	St Vincent's	1951-64	–	–	2	5	2	–

Name	Born	County	Club	Era	All Ireland medals	National League medals (1926–)	Railway Cup medals (1927–)	County Titles	Provincial Titles	All-Star awards (1971–)
Jimmy Finn	1931	Tipperary	Borrisoleigh	1950–59	3	6	2	3	2	—
Pete Finnerty	1964	Galway	Mullagh	1985–94	2	2	3	—	—	5
Johnny Flaherty	1947	Offaly	Kinnitty	1966–83	1	—	—	6	2	1
Aidan Fogarty	1958	Offaly	St Rynagh's	1976–91	2	1	1	8	7	2
Pat Fox	1961	Tipperary	Annacarty	1979–96	2	2	—	—	5	3
Éamon Grimes	1947	Limerick	South Liberties	1966–80	1	1	1	4	2	2
Ignatius Harney	1903	Galway	Tynagh	1920–34	1	1	—	6	—	—
Mick Hayes	1921	Waterford	Butlerstown	1943–53	1	—	2	—	1	—
Jim Hurley	1902	Cork	Blackrock	1925–34	4	2	3	5	5	—
Mick Jacob	1946	Wexford	Oulart-the Ballagh	1969–84	—	1	3	—	3	3
Paddy Kehoe	1922	Wexford	Faughs (Dublin) & Gusserane	1943–56	1	1	—	—	2	—
Dermot Kelly	1932	Limerick	Cloughaun	1951–60	—	—	2	2	1	—
John Kiely	1926	Waterford	Dungarvan/Éire Óg	1948–62	1	—	1	—	2	—
John Killeen	1920	Galway	Tynagh (Galway) Clonad (Laois)	1944–54	—	1	1	2	—	—
Gary Kirby	1967	Limerick	Patrickswell	1986–	—	1	3	7	2	4
Phil 'Fan' Larkin	1941	Kilkenny	James Stephens	1962–79	5	1	5	4	9	4
Eithne Leech	1939	Dublin	Celtic	1959–69	8	—	—	?	9	—
Brian Lohan	1971	Clare	Wolfe Tone's	1993–	1	—	2	1	1	2
Ger Loughnane	1953	Clare	Feakle	1972–1987	—	2	3	1	—	2
Máiréad McAtamney-Magill	1944	Antrim	Portglenone	1958–83	2	—	—	10	15	—

Name	Born	County	Club	Era	All Ireland medals	National League medals (1926–)	Railway Cup medals (1927–)	County Titles	Provincial Titles	All-Star awards (1971–)
Justin McCarthy	1945	Cork	Passage	1964–74	1	3	2	—	3	—
Tom McGarry	1937	Limerick	Treaty Sarsfield's	1956–64	—	—	5	1	—	—
Tom McInerney	1906	Clare	O'Callaghan's Mills	1927–36	—	—	—	4	1	—
Terence 'Sambo' McNaughton	1964	Antrim	Ruairí Óg (Cushendall)	1980–	—	—	—	7	5	1
Paddy Molloy	1934	Offaly	Drumcullen	1955–71	—	—	2	4	—	—
Gerard Murphy	1928	Cork	Midleton	1949–56	3	1	1	—	4	—
Seán Óg Murphy	1897	Cork	Blackrock	1915–29	3	1	2	3	5	—
Willie Murphy	1915	Cork	Ballincollig	1939–49	5	3	7	—	6	—
Donie Nealon	1935	Tipperary	Burgess-Youghalarra & UCD	1958–69	5	6	4	1	8	—
Liz Neary	1951	Kilkenny	Austin Stack's & St Paul's	1968–87	7	—	—	?	8	—
Órla Ní Shíocháin	1948	Dublin	Austin Stacks & Celtic	1964–82	3	—	—	8	6	—
Christy O'Brien	1933	Laois	Borris-in-Ossory	1952–69	—	—	3	5	—	—
George O'Connor	1959	Wexford	St Martin's	1979–96	1	—	—	—	1	2
Dónal O'Flynn	1914	Galway	Liam Mellows	1939–47	—	—	1	5	—	—
Mary O'Leary	1955	Cork	Watergrasshill & Imokilly	1975–84	4	—	—	3	9	—
Margaret O'Leary-Lacy	1947	Wexford	St Ibar's Eoghan Ruadh Buffer's Alley & Oulart-the Ballagh	1961–77	3	—	—	10	—	—

Name	Born	County	Club	Era	All Ireland medals	National League medals (1926–)	Railway Cup medals (1927–)	County Titles	Provincial Titles	All-Star awards (1971–)
Matty Power	1899	Kilkenny & Dublin	Dicksboro' (K) Garda (Dublin)	1922–37	5	2	4	6	12	—
Phil Purcell	1900	Tipperary	Moycarkey-Borris	1926–37	1	—	5	5	1	—
Martin Quigley	1951	Wexford	Rathnure	1969–89	—	1	3	10	3	4
Paddy Quirke	1956	Carlow	Myshall (Naomh Eoin)	1974–90	—	—	1	15	—	—
Mick Ryan	1925	Tipperary	Roscrea & Dicksboro' (K) St Finbarr's (Cork)	1946–54	3	3	3	2	3	—
Seán Silke	1950	Galway	Meelick/Eyrecourt	1972–84	1	1	2	—	—	2
Paddy Scanlon	1906	Limerick	Ahane (L) Liam Mellows (G)	1932–41	2	4	5	3(A) ?(L,M)	5	—
Phil Shanahan	1928	Tipperary & Dublin	Toomevara (T) Young Ireland's (D)	1948–57	3	4	4	1	3	—
Martin Storey	1964	Wexford	Oulart-the Ballagh	1985–	1	—	1	2	1	2
Tony Wall	1934	Tipperary	Thurles Sarsfield's	1953–67	5	8	4	10	7	—
Sim Walton	1880	Kilkenny	Tullaroan	1903–19	7	—	—	14	9	—
Phil Wilson	1939	Wexford	Ballyhogue, Oilgate/Glenbrien & Rapparees	1961–74	1	2	3	2	4	—

Major Hurling Awards

	Up to 1996 (from 1887) All Ireland titles	Up to 1996 (from 1926) National League titles	Up to 1996 (from 1971) All-Star awards	Up to 1992 (from 1927) Railway Cup medals won on pitch	Up to 1996 (from 1888) Provincial titles
Antrim	—	—	5	—	?
Carlow	—	—	—	2	—
Clare	2	3	23	62	4
Cork	27	13	72	173	45
Down	—	—	1	—	2
Dublin	6	2	2	60	23
Galway	4	6	58	126*	?
Kerry	1	—	—	1	1
Kildare	—	—	—	4	—
Kilkenny	25	9	83	144	55
Laois	1	—	1	11	3
Limerick	7	10	40	131	18
London	1	—	—	—	—
Mayo	—	—	—	3	—
Offaly	3	1	32	14	9
Tipperary	24	16	41	150	35
Waterford	2	1	4	90	5
Westmeath	—	—	1	3	—
Wexford	6	4	27	68	18

* Galway had an advantage here, in that whenever Connacht won the Railway Cup, it usually meant at least 15 medals for Galway

Players in *Giants of the Ash*

Kevin Armstrong
John Barron
Paddy Buggy
Frank Burke
Ted Carroll
Martin Codd
Paddy Fox Collins
John Connolly
Brendan Considine
Eugene Coughlan
Dave Creedon
Peter Cregan
Willie John Daly
Mick Daniels
Liam Devaney
Jim Devitt
Shem Downey
John Doyle
John Joe Doyle
Tommy Doyle
Seán Duggan
Dan Dunne
Andy Fleming
Tim Flood
Des Foley
Josie Gallagher
Paddy Grace

Phil Grimes
Jimmy Heffernan
Seán Herbert
Mick Hickey
Garrett Howard
John Keane
Eddie Keher
Padge Kehoe
Martin Kennedy
Jimmy Langton
Terry Leahy
Jack Lynch
Johnny McGovern
Pa 'Fowler'
 McInerney
Paddy McInerney
John Mackey
Mick Mackey
Paddy McMahon
John Maher
Michael Maher
Damien Martin
Lory Meagher
Christy Moylan
Con Murphy
Mick Neville
Matt Nugent

Nick O'Donnell
Jim O'Regan
Jackie Power
Jim Power
John T. Power
Seumas Power
Dan Quigley
Johnny Quirke
Billy Rackard
Bobbie Rackard
Tony Reddin
Christy Ring
John Roberts
Johnny Ryan
Timmy Ryan
Joe Salmon
Jimmy Smyth
Pat Stakelum
Dick Stokes
Jim Treacy
Tommy Treacy
Ollie Walsh
Charlie Ware
Jim Ware
Ned Wheeler
Jim Young

Players in *Hurling Giants*

Ciarán Barr
Willie Barron
Paddy Barry
Vin Baston
Richie Bennis
Din Joe Buckley
John Callinan
Pat Carroll
Iggy Clarke
Seán Clohosey
Jimmy 'Butler' Coffey
Tull Considine
Martin Coogan
John (Ballyhea)
  Coughlan
Éamon Cregan
Frank Cummins
Tommy Daly
Pat Delaney
Tony Doran
Angela Downey
Ann Downey
Jimmy Doyle
Jim English
Leonard Enright
Liam Fennelly

John Fenton
Austin Flynn
Paddy Gantly
Mick Gill
Harry Gray
Jimmy Gray
Seán Óg Hanley
Pat Hartigan
Conor Hayes
Pat Henderson
Brendan Hennessy
Joe Hennessy
Pádraig Horan
Willie Hough
Michael Keating
Jim Kelliher
Jimmy Kennedy
Mick King
Paddy Lalor
Johnny Leahy
John Lyons
John 'Tyler' Mackey
Mick Mackey
P.J. Mackey
Michael Maher
Marian McCarthy

Joe McDonagh
John 'Jobber'
  McGrath
Oliver McGrath
Joe McKenna
Lory Meagher
Kathleen Mills
Barney Moylan
Brian Murphy
Denis Murphy
Jimmy Barry-Murphy
Pat Nolan
Una O'Connor
Seán O'Kennedy
Gerry O'Malley
Paddy Phelan
Nicky Rackard
Christy Ring
Mick Roche
Jack Rochford
Tom Semple
Noel Skehan
Jim Stapleton
Samuel Thorpe
Martin White

Also by Brendan Fullam:

Giants of the Ash

'A great hurling book . . . *Giants of the Ash* has the nation's history woven into it . . . . Conversation courses through the pages as it flows through the living body of the game.' *Irish Times*

'A winner . . . the work of a warm appreciator and a modest recorder, who has done a fine service to the literature of hurling.' *Tipperary Star*

A magnificent record of the game of hurling through the thoughts and memories of the people who played it at the highest level through the century — Willie John Daly, Christy Ring, Mick Mackey, John Doyle and all the big names.

ISBN 0-86327-315-7 Hardback
ISBN 0-86327-346-7 Paperback

Hurling Giants

Another classic from the author of the greatest hurling book of all time. Interviews, photographs, team choices, autographs and players' text all capture the views, memories, nostalgia, fulfilment and friendships associated with a truly unique sport, the game of hurling.

ISBN 0-86327-444-7 Hardback

Available from:
WOLFHOUND PRESS
68 Mountjoy Square
Dublin 1
Tel: +353 1 874 0354
Fax: +353 1 872 0207